GW00360849

STAN RICKABY
UPOVER & DOWNUNDER

A

PUBLICATION

Upover and Downunder by Stan Rickaby
A Britespot Publication

First Published in Great Britain by
Britespot Publishing Solutions Limited
Chester Road, Cradley Heath, West Midlands B64 6AB

Casebound version
ISBN 1 904103 18 9

Perfectbound version
ISBN 1 904103 28 6

Cover design and layout
© Britespot Publishing Solutions Limited

Printed and bound in the UK by Cromwell Press Ltd.

Photos © Stan Rickaby and Colorsport

Dedicated to my dear wife Leni.

CONTENTS

PREFACE

It has taken me seven years to write my autobiography and to get it published. In so doing I discovered just how amazing is the human memory.

I listed chronologically events in my life that seemed to me to be of importance, and which I thought would be of interest to a large section of the reading public. Then I wrote as much as I could about each subject.

It was at this stage that I discovered how my memory was really marvellous. I would start to write, thinking perhaps that I could write maybe a page on a particular subject, to discover that due to an amazing recall ability, I could write several pages. Things and events long forgotten, suddenly appeared bright and clear in my mind. I remembered things which I had not thought of for years, and often in great detail. I refer to these events as stories, and there are 107 of them, some short and some long, but all longer than I first anticipated. In total my book consists of approximately 220,000 words. You will see what a remarkable life I have had so far by reference to the contents page, and briefly on page one, and for me the publication of Upover and Downunder is the icing on the cake.

I am sure that you will enjoy reading it. My first acknowledgement is to my dear wife Leni, not only for her help in reminding me of things past, but also for her patience as I sat writing at my desk hour after hour. However about 30% was written in the most unusual circumstances.

You see Leni, like others of her gender, is a very keen shopper, and most of it is done in the local shopping centre. Now walking around dress shops, supermarkets etc, is not exactly my forte', so I used to take a pen, paper and a clipboard with me, sat on a bench in the main shopping avenue, and wrote page after page, probably more than 70,000 words.

My second acknowledgement is to Linda Gwinnet for trying the original manuscript, from my handwritten foolscap pages. I found her due to an advertisement in the local newspaper where she was asking for typing. I used to take several pages each week, and she became so enthusiastic as she ploughed her way through my script. Linda told me how much she was enjoying "Upover and Downunder" and that she would be crying at the sadness of a particular event and laughing at something humorous.

Therefore Linda was the first person to read my autobiography, and she enjoyed it so much, that she said that it would be a best seller. A good friend and litterateur Patrick Lynch was the second reader and he enjoyed it too. He was followed by my friends and relatives, all of whom gave me confidence to press on. The Professional Footballers' Association helped me by recommending me to Paul Burns and Linda Perkins of Britespot Publishing. Jim Cadman also deserves my grateful thanks for guiding me from a typewritten "Upover and Downunder" to the book which you are reading.

And to conclude, a grandmother, an M.P., a clinical psychologist, a teacher, a priest, two doctors and a University Professor have read it and they all said "I couldn't put it down". I hope that you dear reader will say the same.

CHAPTER ONE
VERY EARLY DAYS

I have had a varied and exciting life, punctuated as most people's have been, by high points and low, successes and failures.

This book traces the story from 'Upover' (or the Northern Hemisphere) where I was born, to 'Downunder' (or the Southern Hemisphere, Australia to be exact), where I now live.

It encompasses being born in the industrial North-East of England where I had a supremely happy childhood, despite the Great Depression and the Second World War, to writing this autobiography in North Beach, Western Australia, via myriad changes of jobs and environments. These include being an infantry soldier in the Normandy invasion and in battles immortalised by such films as 'Battle of the Bulge' and 'A Bridge Too Far'; a career in football that enabled me to travel throughout Europe and experience what it was like to win the FA Cup and to play for one's country; becoming a director of the UK branch of a famous controversial international investment company with connections to Banque Rothschild of France and Dr Erich Mende, ex-Vice Chancellor of Western Germany, and with James Roosevelt (son of Franklin D Roosevelt) as a colleague; and businesses in Cyprus, Gibraltar, Spain, etc. My life has been further enriched by the experience of emigrating to Australia, where we lived in Aboriginal communities on a tropical island in the Arafura Sea, and in the outback of the vast and remote Northern Territory, where temperatures often reached 48 degrees Centigrade (118 degrees Fahrenheit); helping to open the first bail hostel in Australia and working for eight years for what was called the Probation and Parole Department, now Community Based Corrections, in a period of rising crime figures.

Through all of this runs a thread of religion, from being baptised a Christian at the age of three weeks, to the present time of conflicts in the church, which I have tried to serve as a church warden; Sunday school superintendent; church magazine editor; church reader; missions secretary; member of the Western Australia (WA) Board of Missions; organiser of social occasions; and presenter and narrator of the Passion on Good Friday, etc.

It all began on Wednesday the 12th of March 1924: my life that is. No one ever told me what kind of a day it was, but if it was anything like many subsequent birthdays, it would have been grey, with a blustery North-Easterly wind hustling past 26 Hind Street, Stockton-on-Tees, County Durham, cold as the North Sea from whence it came, just ten miles or so away as the seagull flies.

Certainly it must have been a day of much relief for my dear mam, as I called my mother, for I weighed in at exactly 14lbs, or 6.4 kg for the moderns. It may sound like a world record, but it was not even a family record, as brother George weighed nine ounces more when he was born, two years previously.

Born at home, as all but the wealthy were in those far off days, Mam was attended by Dr Anderson of the delightful Scottish accent. By pure coincidence – as it could have been any one of dozens of Teesside doctors – it was he who medically examined me when I was called up in the army eighteen years later, proclaiming that there could be nothing wrong with me as I played football for Middlesbrough FC. He stamped my card 'A1' and off I went.

Grandma would have been in attendance too at my birth, as all grandmothers were for the births of all their grandchildren. She would have been boiling up the water in the big black iron kettle, which sat almost permanently on the hob of the 'kitchen' fire. The kitchen being really the dining-room and living-room in all of thousands of terraced homes built to house the workers of the once new factories of the nineteenth century Industrial Revolution.

The kitchen range was so different to those of today, being made all of steel that needed 'blackleading' (polishing with graphite) in parts, and burnishing with emery cloth in others.

Grandma would have been very used to the procedure by this time. In addition to her own children, my uncles Rob and Oliver and aunts Jessie and Emma plus Mam, she would have had to help at the births of cousins Sidney, Alan, Olive, Phyllis, Vera, and Jessie, plus my brother George.

Hind Street was a well-ordered street, with all of the families trying to bring up their children as well as possible. Not for us neighbours who did not wash too often, or children without boots or with holes in their trousers. No, anyone who chose to live in our street seemed to copy the habits of the then current occupants, and to keep up the prevailing standards of cleanliness and tidiness.

My long association with the Church of England began in the April when I was baptised, and I still have my baptismal certificate. This was at our parish church of St Georges in nearby Yarm Road, and as far as I know, I did not go there again until almost fifty years later to the day, when, back on Teesside with my wife Leni, we attended Evening Prayer in April 1974.

Although we lived in St George's parish, various members of the family went to St Andrew's in Yarm Lane, and I have a photograph of my Uncle George in his Boys' Brigade Officer's apparel. Later both George and I were to attend Holy Trinity Church, also in Yarm Lane, and brother John was baptised there.

As you will read later, I attended Sunday school at yet another local Church of England church – which clearly demonstrates that there were many churches per head of population at that time.

Dad's youngest brother, Uncle George, worked with him and my Uncle Charlie at the South Durham Iron and Steel Co, at the Malleable Works. Incidentally, the Rickabys of the nineteenth century seemed to die quite young. Although Dad, Uncle Charlie, Aunties Edie, Nan, and Maude all lived into their sixties or seventies, three of their siblings and their father, my grandfather Anthony, all died at a young age. Granddad died in 1906 aged 49, Aunt Ellen in 1917 aged 25, Uncle George Anthony in 1915 aged 23, and Uncle William Pearson died in 1899 at the tender age of 17. I have no record at the moment, of my paternal grandmother, but in recent years the Vancouver Rickabys have been compiling a family tree, and I am hoping that they will be able to fill the gaps.

Being a child was so different in my day, compared to today. Mam was always at home. I did not know one mother who worked. Whereas all parents would want as good a standard of living as possible, they were not prepared to jeopardise the safety and happiness of their children for extra money.

Dad never owned a house, a car, or even a bike. We came home from school for dinner (lunch) and Mam had it ready on the table. We came back after school and there she was to greet us, except on the rare occasions when she was at a neighbour's for a few minutes.

I never heard the word divorce, until Nan gave me a ticket for an amateur stage play in Stockton, and the term cropped up throughout the evening – but I just did not understand it.

Home was a place where we were totally secure. We always rented houses, as did nearly all our relations and almost everyone we knew, but we were happy. Mams and dads stayed together 'until death do us part', so there was no cost to the Government for marriage counselling, family courts, child care centres, social workers, drug abuse treatment, or the rest of the paraphernalia of modern society.

People were happy with what they had, not for them four bedrooms, two bathrooms, a swimming pool and two cars leading to gigantic monthly repayments. Instead they caught the bus and lived within their means. Mam's skills were those needed to create a happy home. Mothers were homemakers and they were respected as such by their husbands. They did not try to be equal to them, as there was nothing to compete about. Dad did his thing and went to work, Mam stayed at home and followed her natural vocation of homemaker.

It saddens me that the manner in which such happiness can be pursued and found, has been lost.

Television was yet to be invented and radio, then known as the wireless, was in its infancy. Reading was the favourite source of pleasure, and this must be the reason for my generation being so much more literate than that of today.

Perhaps the people who lived through the twenties and thirties, through the Great Depression and before the advent of so many of the work saving appliances, which are considered essential today, had an advantage in the search for happiness. Although eventually President Nixon was much maligned, I will always remember how he encapsulated this idea when he said that only if you had been in the deepest valley, could you really appreciate the view from the highest mountain top.

Dad was out of work for five years and to keep the house heated, he used to go to a closed down 'slag tip', with a shovel and a sack. The furnaces were shut down, as were all of the steel and iron works, but by patient digging it was possible to find bits of coke and coal. I remember seeing lots of dads doing this. What a pleasure it must have been for them, when the day came that they could afford to have sacks of coal delivered. We just take such things, and much more, for granted.

I have several early memories of 26 Hind Street. One of them seems still quite clear and yet it must have been before I was two years old. The Kings lived next door in No 24, and they had a teenage daughter Molly, who used to love to take me out in the pram. I remember one of these occasions, of her coming to the front door, and of her taking me for a trip to the park.

Ropner Park, named after the family who owned a shipyard on the Tees, was a really beautiful place before the war. In recent years, it has deteriorated and vandals have created havoc, but the flower gardens, the tropical plants around the picturesque lake, the lawns, bowling greens, and the rose garden, were all a joy to behold.

And I recall Molly stopping below a tree on a sunny day, and I lay looking up into its branches.

Despite the economic hardships of the twenties, Mam always managed to have us nicely dressed. I have photographs that prove so, and I have memories too. I can remember quite distinctly, standing on the dining table, whilst my Mam buttoned up my soft leather thigh-length leggings, to keep me warm. She used a buttonhook, which would have no use today, but which might have value as an antique.

One of my fondest memories is of a Sunday in 1927, and it remains vividly in my mind. It was early afternoon when there was a knock on the front door. I answered to find a group of my friends, who asked me if I wanted to go to

Sunday school. There was my best pal Laura Smith, who lived in No 28 next door, accompanied by Dorothy, Jean, and Florence Mash, from No 30. All girls you will notice.

I said that I could not go as I was only three, thinking that I needed to be five, as was necessary for day school. When they said that Sunday school started when you were three years old, I was overjoyed. I ran up the passage crying, 'Mam, I can go to Sunday school'. She got me ready quickly and I was off. I had grown up at last. I could go to Sunday school!

We went to St Gabriel's in Oxbridge Lane, but apparently I could not get my tongue around the name, and I called it St Gravy's. I used to love to hear the stories of Jesus and to sing such hymns as 'All Things Bright and Beautiful, (all creatures great and small)', and at Christmas, 'Away in a Manger, (no crib for a bed, the little Lord Jesus lay down his sweet head).'

I attended my first Christmas party at St Gabriel's in 1927. After lots of games and plenty to eat, we were given an apple and an orange each. It shows how little we got, compared to today, that it is such a clear and pleasant memory.

My fourth birthday was memorable for the quality of Mam and Dad's present. It was a red crane with a cabin, it was on wheels, and the jib's height could be adjusted. My parents must have been better off than usual at the time, as during this period, brother George was given a Hornby Train, which really was something, and Dad bought a gramophone.

I can still see Dad now. It was a Saturday morning and I was up at the top of the street, and looking down I could see him struggling along carrying a huge box. I dashed down to see what it was. It had to be a toy, as didn't they always come in boxes?

I suppose that I was disappointed to learn that it was a 'His Master's Voice' gramophone, particularly when I did not know what such an object was, not having seen one before.

I was not prepared for the magic that was about to happen. Dad wound the thing up, opened what I know now to be louvres, and from behind them came a voice and the sound of music.

This was something different to the wireless I had heard at Mr Smith's – not the Mr Smith next door, but another one who lived next to what was known as the 'bottom common', and who had a beautiful 'red setter' dog. His was attached to a big battery and a 'cumulator', which he used to take to the garage to get 'charged up'. Dad's was a lot bigger, and the sound was really lovely, not like the crackling which came from the wireless.

The first song I heard was 'Let's put out the lights and go to sleep' by Rudy Vallée, and went, 'No more money in the bank; no cute baby we can spank; What's to do about it? Let's put out the light and go to sleep.' I asked Dad how it worked, and for some time he convinced me that there were little men and women inside the black box that I could see inside the louvres. Eventually, I found out that Dad had put a record on the top and that he used to 'change the needle' (although I thought he was pulling my leg, because his needles did not have holes in them), and that if he did not wind it up properly, the music would get slower and slower. But I really did believe about those little men and women. When no one was around, I used to peep inside the louvres, wondering....

One day the Mr Smith with the wireless let me listen to the 'big fight', perhaps it was Jack Dempsey and someone, but we did not hear a word for the crackling.

We were all good neighbours and genuinely took an interest in one another. Help was always available whatever the problem. I recall one Lenny Mash from No 30, who used to wear black leather leggings up to his knees. Quite a few wore them, particularly if they were to do with horses (although I do not think Lenny was), and the habit was continued by the early chauffeurs. Lenny's immortalisation in this book was not for any equine reason however, but because he taught me to tell the time. He must have been about sixteen years old then, quite old, and he had been given a pocket watch for his birthday. We were out on the pavement and I was playing 'top and whip', at which I was most adept, when Lenny showed me his watch. 'I wish I could tell the time,' I said, and so he taught me. I actually learnt it whilst standing on the pavement in front of our bay window, and I never forgot it.

In one way or another, the years seemed to be broken up into seasons. In addition to the obvious cricket and football seasons, there were times in the year when we played the previously mentioned 'top and whip'. For the uninitiated, the whip was a stick about half a metre long, with a metre of string to do the whipping. The tops were of two kinds. One was about 4cms tall with a flat round top and the other was fat and squat. The first was the best and we called them 'window breakers' for obvious reasons. We would spin them with the fingers first, and whip them to keep them going. With practice you could whip them into the air. It was all great fun.

Then there was 'booling'. The best 'boolers' were made of wood and were about 80cm diameter. We raced around the street hitting them with a stick, and we became very skilled at 'steering' them through gaps and around corners.

Cigarette cards were used in many ways to create enjoyment. Apart from collecting cards and swapping 'doubles' to complete sets, we devised various games where we 'flipped' them. For example, we would set up 'stalls' in the schoolyard, and the stall owner would stand up a spent cartridge or bullet case, and those who flipped a card and knocked it down would get two cards as a prize. Another game was where two of us would kneel on the ground about three metres from the wall, and flip cards one after another. If your card, or part of your card, was over any part of the cards already flipped, you picked them up. This generally went on until one of the players (there could be any number of players) had won all of the cards.

'Jarping' chestnuts was an autumn game, more about that later, but the important thing was that we used to have great fun without spending more than, say, a penny for a top and whip.

George's Hornby train was the reason for a lifetime of guilt for me. I was never allowed to play with it, as 'Stanley would be sure to break it', so it is not difficult to imagine my feeling when I got home one day to find no one home. Mam must have been next door, so here was my chance. It was in the top drawer of a built in chest of drawers in the left-hand corner of the kitchen, next to the fireplace, and hidden, as I discovered, under some knitting wool.

I got it out, wound it up, and put it on the kitchen table. I did not bother with the rails or the carriages, as my intention was clear – to crash the engine off the table and on to the floor. I could not resist the chance of seeing it tumbling off, to see if it went over and over in the air.

The crash was as spectacular as I expected it to be, but when I tried to do it again, I was horrified. It would not go. I had broken it! I put it back in the drawer, covered it with the wool, and denied all knowledge of it being broken. And I never ever recanted.

CHAPTER TWO
OXBRIDGE LANE SCHOOL

It was whilst living in No 26 that the great day arrived: the day I went to school. I was five, and Mam took me to Oxbridge Lane Elementary School, just five minutes walk from home.

I can see Miss Flintoff now. Bespectacled, hair in a bun on top of her head; wearing a long black dress, she looked like the archetypal headmistress of the Dickensian era.

She did not need modern day psychological training to know how to put me at ease. She merely sent for a cup of hot malted milk, told me that I would get one every morning playtime (the latter word attracted me), and I was wishing Mam would go and leave me to get on with it.

I was taken across the road to the hall of St Gabriel's, as that was where the 'bottom' class was housed. I was well behaved and people liked me, so I have never understood why I pushed a girl off her seat and on to the floor. We sat two at a desk, and I deliberately pushed her off. My punishment was to be sent to the cloakroom, and I stood amongst the coats and caps hanging on hooks, until I was sent for and told to resume my seat.

A favourite game we used to play on our way home, was to climb on top of a wall near the railway bridge in Oxbridge Lane, and slide down it on our bottoms. Mam must have been puzzled as to how frequently she had to patch my trousers.

Eventually I was 'put-up' which meant I went to the main school, across the road from the church hall. I had played football on the common next to Mr Smith's since I was two or three, so I was delighted to find that before school, and at every playtime, there was a twenty-odd-a-side football match with a tennis or rubber ball. I joined in and I improved my skills very quickly, as all the boys could play well.

I knew all my arithmetical tables when I was six, and I could read almost anything. The tables were on the classroom walls and the first thing we did every day was to say them aloud. Similarly, difficult words were all around the walls, so that we learnt to spell them at a young age. I can still picture the word 'people' for instance and we were encouraged to say 'pee-ople' so that we spelt it correctly.

We used to have to sing, and Miss Pennock played the piano for us. One day we were singing, 'Sweet and low, sweet and low, wind of the Western Sea', when the music stopped ... Looking at me our teacher said, 'Stanley you are flat!'. I thought at first it must be a compliment, but she gently asked me not to sing – as it put others off! I was bitterly disappointed, and I remembered this sad occasion a couple of years later, when at my next school I was put in the 'Teddy Bears chorus', which stood in a row next to the radiators in the school hall, with orders not to sing.

Nothing has changed. I still cannot sing. I am still flat, and to add to that I have been told that I am 'tone-deaf', whatever that means. Ah! well!!

There is much more violence in the world today than there was of yore, but I suffered on a number of occasions because I was of a peaceable nature. This was known to a few rough boys at school and they used to make me run the gauntlet to get home. They would wait for me and hit me as I tried to get past them, as I ran down the backstreet behind the school.

Laura Smith and I were of about the same age, and played together from the earliest days. We were in and out of each other's houses, and our respective mams never had to worry about us, until one day ...

We decided to go for a walk as Laura said that she had an Auntie in Hartburn, which today would be referred to as a garden suburb. For two four year old tots it was quite a feat to walk all that way, about three miles, but an even greater achievement to find Laura's Auntie. All the credit for the latter went to Laura, as she alone knew where to go.

When we got there, Laura's Auntie was duly horrified to think that we were on our own, and after a rest and a drink, for it was a summer's day, she walked us back home. Pandemonium reigned on our return, as the police had been notified, and 'Bobby' Downey was deputed to search for us.

We were chastised and told never to do it again, and we didn't. It wasn't my last brush with PC Downey however, as when I was two or three years older I used to spend a lot of time at Ropner Park. During the light evenings, we would play cricket or football. At the appointed time the bell would ring for everyone to vacate the Park, and they were given reasonable time before the huge, ornamental, but spike topped gates were locked.

Of course, we would leave it too late on occasions, and the local PC (the self-same PC Downey) would see us locked in, and have to go and fetch the park-keeper to let us out. This was always accompanied by a lecture, but the only real remedy for our recalcitrance was when we grew a little more, and acquired the skill of being able to climb over the gates.

In 1930 we moved house, but not very far; merely about sixty yards and on the other side of the street to Number 69. I do not recall the move or the reason for it being discussed by my parents, but the obvious advantages were a bathroom and a very big back yard. The bath was enormous and its feet were like huge claws, and I was always a little afraid of them. The reason for the yard being so big was that next door to us was a garage, most unusual in the thirties, although it probably was built to stable horses, and our two yards were not separated.

It was wonderful for playing my two favourite games, football and cricket. The backstreet too was twice as wide, at least, as other backstreets, so I was very pleased with the change.

Two very important events happened whilst living at No 69, even though we probably only lived in it for about two years. The first was during the Easter holidays of 1931, when Mam dropped what was to me a bombshell. She told me that I was not going back to Oxbridge school: I was joining George at Holy Trinity Higher Grade School.

I was very disappointed because I was reading a book at Oxbridge, and I was looking forward to finishing it as it was so exciting. It shows how advanced we were when I was at school, as although still only six I had already read many books. On my seventh birthday, Uncle Charlie bought me the most beautiful book I ever owned. It was a blue hardback, about three inches thick, and was about Robin Hood, and I read it avidly.

CHAPTER THREE
HOLY TRINITY SCHOOL

The other important happening at No 69 was a happy event: the appearance of my brother John. He arrived whilst I was at Trinity school, on 5 May 1932. Mam was in bed 'poorly' (as we described being unwell in the North-East of England), and sometime in the morning our family doctor, Dr Anderson, had 'brought John in his black bag'! I was delighted to have a baby brother, and eventually I was allowed to push him in his pram when I used to 'go messages' to Mr Hilton's corner shop, which was only a hundred yards away.

Mr Hilton sold the most delicious sweet I had ever come across at that time. It was called a 'Ginger Butter', and after a little sucking it went soft in the centre, allowing the lovely ginger tasting cream to ooze out. And thereby hangs another tale, another sin, another confession.

One day as I pushed John's pram, I saw a glint of something shining in the bottom, and it turned out to be a silver threepenny piece. They were really tiny, and one had become trapped between the two or three boards which made up the base of the pram. I removed it and guessed immediately whence it had come. There was a very pleasant custom whenever someone, adult that is, saw a baby for the first time. They invariably gave the mother a piece of silver, most commonly a shilling or a sixpence, by placing it in the child's hand. Then to prevent it from being put straight into the infant's mouth, the mother would put it in her purse.

In this case, it had been dropped. Looking back, threepence could buy you a seat at the cinema, or a two ounce plus a one ounce bar of Cadbury's chocolate, or five Players cigarettes, or half a pint of beer, or three morning newspapers. I would imagine that Mam would have missed that coin eventually, and she must have been really puzzled as to what had happened to it.

Well, it finished-up being spent in three trips to Mr Hilton's, all to buy a 'pennorth' of 'Ginger Butters', such was my addiction to sweets. Every trip I felt guilty, and it has haunted me ever since.

It seemed that from a very early age I was the one who always 'ran the messages'. Even before I started school, I used to go to Miss Duffy's in Alliance Street to get a variety of goods, but apparently I had a poor memory. Mam reckoned that I would quite often forget what I had gone for, and so I would just say, 'I'll take an ounce of yeast!'

Everyone baked their own bread in the kitchen in those days, so the yeast would always come in handy sooner or later.

It was about this time that I was discovering my natural ability in ball games. Our backstreet, being wider than normal, became a football pitch in the winter and a cricket pitch in the summer. Almost every boy could play well, and in consequence the general standard was high and we all helped one another to play even better.

Ropner Park (being only a five minutes walk from our house) was a mecca for us on weekends, in the holidays, and after school on the light nights. In those early days I never owned a cricket bat or ball, or a football: but I never failed to get a game.

My cousin Frankie and I used to go there together whenever he visited us. Although he must not have continued with sport when he left school, he was an excellent cricketer and footballer. We would always manage to get a game and on the same side, and if it was football we would combine to score lots of goals, or if it was cricket we would get all of the runs and bowl most of the batsmen out.

One day I recall Frankie bowled the last player out, by knocking two stumps out of the ground. Although the game was over, I asked the batsman if I could have a bowl at him, and I knocked down the remaining stump.

Norman Fowler was several years older than me, and he played football for Oxbridge Lane School. He was a hero to all of us smaller kids, as he also played for the town, the county, and I think also for the England Boys Team. We were thrilled when we learnt that he had been signed by Middlesbrough Football Club, a top First Division team and our local favourites. One day he was in the park kicking a ball about with the lads, so I joined in and actually tackled Norman, taking the ball from him! Well, I told everyone I ever met. This really was my claim to fame.

Another top school player was Norman Geldart, and I will never forget the time he let me carry his football boots for him. I tied the laces together, put the boots around my neck and proudly walked home with Norman, who must have been twice as tall as me, but I gazed up into his face all the way, demonstrating my hero worship of him.

Joe Cumber was another one of the 'big lads' I knocked about with at that time. Actually, when compared to his peers Joe was small, but he was a very good left winger. More importantly, he let me play with him and his mates in their back street, which was also a wide one.

One day I was playing wicketkeeper, and in my keenness to try to stump everyone, I always stood right up behind the wicket (which was in fact a wooden box). This time I was too close, for as the batsman swung his bat back, he hit me on the right eyebrow. I went down as though poleaxed and I was bleeding profusely. Joe took me in to their house, and his oldest brother managed to stop the bleeding. I suppose I should have had a stitch in it, but we were not sufficiently sophisticated in the early thirties.

There were two interesting sequels to this incident. One was that the batsman, who learned his craft in the backstreets, eventually became Captain of Somerset Cricket Club, and later was on the County Club Committee. Not bad from humble beginnings. His name was Harold Stephenson, or H H Stephenson as he appeared on Somerset's batting list for years, or as he was known and respected throughout the sport of cricket, 'Stevie'.

In the 1991 'Wisden' (the Cricketers' Almanack which contains all of cricket's official records since the game started – or since 1864 at least), Harold is listed as the 16th highest ranking wicketkeeper from the point of view of catches taken and stumpings made. These totalled 1082 in 16 seasons, compared to Godfrey Evans, England's keeper at the time, who totalled 1066 in 30 seasons. If we take out the 6 War seasons, leaving a total of 24, we find an average of 44.4 wickets per season for Evans and 67.6 for Harold. So why didn't Harold play for England when his average was 50% better than that of Evans?

Years later I was honoured to be asked by him to play in an 'All Stars' football match at Yeovil, for his benefit year.

A further sequel to the split eye, albeit delayed action, happened about forty-five years later. Whilst living in Perth, Western Australia, I was on the executive of the Soccer Federation of WA and I had to ring the President of Subiaco Soccer Club for a reason I have now forgotten. His name was Cumber. As soon as I heard his voice, I knew that it had a Teesside accent.

I asked him if he had two brothers, Tom and Joe, and he replied, 'Yes, why?' I said, 'Do you remember a kid getting his eyebrow split open in your backstreet, by Harold Stephenson?' He remembered immediately. We said that we must meet again, but we never did.

Of the four houses that I lived in during my childhood, 69 Hind Street was the house that I liked the best. It was spacious inside; as I have said before it suited my love of ball games; and it was near to Spring Street, which led to my beloved Ropner Park by way of the bridge over the Stockton to Darlington railway line – which, incidentally, was the first railway in the world.

When I was about seven years old, two or three of my pals suggested that I should join the Cubs, as they had done. Of course, I agreed. Who wouldn't want to wear their smart uniform?

It was summer and that meant long light evenings, so at the appointed time we all set off and walked past the magnificent massive horse chestnut trees in Hartburn Lane, to what I already knew to be the Scout Hut.

Due to my keenness we got there very early, and we played around outside to fill in the time. Whilst this was happening, it started to rain, so we sheltered inside some big white pipes, which were lying by the hut, prior to their being put into the ground – for sewage, I think. Eventually the Cubmaster arrived along with the rest of the boys, and one of my pals introduced me to him. What happened next seems as unbelievable nearly sixty years on, as it did then.

This heartless person took one look at me, told me I was too fat, and that I could not join. I was so upset that I cried, and the incident is still so deeply etched in my memory.

Hartburn had quite a variety of memories for me, almost all happy, with the Cub episode the only exception. In my early days of little travel, when what are now populated suburbs were 'out in the country', this beautiful rural area of Hartburn was a place I only visited spasmodically. Climbing over stiles and walking through meadows ablaze with gorgeous golden buttercups and white daisies, we would make for 'Sunnyside', where there was a stream. Playing in it, or lying by it was – in today's terms – equal to staying in the Lake District.

Dad and I walked together, and he would tell me stories of when he was young, One day when I had a chest and nose cold, we went looking for a road gang who he had been told were laying tarmacadam around Hartburn, as 'breathing in the tar fumes was good for the chest'. We found them, and it did me good.

In the thirties, welfare services and help for the disadvantaged was thin on the ground, but during the mass unemployment era, free milk was given to children whose fathers were 'on the dole'. The children of employed fathers paid a 'ha'penny' a day, and during this time my Dad got a job. He had to travel to West Hartlepool everyday by bus, about fifteen miles, but he was only too pleased to do this, and in fact he worked there as chief stocktaker for the steel mills until he retired with ill health, when aged 63.

I kept on forgetting to tell the school about my fathers job, and after a week or two I was terrified to do so, as I should have been paying for the milk. I kept putting it off, but eventually plucked up courage and found the teacher to be understanding.

Advertising was not what it is today, but I do remember a huge Ford car ad. It was a picture of the 1933 model spread right across the window of a showroom, which I passed on the way to school.

Another fond memory is of walking to Holy Trinity Church for Evensong. I loved going, but one evening I did something which I regretted and worried about for a long time. En route there was a sweet shop which sold some beautiful chocolate toffees. Mam always gave me twopence to put in the collection. One night I just could not resist the temptation, and I spent one of the pennies on some toffees and ate them surreptitiously in church.

It was at about this time that I started to think a lot more about Jesus, and for a while I actually wondered if I was He. I hoped that I was, but ...

In 1934 all of our class went into double figures as we all had tenth birthdays. I cannot remember anything about mine, but I remember well that of John Bowron.

John had always been a thorn in my side, because he had always beaten me in positions in the class. John was first and I was second to him as usual. This had gone on for three years, ever since I started at the school at the age of seven. No matter how hard I tried the result was always the same.

Mr Bowron was a 'Monumental Mason' and he had a business in Yarm Lane, Stockton, making headstones for those bereaved who could afford them – as such he was one of the better-off people in those days, and where they lived confirmed this to me.

Almost everyone I knew lived in a street. A street was a long terrace of two storey houses, all the same design, with the front door on the pavement and a brick walled, concrete floored backyard which housed the lavatory and the coal house. Invariably they were rented, with the 'landlady' or 'landlord' picking up the rent weekly.

But the Bowrons were quite different. They owned their house. It was in a road not a street, Osborne Road to be exact, and it had gardens back and front, albeit rather small. It was also in a very pleasant location by the gates of beautiful Ropner Park.

My one and only visit was for John's tenth birthday party which was, incidentally, the one and only birthday party I ever went to, until we were giving parties for our own daughter.

I could not believe that people could be so rich. Instead of us guests all giving John a present, we were all given one, and the way we received them was so exciting. They had something quite unique, to me at least. It was a bran tub. I had never heard of one before, and when we were told that we put our hands into the tub, and we could take whichever gift we wished, it was almost frightening. Suppose I was unlucky and picked out something that was not worth much, and perhaps there were much more expensive presents I had missed!

Anyway, 'here goes' I thought, and plunged in my hand. After a few seconds of rummaging about in the bran, I grasped a small but quite heavy circular object. It was wrapped in blue paper, and I slowly unwrapped it. It was a pencil sharpener in the shape of the globe, and with a world map on it. It seemed heavy because it was made of some alloy including lead.

I was thrilled with my gift, and could not get it home quickly enough, but not before I had eaten large quantities of such delicious dishes as custard, jelly, and cream cake.

Whereas 'Teessiders' were as friendly and generous as any people in the world, this did not often stretch to birthday parties, no doubt because of the expense. It was an industrial working class area, and having suffered from unemployment, there was little money about.

Birthdays for me were mostly home affairs, with maybe a few cards, but generally presents were from Mam and Dad, Auntie Nan, and sometimes Uncle Charlie – who also came at Christmas, and brought us a large tin of Quality Street the same size as the shops used to serve from, when selling them loose. This was real luxury.

Our visits to Uncle Charlie's home were special treats. We used to go by train to Dinsdale, where Uncle Charlie would either pick us up in his car, or in nice weather we would walk the mile or so to his house. He had a large beautiful house standing in magnificent grounds, with its own bowling green

I used to like to play with my cousin June, who was my age, and go walking with her and her sisters, Mary and Winnie. We would walk down the road to the River Tees, which lay in a delightful wooded valley, on the north bank of which was the ancient village of Middleton One Row, so named because at that time there was indeed one row of houses.

Spring was particularly beautiful, as the river banks held clusters of daffodils and bluebells. It was a glorious sight with weeping willow trees reaching down from the banks to dip in the water. We would skip along, and laugh, thoroughly enjoying simple pleasures, which included picking some flowers to take home.

Auntie Margaret, who lives at Barnard Castle, used to make us a lovely tea which always included desserts such as jellies and cakes, luxuries to me in those far off days.

Uncle Charlie would walk us back to Dinsdale Station, and I can still picture him waving to us as we set off for home. I do not recall George coming with us, but Dad only had to ask me to go with him and I was ready and waiting.

I loved Holy Trinity and not because we got extra holidays! Holy days were truly holidays, such as Ash Wednesday and Ascension Day. We used to go to church at 9 o'clock, and then after the service we went home.

Religious instruction was a most important subject, and in addition to lessons when we studied such prophets as Jeremiah and Amos, we held an assembly first thing every day, followed by a short service. This always included one or two of the canticles: Magnificat, Venite, Jubilate Deo, Benedicite, Nunc Dimittis, etc.

CHAPTER FOUR
WE MOVE TO NORTON-ON-TEES

To continue about the virtues of Trinity – we were taught good manners, to touch our caps to elders we knew, and to be proud of our school. Our school hymn was entitled 'Hold High the Flame for the Honour of Trinity'. During my stay at Trinity we moved house again, this time to Norton-on-Tees, which was only about three or four miles away. A beautiful village, it is older than Stockton, but it has been swallowed up by the latter during Council boundary changes. I was never made aware of the reasons for our moving house.

Today moving house is relatively simple, with huge furniture vans carrying all of the household effects: but all of our moving was carried out by my Dad's cousin, Alfie Ward, who had a horse and cart which he used primarily for his fruit and vegetable business. He called on houses and rang a bell to signify his presence, and in addition he doubled as a furniture carrier when required. When acting in the latter capacity for us, it always seemed to rain. I remember Mam trying desperately to dry mattresses, blankets and sheets which were sodden. Obviously our Alfie did not have any weatherproof tarpaulins.

Initially I was quite unhappy about the move because it meant saying goodbye to my pals; pals whom I had known since I learnt to toddle. At that time Norton was worlds away from Stockton, a different place altogether, and as I did not even have a bike, never mind the family having a car, it was the end of a chapter in my life.

I missed Ropner Park, and all of the 'commons' and back streets where we played, and looking back, except for occasionally 'bumping into' people in town (Stockton) in later years, my pals were lost forever.

However, there were compensations, and soon I was discovering my new habitat. Norton High Street was really beautiful and later on, in the fifties I think, the magazine 'The Listener' had a photograph of it on the cover entitled 'One of the prettiest villages in England'.

Beginning with a magnificent display of daffodils, crocuses and snowdrops in early spring, we had flowers through to the autumn. The central main street had a row of trees down the centre, and lawned gardens on either side, and then another carriageway, a pavement and then the houses. Some were several hundred years old, and had ancient gardens behind that we could only glimpse, but which were lush and gorgeous.

At the top of the High Street was Norton Green, a magnificent village green that had seen the Saxons and the Normans and all of the changing populations since. The Church of St Mary the Virgin stands on the highest point at the back of the green, and the villagers had worshipped their Saviour there for a thousand years and more. The present building dates from 1100AD. A few years before in 1082AD, the then church became a collegiate church consisting of the vicar and eight monks, due to the Bishop of Calais transferring the secular monks from Durham. The effigies of Baron de Blakiston and his wife, in local stone, have lain by the altar since 1200 AD. Whatever time of the year, the church was a joy to behold, as the creepers covering most of the walls changed colour from green, through gold, to a magnificent red. John Walker, inventor of the first match, is buried in the churchyard as was Napoleon's brother, who apparently died in the village whilst a prisoner of war.

Always eager to worship my God, I first went to a Church of England church in Norton Road, but I was not comfortable there. I then tried the village church, and I liked the Sunday school from the start. It was held in the 'schoolroom on the green', next to the village blacksmith's shop. The vicar was in fact a Canon, Sturt by name, and he was an Australian. Having lived in Western Australia for fifteen years I have realised how well known the name is. He was a big man and he had difficulty in belting-in his very large girth, as he stormed up and down the aisle to make his point. He had been a padre in the army during the first war, and we were held spellbound as he recounted his days in Flanders.

As I have written previously, horse drawn carts were in vogue then, and most household supplies, such as fruit and vegetables, coal, fish and milk, were delivered in this way. The rubbish was also picked up similarly, and the rubbish cart and the coal cart both used the narrow back street. The horses were huge, Clydesdales I believe, with great big feet, and I used to be scared stiff as I tried to pass them.

The cartwheels had a steel or iron 'tyre' that was put on by the village blacksmith. We used to love to watch him. He would heat up the tyre in his forge until it expanded, and then put it on the wooden wheel. To cool the tyre to make it fit tight, he used to 'bool' it across the road and straight into the 'Duck Pond'. I never saw a duck on it, but I often saw the clouds of steam created by the Smithy's cooling process. I reckon that with today's volume of traffic, this ancient procedure would be banned.

The Green has been the venue for village childrens' sport since games were invented. I soon got admitted to the football and cricket matches. The latter were played on 'wickets' which were worn areas, all bumps and hollows, and the ball did all kinds of tricks. The rest of the grass was too long to pitch a wicket on, so year in and year out we used the same bare patches.

Football was also difficult due to the grass tending to be long, and there were added problems due to the 'pitch' being enclosed by tarmacadam roads. Cars were a danger, as the boys chased across the roads after the ball, and more than one ball was burst by being run over by them.

Dad knew every flower, every bush or tree in the hedgerow or the meadows, and he would tell me all about them. He could see delicate wild violets almost hidden behind mounds of grass, when I could not. Primroses of course were easy to see, and so were wild plums when he pointed them out to me, but I had probably walked past that hedgerow on numerous occasions without noticing them. Often on a fine Sunday morning, we would walk through the country lanes to visit Sep Hall, a friend of my Dad's. Mr Hall had a beautiful garden, and Dad revelled in discussing the progress of the many varieties of vegetables and flowers with his friend. We always finished up in the garden hut, which was comfortably furnished, and whose walls were covered with prize certificates from many years and many types of flowers and vegetables.

I have to confess that I used to find the garden tours rather boring, but Dad never knew that. His own garden was at first extremely limited, being merely a bricked up corner of the concrete backyard, containing nasturtiums and night scented stock. The latter also grew out of the moss, which nestled in the gaps in the mortar between the bricks of the backyard walls.

One day Dad had great news. There were half a dozen gardens at the bottom of the street that were rented out for a few shillings a year, one was vacant, and he had applied for it and received a positive response. What a wonderful job he made of it. It was fresh berries and vegetables for several months of the year, and flowers in profusion, especially marigolds, which were his beloved 'Meg's' favourites.

Fruit trees grew very well in our area, and 'Worcester Pearmain' apples and 'Hazel Pears' flourished in the many local orchards, but why were the pears so hard and the apples so sour? Probably because they were unripe when we went 'scrumping'! Yes, I have to confess that after a game of cricket in Mr Page's fields, it was difficult to resist the temptation to nip over the wall and sample the produce. Many years later, I was to be the one who berated aboriginal boys for taking mangoes and pawpaws before they were ripe.

Oh! Happy days.

In September 1934 I was 'put up' into Standard 5, Mr Burdon's class. I still have an end of term report. 'Number in class - 58, position in class - 2nd.' That John Bowron again! Recently, here in Western Australia, they were talking about the need for classes of 14! You could hear a pin drop in our classroom, and 'Daddy' Burdon had total control. He also had a wonderful record of his pupils winning scholarships.

I was still playing plenty of football, mostly in Norton Recreation Ground, and although I knew that I was better than most of the lads, I was both delighted and surprised to learn that I had been chosen to play right back for my school, Holy Trinity. As I was just ten and the rest of the team were up to fourteen, I could not have been more thrilled. On the Friday I was given my school shirt, shorts and stockings, and in the evening I went to the 'Rec' and wore all my gear, to show off that I was to play for the school!

Our first game was against Richard Hind School, which was the school where children went who had just missed out in the scholarship examinations. We won 1–0, and as it was my very first proper football match, it was a red letter day.

We had a game every Saturday at different grounds around the district. We were one of the poorest teams in the league, but as a full back I saw plenty of action. I always arrived at about 9.00 am – even though the kick-off was at 10.00 am – in the hope that someone would be there who owned a ball and we could have some practice before the game. This meant that I would have done a lot of running prior to the match, but at that age it did not seem to matter.

Whenever I went to the 'Co-Op' to get Mam's groceries, I used to look in Mr Chilton the shoe repairer's shop window. You see, he had made a football, and there it was in the side window, priced five shillings. Now this was a lot of money and when I mentioned it to Mam around about October 1934, I did not expect her to be able to afford it.

To my delight, she said I could have it for Christmas, if Mr Chilton agreed to my taking him sixpence a week for ten weeks. He said 'Yes', and I gave him his 'tanner' every Friday evening when I did the grocery shopping.

Digressing for a moment, I recall very clearly my weekly excursions to the 'Co-Op' in Norton High Street. How completely different is the 'supermarket' of today compared to the grocer's shop of the thirties. Then they closed at 8.00 pm on Fridays and Saturdays, which were the busy days due to everyone being paid on a Friday. I remember that when I bought flour, which was just about every week, I used to get two half stones or fourteen pounds (6.4kg), and the grocer would weigh it in front of me with great alacrity. He also weighed most of the items I bought, including sugar, butter and margarine, and finally the whole order was parcelled in brown paper and tied with string. Having watched this parcelling so often, I learnt to do it myself, and every Christmas or birthday gift we have ever given has been wrapped à la 'Co-Op'.

Back to the football, which I duly received for Christmas; Stanley Nelson and I used to take it over Page's Field and play for hours. Sadly it did not last long. I took it to our first school match in the New Year, and after a good kick about, I had to join my team on the field. I asked one of the boys with whom I had been playing to look after my ball, I didn't know him, but he seemed nice enough. Soon after we kicked off I glanced across to where he had been standing, but he was no longer there. As I looked towards the exit road, I could see him running away with my ball under his arm.

It broke my heart to have to tell Mam. It was the only football I ever owned.

My first match in front of a crowd was in the semi-final of the Stockton Schools Cup, when we played Tilery on Stockton's ground, the Victoria Park. We lost 3–0, but that did not matter as I had played against 'Rocker' Lakey – who played for both town and county – and on the town's main venue. This meant an enormous amount to me.

Many years later when I played for England, I had dozens of letters and telegrams from all over the place, but none of them equalled a book I received entitled 'A Boy's Religion'. The dust cover was in the school colours of claret and light blue, and it was written by Holy Trinity's vicar, the Reverend S Layton Petrie, and suitably inscribed by Mr Hewitt, the headmaster.

Here in North Beach, Western Australia, I once loaned it to a church member to read. I have forgotten who it was – except that he would have been connected with our Sunday school, as I remember how I said that it would be an excellent source of lessons for both boys and girls. It was never returned, and of all of the trophies and souvenirs I received during my career, this book was the most important. I am still searching for it as I regard it as an heirloom which I want to pass on to Toby Gardner, my dear grandson, and then ad infinitum.

As I have written previously, Dad was on the dole for five years, and obviously things must have been difficult for Mam. In later years, Auntie Nan (who lived with us in the nineteen twenties and early thirties) told me that she remembered Mam and Dad quite often going without a meal, so that George and I had sufficient to eat. By the time she told me this, my parents were dead, and the revelation really upset me and reiterated what I already knew: that they were the best in the world. It brought tears to my eyes.

On a brighter note, in the summer of 1935 I was pleasantly surprised to be a regular player in the school cricket team, once again playing with and against thirteen and fourteen year olds when I was just eleven.

All the boys in the North-East of England wore black lace up boots; shoes were some kind of an upper class luxury. Dad always polished ours daily, and soled, heeled and studded them as required. I can still smell the melting wax with which he sealed the slight gap between sole, heel, and upper. The 'studs' were about a quarter of an inch across, and helped to prevent the wear caused through us sliding around on the pavements and in the schoolyard. Boots were also a great advantage when playing football, though I was nine before I had a second-hand pair of football boots. However, the black boots did not last forever, they wore out and we grew out of them. One day Mam went down to Stockton Market and came back with a bargain. Everything she bought had to be a bargain, being so short of cash. Did they fit? Yes, they were very comfortable. But they were brown. 'Brown boots! I arsk yer, brown boots!' as Stanley Holloway (the actor comedian) used to say in one of his monologues. What Mam did not know, was that everyone else knew that only cissies wore brown boots! But how could I tell her?

At Stockton we had separate boys' and girls' schools called 'Stockton Secondary School (for Boys)' or '(for Girls)' respectively, where the students were coached to sit the Matriculation and the School Certificate examinations, sponsored by the Northern Universities Joint Board. I would guess that there were about fifty places for boys and the same for girls every year, and then a similar number of the next best students were offered places at an intermediate school, Richard Hind Central School. After two years, the best of the latter were able to change to the Secondary School.

CHAPTER FIVE
STOCKTON GRAMMAR SCHOOL AND REDCAR INTERLUDE

In addition to the Secondary schools, there was a private school called Stockton Grammar School, where the majority of pupils were fee paying, but there were also twelve scholarships awarded each year. These were eagerly fought for, and both George and I were successful in passing the entrance examination. We also passed for the 'Sec' school, and therefore we had a choice.

George was completing his second year when I passed, and there was never any doubt that given a choice, it would be the 'Grammar' for me too. However, I have often wondered what I would have done if the 'Grammar' had not played football. You see the 'Sec' played rugby, so apart from any other consideration I would have selected the 'Grammar'.

Actually, there were two written examinations for the 'Sec', the second providing you got through the first, and then the interview. I knew I had passed both of the written exams, which consisted half of arithmetic and half of English grammar, because I knew all of the answers, and I was finished so early that I was able to check everything and still have time left over. In the first arithmetic test however, one of the early questions was just to write a seven-digit number in words, with the number seven as one of the seven numbers. As I left the classroom I realised that I had spelt it 'severn', the way the Bristol river is spelt, and I was quite upset.

I remember nothing of my interview with Mr Ridley, head of the 'Grammar', but I do remember a question asked of me by the 'Sec' headmaster. The interviews were really just to give the head the opportunity to meet you, and for him to decide if you were the kind of boy he wanted in his school. To do this he got you talking and I was first asked if I knew the name of the famous person who had just died.

On my way to the school that morning, I had passed a newspaper shop in Nelson Terrace where the school was situated, and on the placard outside of the shop were the words, 'Lawrence of Arabia dead'. No problem, as they say in Australia. The remainder of the interview went very well and I knew I must have passed. And I was quite right, I had.

Redcar is a small town on the coast of North Yorkshire, and these days there are still families who go there for their holidays, most staying in boarding houses on a bed and breakfast with evening meal basis. However, over the last two or three decades, Spain and the rest of Southern Europe have become very attractive holiday locations, with their very competitive packages of travel and accommodation, and in consequence the 'working man's' holiday spots have suffered.

But when I was a boy, Redcar was a true holiday resort with many attractions. Coloured lights were strung all along the 'front', as the area that encompassed the promenade adjacent to the beach was known, and crowds of people walked back and forth along the 'prom'.

Ice cream kiosks, and cafes serving fish and chips plus peas, bread and butter, and a cup of tea for a shilling, did a roaring trade. Amusement arcades with garish flashing lights attracted children like me who fondly thought that it was possible to win, when in retrospect it is obvious that the opposite was the case.

My first visit was with the Sunday school, and there would not be a church in Teesside that did not go to Redcar for its annual outing. 'If wet, in the Hall', was an expression we all knew well, referring as it did to the meal which we called 'tea'. If it was fine (and unless my memory is playing tricks, it generally was), tea would be had on the 'sands', the term we always used for what most now call the 'beach'.

Then on one occasion Mam took George and me for a whole week to a boarding house at Coatham, the northern suburb of the town. Dad did not come. He was notorious for always preferring to sleep in his own bed, and he always did until many years later, when he stayed with us after we moved to Birmingham to live.

Workmen used to get one week's holiday, which generally in the case of Teesside, was the first week in August, when it was Stockton Races. Most works closed down for the Races, and it was often lovely hot weather. The week was looked forward to by the populace, as most men worked very hard in terrible conditions of heat and dirt, in the foundries, machine shops, shipyards, and chemical factories of the great industrial area.

Of course, working and having only one week's holiday was tough, but much preferred to the then recent period of five years when there was massive unemployment. Forty-four hour weeks were looked upon as very reasonable, as many worked on a shift system of 6.00 am to 6.00 pm in such as the steel foundries. Sometimes they had to work weekends too. Hard work was a man's expectation in the nineteen twenties and thirties.

It is not difficult to imagine the delight I felt when Grandma and Granddad, who had lived in the Tilery district for many years (as had most of their family), announced that they were moving to Redcar! It really was quite remarkable, and a very brave or risky act depending on your viewpoint, for no one moved far away from their roots. Then, hardly anyone had a car, and to move 15 miles was virtually unknown.

I am not sure what Mam and her brothers and sisters thought, but with dreams of staying at Redcar on holidays, I certainly considered it a great idea. Consequently, for two or three years, until my grandparents managed to get a Council House back in Norton, where we were, I had a great time. My cousin Frankie had been brought up by Grandma and Granddad, and he and I were good pals. He was a couple of years older than me, bright, and as I have already written, good at cricket and football. So every time we went to Grandma's we thoroughly enjoyed our time together. Living there, Frankie got to know everything that went on.

I used to go there at Easter, in August, and in early October, and we used to play lots of sport. Redcar sands were magnificent for both football and cricket. The tide went out several hundred yards and left the surface quite hard. At Easter and in October, full games of soccer were possible, and most days there was a game going on. We never had a ball, but all we had to say was 'giz a game?' or, translated into English, 'Please may we have a game?', and you were in, one kicking one way, and the other, the other way.

In August excellent games of cricket went on, and being better than most, we used to get plenty of batting and bowling.

Redcar pier was an attraction, and a walk along it was a 'must' every day. Most adults paid a penny, but I must confess that we used to climb on as most of the local boys did. Sometimes we would go fishing, with varying results, or just watch the many holiday-makers who looked upon fishing off the pier as a main part of their holiday.

On Friday nights Redcar water polo team had a match in the outdoor swimming pool, and I regret to have to record that Frankie knew where to climb over the railings without being seen. We gave the home team such enthusiastic vocal support, so I suppose that that was worth something.

Another free entertainment venue was the 'Pierrots' on the front. A variety group, they used to put on several performances including one in the late evening. This was our favourite, as there was something very exciting about going in the night, with the moon and stars as the backdrop – we really were stepping out, as we mingled with the adult holidaymakers out for the evening.

The audience sat in deck chairs on the sands, and before the show commenced, the attendants came around and collected the threepence or sixpence, or whatever it was, for admission. This we could not afford, but Frankie knew how to avoid paying. The show changed frequently, so every summer we were able to go quite often.

One sketch was funny enough to stick in my mind for well over fifty years. 'Two gentlemen were praising the virtues of their respective servants, and they decided to have a contest to prove whose was the quicker. Both servants were given two one-shilling pieces and told to go to Saltburn-by-the-Sea, a few miles to the south, and each buy a pound of sugar and a packet of tea, and the one who got back the quickest, was the winner. The two employers sat chatting, waiting for the first servant to appear. Eventually, one walked in and his boss was ecstatic. "Terrific", he said, "I knew that you would win. Now please give me the sugar, tea, and the change", he requested. "I am sorry but I have not got them," the servant said, "You see, when I got there I could not remember which was the shilling for the sugar, and which was the shilling for the tea!"' I must have been easily pleased.

Another tremendous favourite for all ages was 'Sunshine Corner', a religious group who preached, and sang hymns, mostly of a children's type. Children sat on the sands, adults in deck chairs, no admission fee, but a collecting box was handed round, and children prepared to sing a song would be given bars of chocolate etc. Mam had a cousin in Redcar and her daughter was often rewarded in this way. In later years, she trained in London as a singer and maintained herself by appearing on TV with the George Mitchell Singers, who were very famous at that time.

Despite our sins, getting into places for nothing, both Frankie and I loved to sing songs about Jesus, and listen to the Gospel stories at the Sunshine Corner.

'Now Lazarus was a very little man, a very little man was he, and he climbed into a sycamore tree, for the Saviour he wanted to see.' 'Sunshine Corner it is jolly fine, it's for children under ninety nine', are just two of many we learned there. They were on the Redcar beach for years and did a great work bringing Jesus to the people on holiday, but sadly there was a scandal about them later, something to do with the funds. Nevertheless, for me it was still a great event in my life.

Sometimes we would hitch a ride with a local fisherman when he was going out to collect the crabs from the crab pots he had strategically placed. In those days, there were a lot of professional fishermen with their boats parked up on the sands. It must have been a very hard life, as the North Sea in winter must be one of the coldest and least hospitable places on the earth.

One particularly bright memory is of a walk under the pier, one Friday evening at the end of August. As the holiday was over and I was returning home on the bus on the Saturday, I was spent up. I would not have had much to start with, as my weekly pocket money at that time was two-pence. I saw something shining in the shallow water, through which I was wading, and I stooped to pick up....a shilling! For the moderns it equalled twelve pence or six weeks' pocket money!

My last memory of Redcar was to do with food. A hundred yards from Grandma's in Lord Street, was a bakery, and they made a particular flat round bread that is still today the most delicious bread I have ever tasted. But now it is back to school and back to Norton-on-Tees.

I have already written of Harold Stephenson, my split eyebrow, and his playing for Somerset as a wicketkeeper-batsman. Having moved to Norton, one could hardly anticipate being involved with a similar person, but as you will see, remarkably I was.

A lot of lads around Norton were good at football and cricket, and we all knew one another as we played together on Norton Rec., Norton Green, or up the Showfield.

One of these lads, whose first name was Dick, was on the small side, bandy-legged, left-footed at football, and a left-handed batsman at cricket. We had often kicked a ball about or taken part in the cricket on the Green, but one Saturday we were up Junction Road to watch a local football match. I cannot remember the name of the local team who played on that particular ground, although it could have been Kendrews the builders.

I do remember the name of their opponents however, and that was Stillington St Mary's. Stillington was a village three or four miles from Norton. Dick and I had our football boots on, and before the game, we joined in with the players and had a 'kick-in'. Not for us to miss a chance of kicking a ball about.

As we were enjoying ourselves and obviously showing that we could play a bit, we were approached by the secretary of the visitors' team. They were two players short and would we like to play for them? What a silly question! We couldn't say 'yes' quickly enough.

Dick was a year or two older than me, but we were about the same height at the time, and that was rather small, especially to play against some large raw-boned local amateurs whose enthusiasm was not matched by their skills.

I played on the right wing, and Dick was on the left. We played really well and we won. After the game we were asked if we would play regularly for them. I cannot remember Dick's reply, but I eagerly accepted the invitation. At that time I had only played for the school. What an opportunity!

During the following week the club secretary called at our house to sign me up, but my Dad overheard the conversation and told us both that there was no way he would agree, saying that I was too young. In retrospect, he was obviously right, but at the time it was a body blow. Incidentally, we had broken the rules by playing for St Mary's as we were not registered players, and we had played under false names!

Dick Spooner, to give him his full name, or R T Spooner as he appeared in Warwickshire's batting order for years, including their championship year, was our bandy-legged 'cuddy whifter', as we called all lefties.

Dick also played batsman-wicketkeeper for England. He played during the long reign of Godfrey Evans as England's wicketkeeper, and therefore only played on tours of the sub-continent, but he was capped for England nevertheless – as I was at football. It shows how much talent there was amongst us kids in those days.

Late in the following summer, that of 1938, a most important thing happened. I was playing in the usual 12–15 a-side match up Norton Avenue Rec., when three men who were watching, stopped us and asked us a marvellous question: Would we like to form a team and play in a league? Would we?! We were so keen that Eamont Road Club (as our club was named) put out two teams, A and B in the Stockton Minor League (for ages 14–16), and a team in the Junior League (for players aged 16–18).

We were very successful and I was in the 'B' team, which turned out to be the better of the two younger teams. We won the league and every cup we went in for. In fact, we even made the national newspapers: and this brought a fascinating development.

In 1939, we received a challenge to play a team from Cambridge at Easter. Now at that time the furthest I had ever travelled was the fifty miles to Scarborough, and many of the team had been no further than Redcar, a full fifteen miles from home. Cambridge was two hundred miles away! Unbelievable!

We assembled at the home of Mr Moore – one of the committee, whose son Charlie was our high scoring centre forward – on the evening before the trip. A team photograph was taken and instructions for the journey given. We were to play the challenging team on the Saturday, and then a team chosen from all of the teams in the Cambridge League on Easter Monday, on Cambridge City's ground, which to us was like playing at Wembley.

We won both games easily, even beating the selected team 6–0, but the most outstanding memories were threefold. The first was the train journey. We went into the guard's van and devised a game of football using a tennis ball. We were so excited: it really was the trip of our lives. The second was to do with where we were accommodated. Jimmy Jones, our centre half and the humorist of the team, was my partner as far as billeting was concerned, and we stayed the weekend at a house in Cherry Hinton, a village just outside of Cambridge. Strangely, 25 years later we were to live in Cherry Hinton Road.

Our hostess was very welcoming when we arrived on Good Friday, at about 5.00 pm. We were immediately served tea – on our own at a small table in the kitchen. To say that we were surprised indeed shocked at the crockery is an understatement. In this modern, bright, semi-detached house in a prosperous suburb of our greatest university city, our cups were without handles or saucers. The handles had been broken off at some time, but apparently they were considered good enough for us.

During the following day, the lady of the house said that she wanted to talk to us. She was most embarrassed and so very apologetic, and she told us a remarkable story.

She said that when she was told that we were coming down from County Durham, all she could think of was coalmines, dirt, and squalor. She expected us to be ill-mannered, dirty, and unused to such as nice crockery. Remarkably, she thought we used enamel mugs, and I recall Jimmy saying to me during our first meal that she would probably use old jam jars next.

It was an example of the parochialism of the pre-television and the early wireless days. The majority of the population had never been away from their own communities. Another illustration of this fact was to do with accents and dialects. They varied throughout the country, and indeed villages ten miles apart could speak quite differently. This phenomenon, of course still continues, although not to the extent it did. Perhaps it emanates from the lack of mobility and communication in those earlier days.

Anyway, for the remainder of our stay, we were given cups with handles and saucers, and the landlady could not do enough for us.

The third memory and unique occurrence was the great commotion caused by the police rounding up German students, presumably for deportation. War must have already been on the horizon.

All Christmases have been the same to me, in the most important way: the celebration of the birth of Jesus Christ. I have never tired of the Christmas story, from hearing it from Mam as a small boy, through St Gabriel's Sunday School, via Holy Trinity and St Mary the Virgin; the post-war Christmases in Todtglüsingen and Braunschweig (Brunswick), where 'Silent Night' was sung in the original German. 'Stille Nacht' brought me out in goose-pimples through the emotions of the time, that at last peace had come to the earth and that we sang about 'Himmlischer Ruhe', heavenly peace, in the language of our former foes, and in their homeland.

But one Christmas is to be remembered by a very sad happening. Mam was the epitome of the careful housewife and mother. She saved for Christmas, so that we could have that little extra in food and presents, which were special, as was the occasion. On the Saturday before the holy day, she would go to Stockton market – which incidentally had been held since the fourteenth century – and buy lots of fruit and delicacies, even a bottle of 'port wine' to go in the gorgeous crystal decanter (which now has pride of place on top of our cocktail cabinet), and for the children, 'Stones Green Ginger Wine'. Christmas 1938 should have been such a time.

However, it was not to be. Mam had her purse stolen whilst looking around 'Mrs Stott's stall', a favourite venue of hers. It was found later in the ladies' toilet in 'Spark's Cafe' opposite. Everything was left in except the twelve pounds she had assiduously saved. Dad said, 'Never mind, love', even though it was all the money they had. But that was Dad.

It is common knowledge that these days children often leave school and they still cannot spell, some cannot read properly, and it seems to me that few are skilled at mental arithmetic. I wonder why this should be. On these dreadful 'talk back' radio programmes we often hear people calling themselves 'educationalists', propounding theories regarding how much more advanced are today's children. But in what way?

Rather than attempt to prepare a list of their faults, it would be better for me to try to relate how we acted and were treated sixty years ago. First and foremost we were taught to respect our elders, including, of course, teachers. Being told 'not to cheek your elders', or to 'speak when you are spoken to', may suggest that we were impolite, but all of the children I knew at school or elsewhere, rarely needed such admonishing.

When in the infants' classes, all that the teacher needed to say before the start of a lesson was 'Quiet, please, children', and in the ten years and upwards classes, the entry of the teacher was the catalyst. Of course, the cane – now banned in most places as corporal punishment – was feared and rightly so, but it must have helped to maintain discipline. Classes were all very large, but this was never a problem.

I recall that they were split generally into four sections, each with an appointed monitor whose duties included giving out books and material and collecting them after the lesson. Broadly speaking, the subjects were arithmetic, reading, writing, spelling, poetry, drawing, singing, English grammar, scripture and practical botany – growing plants from seed etc. There was concentration on the important subjects and very little, if any, homework.

Handwriting was done initially using an HB pencil, and we were taught to press hard on the down strokes and to press lightly on the up strokes. Eventually came the transition to pen and ink, the latter being navy blue and was to be found in the small pot inkwells that fitted into a hole in the desks. The pens were made of wood with a metal nib holder, and the nib was removable. Blots were the biggest problem, and were accompanied by a good telling off.

Drawing required the use of coloured chalks and thick dark brown or black paper. I recall being sent home on one occasion to fetch a candlestick for the class to draw. Made of enamelled metal, it would be hard to find one today.

During this time, as always, I was kicking everything from a tennis ball to a tin can, and I generally carried a ball stuffed into my pocket. When I was at Holy Trinity a tremendous thing happened. We were all told to assemble in the school hall to greet an old boy from the school. This kind of thing happened several times, but the visitor was never as significant as this one.

He was George Allison, the Manager of the mighty Arsenal Football Club. Oh what joy! To see him in the flesh!

I never met him in later years and no doubt he has been dead some years now, but he had a great effect on me.

From then on, when I used to kick my tennis ball against our backyard door, avoiding the cross members, and keeping it going, left foot, right foot, I always said to myself that Mr Allison was watching. I could imagine him standing behind me, admiring me as the ball went backwards and forwards. I am sure that this gave me the determination to succeed.

The summer holidays had started as usual about the third week of July, and I enjoyed them as always, mostly with Peter O'Brien, my school pal. Incidentally, he was one of three brothers, one of whom – John – was a pilot, killed in the first 1,000 bomber raid on Germany, and Peter himself died in his thirties. We followed our usual leisure pursuits, which included walks over the fields to Thorpe Thewles, and Wynyard the home of Lord Londonderry.

We often visited his country seat or estate and we enjoyed the beauty of his woods and lake, although his Lordship never knew, probably because we did not use the main gate, preferring to climb over the fences. Often we would get up early and go looking for mushrooms, and then sell them to 'R T Trotters', the general store in Norton Village.

Other times we would ride on our bikes around the country lanes to villages such as Bishopton and Carlton, the former being of special interest to me, and the latter was where we knew of the best spot in the countryside for brambles (blackberries). My grandfather Anthony Rickaby, had been the village policeman at Bishopton for many years. I remember going there on the bus with my Auntie Nan, when she got talking to an old man who said that he remembered P C Rickaby. Nan told me that if there was a knock on the door when father was out, mother would go to the door with one of his helmets in her hands pretending to be polishing it. Gypsies and others beat a hasty retreat.

My bike, a Royal Enfield, cost five shillings, and I know that I was a bit put out because brother George's cost seven shillings and sixpence! Mine had a buckled front wheel and it was so bad that a few people tried to straighten it without success. Every now and then I would feel ashamed of it being rusty, and I would take it apart, clean and oil it, and put it together again. My dad always reckoned that when I had finished, there were sufficient parts left over to make another bike. I was no mechanic, but Dad did exaggerate.

Sometimes we went fishing for roach. I used to borrow George's rod and line, and Peter and I would sit underneath a big tree, which towered over the beck (stream) at a spot where it had widened to create a large round pool. It always seemed to be hot and sunny in those days, and we spent many happy hours watching for the float to bob up and down, signifying that a fish had been attracted by the maggots we used for bait.

Peter was a great diver and swimmer, unlike me, and he would climb the tree and dive into the pool from quite a height. I tried very hard to swim, and I had taken lessons at school, but despite this and going around with one of the school's best swimmers, I seemed to get no better.

We also used to ride to Seaton Carew, which was about ten miles away, to swim in the sea. We would often do this on a fine summer's evening and invariably we would be riding back in the dark without lights, not having the money to buy a new battery for the headlight. Many's the time when a 'bobby' would shout to us to stop, making us pedal even harder.

It was a good job that we were never caught, as the fine for riding a bicycle without lights was five shillings – the cost of my bike!

Many a day we would go to Norton Showfield to play football. There had not been a Show there for donkey's years, but it still retained its name. As long as there was a game going on we would just join in. If there were only a few of us, we would play 'three pots in'. This meant that one would play in goal, formed by two piles of coats, and the others would compete against each other. The first player to score three goals would then become goalkeeper, and the game would start again. It was wonderful practice for the skills of dribbling, tackling, and shooting, as well as goalkeeping.

On one side of the Showfield was Stockton Rugby Field, and on the other side Norton Tykes played cricket in the summer, and Norton Mixed Hockey Club played hockey in the winter. I have never seen or heard of mixed hockey since. This is surprising, as it seemed to be a game where both sexes gave a good account of themselves. I believe that of the eleven players in each side, six were male and five female.

Norton Tykes was very much a social type of cricket club, playing mainly village teams out in the country on a friendly basis. Most of their games were on Sunday afternoons and they practised most evenings. I was not a member, but they were happy to let me join in the practices. I also served as an umpire on many occasions, sometimes with unfortunate results.

There were three O'Neill brothers in the team. Peter was captain, Hubert was a very good fast bowler, and Terry was an all rounder. Hubert was prone to bowl the odd no-ball (overstepping the crease), and of course I would call out 'no-ball' – much to his annoyance.

Other players included two fine all round sportsmen, named Alec Grant and Horace Hale. Both were excellent cricketers and, in addition, they both played football for Stockton, in those days a Northern League team which was one of the most famous in England. Alec was a fine goalkeeper and Horace a very fast outside right, who no doubt would have gone on in the game, but for the onset of war. He was also a professional sprinter, and I used to train with him often.

Alec went into a Guards Regiment, and it was probably in the first year of the war that I had an awful shock when I saw him on crutches in Norton High Street. He had lost a leg in France.

I think that I was as good at cricket as I was at football, and sadly, this normally friendly outfit was very much responsible for me not continuing in the game. At the time, I had already played a few games for them, generally when they were short of a player, and on this particular day we were playing in the Middlesbrough area. We had got the opposition out for 109 and I was last man in. When it was my turn to bat, we were being well beaten, with fewer than 40 on the board. I joined skipper Peter at the wicket with the game virtually over.

I batted very well as did Peter, and we saw the 100 up, but when a few runs short of their total, Peter was run-out. I did not think it was my fault, but I was not ready for what happened when we got back to the pavilion. I was only fourteen, and whilst expecting the captain's plaudits for a stand of over 70 runs, instead he blamed me for running him out and losing the game.

I was very disappointed and worse was to come. Shortly afterwards I was at the ground practising, and when we finished, the two footballers, Alec and Horace, said that they were going next door into the football field for a 'kick in'. Of course, I was with them in a flash.

After practice I went back to the pavilion to collect my sports coat, which I had hung on a coat hook. Most of the members had gone home, but one of those remaining said to me, 'Peter is mad with you.' I said, 'What for?' He then told me that Peter had said that I had tried to steal a pair of batting gloves, which he had seen sticking out of a pocket of my coat.

I was shattered. It was normal procedure that at the end of each session at the nets, we would all carry wickets, balls, bats, leg guards, and batting gloves back to the pavilion. Obviously, I had carried a number of things, including a pair of batting gloves, and in a rush to get a game of football, I had hung up my jacket with the gloves still in the pocket.

I never went near the ground again, and I never heard from Peter O'Neill. The other club in the village, Norton CC, charged a membership fee that I would not have even asked my parents for. They had enough expense keeping the two of us at the grammar school.

CHAPTER SIX
THE WAR BEGINS

Shortly afterwards the war started, and I probably played cricket three times during the next eight years till my demob, when I decided not to play anymore.

As most would know, the war started on 3 September 1939 at 11.00 am. I was glued to the radio as all of Britain were, and I heard the words of Neville Chamberlain finishing with, 'We are at war with Germany'. It was a sunny day and I felt excited one moment, and then I felt as though we were doomed the next. We had already heard of the air raid danger, and air raid shelters had been erected in gardens, and in our case, in the backyard.

I went out in the street to see what it looked like, now we were at war, but of course it was no different. We soon had another shock to the system, when the air raid sirens went off. It turned out to be a malfunction!

The only good news around was when we had a letter from the school to say that the summer holidays were to be extended several weeks, whilst the school buildings were being strengthened against air raids! When we went back they had strengthened the cloakrooms to act as shelters, and we had to practise what to do if the air raid siren went off. Of course, gas masks were part of the drill, as it was expected that we would be subjected to poison gas attacks.

Looking back, I suppose we were to some extent prepared mentally for war. The year before when Germany invaded Czechoslovakia, I remember I was at Auntie Nan's house, when the newsboys were shouting 'Special Gazette' around all of the streets. I had only experienced one 'Special' before, around about 1931 when there was a riot at Dartmoor Prison, and with so few people having wirelesses (we did not call them radios), the quickest way to get red-hot news circulated was via newsboys and the 'Special Gazette'.

In 1938 I recall the thrill which I felt when I heard the boy shouting, 'The Germans invade Czechoslovakia', but after a year of daily news re the danger of war, when it did happen, I realised the seriousness of it.

For some time the local 5th Battalion of the Durham Light Infantry had been training as a searchlight unit, and every night at the Drill Hall at the bottom of our street, we would see the 'Terriers', as they were known, practising. The Territorial Army was the Army Reserve, training in peacetime, to be called up when war looked to be imminent.

A few weeks before the declaration of war, the Drill Hall became a place of sadness, because the 5th Durham Light Infantry (DLI) was mobilised, and all the 'lads' as we called them, went off in army trucks leaving behind sweethearts, mothers, wives and children.

Two of the first to go were my Uncles Rob and Oliver, my mother's two brothers, both of whom left several children looking forlorn as the trucks disappeared down the road to Stockton Station. People were remembering what was only 25 years before that time, when the DLI had more battalions in France than any other County Regiment.

Rob and Oliver were to have a tough war, fighting up and down the desert in North Africa, then the invasion of Sicily, and finally battling all the way up Italy. Fortunately they returned unharmed in body, if not psychologically.

About two or three miles away from us at Billingham, was the ICI (Imperial Chemical Industries) works, a huge complex employing 25,000 people, and we realised that this just had to be a prime bombing target. To protect the industrial areas of Teesside – a great centre of steel making, the manufacturing of all things made of metal, plus the chemical works which had a large Coal Oil plant – was very important for the war effort. Bringing crude oil from such places as the Middle East was obviously going to be hazardous, so ICI was going to be a vital producer of petrol.

Incidentally, in the eighties, when new methods of energy production have been very much in the news, I do not think that I have heard the Coal Oil method mentioned.

To help protect the area's people and factories, the army installed a large number of searchlights, batteries of anti-aircraft guns and balloons. The balloons were grey and long with fins at the rear, and were tethered to the ground by steel cables. It was the cable that was the important component. Due to the circle of steel cables, German planes could not come in low from the sea and bomb with accuracy. If they tried it, the balloon cables would bring them down.

In the event they certainly did the trick because, despite many attempts, ICI worked at full capacity throughout the war. The nearest the Luftwaffe got was on their first raid on England.

The first raid on Britain was, in fact, on the Firth of Forth in Scotland, and the next was on Billingham. It was at about lunchtime one day in the spring of 1940. The air raid sirens had gone and for the first time we heard that dreaded whistle of a bomb falling to earth. A Dornier bomber had come in low over the North Yorkshire coast, and had off-loaded its stick of bombs.

We heard the whistles and then the crumps as they exploded. Our house rocked as though shaken by an earthquake, and our windows and those of other houses in the street were the first to be damaged in England. The bombs had dropped on what we knew as Billingham Bottoms, the low-lying land in the valley between Norton and Billingham.

We had been advised to protect ourselves from injury from splintered glass, by criss-crossing all windows with strips of brown sticky paper; and it certainly worked.

This was also the first time that we heard the gun battery known to us as 'Kia Ora' firing. They were of a large calibre, and we knew that when they fired we could be in trouble, as the enemy planes had to be by then very close. We could always hear the coastal anti-aircraft guns having a go as the bombers crossed the coast, but when 'Kia Ora' got involved, we used to duck for safety. Incidentally, the name of the battery came from the name of the large country house outside of Norton where the guns were sited. Strangely, ICI took it over during the war for extra office space. It must have been horrific for the staff when the batteries fired during office hours.

It is amazing how one adapts to almost anything. We even grew accustomed to air raid sirens, and to how much time we had before we should take cover. We would hear the coastal batteries around by Hartlepool, about ten miles away as the bomber flies, and this meant that if they were coming our way, they would be overhead in about two or three minutes.

Our air raid shelter was of very thick brick, with a reinforced concrete roof, built up against the back of the house, in the backyard. Before my brother George went in the army, he always disdained its protection, and slept on during the raids. Mam used to be terrified for him, but he had an opinion on what were the chances of being hit, and they did not warrant losing a night's sleep!

As it turned out, he could have slept in his bed for all of the war, and he would have been unharmed. Not so for Mam and Dad. When 'the bomb' dropped in Benson Street later, a large piece of a wall came through the roof and went plumb through the middle of their bed. George's bedroom was full of acrid brick dust, but he had worked out his risks correctly.

As I write this bomb story, I am well aware that people in the East End of London could write dozens like it, but it is worthy of record for sociological reasons as well as for being a matter of fact.

We were in the shelter, where we often retired – during periods of much aerial activity, and particularly if there was a 'bomber's moon' when it was like daylight

– instead of going to bed. Dad was at Hartlepool on the night shift, so there were just three of us, Mam, nine-year old John, and me.

The siren had ceased, and we had heard the distinctive throb-throb-throb of German planes as several passed over to the accompaniment of heavy anti-aircraft fire. We were always grateful when the last throb ebbed away in the distance, without us hearing the dreaded whistle of a bomb – or bombs – falling. We always said that if you could hear the whistle, you were safe, that it had missed you, because the bomb would hit the ground before the sound of the whistle reached you.

This was not much consolation: as what about the rest of the salvo! We had not heard them yet. Then a strange thing happened. There was a tremendous thud. The house shook. Then came the whistle. But what about the explosion?

A deathly hush was suddenly pierced by screams of, 'Help, help', and then the earth shook, followed by the noise and the blast of a tremendous explosion. It had been one of the cruelest forms of attack on a civilian population. The bomb was huge and was of the delayed-action type. People would rush to the scene to help, and the delay was intended to kill them too. So ambulance workers, Red Cross volunteers, policemen, air raid wardens, etc, were specific targets: attracted by a bomb penetrating a building and obliterated by the delayed detonation.

The bomb had gone straight through a house diagonally opposite the front of ours, and had buried itself deep in the ground. The house had collapsed, trapping Mrs Fisher, her sister, and her son Ernie, and it must have been the Fishers who were screaming. They were all killed and it was said that very little of them was found. Many houses had been destroyed, and many more badly damaged.

Now Ernie, who was fourteen, was a pal of mine. He worked for Newman's in the village High Street, delivering groceries on a push bike. I used to go with him sometimes, especially in the autumn, when the horse chestnuts were about. Ernie used to go to the big houses on Norton Green, houses with back gardens centuries old. Some of the chestnut trees must have been there for centuries too, and it was fascinating to think that generations of village lads had enjoyed 'jarping chestnuts' from the fruits of the same trees. For the uninitiated, 'jarping' involved drilling a hole through the nut, putting a string through it with a knot at one end to stop it coming off, and then challenging your pals to a contest. 'Jarp yer!' was the cry. Then in turn each would aim his chestnut to 'jarp' or strike the other, until one broke and fell off the string.

The winner would then enquire of the other how many chestnuts it had broken, and add that number to his own score. As one can imagine, the truth was exaggerated, with claims of nuts being such as 'conker 110' being quite frequent.

A final comment on this autumnal sport is that God's beauty is never better portrayed than in the humble horse chestnut. The various shades of brown run into one another as do the tide-marks on the beach.

My last memory of Ernie Fisher is very pathetic. It is of his bike. A bike, which he was happy to loan me before I got one of my own, and which was his pride and joy. It was on the roof of a house, four or five away from his own.

After the bomb went off, it was not long before the siren wailed the 'all-clear' signifying that the raid was over. We were safe, but this was the village where Mam's parents lived, along with her sister Emma, two brothers, and a niece – all in separate houses,. Her sister lived in Benson Street, where the damage turned out to be the worst, and her niece lived nearly opposite us in Pine Street.

It was not long before the best and the worst was known. The moon was full and its light made the night like the day, so that when our backyard door opened, it was easy to see the people who entered. There was Auntie Emma, cousins Alan, Sidney, Vera, Phyllis and Olive, all in pyjamas or nightgowns, covered in soot.

They were all uninjured, and when I saw the ruins of their house, this ranked as a miracle. There was not one outside wall intact. However, the cupboard under the stairs was still standing, although covered in bricks and bits of timber. This is where Auntie Emma and her family had sheltered! I recall Sidney saying, 'It (the bomb) must have come down with carpet slippers on.' Cousin Jessie was safe too, so our portion of the family had survived.

Shortly afterwards we knew that all were well. Granddad must have run the couple of miles from the other side of Norton, for he arrived breathless, after being told that Pine Street and Benson Street – where ten of his own flesh and blood lived – had been bombed. It was even worse for Grandma, for in those days when only the wealthy had telephones, she had to wait until Granddad returned with the news. The latter was able to tell us that Uncles Rob and Oliver's families, all in Norton, were safe too and that their area had not been bombed.

The damage to our house was quite extensive, but we considered ourselves lucky when we saw Benson Street through a large gap in the houses that used to face us. Our bedrooms were wrecked and the 'front room' downstairs was badly damaged.

Mam's usual philosophy saved the day. 'As long as we are all safe, we can always get another house', 'Don't worry, worse things happen at sea', etc! Of course, Dad was the next one.

When he finished work at 6.00 am he was told that Norton had been bombed. His 'United' bus could not get him home fast enough, and I can remember his face when he found us all well.

There was much cleaning up to do. Much 'make and mend'. Auntie Emma's family had lost most of their clothes. They had just disappeared in the whirlwind, as had Sid's bottle of champagne, being kept for 'when the war is over'.

The Maison de Danse dance hall in Stockton was a bomb relief centre, and I went with cousin Alan to get a new set of clothes, as most of his had gone.

I suppose every cloud has a silver lining, but Mam's silver lining was clouded by guilt. Whilst most houses only had gas for lighting and cooking, we were rather modern, having electricity, but just downstairs! Upstairs it was a candle in a candlestick for illumination.

We had to live downstairs until the bedrooms were rebuilt, and a new roof put on. One day when a good deal of progress had been made upstairs, the electricians arrived. The wiring in the 'front room' (downstairs) had been damaged. They renewed the wiring and then proceeded upstairs and wired up all three bedrooms and the landing, putting in lamp holders and electric globes.

Mam was horrified. It was not our house. We rented it. So it was not of pecuniary gain to us, but Mam did nothing to stop 'the men' putting in what was not there before! I think she took that worry and the guilt with her to the grave.

Earlier I referred to almost all of the family living in Norton. This was commonplace. Families lived close together; when one married he or she rented a house as near to their mam as possible; and all of their houses were 'homes' to all, meaning that in those days of unlocked doors, we just walked in and out of each other's places. Helping one another was a way of life.

Being a member of an extended family was great and, although it still occurs in the Eastern countries, and perhaps in remote outback towns here in Australia, it is virtually non-existent in more 'sophisticated' communities, such as Perth, Western Australia.

Quite remarkably, life carried on almost normally, despite the fact that there was a World War going on, and this normality, of course, included school.

I am sure that I am not alone in confessing that I did not take advantage of my grammar school education, not fully anyway. When at Holy Trinity we had hardly any homework, and I found that learning in the classroom was easy. The first day at Trinity, I was given seven different kinds of arithmetic, and in just the time it took to write the answers, I got them right.

I do not think that I ever got a sum wrong, and I was always top at English, so when I arrived for my first day at the 'Grammar' I would have been the most advanced of all of the new pupils. There were many new subjects in the curriculum, including Latin and French, and looking back I should have taken them all in my stride, but right from the start I used to rush my homework. Consequently, I failed to learn the basics, the grammar and vocabulary in the case of the new languages, and of course without the right foundation, nothing can be built.

I always managed to scrape through and, for example, when I went to France during the war, I found that I could hold a conversation, even to the extent of being complimented on my accent on occasions. This made my regrets even greater, as it became obvious that with a bit of effort I could have done really well.

In later years I found that the Latin I had learned was a great help in knowing my own language better, and in my first visit to Spain I was able to understand the gist of what I read in the newspapers, as there were so many words derived from Latin. When Francis Chichester sailed around the world it made front page news, but not for the right reasons. Instead of praise for the intrepid circumnavigator, the writer immediately linked his Christian name with one Sir Francis Drake, and went on to criticise him hysterically, referring to him as a pirate. It was really ridiculous, but it was obvious that the Spanish were still anti-English deep down, although as hosts to British holiday-makers they were very hospitable.

The modern younger generation must get tired of hearing how hard it was 'when I was at school' from their parents, but there is a lot of truth in it. For example, when I took my School Certificate examination, I spent every night, all night, in our air raid shelter, unable to sleep properly. By the end of the week I was worn out.

And to get to school there were no lifts from parents as cars were almost non-existent, and we just had to get there as best we could. For me, this included catching the bus, or if Mam could not afford it, walking (which was perhaps the most common), or going on my roller skates, or later on, by bicycle (that is if it happened to be rideable). I seemed to have the propensity to ride over any nail or piece of glass on the road.

To conclude my account of my school days, a few little anecdotes.

Playing in an inter-form football match, as I scored my tenth goal, out of ten, the teacher/referee told me that if I scored another he would send me home. Then at the end of the year assembly, whilst reporting on the football team's performance, Mick O'Donnell the Latin master said that Rickaby would be a good player, if he were not so selfish. It seemed that our school preferred good 'triers' to good players. Mick failed to say that I scored almost all of the goals in inter-school games.

I was also once in hot water on the cricket field, when I was fielding and ran like mad to save a boundary. I then intended to try to run a batsman out, but after all of my effort, I looked up to find no one at the wicket to receive the ball. However, a boy called Hutchinson was actually standing between me and the stumps with his back turned, so I hurled the ball to just miss him, but so that he would get the message.

Unfortunately, a teacher umpiring on the next pitch got a different message. He said that I tried to hit 'Hutch', but my telling him that I would have hit the disinterested fielder if I had wanted to, only served to upset the master more, and he then sent me home.

Anyway, I did pass the School Certificate examination, and my last visit to the school was to receive a piece of parchment on Speech Day.

I suppose my only lasting claims to fame as far as Stockton Grammar School is concerned, were to be the only Old Boy to play football for England, and to have jumped 17 feet one inch in the junior long jump, a record which stood for many years and may be still standing.

Another sporting achievement (drawn from a large number) was when I first ran in the cross country race. I had done no training, and I had no idea of the route. The rest of the competitors had been practising on the actual terrain, so I ran behind the front pack and, when we entered the school field where the tape was, I just sprinted ahead and won easily.

We went on three trips during my time at the grammar school, the first being to a match factory at West Hartlepool. It was very interesting and it was my first experience of mass production. We saw the timber arriving and the matches leaving to be delivered to wholesalers.

What were in fact tree trunks came in on big lorries. They were then automatically stripped of their bark and cut into 'slices' the exact width of a match. A cutter then came down and cut the 'slices' into thousands of matchsticks which, still held together, were dipped into a few different substances that formed the flammable 'heads'. The match boxes were made of the same timber as the matches, and women filled the boxes and another machine wrapped up a dozen boxes at a time. Finally we saw them being made into orders and being put in a van for shipment to a wholesaler.

Our second trip was to Edinburgh, and I was sick most of the way there and back, but I enjoyed our tour of the Scottish capital, particularly the Zoo and the museum. Being a sweet tooth, I found a new confection, Edinburgh rock, which was quite different to the English type. I bought Mam a handkerchief in the Stuart tartan. I always bought her something.

The third trip was the best. It was to the Roman Wall, only 45 miles north and of tremendous interest. It was built by Emperor Hadrian in the second century AD, and stretches right across England, from Wallsend on the East Coast to Bowness on the West Coast.

There are a number of forts in between, and some of them have been converted into museums where lots of artefacts dug up along the wall are on show. The exhibits are extraordinary, as the designs of so many of them have hardly changed over two thousand years. Objects such as bottles and vases for instance, look as though they are of recent manufacture, and the manual sheep shears, which have only been superseded by electrical shears in recent years, were almost identical in those distant days.

It was very exciting to stand on top of the wall, which is about six feet high and eight feet wide, and look out on precisely the same view as did the Roman sentries.

Another memorable occasion was when I went to Leeds with Peter O'Brien to see England play Australia at cricket. It was on Saturday, 23 July 1938 and the Headingley ground was packed. We sat on the grass and were thrilled to see the great Don Bradman score a century, 103 to be exact. He was magnificent, and another great player playing that day was Wally Hammond, perhaps the greatest of all players.

Today when a player takes a catch there is such a fuss made. He throws the ball sky high, and the rest of the team rush at him and pat him on the back, and even worse, they pat each other's palms. At Leeds that day, my hero took two slip catches, and on both occasions I saw the ball 'snicked', and like everyone else my eyes moved to the boundary. For a moment it was a mystery as to where the ball had gone, until Hammond was seen calmly and without fuss lobbing the ball to the wicketkeeper.

When Stan McCabe was batting, the ball hit his pads and I think just about everyone in the ground, including the English fielders, shouted, 'How's that?',But the umpire just shook his head. The very next ball seemed to do the same, and a lone voice shouted, 'How's that?' There was deadly quiet for what seemed an eternity, until a wag in the crowd shouted to me, 'That's right young 'un, give him out!' I wished that the ground could have swallowed me up.

My village cricket team, Norton, was always very good. The captain in my school days was DCH Townsend, who played for England when he was at the university, and thus followed in the footsteps of his father. They were one of the very few father and sons to represent their country.

Another great village sporting family was the Walfords. David captained Great Britain's hockey team in the 1948 Olympic Games and his brother Michael also played in that team. Michael also played for Somerset at cricket and had he not been a full-time schoolmaster in Dorset, he would have been one of the greats of the game along with May, Cowdrey, and company.

Jim Grigor was a great slow bowler, left arm, and playing for Durham County, the only Minor County to play 'the tourists', he bowled Stan McCabe at Sunderland in 1938. Then there was Dick Spooner ...

CHAPTER SEVEN
I LEAVE SCHOOL

I left school in July 1940 with little idea about what I would like to do. We had received no advice on careers, and I was so ignorant in this regard that I told people that I would like to be a draughtsman, although I knew nothing about the profession. I applied to ICI, the largest employer in the area, for a job as a junior clerk, but all I got was a note of rejection.

The 'Evening Gazette' advertised for a 'Junior Reporter' and due to my application and the mentioning of Uncle Charlie's credentials, the editor, who lived in Stockton, gave me an interview.

One had to learn shorthand and start by attending the Local Courts and reporting the lesser cases. Saturday afternoons were to be worked on occasions, for reasons I have forgotten, but I know that this was a negative point as it would have interfered with my football. This, and the starting wage of seven shillings and sixpence per week, resulted in my turning down the post, which was in fact offered to me.

I was also thinking of Mam, and I considered that my contribution to home expenses should have been more than seven and six. Looking back, that was a mistake, as I have realised since that it would have been eminently suitable for me. Strangely, nearly fifty years later I was to write a weekly newspaper column.

Head Wrightson and Co Ltd, Teesdale Ironworks, Thornaby-on-Tees, eventually took me on as a wages clerk. I got to like the work, but not the hours: 7.30 am to 5.00 pm Monday to Friday and 7.30 am to 12.00 noon on Saturdays.

I liked the mental arithmetic involved in the job, and I was far more efficient than any of my colleagues. There was also a lot of routine and repetition, which could be boring, but all in all it was interesting.

I was able to get around the works, which covered an enormous area, and included a shipyard, blacksmith's shop, machine shop, iron foundry, brass foundry, steel foundry, fitting shop, and a number of works offices. How all the workmen could work with cold steel on a freezing day or night I did not know. The hours in the steel foundry were 6.00 am to 6.00 pm Monday to Thursday and 6.00 am to 5.00 pm on Friday for the day shift, and 6.00 pm to 6.00 am on the night shift with Friday nights 5.00 pm to 6.00 am. And how those poor devils worked. For rush jobs they also worked weekends.

My Auntie Emma, Mam's sister, started the war as a welder, and finished it as forewoman welder building all welded ships. Granddad spent the war on security duty on the main gate, and cousin Jessie worked in the shipyard office, all of us at Head Wrightson's.

Every now and then I used to be called to the Company Secretary's office. This was the holy of holies and normally such a visit was for a rise or the sack, but in my case it was because Uncle Charlie was visiting the company. He worked during the war for the Ministry of Works, Iron and Steel Control, and I know that for all of the war he fixed the price of iron and steel for the whole country. I used to have a chat with him and the boss, and I used to feel quite proud.

The switch for the Air Raid Siren was in our office, and so we used to receive the 'red alerts' and I used to work the siren. Then off we would troop to the air raid shelters. To show how we even got used to air raids; consider the fact that I used to quite like the change, and the opportunity to have a chat with otherwise busy colleagues.

One of my footballing pals worked in the shipyard, Bill Harburn was his name, and he was an apprentice plater. He was also quite a wag, and he used to make me laugh at the method he had of making extra cash. In the war, with a shortage of meat, many people, myself excluded, would find rabbit an attractive non-rationed addition to their meat supply. Bill used to raffle a rabbit every week. Nothing extraordinary in that you might say, and you would be right, but it was the way he went about it. Low in funds, he would invest twopence on a book of raffle tickets. He would then sell the raffle tickets at twopence each, until he had sufficient to buy a rabbit from a local shop, plus enough profit for himself, and then he would get someone to draw the winning ticket. I think of Bill in two totally opposite ways: one as a happy go lucky, charming, smiling friend, and the other in stark tragedy.

One day in the 1970's Leni and I were watching the news on TV in Perth and one of the main stories was of the re-opening of the Westgate Bridge in Melbourne. It had crashed about ten years before, and many workers were killed. Included in the ceremony was the unveiling of a plaque on which was listed those who had been killed. As the camera panned in on the names, it rested on 'William Harburn'. It was an awful shock, and we also saw the old newsreel showing the dead being carried out on stretchers. They had been suffocated in the mud.

The shock was not that we did not know that he was dead. We had heard of his death whilst we were still in England, but we remembered it as being on the Sydney Harbour Bridge, wrongly, as it transpired.

It was so eerie and traumatic to see poor Bill brought out on a stretcher about ten years after the event. It was a great shame, particularly as he had done well, including playing football for Australia.

Another Head Wrightson employee was a member of the football fraternity. Jackie Carr worked in the blacksmith's shop, and he was an all time great for Middlesbrough FC, playing before and after the First World War. My dad told me stories of Jackie's great prowess and of his mischievous nature, including when he sat on the ball and he invited the opposition to come and take it off him. I used to feel so sorry for him, that he was getting old, his career was far behind him, and I was just starting. Indeed, it was whilst at Head Wrightson that I played my first game for Middlesbrough. Now, of course, I am as Jackie was. Life passes quickly.

Another Head Wrightson football story is worth recounting. The works always had a good football team, and indeed, they did well in most sports as they had excellent clubrooms and sports grounds. When men worked all of their lives for the same firm, they had a pride in the company, and in return, in addition to the security of the job, they were provided with welfare and sports facilities. 'The Club' was always an important feature.

Jeff Earnshaw was a fine example of the above, working all of his life for 'Head's', and a leading 'club' member. He ran the football team, and played himself in the late thirties and early forties. Their greatest accomplishment to 1941 was reaching the North Riding Amateur Cup Final (The North Riding being the northern part of Yorkshire). They were to play their arch rivals Bon Lea, another works team, on the Victoria Ground, which was the home of Stockton Football Club.

Quite against the rules, Jeff asked my pal, Johnnie French, and me to play in the final! We were both Middlesbrough players and not having been registered 'Head's' players for that season, we were ineligible.

However, never refusing the chance of a game anywhere, we played, presumably under assumed names! We won, and playing centre forward I scored three! What a night!

It was followed by a celebration in a local pub, and this was significant for the following reason: I had my first glass of rum, and it made me so sick that it was also my last!

A few years later, in the campaign in Europe, we were quite often offered rum when it was very cold, and/or when we were soaking wet, and I could not even bear the smell. But enough of rum – for both drinking and writing!

To return to my football career proper. After the Cambridge trip, we only had one or two games to play before the season was over. During the summer of 1938 I played cricket for the school, and as mentioned before, had that unhappy experience with Norton Tykes.

By the time July came around the ad lib games of football began again in Blue Hall Recreation Ground. Shortly afterwards our committee started to organise for the new season and they recruited some very fine players. Three of them in particular became firm friends of mine: Bill Harburn and John French, both referred to earlier, and Len Franklin. We were still in the Stockton and District Minor League, as the oldest of us was fifteen. We got off to a great start to the season on 2 September 1939, but the next day the war started.

Everything was chaotic. The whole of the Stockton and District League, both minors and juniors, closed down. I thought then that this was ridiculous and I still think so. We had a great team, but no one to play.

It was then that our committee put on their thinking caps, and they came up with the idea of playing in the Middlesbrough Junior League (the minor section having also closed down). Most of the players were seventeen or eighteen, quite a big difference to us fourteen and fifteen year olds.

I cannot recall the reasons, but the committee seemed to fall out with one another, and although we got on well with all of them, we finally had to decide to go with one or other of the factions.

The one we chose came up with a new name 'Middlesbro' Crusaders', and so the 1940–41 season began with us in different colours.

We had a great season and our best feat was to beat South Bank Juniors 4–3 on their own ground. They were a Middlesbrough Football Club nursery team, and all seventeen or eighteen to our fifteen and sixteen years of age.

The sequel was that during the summer of 1941 five of us, Bill McLean, John French, Len Franklin, Bill Harburn and I, were asked to sign for South Bank, and this meant that if we were good enough we would sign for Middlesbrough. What a thrill this was, and it laid the foundations for perhaps the most successful season any team ever had. We all won a place in the team, so we were joined by six of the regular South Bank players, several of whom had already played a few games with Middlesbrough's first team.

We played 37 games, of which we won 36, lost 1, scored 409 goals, conceded only 24, and the team who beat us in the North Riding Senior Cup was a team containing several professional players, and they were lucky to win.

We won three cups in addition to the League, and during the season, Arran, McLean, French, Gilbraith, Franklin, and I, all played in Middlesbrough's first team at least once.

My first game was at Newcastle United, a day never to be forgotten. I had a telegram that read, 'Can you play at Newcastle Saturday?'. What a silly question! I hardly slept a wink on the Friday night. A taxi picked me up and took me to the station, where I joined up with the team. I was so nervous. Here I was in the same team as Bobby Baxter, Middlesbrough and Scotland's captain; Dave Cumming, Scotland's goalkeeper; Bill Forrest, Middlesbrough's famous left half; and other well known professionals. Bill McLean was also playing in his first game.

Taxis took us from Newcastle station to the 'County Hotel' where we had boiled fish for lunch. I could hardly hold my knife and fork for nerves. Then off to St James' Park, one of the holy of holies of the football world.

As the taxi stopped by the players' entrance, I looked with interest at the long queues of supporters, and to my amazement I actually saw my dad going through the turnstiles. Out of all of the turnstiles and all of the people and the time factor, it was a great coincidence.

He had told me that he could not come to the match because he was working and, although I wanted him there, his absence would have taken some pressure off me. Of course, I could have got him a seat in the grandstand, because players were always given two seats, but dear old Dad did not want me to worry about him. But there he was!

Wearing the magical red shirt with a white collar, white shorts, and red and white hooped stockings, was a dream come true. I must have been so naive and impressionable, as I thought it really luxurious to be given 'Brylcreem' to put on my hair.

Within a few minutes of the start I had to take a corner kick. I put the ball by the corner flag, walked backwards a few paces and stopped, prior to running forward and lofting the ball into the goalmouth. As I stopped, I looked behind to see that if I had taken one more step back, I would have fallen backwards over the low concrete wall, and down three or more feet to land on my head on the hard ground!

Whenever I played there in later years, I used to look at the spot where my career nearly ended, and wondered if any one had done the same.

Strangely, my first 'away' game for West Bromwich Albion eight and a half years later was on the very same ground; the ground that became my favourite. There is nothing better in sport throughout the world, than to play in front of a packed ground of 'Geordie' spectators.

Another game at St James' Park a few years later was to be the precursor of a most surprising event, about which I will write later!

Johnnie, Lenny, Bill, and I certainly deserved to get on in our favourite game of football, for when we played for South Bank we used to get there by catching a bus to Middlesbrough and then a 'trackless tram' to South Bank. It took well over an hour, and as we trained on Tuesdays and Thursdays, and played on Saturdays, it was quite expensive too.

Of course, due to the wartime 'blackout', except for the very beginning of the season, and at the end, it was dark. We trained from 7.00 pm to 9.00 pm and, except on moonlit nights, it was pretty miserable. When the moon shone, we used to play with white painted footballs, an innovation at that time, and we used to really enjoy ourselves.

At the end of every session, we had to do a hundred skips without 'clicking', and old Jack Cottrell used to do the counting. Even if you clicked on ninety-nine, he would make you do another hundred. It certainly made us smart skippers.

The same Jack must have been the worst psychologist in the world, because one night after training he really upset me, although I did not show it. I was seventeen and playing really well, hardly the time to be told that 'if we had had you a year or two earlier, we could have made a good player out of you!'

Quite often there would be an air raid warning during training, and this meant there were no buses, and we had to walk home about ten or twelve miles. If the anti-aircraft guns were firing, there was always a danger of being hit by shrapnel. We really must have been keen.

Lenny Franklin introduced us to the world of racing whilst on a 'trackless', one Saturday. He said that you could make a lot of money at the 'over the sticks' (his expression for steeplechasing) by backing the first, third, and fifth favourites, then 'doubling-them-up' and then a 'treble'. It sounded doubtful to me, but I put in my shilling for a few weeks...

It was amazing how we got used to life in wartime. We laughed and joked and enjoyed ourselves, despite the air raids and the frequent air raid warnings. We knew by the sound of the engines whether an approaching plane was 'one of ours' or 'one of theirs', and we became disciplined to the extent that we still went to the cinema in the blackout, knowing that there was always a chance that we would have to leave, if the siren sounded.

Cinemas were busier then than at any other time, and we always had to join a queue to get in. In Stockton we had six cinemas, and we had to queue just about every time at every one. In fact, sometimes we would go to one specifically because it had the shortest queue.

One of our favourite haunts was Pacittos Ice Cream Parlour, and our favourite treat a vanilla ice cream with strawberry sauce. Some time around 1941 or '42, the Government played a foul trick on us. They banned ice cream for the duration of the war. What a blow! However, we made the most of the last evening. The Pacittos' said that all of the ice cream had to be eaten up before they closed. Of course, we were extremely helpful in this regard, and decided that however long it took, we would be there to the bitter end, or was it the sweet end? Never was so much ice cream eaten per person in one evening, before or since.

It really was the end of an era, because apart from our close group of friends, Lenny, Johnnie, Bill, and I, we knew lots of others who frequented the Parlour, and after this finale we saw them no more.

Compared to today, our teenage pursuits, even at eighteen, were mild in the extreme.

Stockton High Street, the widest High Street in the country, was most popular for lads and lasses. They walked along the broad pavements in the long summer evenings, and on Saturdays and Sundays, eyeing one another up and down, and if in luck pairing off. If this happened early enough it could result in a trip to the pictures to sit in the back row. This was just the ultimate in daring and was something to boast about. And then of course there could be 'taking her home', which was mostly walking as the buses did not run very late in the war.

Quite a few young people smoked in those days when Woodbines were ten for 4 1/2d, though not many drank beer until late in their teens. My biggest privation was the scarcity of sweets and chocolates. They were rationed to two ounces per week, and this could mean one small bar of chocolate. I relied on Mam and Dad to help me out, but it really was frustrating for me!

By the summer of 1942 I began to expect my calling-up papers. Eventually I had to be medically examined, and as I have written earlier, my own doctor just happened to be on duty, so with his prior knowledge of me, he passed me immediately.

CHAPTER EIGHT
I JOIN THE ARMY

Eventually the order came. I had to report to the General Service Corps at Blackdown Camp, Deepcut, Surrey, on 15 October. I suppose, like millions of others, it came as a shock despite all the expectation and preparation of the previous months. The football season had started and Middlesbrough Football Club had created a new team called the 'Colts'. I had played all of the games to that date, and an important thing had happened. After several seasons as a forward, I had changed to right back due to the No 2's injury in a game, and as it transpired, this was to have a great effect on my future. Although I played at centre half later in my army career, it was at right back that I eventually played for West Bromwich Albion and in representative games for England and the Football League.

I travelled by the night train to London from Thornaby, and on the afternoon prior to my departure I went with Mam to the 'Globe Cinema' in Stockton to see Bing Crosby in 'Holiday Inn'. It was a most beautiful film, and whenever I hear any of the music from it, my thoughts go to my Mam, and how that afternoon turned out to be our last together as mother and single son, for when I was to cast off my khaki uniform, it was as a married man.

It is a pity that when we are young we do not really understand the deeper feelings of our parents. Only later could I appreciate how she must have felt that last day. Her second son was off to the war. Her first was already there. Would they survive? Would they return? I know now that she and Dad must have put their arms around each other, and tried to comfort one another. But words would have done little good.

I arrived in London early in the morning. This was exciting as I had not been to the capital before. I went by 'Underground', which was another thrill, to Waterloo Station, where I was to get a Southern Railway train to Brookwood in Surrey. I had only seen LNER trains before. Everything was new and different, but this was only the first and newest of the many experiences to which I was about to be introduced.

I had led a very protected life so far, in a quiet and happy home, full of love and support. An extended family of aunts, uncles, cousins, grandparents and friends surrounded me; and I had never really had a problem.

Suddenly I realised that this was all over. I had been pitched into the real, hard world, particularly when I alighted at Brookwood. I lost my freedom in a very few minutes. A tough looking sergeant with a loud hailer called out that anyone for Blackdown Camp should get into the first three-ton lorry outside the station.

I had travelled down with a lad called Pass, a footballer like me, who was en route to another camp in the same area. He was also from Stockton, and his father 'Marky' Pass was one of my childhood heroes when he played in the FA Amateur Cup Final against Kingstonians.

We said our goodbyes and with a few more recruits, I climbed into the army lorry. The journey was not very long, but my main memory was of the bumping along country roads as we sat on the bare floorboards.

On arrival I was shown to a barrack room, which was my first intimation of the fact that privacy was a thing of the past. The thought of sleeping in a room with twenty or so other male human beings appalled me. What I did not know was that it was far better than the norm, and that I would have done myself a favour by endeavouring to stay there.

Still in our civilian suits, we had our first army meal at 12.00 noon, and to my surprise we were served by ATS (Army Territorial Service) girls, and the food was good and there was plenty of it.

Later in the day we were taken to what was peculiarly called the 'Quartermaster's Store'. So this was what the song meant. I was not to know that I was about to be conned.

In line, we were issued first with a kit bag, and then we filled it with clothing and boots. Two battledresses, three shirts, three sets of underwear, etc, and various items of cleaning materials – such as a button brush, a shoe brush, and a piece of brass which was used to protect the greatcoat and forage cap buttons from polish – were given, but all in a great hurry and without the opportunity of checking. When it was too late, that is when my kit was checked by my next unit at Colchester, a large number of items were missing and I certainly had not lost them.

I had to pay for those items and it was said that I paid double. I paid for those that I 'lost', as a penalty for carelessness, and I also paid for the replacements. And my income was only fourteen shillings, as I allowed Mam seven shillings a week!

October 16th 1942 was a dreadful day. I was given a box on which I had to write my home address, and then pack in my civilian clothes. So this was indeed the end of my civilian life. Whether I would ever regain that status, I could not know. It was all so traumatic and for the first time I fully realised that apart from any other factor, I had totally lost my freedom. From now on I had to just obey orders. I was awakened in the morning, and I had to march to breakfast just before 7.00 am. I obeyed orders all day, had a short respite of leisure some evenings, to complete the day by mandatory 'lights out' at 10.00 pm.

An historic event occurred on my first army awakening. I polished my boots. I got the black polish everywhere. You see Mam or Dad always cleaned my shoes, which awaited me every morning. Even worse, the commanding officer demanded that we 'bone' the toes and heels. This meant hours of the proverbial 'spit-and-polish', until the surface of the leather gleamed like polished metal.

My first Sunday morning in His Majesty's Armed Forces was disappointing. I had looked forward to Church Parade, which was compulsory for C of E's (Church of England), but from which all Catholics were excused! However, I was on what was called 'fatigues', which translated meant being on hands and knees whilst scrubbing every square inch of the greasy, smelly kitchen floor. I could have cried.

I slept well on what proved to be the most comfortable bed of my service as an infantryman. It was sprung and the mattress consisted of two of what were called 'biscuits'. For leisure we had a 'Red Shield Club' where we played billiards, snooker, and table tennis, and could get a nice cup of tea for a penny.

We learned all of the basic foot and rifle drills, and by the end of the six weeks of basic training, we were quite smart. Our first encounter with a rifle was with a .22, which had very little kick, but which was good enough for us to be able to learn how to hold it, and how to fire standing, kneeling, and lying prone.

Later on we had quite a thrill by being taken to the rifle range to fire the SMLE .303; but it was no ordinary range. In fact, I can boast that, instead of aspiring to one-day shoot at Bisley, the Wembley or Lords of rifle shooting, I fired my very first .303 round at this Mecca of the sport.

I learned a new sport when I was at Deepcut. Some evenings I used to walk through the beautiful Surrey countryside, with its October autumnal shades of golds and browns crowning the majestic beech trees, and the horse chestnuts, which would have been greatly prized a few years earlier in my conker days, to a pub in the then tiny village of Frimley Green.

Never a beer drinker, I would sip a 'shandy' all evening whilst I played 'Shove Ha'penny' with the locals. Why it is not a worldwide sport I do not know. It is so very skilful. The old country yokels at Frimley were past masters. It was played on a slate board, about a metre long and 40 centimetres wide. Horizontal lines across the board had different scores, the highest being the top line. Highly polished ha'pennies (half-pennies) were used, and the aim was to achieve the highest score by landing the coins in the top positions on the board.

I have forgotten how many coins were played, but the art was to cannon off coins already on the board, in order to knock your opponents out whilst remaining in a high scoring position yourself.

To play, you place a coin so that it overlaps the bottom of the board, and then you strike it with the heel of the hand. I used to love to play and I became quite good at it, but nowhere near as good as the locals.

Basic training was only six weeks, but we certainly packed a lot into that time. Half way through the course we were given thirty six hours' leave, and I went up to London on a Saturday afternoon. I had to be back by 'lights out' on the Sunday night. I stayed at the 'Union Jack Club', and I felt quite sophisticated walking around Trafalgar Square and other streets and squares about which I had only read. I went to the 'Odeon Cinema' in Leicester Square and saw a musical film, the title of which I have forgotten. All very exciting!

There were personnel from all of the Allied forces at the Club, and I found it quite uplifting to chat with Americans, Canadians, Aussies, Kiwis, etc. It was good for the spirit to feel a part of such a tremendous enterprise.

Another highlight of my short stay in Surrey was my attempt at winning the Army Cross Country Championship. It was run at Aldershot and there were 200 entrants, many wearing club and university vests, whilst I was in army vest and shorts. I had no idea of the route and I had never run ten miles before, but I was determined to do my best. The first few miles were through forests and beautiful meadows, and it was stimulating to see all of the autumnal colours. The worst part was towards the end, when we ran for two or three miles along a concrete towpath by the side of a dead straight canal. We passed under several bridges, and I was overtaking runners all the time, the realisation surfacing that there could not be all that many in front of me.

The race ended in a field. As soon as I entered, I could see the winner finishing and I overtook more and more in the rush to the tape. They told me I was tenth, and obviously, I could have even improved on that if I had known something about the route, such as how long the concrete path was, and how far we had to run when we entered the field. Nevertheless, I was quite proud to be tenth.

Every day we did Physical Training (PT), although quite often I did my exercise with the football, cross-country, or boxing teams. I had always looked upon rope climbing as being very difficult, and needing great strength to climb high, but during PT we were taught how to climb properly in a way which made it really easy. The method is to climb up with both hands gripping the rope, then with the rope below the hands running between the knees and behind the heels, lean back and raise the knees until you are in a sitting position. Then you grip the rope with the knees whilst climbing hand over hand until you have reached as high as possible, and just keep on repeating the process.

Like all recruits, I felt as though I stuck out, as such, like a sore thumb. My uniform looked so very new, as did my boots and, of course, I wore the badge of the General Service Corps, which told everyone that I was a 'rookie'. It was rather strange, but we all tried to pretend that we were experienced soldiers right from the start.

The battledress with which I was issued had been left in the disinfectant too long. All uniforms were treated, but mine was stiff with it, and took even longer to appear old, and I did everything I could think of to achieve that august state.

After two or three weeks, we were all interviewed to be asked if there was a particular regiment we wanted to be in. They could not guarantee to accede to a particular request, but they would try.

Now as I was a decided acquisition to the football team, the boxing team, and the cross-country team, the Sports Officer recommended that I should be found a place on the permanent staff of the depot.

There were two reasons why I could not accept, although there were many times later when I wished that I had. One was that brother George was an Infantry officer in Burma, and he said that the Infantry was the arm of the service for real soldiers! The other was that our local Home Guard back home were all in the Light Anti-Aircraft Regiment of the Royal Artillery, and who wanted to be in the same mob as the Home Guard? You see, in addition to their six week basic training courses, they trained Royal Artillery 'Gunners' on Bofors Light Anti-aircraft guns, similar to the Home Guard – even to the leather ankle gaiters which definitely were 'Home Guardish!'

Thinking about it later I reckon that the Sports Officer and the interviewer must have thought me mad electing for the footsloggers. Maybe I was the only one who ever did.

The day came when the postings went up on the notice board. 'Private S Rickaby to the 15th Infantry Training Centre, Hyderabad Barracks, Colchester'. I left what proved to be equivalent to the Dorchester Hotel, compared to every other camp or billet I ever lived in during my service.

I quite enjoyed the temporary freedom of going up to London by train and then going across London to get the train to Colchester, Essex. It was a bitter cold day at the end of November and when I got out of the train at my destination, it was drizzling a kind of freezing rain.

I had a full kit including a rifle. My kit bag weighed a ton, or seemed like it. I left the station having found out that Hyderabad was up the top of the hill, and I gritted my teeth as I battled against the rain, which soon soaked me. In the cold, and with all my gear, the hill seemed like a mountain. It must be one of the longest hills in England, but at last I saw the forbidding gates of Hyderabad Barracks ahead of me. I reported to the guardroom, and the orderly sergeant, recognisable by his red sash worn diagonally across his chest, took me down to my barrack block.

There was an orderly corporal waiting for newcomers, of which I was the last, and he took me to my barrack room. Remembering the relative opulence of Deepcut, I nearly cried when I saw it. Hyderabad had been built for one war or another. Maybe it was the Napoleonic. Anyway, worse was to come. The corporal gave me two sacks, one large and the other small, and torch in hand he told me to follow him.

He said we were going to the stables. I thought he was kidding. When I saw all the straw in what were in fact stables, I looked for the horses, but apparently they had left some time ago. When I was told that the idea was to stuff the straw into the two sacks, as they were to serve as my mattress and my pillow, I could have cried, and just hoped that they had changed the straw since the horses left!

On the morrow it was confirmed that I was to be in the Carrier Platoon. This meant learning to drive and maintain a Bren gun carrier, then learning how to use it in action.

It was soon discovered that I was a footballer, and I was picked for the unit team. One of the team was Eric Parsons, and we were destined to see quite a bit of each other in the years to come.

Eric was a West Ham United outside right, and I had played in the same position for Middlesbrough. So for us both to be able to play for the 15th Infantry Training Centre, one of us would have to change. I volunteered to play on the other wing at outside left. This was very good for me in the long run because, for the uninitiated, it meant that I had to use my left foot most of the time, thus developing it to be as good as my right.

We got to the final of the Old Contemptibles Cup Competition, and we played on Colchester United's ground and drew 1–1. The following week we played again and drew 0–0, so it was decided that if there was a draw the third time, we would play a half hour of extra time.

Lo and behold, we were drawing at full time. I cannot remember the score at that stage, but my photograph of the team with the trophy tells me that we won 4–3. What I do recall well is that I was the hero. I scored the last three of our goals.

I certainly enjoyed my football at Hyderabad Barracks. The Regimental Sergeant Major was a real Tartar to the many hundreds of new recruits who were training there. Some of them were in the General Service Corps, and they were receiving their first six weeks initial training prior to being tested in a variety of ways, to decide for which branch of the army they were best suited. Others, like me, were in the second stage of their training.

On Saturday mornings, both groups came together for the grand drill parade. Everyone was in best battledress, rifle cleaned to perfection and ready on the hallowed 'square' by 8.30 am. From then until 9.00 o'clock their respective Platoon Sergeants checked and rechecked that there were absolutely no imperfections in their clothing or equipment.

At the appointed time (to a second) the RSM arrived on what was in effect his stage, and everyone felt a shiver go down their spines. Everyone that is except the football team, who just by coincidence had been told by the same 'tyro' to report to the sports room, to make sure that their boots, of the football variety, were in good order. Being a good player certainly had its advantages.

The methods used to decide which job you should be trained for are worthy of comment. 'Aptitude tests' is how the system was known. I had a good idea how I would make out. I was the one who could take things apart, but could rarely put them together again. If I did, I seemed to always have pieces left over. Remember?

Another of my attributes which was particularly appreciated in the winter at the training school, was the way in which I kept the stove going in the woodwork room. I would carefully measure and perfectly mark the mortice and tenon joints, with a joiner's precision, and then proceed to saw and chisel them until one fitted snugly into the other. But what always seemed to happen was that at first they were too tight, and then they were so sloppy that I could almost put my finger in the gap. Another bit of fuel for the stove, and hence my popularity.

Such abilities were aptitude tested, as was that of a knowledge of mechanics, particularly as applied to auto engines. Of course, I could not go wrong there. I had observed on countless occasions at the filling station at the bottom of Pine Street, what they did to make a car go. They put petrol in one hole, oil in another, and water in a third; they all mixed together and then you turned the starting handle which possibly did the mixing, and off it went.

With such superior automotive knowledge as that, and being particularly adept at putting square pegs in round holes, the army decided that I could do the most good for my country by being sent to Colchester, to take a driver mechanic's course in the Bren gun carrier platoon. QED.

The dreaded day arrived when I had to take my first driving lesson, and two of us were taken out in a 15cwt Bedford truck. The driving instructor wisely put my comrade in arms at the wheel first. To my chagrin, he merely did a number of things with his hands and feet, none of which conveyed anything to me, and there we were on the way to Halstead. Of course, he had done it all before in civvy street.

My experience of riding in a vehicle at all was limited to one trip down Pine Street with Uncle Charlie, and two or three in the back seat of a taxi when being transported from the station to a football ground. Other than that, I had been in the back of an army truck a few times, but you do not see much of those perplexing foot and hand movements from there.

Then it was my turn. Wisely, we set off on a hill, downwards that is. My instructor talked about gears, clutch, brakes, and various other esoteric terms. Now to my credit I had heard of most, if not all of them, but what did they mean? He was very patient, and he needed to be, but what had he done to the truck? When the other chap drove it, it went smoothly, when I tried it went like a kangaroo!

I never went out with this instructor again, and I often wondered why. My next lesson was in a Bren gun carrier. I think it was for the protection of the new instructor, because I noticed that all other road users got out of the way when they saw a Carrier approaching, and probably particularly when I was driving. You see a Carrier was a tracked vehicle and looked like a small tank.

Eventually it started to make sense to me, but my biggest problems were threefold. One was trying to change gear downwards, say from fourth to third. In those days you had to do what was known as double-declutching, and almost regularly during the performance of this virtually impossible task, I used to stall the engine, which was problem number two. This led directly to number three, because the only way to restart it was to get out of the vehicle, unhook the six-foot long starting handle, place it in the hole at the front, then push it through to the back where the engine was, fiddle about to connect it to the engine, then turn the handle. Sometimes it took ages. I would then climb back in and hope that it wouldn't stall again for a while.

Another arduous part of our training was to report to the Carrier Yard to learn to maintain the vehicle, other than the engine. The latter was dealt with more in the classroom and then the workshop. No, the joy of the Carrier Yard, and I went down there every morning Monday to Friday during November, December, January, and February, not the warmest months in England. I was to discover just how cold steel could be when it has been out all night in the frost, and sometimes the snow.

I recalled how happy I used to be when I worked in the Time office at Head Wrightson's, with its open fire, knowing that most of the workmen had to put up with working with ice-cold steel. Now here I was doing the same thing. If it was very cold, your fingers would stick to the metal and you had to pull them off, leaving some skin behind. The physical work was an aid to fitness however.

To practise for active service, when everything would need to be done in a hurry, we used to have to take off the tracks and the sprocket wheel which drove the carrier, and put them back on as quickly as possible. This was heavy work and helped to develop muscles I didn't know I had.

Carrier drill, when we used to mount and dismount at great speed, was also a great test of your fitness.

Driving practice used to be quite enjoyable, once I became more competent, although prior to this being achieved, I had my one and only accident.

We used to go off on trips down the road that led to Halstead, and we would all have a turn at the wheel, but the event we looked forward to was when we stopped for a mid-morning break at a roadside cafe. A cup of tea and a rock bun or two was the fare, but oh the rock buns! I can still taste them. They were delicious.

On the way back one day, somehow or other I managed to knock down part of the parapet of a small stone walled bridge on a narrow road. Someone said that there must have been something wrong with the 'lock'. Now I did not know what a lock was. I knew what it wasn't, i.e. a lock on a door, but I did think that it sounded a good excuse, so I stuck to it.

Of course, when it happened, the Carrier slewed across the road, ran into the wall, knocked off a few stones, and stopped precariously with one third of the vehicle hanging over the stream that ran beneath and, as you might have guessed – the engine stalled!

Remembering how difficult it was to restart under normal circumstances, it is easy to imagine what it was like in this rather unique situation.

After a few minutes of reaching upwards and outwards from the bank of the stream I managed to get the end of the handle into the appropriate hole, and with one chap in the driving seat, and two in the back to act as ballast, I eventually turned the handle sufficiently to get the motor to start.

The relief was tremendous, but this was not the end of the matter. I was told that anyone who was involved in an accident was automatically 'put on a charge'. In five years in the army this was the only time it happened to me, and I cannot say that I enjoyed the novel experience.

It seemed that I would have to prove myself 'not guilty' rather than the other way round. I had to report to the Company Commander's office, and the Sergeant Major marched me in 'at the double', knocking off my cap in the process.

I had a trick up my sleeve didn't I? Yes, I just said that there must have been something wrong with the lock. I don't think that the Captain understood what it meant either, so rather than show his ignorance he said that I was not guilty! I picked up my cap and I was off.

Physical training was an important part of our development, and we were scheduled to be in the gymnasium every weekday from 3.30 pm to 4.30 pm. I was never keen on PT as such. I would run miles and play games for hours, but I found doing exercises boring. Maybe it was because I always found it difficult to touch my toes. I put it down to my legs being long in proportion to the rest of my body.

It would appear that I was not the only one who was less than keen, because if we were out in the country in the afternoon doing various types of training, it seemed that we were all endeavouring to take our time in completing whatever task we were involved in. Consequently, quite often we would get back to the barracks at about the time when the sergeant would decide that it was too late to go down to the gymnasium.

Awaiting us there, and I do not think that he was disappointed when we failed to appear, was PT Instructor George Lambert, well known before the war and again afterwards, as Gloucestershire's opening bowler. He was also a very good footballer and played full back for the Training Centre.

I saw George quite often in the immediate post war years when I used to go to Edgbaston, Birmingham, to see him playing against Warwickshire. On one occasion he told me about one of my great boyhood heroes, Wally Hammond, one of the greatest cricket all-rounders the world has known. George would admit that modesty was not one of his outstanding virtues when he was young, so this story is really to support that admission.

He was invited to go to the County Ground at Gloucester for a trial when he was an aspiring young fast bowler. He knew that he was good and he was going to show them that he was.

To put him through his paces, they asked the great man Walter Hammond to go with him to the nets, and George was asked to bowl against him.

This was his big chance. He took a long run, charged up to the bowling crease and really let fly. As George told it, Wally obviously had decided that this raw but fast, dark haired youth, needed putting in his place.

To George's utter amazement the master turned his bat so that only the edge was showing, and he straight drove the ball past him like a rocket. For non-cricketing readers, this meant that instead of using the face of the bat, which is 5" wide, he used the edge, which is only about 3/4" wide! George concluded the story by saying that it was the best lesson he could have had.

The last time we met was on a very pleasant occasion. Gloucestershire had given him a benefit, which meant that all kinds of events were organised to raise money to reward this really excellent servant of the County. One such event was a Ball in Bristol to which I was flattered to be invited as an 'honoured guest', and I spent the evening with three stars of the stage and television. They were Eve Boswell, Eric Morecombe, and Ernie Wise. I was trying to talk about the stage etc, but Eric and Ernie always steered the conversation to football.

Returning to Colchester and to 1943, at the end of our course we had three tests, all of which I dreaded. They were driving; a written test on the V8 engine, which powered the Bren gun carrier; and the most dreaded and impossible of all was having to drive in the dark, knowing that at some stage the Sergeant examiner was going to do something to make the vehicle break down.

You had to use a torch and decide where the fault lay, and then put it right.

Incredibly, I passed the driving test with flying colours. I do not know why, but everything went right. I double-declutched and did not stall the engine. I could hardly believe it.

Then the written examination. All I can say is that, unlike when I took my Matriculation examinations at Stockton Grammar School, people were not prevented from talking to their neighbours. I was near a lad called Andrews from Portland, Dorset, who had the broadest accent I ever heard. By this time I had got used to it, and as his brother had the only garage in that remote outpost of Southern England, Andy was a whizz, and passed on information to me as required.

However, my biggest stroke of luck was on the night when I had to find the fault when the engine was tampered with.

I remembered the two golden rules. If it stops suddenly, it is an electrical fault; if it splutters before stopping, it is petrol. But even though these facts have stuck in my mind to this day, I was no wiser. 'So what?' would have been my response.

The army must have needed me as a Carrier driver, because there I was driving along merrily, when the Carrier stopped. Now did it stop suddenly, or did it stop gradually? I asked myself, but no answer came.

Reluctantly I got in the back and uncovered the engine. I shone my torch on the engine, almost as though I knew what I was doing, and incredibly, as I waved it around, I saw a glistening drop of petrol fall through the beam!

It must have come from above, was my rather smug analysis, so I deftly raised the torch. There it was! A petrol pipe had been unscrewed from something or other. I nonchalantly reconnected the pipe to the joint from whence it had been unscrewed, then I merely replaced the engine cover and waited for the plaudits! Yes, I had passed. They certainly must have been needing me.

From then on I was allowed to wear a wheel on my sleeve. I could not get to the shop quickly enough. I think it was because an extra badge seemed to convey some sort of seniority. My battledress was starting to look as though it had been worn some time, that I was no longer a recruit, and the badge tended to set the seal. It all seems a little silly now, but that was how it was.

Having won the Colchester Old Contemptibles Cup, and my having scored three goals in the final, other players in the team, most of whom were on the permanent staff, reckoned that I was sure to remain at the 15th ITC.

Had not the powerful Regimental Sergeant Major sat with the team for the official photograph? One would have thought that it had been the FA Cup we had won. Word was leaked that he had asked my Commanding Officer not to put me on a draft, but to put me on the staff.

The ITC at that time was primarily for the purpose of training soldiers for service in North Africa, and every few weeks contingents would leave the barracks en route for the desert.

The Company Commander, I can see him now, was a captain in the Somerset Light Infantry. There were two factors about the Light Infantry regiments that set them apart from lesser mortals. One was that they marched at an incredible speed; and the other was that they wore their caps, forage caps to give them their right name, dead straight. This looked quite ridiculous, and at every opportunity we would wear them on the side as did all other soldiers, but not in the barracks and certainly not in the sight of our Captain.

He was the strictest disciplinarian I ever came across. Silver haired, he had an excellent body for his age and I am sure that he must have been called out of retirement. He strode around, seemingly looking for something to complain about. His kit inspections were terrifying. We had to lay out all of our kit on our beds to a symmetrical pattern and woe betide if, for example, your spare pair of boot laces were not coiled to perfection.

'Footballers have as much right to die in the desert as anyone else,' he told the RSM when the latter suggested my retention. And, of course, he was right, and particularly as he was wearing his World War 1 medal ribbons. How could I argue?

It did not exactly cheer me up, but I awaited my draft orders. This did not take long. I was to go on an infantry 'toughening-up' course, with the Oxford and Buckinghamshire Light Infantry, at Woodhall Spa in Lincolnshire, prior to joining an active battalion of the Somersets.

CHAPTER NINE
I AM A TRAINED SOLDIER

On arrival I was allocated a bed in a wooden hut. Toilets were referred to as latrines and were primeval, lacked privacy, and would only have been attractive to those who liked a chat as they went about their evacuations.

Woodhall Spa's main claim to fame is its golf course, which is apparently of championship standard, although I never got to see it. For me the best thing about Lincolnshire was the Forces Club at nearby Horncastle, and in particular, its jam sandwiches, which were the best I have ever tasted. And I would claim to be a connoisseur. There was a lock by a mill and as long as I could put my foot on the bottom, as usual, I used to try to swim.

However, the most important reason for our being with the 4th 'Ox and Bucks' was to take part in manoeuvres under simulated battle conditions. This happened when we travelled to Yorkshire to Fylingdales, where there is now an early warning system or something top secret, to put into practice that for which we had been trained.

There were two unique events on these Yorkshire Moors. One was that all of the exercises, the manoeuvres, etc, which we went through, were all with live ammunition. It was one thing to fire it ourselves, but to have it fired at us, well nearly at us, was another thing. Our opposition fired over our heads, supposedly to get us used to the bark of the guns and the whine of the bullets as they passed over, as though anyone can really 'get used' to that.

Then artillery and mortar fire from weapons from 'our side' whistled over our heads to land and explode a couple of hundred yards ahead. I suppose it did achieve something, but you did have the comfort of knowing that you were not the target, when in real action...

The second of my unique experiences happened on Day 2 on the Fylingdale's Moor. We slept in 'bivouacs', which if I have remembered right were groundsheets somehow supported to perform the functions of tents. As per active service practice, we were awakened an hour before dawn to 'stand to', on the basis that the enemy would invariably attack at dawn.

I was standing there waiting for something to happen, when I noticed that it was getting lighter. Suddenly, over the top of the hill in front of us, a miracle occurred. An orange ball of fire started to peep over it. It got bigger and bigger. I could not restrain myself, for I was witnessing my first dawn and sunrise.

In my life to that date, I had been in bed asleep when the sun rose in the spring and summer months, and in most of the autumn too, whilst in the winter, clouds and streets upon streets of houses would have blocked it from my view. And so far in the army, Reveille had mostly been after dawn, and when it wasn't, high barrack blocks would have hidden the sun. I was to see many more in Normandy, but I did not appreciate the beauty then, as they were to signal long days of danger and stress.

No, that first great sunrise in Yorkshire is a lifelong memory of the beauty of nature.

This was my first visit to the Yorkshire Dales, hardly under ideal tourism conditions, but it introduced me to that most beautiful part of England. The Yorkshire Dales is an area that must form part of the itinerary of anyone seeking to explore the beauties of Britain. Since very early on, my Dad had talked about the Dales, and I was always fascinated by his reference to 'fields and fields of daffodils growing wild in the early spring around Farndale.'

Another dale of which I had heard, but at that time not seen, was Wensleydale, the home of that wonderful crumbly white cheese, which I bought for Mam at Mr Lowe's milk, eggs and poultry shop. Mr Lowe used to cut it into segments from a huge circular specimen that must have been well over a foot across. Of course, this dale must be the best known in the world as the television series, 'All Creatures Great and Small' was filmed there. But I am digressing, although who wouldn't when the mind's eye is bringing back images of such beauty?

Back to Lincolnshire and Woodhall Spa, for a few more reminiscences from the wartime.

I used to like to get away from it all by going to Lincoln. The train journey to this Roman city was by the side of a long straight canal, and I used to marvel at the number of fishermen casting their lines. Whether they ever caught anything I do not know, but they didn't when I was watching them. I liked Lincoln's cobbled streets and its beautiful cathedral. I am not sure if the waterway there is a river or a canal, but my memory of it is of walking along disconsolately near its edge, on my own, and feeling pretty low. There never seemed to be anyone around on Sunday afternoons, and I used to be provoked to sing a Bing Crosby song of the day. It was the 'B' side of a hit record, the name of which I have forgotten, but it went, 'Once we walked along, down by the river,' and I can remember the tune right through. Recently I tried to get a record of it, but it was not possible.

My penultimate Lincolnshire memory is of an exercise in which we were involved. We were to attack Boston Spa on a particular Sunday, and it was to be defended by the local battalions of the Home Guard. It was really for their benefit, as they had been developed from the Local Defence Volunteers (LDV), and their duty was to defend their town against the Germans in the event of an invasion. Since the British retreat to Dunkirk and subsequent return to Britain, such a possibility had been on the cards, and we were to try to catch Boston's defenders unawares.

It poured down and we were soon frozen and soaked to the skin as we progressed towards the outskirts of the town. We were to use blanks to make it all more realistic, and we threw firecrackers, which made a bang and substituted for hand grenades.

We were soon in action and we were adjudged by 'umpires' as to whether or not we had won an encounter. Using hedgerows and ditches for cover, and remembering all of the tactics we had learned during the hundreds of hours of training, we advanced bit by bit. Soon Boston was in sight and resistance was much stronger.

By this time we were thoroughly wet, cold, and miserable; and it was still pouring down; only mid morning; and many hours still lay ahead of us. One of our number offered a solution to our misery. He said that he had heard that if we were captured by the Home Guard, we would be taken to their headquarters and well looked after.

So, just by chance, in our next skirmish we were adjudged to have been defeated, in fact, killed; dead. The umpire made a big thing about it, but the result was that one of the Home Guards escorted us to their HQ.

It was in a club room, and as we walked in we knew that luck was on our side. It was lovely and warm due to a large wood burning stove in the middle of the room, from which came the smell of toasting bread. We had a great day. We got dry, we ate well and we were treated almost like heroes. Losing was certainly better than winning, and in the afternoon, we had a good sleep before being returned to our unit, for transport back to Woodhall Spa.

A final comment about Lincolnshire. It was the worst place I ever knew for what were called route marches, because being so flat, we could always see miles ahead, whereas in hilly country the roads had lots of bends, and it did not seem so bad, as you never knew if the next bend was the last or not.

As I write, we are contemplating moving back to England, and due to our daughter's love for the Lincolnshire/Norfolk area where she hopes to settle, we have started writing to estate agents in that part of the world.

Strangely, the most attractive replies re house prices have been from Boston. So maybe I shall return to the scene of our wartime battle! And in triumph instead of ignominious defeat.

However, as far as this book is concerned the war is still on, and it is in fact the summer of 1943. It is a critical year for the Allies and there is much optimism around. El Alamein was an important victory, and it seemed less likely that I would see the sands of the desert. Instead I was to see the sands of Perranporth, to live in the Ponsmere Hotel. The sands there were not mined or 'barbwired' against a German invasion, which had been a possibility for the preceding three years, though not really via the North Cornwall coast. It was considered that Hitler would never travel so far.

This was not so bad after all. Prior to joining the army the furthest I had been was Cambridge, and the furthest seaside resort was Scarboro', which was about sixty miles away. Now, all paid for by His Majesty King George VI, I had travelled all the way to Cornwall and was living in a hotel, something I had never done before.

Of course, it was not quite as good as it sounds. There was no furniture in the hotel, and no carpets on the floors, which we slept on. The palliasses, or 'biscuits' as the army called them, were quite comfortable, and I really would not have minded seeing the war out there in the South-West of England.

We did a lot of military training, starting early in the morning, so that we could enjoy the beach in the late afternoon and evening. For the first time in my life I got brown with the sun. Before breakfast, we would do PT on the sands and finish with a dip in the ocean.

It could not last and in late July, we received our orders. Somehow I had been lucky enough not to go to North Africa, and North Cornwall was very much preferred.

Our next destination was Inverary, on the west coast of Scotland, in Argyleshire, the seat of the Duke of Argyle. It was one heck of a long way and it took us a couple of days by train, being delayed at Crewe, Preston, and Glasgow. Naturally, we very much enjoyed the journey. Sleeping or playing cards in the compartment was preferable to any amount of army training.

We were accommodated in Nissen huts, of which I had only heard before, and they were situated in the grounds of Inverary Castle.

Although it was high summer I do not think there was one day during our six weeks sojourn when it did not rain, but the most remarkable feature of our life up there was to do with the clock. I am not sure what it was intended to achieve, but the timetable to which we adhered was as follows: 6.00 o'clock Reveille (i.e. get out of bed), 6.30 a run around the camp for a quarter of an hour, then a shower, and to breakfast at 7.00 o'clock.

On parade at 8.00, which could be for drill, or most days it would be for some aspect of military training. This would continue until lunch at 12.00, which was in the camp dining-room, or if we were out of camp, we would eat sandwiches.

There was very little variety in the sandwiches whichever unit you were in. It was mostly one of cheese and one of jam, and the method of creating this haute cuisine is worthy of mention.

The cook would cut the bread into very thick slices, like doorsteps, and then he would melt the margarine until it was liquid. Using a shaving brush he would 'paint' the bread with the liquid, let it set a while, then apply large chunks of Cheddar cheese to one and lashings of red jam to the other.

I always assumed that the shaving brush was reserved for this one operation, and did not double as the brush used by the cook when shaving.

Cigarette smoking was virtually encouraged by the army, as there were always a number of stops for a smoke.

At 5.00 o'clock we had a cooked meal, and unless there were special duties, we were finished. The Naafi, the Forces' name for what was a large cafeteria, was a favourite haunt until the last bugle call of the day signalled that it was time for bed.

Nothing too unusual about all of that, you would be excused thinking. How about if the 6.00 o'clock breakfast was pm and the 5.00 o'clock hot meal was am and 'lights out' at 10.00 am.

Well that was how it was. I do not know why we did it or if it was successful, but 'ours was not to reason why'.

Actually, we were a Combined Operations Brigade composed of a battalion of Royal Marine Commandos, our battalion, and a support regiment. We were being trained to capture an island in the tropics, and we used to go out into the bay in a large ship, then climb down scramble nets into the infantry landing craft, and land on the Inverary beaches. We did this time after time, always during the night (our 'day') and it could really be cold, especially when what the locals called 'Scotch Mist' (a thick drizzly mist) came down, soaking us.

The personnel around Inverary included a number of sailors from the Royal Navy, and altogether we numbered several thousand men. Females were limited to one, an RN Signals Officer! I never saw her, but I guess that she could have felt outnumbered.

When we were fully competent in methods of landing, dashing over beaches, and climbing cliffs, we were on the move again. The rumour was that we were to capture Madagascar. I did not even know where it was.

Our next stop was a place called Haggerstone Castle in Northumberland, near Berwick-upon-Tweed. Again it was Nissen Huts, but we did have Berwick to visit, and it had all of the amenities a town had to offer. Every evening several three-ton trucks took whoever wanted to go to this most northerly of English towns.

Prior to this move, I had been involved in normal infantry training, but I was pleased to be told that I was to be the Carrier driver for 'D' company. Apart from the Carrier Platoon, which was always part of what was known as 'S' or Specialist Company, each of the companies A, B, C, and D, had their own vehicle.

However, most of my time was spent with the Platoon. We were quite excited to learn that we were to be issued with new vehicles, and that they had to be 'run in' prior to embarking for our invasion operation.

This was achieved in quite a pleasant way. Most days we used to drive through Berwick, over the Tweed bridge, and then we took the coast road to Dunbar, where we had lunch, before returning to Haggerstone Castle.

We had a number of 'Don R's', which was the army term for Dispatch Riders, and they had new motor cycles. They also ran them in, but two of them never made it to the end. Unfortunately, one was killed on his way back to camp one evening, when he crashed. The other was a regular soldier from pre-war, and he was a Geordie from Newcastle upon Tyne. He decided to run in his bike in a different way. Instead of going north to Dunbar, he went south to Newcastle, and we never saw him again.

Embarkation leave meant two things, one good and one bad. On the one hand we were getting nineteen whole days of leave back home, and on the other when it was over we were returning to a rather frightening event. Invasion. We had heard a lot of the fears of the Germans invading us, but now our minds were turned to being the aggressor, and in the cold light of day it was scary.

The football season started and I played my first game for the battalion. By coincidence, a lance sergeant in the Carrier Platoon, who was the NCO in charge of me, was also a professional footballer. His name was Bert Head and he played for Torquay United. In later days he was to manage Torquay and then Crystal Palace, where he performed miracles and got them into the First Division. For the battalion he played inside left and I played inside right, and in our first game we won 8–0, Bert scored four and so did I!

Map reading was going to be important on this mysterious tropical island of Madagascar, and so we did a lot of work in the 'classroom'. When considered good enough we were put to a test. The method of testing was quite novel. We were taken out in the back of trucks with the canvas secured so that we could not see out, and only the driver or the NCO accompanying him could release us. After about a quarter of an hour, the truck stopped and we were let out.

We all had ordnance and survey maps, and we were to use them to decide where we were and to find our way back to camp.

The truck drove off and left us in a country lane. Now we should have walked across the fields until we saw some land marks which we could use to determine where we were. These were such as churches, high points, streams, woods etc.

However, we had a better idea. We did as instructed, and walked across a couple of fields until we came to a main road. Then we sat in the hedge until a truck came along. He stopped for us and we asked him the way to Berwick. To our delight, that was just where he was going.

We jumped in the back and he deposited us at the 'Red Shield Club', where we ate our sandwiches, had a cup of tea, played a few games of snooker, and then walked to the bridge over the river. We flagged down another truck, and he was on his way to Newcastle. This meant he passed the end of the road that led to Haggerstone Castle.

He dropped us off and we marched in single file the one or two miles back to camp, to be congratulated on a job well done!

Then it happened! The battalion commanding officer got us all on parade and announced that the objective for which we had been training so very assiduously, had been captured by the Canadians!

It was strange how disappointed we were. It was a real anti-climax. But nothing could have been more anti-climactic than his next announcement.

Instead of continuing as a Combined Operations unit, we were to be allocated to, of all people, the Northumberland War Agricultural Committee, to help them get in the harvest! How incredible!

Most of the Battalion were from Somerset, a farming county, and the prospect of going farming was most attractive to them.

Now I did not know a stook from a stack, wheat from barley, threshing from ploughing, and the thought of farm labouring was repugnant.

I soon discovered that I was definitely a 'towny', and that farming was for the peasantry. The system was that we caught a truck at 7.00 am every weekday, and the driver would drop off two at a time at the various farms on his list.

Consequently, I was taken to one of these farms, to find out to my regret, that the job we had to do to start with was called 'stooking'. To explain, some machine or other had gone around all these seemingly hundreds of cornfields and cut down the corn and somehow had left it in bundles with a piece of string around the middle. Now there were large numbers of these sheaves, as I think they were called, and we had to pick a few up and lean them against one another in a ring, so that the wind could blow through to dry the stalks, and the sun could dry out the ears of corn.

I thought that it was the most back-breaking job in the world, but I was wrong because shortly I will tell you of an even worse job which we had to do in the service of our country, and country is the operative word. I had never seen so much country.

Round and round we went, stooking all this corn, and I was soon aching everywhere. Also, the stooks contained lots of thistles, which played havoc with my arms and hands. At the end of the day I was very sore and I used to spend the evenings getting the thistles out of my fingers.

On some farms there were Italian prisoners of war, easily recognisable by their uniforms, and they eventually became part of the farm family. We were quite jealous of the way they were treated compared to us. The POWs always had a hot lunch with the farmer and his family, whilst we ate our 'one-of-cheese and one-of-jam', in the farmyard, sitting on anything that was convenient. We found the reason for this different treatment. The farmer could either pay the army one shilling and sixpence per day for our services, or they could give us a hot meal and sweet, but they chose the former.

Northumberland farmers were definitely not our favourite people. Time used to go so slowly. We would get started about 7.30 am and we would work and work for seemingly hours and hours. No one had a watch as it would not have been practical. If it was not broken during training, it could have been 'lifted'. There were all kinds of people in the army.

So we would look out for someone walking down the lane by the side of whatever field we were in. I would dash over to find the time and I would always think they were joking. They would say things like 9.30 am, when I 'knew' it must have been 11.45, lunch being at 12.00 noon. It was heartbreaking.

One day I decided that I could no longer bear such disappointment. We stooked and stooked, sweated and ached, as round the field we went, until I just knew it was about lunchtime. And there was someone walking past. I dashed across and confidently asked the time. He said, 'ten o'clock'. I was crestfallen.

Eventually, we stooked all of the corn, partly due to lots of my rural mates actually doing it on Saturdays and Sundays to earn a few bob. I needed those days to recover.

To my bitter chagrin, I discovered that stooking the corn was not the end of the process. Threshing or 'thrashing' as the Northumbrian farmers called it, was the next boring, back-breaking job, part of the chain which presumably finished up as a loaf of bread.

A tractor and trailer would go round the cornfield, and we would use pitchforks to toss the dried stooks onto the trailer. I noticed that the farmer always seemed to be doing the driving by the way.

Then when the trailer was full, we would follow it to a strange machine, which was to do the threshing. Naturally, I was the one who spent the day tossing the heavy stooks on to the top of the thresher. This happened for two or three days, but then I had a real stroke of luck.

They put me up top where I was given a sharp knife. I cut the strings on the stooks and dropped the sheaves into the machine, where the ears of corn were stripped from the stalks.

I had only been up there a short while when it happened. I stuck the knife in my knee. Not on purpose, of course, but the result was that the farmer took me back to camp to the Medical Officer.

The doctor put a few stitches in it and put me on what the army called 'Attend B', its exact meaning eludes me, but it resulted in my being excused all duties for a fortnight. Two weeks rest from the chain-gang. Unbelievable!

But the torture was not yet over. Have you ever picked potatoes? When the harvesting was over, the spuds were waiting for me. Fields of them, and the system was barbaric.

A machine came along and turned over two rows of potatoes. There were lots of us, including Land Army girls. At first that seemed great, but it worked against us, as we had to keep up with them. They were squatting down, singing and chatting happily as they threw the potatoes in sacks, whilst my back felt as though it was breaking. I would just have thrown the last spud in, and be about to stand up to relieve the pain in my knees and back, when this damned machine would return to turn over two more rows.

My delight knew no bounds when at last the final potato was harvested. This also was the finale of my agricultural career.

One of the rural brigade was a Corporal Ballard, a farmer from Herefordshire, and the strongest man I ever met. When working on the Bren gun carriers, we would sometimes remove the sprockets, which were the drive wheels for the tracks. They were very heavy, and we would have great difficulty in dropping them down to the floor after removing the tracks, and also putting them back on. Not Corporal Ballard. He could lift them above his head.

Another forte of his was rabbiting. Whereas mere man would use ferrets to put down the rabbit holes to drive them out, or shoot them with shotguns; our man from Herefordshire needed nothing extraneous to achieve the same result.

He knew the habits of rabbits! He would go into a field on a summer evening, and there would invariably be a few patches of longer grass, and he could spot their 'runs'. We would be stationed at the end of these runs, whilst our Corporal stamped about and shouted all over. Initially we were amazed to find that the poor bunnies, in their attempts to escape, would scurry along the runs and we would merely bonk them on the head. Corporal Ballard would then put them out of their misery. One night we took more than twenty to the cookhouse. But that was another rural pursuit which started and finished in Northumberland for me.

Not being needed by the farmers, we moved again, this time to Bedlington, still in Northumberland, but nearer Newcastle upon Tyne. The weekend the battalion moved – and by the way, the army always moved at the weekend, resulting in the troops missing out on two normally slack days – I had a 48 hour leave pass.

I was to report back to the new camp on the Sunday before midnight. That evening I caught the United bus from Stockton to Newcastle, with the intention of getting another bus to Bedlington. It was getting foggy when we left Stockton and during the journey it got much worse, making the bus so late that by the time we arrived in Newcastle, the last Bedlington bus had long gone. There were trams still going part of the way, so I caught one and it took me to Gosforth, which was about half way.

Then I walked the rest of the journey and arrived at the camp gates after midnight. As the battalion had just got there that day themselves, the lads in the guard room did not know which Nissen hut I was to live in. So they put me in the headquarters hut, and thereby hangs a tale, or should it be tail?

By then I had heard about 500 Reveilles blown on a bugle at 6.00 am every morning, and as I cursed every one of them, I had a mental picture of the bugler standing to attention at the flagpole, as the Union Jack was being struck.

The wretched noise woke me on my first morning in Bedlington, and I could not help thinking – as I cogitated over the dreaded prospect of getting up, getting shaved in freezing cold water, and making my bed – that the bugle seemed to be in close proximity. I gazed at the door from my upper bunk. To my amazement I could actually see the bugler, well the back half of him, well not really all of the back half, more like the bottom part of the back half, as the top half of his body was thrust out of the door, that is the half which included his head, and the bugle. In fact the most evident thing I could see was his shirt tail. Greatly amused I watched him until he played the final note. He then got back in bed and I just turned over and went back to sleep.

Breakfast was at 7.30 am and the lads of headquarters hut were the last in the line.

Incidentally, the staple breakfast diet was always porridge, which filled you up every time, and could even taste nice. It was followed by sausages or egg and bacon, and it was certainly needed, as the lot of the infantryman was not the easiest.

We did not stay in the Northumberland mining town long, but whilst there the lads who were almost all from the South-West of England, found out what Geordie hospitality was like, and there were many marriages with the local lasses. Just before we moved, I was given leave and something rather extra special happened.

Rosie Ward had her 21st birthday party on the Saturday night when I was home on leave. It was around about the 10 December 1943 and it was just by chance that I happened to be home and able to join in Rosie's celebration. Rosie was the daughter of Annie Ward, one of the three Ward sisters who were Mam's best friends, with their relationship going back to when Mam was fourteen and worked with Annie and sister Bella in Robinson's cafe in Stockton High Street.

Robinson's was one of the original department stores and was known as an emporium.

I was always shy with girls, possibly because I had no sisters, but Rosie was an exception, as I had known her all of my life. Looking back maybe our mothers would have hoped that we would have made a match.

If so, that 21st party threw a large spanner in the works, for it was at Rosie Ward's that I met the young lady who was to become my wife. I can see her now sitting on a settee, pretty as a picture. Life is so strange. Leni only decided to go to the party at the last minute, invited not by Rosie, who she did not know, but by her cousin Doreen, with whom Leni worked as a bus conductress for Stockton Corporation Transport. And I just happened to be home on leave.

At the end of the evening I disclosed that I was a soldier, and we exchanged addresses as our attempts to make a date for before I returned to camp were nullified because of Leni's hours on the buses. However, fate played yet another welcome trick. On the following Wednesday I was walking around Marks and Spencer's store, when I bumped into Leni and her mother. Her shift had been changed, but no one had telephones in those days, so it was difficult to contact me as I had only given her my army address.

We arranged to meet on the Thursday evening and we went to the Globe cinema – with her friend Doreen! It was love at first sight and at the time of writing we have been married nearly 48 years.

My stay in my native North-East did not last much longer.

Our next stop was as different as chalk and cheese, from a Northumberland hut in a Geordie mining community, to a hotel in Durley Chine in fashionable elitist Bournemouth!

Yes, we moved into the Durley Dene Hotel, a hundred yards from Hampshire's top resort's golden beaches. Of course, it was January and not the holiday season, but it was very pleasant to walk along the promenade when off duty.

Virtually all of the furniture had been removed from the hotel, and we slept on mattresses on the floor, but it was comparative luxury. We did not do much training, drill parades being some of the apparently important activities, but we thought that the reason for this was to show the American infantry, who were in the hotel across the street, how it should be done.

The street between the hotels became a barrack square as we both showed off our abilities at drill. We thought our allies were hopeless compared to us, and I still think that to this day. By the way, I am only referring to drill.

I took the opportunity to look up Mr and Mrs Smith, who had the red setter; the first wireless I ever heard; lived next to the bottom common in Hind Street; had a son Leslie; and who had moved to Christchurch, which is near Bournemouth. Les was away in the forces, but it was nice to be able to bring one another up to date with the news.

There was an excellent Forces' Club in the town, where I used to go and have a game of snooker. But the people! How they looked down on us soldiers. It was particularly evident on the trams, where it was impossible to make conversation with anyone, and it was obvious that we were a dammed nuisance and a disturbance. They did have a couple of bombs dropped on them by the Germans whilst we were there, and we almost felt like doing the same.

I went on leave from Bournmouth and during my time at home, I received a telegram from my unit telling me to report to Beaulieu at the end of my leave. That was all. I had never heard of such a place, the name suggesting that it was in France. But we had not yet had the Second Front had we? At least I had not noticed.

It turned out to be a small village in the New Forest, and on arrival I was shown to my Bell Tent – after the Durley Dene Hotel! The reason for being there was unusual and unexpected. After all of the invasion training we had undergone, we were to be the servants of other units who were waiting to go on the Second Front, whenever and wherever it was to occur.

My job was to go around all of the vast number of tents, filling their lamps with paraffin! We all had maintenance work of one kind or another, and although it was acceptable in some ways, for example it was not stressful or hard work, it was a let down in others, particularly as we had missed out on our island operation, when we were up at Berwick.

We were able to explore the New Forest and to discover how truly magnificent it is. The people in the small Hampshire towns in and around the Forest were very friendly, and it proved to be a pleasant interlude.

One of my pals in our tent was a certain Lance Corporal Sissons, a Yorkshireman who spent most of his leisure time studying 'form'. He had a book with all of the race meetings for the previous year in it, and he would ask me to 'test him'. I would open the book at random, and let us say it opened on the page of the Ascot Gold Cup for instance, he would tell me the names of the first, second, and third horses, plus their jockeys, owners, and trainers. I was dumbfounded that he had such a marvellous memory, but that he did not put it to better use. He reckoned that in this way he knew the form of all of the horses, enabling him to predict the winners of future races. More about our tipster later.

CHAPTER TEN
THE DURHAM LIGHT INFANTRY

This rural retreat could not last, and it didn't. We were split up all over the place and, with others, I was transferred to my County Regiment, the Durham Light Infantry, the 11th Battalion stationed at Thetford, Norfolk, and awaiting D-Day. So I was to take part in the great invasion of Europe.

Luckily I was put into their Carrier Platoon, and we began preparing the Carriers for the invasion. In the event of them being dropped off in the water instead of on the actual beach, we had to make them watertight. This took a lot of painstaking work as, for instance, every rivet had to be sealed, and there were hundreds of them. When completed we had to test them in a local pond, until all was satisfactory.

We did plenty of physical training and played lots of football. We were extremely fit, and when eventually things slackened off, we were given home leave and we relaxed in the very fine weather, awaiting the big day.

One of those who accompanied me to the DLI was 'Siss', our inveterate tipster. 'Housey Housey' (Bingo) was very popular in the Naafi Canteen. One night in midweek, between pays, when money was so tight that, in my case, it was non-existent, Siss announced that he was going to play Housey and was I coming? Knowing that I was without funds, he kindly said that he had three shillings and I could have half of it. I thanked him, but declined. Instead I waited a while and then went over to see how he was getting on. He had a shilling left, and he proceeded to buy two cards in the next 'House', one for me and one for himself.

Insisting that I should have a card, he persuaded me to play, and incredibly I won three pounds nineteen shillings and sixpence, or nearly six weeks' pay!

Immediately Siss had further plans for our road to riches. Was not tomorrow a day off, and were not Newmarket Races on?

So here was a great opportunity for our arch tipster to demonstrate his skills, in practice, with real money, instead of in theory as he had done for months, with imaginary money.

We hitched a lift to the famous racecourse and got there early to give Siss the chance of getting used to the atmosphere. He bought the 'Sporting Life', and sat down under a tree to sort out the eight winners. He insisted that we were to share the ultimate proceeds because hadn't I won the bingo, even though it was his sixpence?

We could afford nine shillings in each race, so we were all ready for our coup. 'I am just going to have a chat with a few people,' he said, prior to placing his first bet. Siss liked this part, swapping his book-learned knowledge with some of those professional tipsters and punters one sees at all race meetings.

Anyway, he was put off his own deliberately considered selection, and he put our first nine bob on a donkey, or so it looked as it jogged past us as we leaned over the rails on the free part of the course. Time has eroded the memories of the next six races, all but the fact that we lost every time. For sure, my partner hardly ever backed his fancy, not that I can remember how many of them won, if any, but I do remember vividly the last race. And who wouldn't, had they been with us?

This was our last nine shillings, we would hitch a lift home; and it was pay-day tomorrow, so let us have one grand last splash. And this time I went to the bookie with Siss, to make sure he backed his fancy. I was quite proud of him as he talked to the bowler hatted gent, with the big leather bag and the blackboard on which were all of the horses' names. He sure knew his stuff, and in race language, which was mostly foreign to me, they agreed what the price was to be, seven to two, which explained meant that for our nine shillings we would get back two pounds and sixpence.

It was the shortest race of the meeting. Was it six furlongs? Anyway, we saw our horse go past en route to the start, and Siss, being a good judge of horseflesh, was very satisfied that it was fast enough, and strong enough, to carry our last nine bob.

Being a short race, we leaned over the rails and could see the horses getting into position for the start. We knew our jockey's colours; in fact I think Siss knew everything there was to know about horse, jockey, trainer, and owner.

'They are off', shouted a few thousand people, and we peered down the course. We could see the melee of horses, and very soon we could hear that exciting clatter of hooves as ten or more horses charged towards us; charged passed us, 'But Siss, I didn't see ours'. 'Neither did I' he replied, so we looked forlornly down the course. A horse was coming towards us on three legs, the fourth sticking out grotesquely. There was a hubbub behind us and we were pushed out of the way as a truck with a trailer attached went on to the course.

They pulled up our horse right in front of us; shot it dead, put it on the trailer, and took it away.

I have not backed a horse since.

And Siss? We went to Normandy in the same battalion, but in different companies, and I never saw him again.

Until about 1950. I was playing against Tottenham Hotspur at White Hart Lane. At the end, as I was leaving the field and passing through the tunnel under the stand, someone leaned over the tunnel parapet and shouted, 'Hi ya, Stan'. I looked up to see Siss, with a great big grin on his face. I called to him to see him afterwards, but to my bitter disappointment he did not come to the dressing room, and I have not seen or heard from him since.

But most important, I found out that he had survived the war.

Now back to Thetford. From a more leisurely routine than previously, suddenly we were back on the parade ground and cleaning our equipment and polishing our boots. This was disconcerting, because we had thought that we had put that behind us.

Then the rumours started to fly, and they settled on the fact that we were to be inspected by none other than the Commander-in-Chief Allied Forces, General Dwight Eisenhower. The great day came and we were on parade, with officers and sergeant majors nervously dashing about, making sure every rifle was clean, there was no dust on any boot, etc, etc.

Suddenly a jeep was seen to be entering the parade ground. We were called to attention, and the Regimental Band struck up 'God Save the King'!

Yes, it was King George VI.

It was often said that the King was not very strong, and it must have been for this reason that he appeared to be wearing some make-up on his face as he inspected us.

Getting into the battalion team was a bit of a problem as there were so many good players, including two from Manchester United, two from Leeds United, one from Norwich City, and one from Sunderland. I managed to get in as inside right, and we played our tenth battalion, who were in our brigade. They also had a number of professionals and, in consequence, the game (which we won 2–0) was of a very high standard.

That year the Wartime Cup Final at Wembley was between Charlton Athletic and Chelsea, and the Durham Light Infantry had either five or six playing in the game.

Incidentally, the next and final time the two battalions were to play each other was a couple of months later, in a field in Normandy when the brigade was pulled out of the front line for a rest. My main memory was of their right back, either Jack or Colin Shreeve of Charlton Athletic, who was one of the Cup Final players. His bit of one-upmanship was having his army boots laced with white football boot laces. Where he got them from I do not know. We all played in khaki shirts, trousers, and army boots, and played as though it were a Cup Final.

We were in a closed camp, but for a while we could go in and out as long as we were off duty. When suddenly we were told that we could no longer leave, we knew that the invasion of Europe would soon be on. Another indication that D-Day was near, was when we were told to put any personal effects we might have in our kitbags; such things as civilian shoes, pyjamas, letters, etc. We then labelled them and addressed them to our homes; and who could help wondering whether or not we would be able to re-open them one day.

Then our movement orders came, and we marched to Thetford Station for the trip to Newhaven, from where we were to sail; and the road was lined first with the Naafi girls from our camp, and then the townspeople, many of whom had tears in their eyes.

CHAPTER ELEVEN
NORMANDY

I cannot say that we were particularly happy that the moment of truth had arrived. Much had been talked and written about regarding the 'Second Front' – which the Russians had pressed for to relieve the pressure on them, and which was vital for the Western Allies to be able to stamp their authority on the peace treaty – when it arrived. All the training and planning was over, now we were going to find out what it was like to be confronted by real Germans and real bullets.

We were taken to an enclosed camp near Newhaven to await our turn to cross. Early in the morning of 6th June, D-Day, we heard the first radio news. Amongst others, 30 Corps – our Corps – had got its first few brigades ashore and, as far as the infantry was concerned, this meant '50 Div', the great Tyne Tees Division which had been in the desert, Sicily, and Italy, and which included three battalions of the Durham Light Infantry, namely the 6th, 8th, and 9th.

We, the 11th, and the other two battalions of our brigade, the Tyneside battalion of the Black Watch Regiment and yet another DLI unit, the 10th, were kept waiting. We heard it was due to bad weather in the English Channel, and we were put on the big assault craft and taken off again two or three times. Eventually we left in the dusk of I think the 10th of June, quite a while later than planned, and by which time we should have taken our first day objective, a Norman town called Tilly-sur-Seulles.

It seems in retrospect that the true story of how the invasion went was never told, because Tilly was not taken until the 19th June, and our 'D' Company were fitted out with folding collapsible bicycles, presumably to ride to Tilly! They left them on the beach.

But back to our re-embarking the big assault craft, which was to take us across the Channel. We made ourselves as comfortable as possible and settled down for the night. I said prayers for a long time, but this was very confusing. All I could really pray for was allied victory, to right the wrongs and stop the terrible things that were being done by the Germans. I prayed for my deliverance, but with the question, 'Why me?'

During the night we were given two self-heating cans, one of cocoa and the other of soup. I had not seen a self-heating can before, and I have not seen one since, but they were rather clever. Similar to a firework, there was a sort of fuse protruding from the top of the can, and when you put a lit cigarette to it, it started to smoulder. Very quickly you could feel the can heating up, and it was welcome to warm the hands, as it was quite cold in the Channel during the night. Its main purpose of warming the inside was also achieved, and had it been on a happier occasion, you could say that they were very much enjoyed.

Sweet chocolate and rich soup, however, when combined with the up and down movement of the landing craft, created the perfect recipe for seasickness. Maybe this was the idea, to make us want to get off on the other side. What a dilemma. On the one hand the only relief for seasickness was to get off the boat, and on the other, it meant landing on the Normandy beaches.

When the sun started to rise over the European mainland, the sight before our eyes was incredible. It was probably the largest collection of ships in history.

Simultaneously we experienced for the first time what it was like to hear the deafening roar of heavy guns, as the Royal Navy warships pounded targets well beyond the beaches. The flashes and the thunder of heavy artillery were to be with us night and day for a long time.

German heavy guns were also firing non-stop, trying to stop the continual landing of troops and supplies on the beaches of Arromanches. German planes made occasional sorties across the beachhead, and our anti-aircraft units let fly at them.

It was a terrible cacophony of noise and, if I was to say that it was not terrifying, I would be deluding myself.

The time came for us to get off. The landing craft moved ever so slowly inshore and then we heard the noise of clanking heavy chains, as the front end was lowered, theoretically on to the beach, so that we just ran off onto firm sand, but in fact into about five feet of water.

We were equipped with 'Mae West' blown up life belts, so the planners guessed right, that perfection in the landing techniques would not be achieved every time, if at all. For the moderns, the reason for the name was because of the famous film star's plenteous bosoms.

Keeping our weapons up high, we pushed through the waters of the Channel until we reached the beach, swapping the danger of drowning, and some did, for that of the Germans' first line of defence.

The immediate weaponry of machine-guns, coastal artillery, etc, had been eliminated, as had some of the minefields, and we crossed the sand to the bottom of the cliffs through one of the mine-swept sections. The whine of shells, the screeching of mortars, the perpetual gun flashes followed by the bang of the guns, and the noise of the shells as they exploded ahead of us, introduced us to the world of the infantryman in action.

It was one thing to be told of these things in training and to experience manoeuvres on Fylingdales Moor in Yorkshire, conducted with live ammunition – but when some of those bullets, mortar bombs, and artillery shells were intended to kill you, it was a very different story.

As we climbed the cliff a strange thing happened. One would not expect to take part in an everyday mundane conversation during one's first hour of active service, but I did. Ahead of us were some Royal Marine Commandos. One of them shouted down to us, 'What mob are you?' I replied, 'The Durham Light Infantry,' and he asked a further question, 'Anyone there from Stockton?' I shouted back, 'Yes, I am.' He said, 'I am from Bowesfield Lane.' Now this was only half a mile or less from where I was born. 'I'm from Oxbridge,' I said. And that was it. They went their way and we pressed on to take up our positions.

We eventually stopped a few hundred yards behind the forward troops, and were told to dig in. The first slit trench of what was to be a great number before the war ended. German fighter-bombers had flown several sorties over us, one so low that I could see the pilot's features quite clearly, and they had been greeted with a great variety of small arms fire, the first time we had fired our weapons in earnest.

We 'dug in' in a cornfield, which was surrounded by the hedgerow special to Normandy, known as 'Bocage'. There were four Sherman tanks in the field with us, American, but manned by a British crew. Just as it was getting dark there was a bang, whistle, and crash, and up in flames went a Sherman after a minute or two. Then it happened again, and again. All four 'brewed-up' and burnt all night to the accompaniment of exploding six-pounder shells, and machine-gun ammunition.

A Tiger tank had been hidden camouflaged in a 'Bocage', which consisted of two parallel rows of quite big trees with a small 'valley' between. The terrible Tiger with its ferocious 88-millimetre gun, which the Allies could not match at the time, had been driven deep into the hedgerow, and the protruding monster gun covered with camouflage netting. This was just the first of what was to be many examples of the power of the Tiger tanks and the cunning of their crews. They easily outgunned the Sherman, which they called unofficially 'Der Tommy Kucher', translated obviously as, 'The Tommy (British soldier) Cooker', and they really were. This first tremendous example of German tank power worried me, as I could not see how we could beat the Tiger.

But I did not know about the Royal Air Force's Typhoons, until subsequently we saw them attack the Wehrmacht's tanks by diving straight at them whilst releasing the rockets which pulverised those steel juggernauts. Then later in the war, the seventeen-pounder guns of the Cromwells and other tanks evened up the equation to some extent, but the Tiger was always our main worry.

Other memories of those early Normandy days included the long warm nights, when the vast variety of insect sounds, including the crickets and bullfrogs, drove us mad as we tried to sleep in the slit trench for our periods of two hours off, sandwiched between two shifts of two hours on every night.

As attacks by the enemy were most likely to start at dusk or dawn, we all had to 'stand to', that is be alert, for an hour before those two occasions.

A pungent memory of those awful days was the terrible smell of dead cows. Killed by shellfire or bullets, they would swell in the summer heat to gigantic proportions, and oh the smell. Other cows would escape the guns, but would suffer from not being milked. Their udders would be enormous, and only the efforts of soldiers from the country, milking them, prevented many more from dying through milk fever.

Our section's first death was our section commander, a corporal whose name I have forgotten. But I can remember the name of our second in command, Lance Corporal Smith, who took the corporal's watch and other personal effects, and who none of us believed, when he said he was going to send them home to the corporal's girlfriend.

There are many incidents and situations worthy of record, one of which had a most remarkable sequel. My partner in the digging of a slit trench one day, was named Allenby Chilton. He was about six feet three inches tall and immensely strong. We had just captured a hedgerow, which was the way we progressed in Normandy, as all hedgerows were excellent strong points from which the Germans could defend. It was obvious that many trenches had been dug in preparation for our invasion, because they were so well equipped.

But we had to dig as we went, in the main. Sometimes we could take over enemy trenches, but generally they were facing the wrong direction. On this particular day we had to dig our own, and it was necessary to dig quickly, as the Germans always shelled and mortar bombed us in an attempt to catch us above ground.

We were doing quite well whilst perspiring profusely in the hot June sun, when we heard the dreaded whine of what we called 'Moaning Minnies'. These were mortar bombs, I think they were fired twelve at a time, and special fins made a horrific whining, screaming noise.

Allenby and I jumped straight into our partly dug slit trench, just as the mortars were landing around us. I got my body, head and shoulders below ground level. This was our intention so that we could not be wounded except from a direct hit, but my comrade, being three or four inches taller than me, left his shoulders exposed.

He was hit by shrapnel and was bleeding profusely. Very soon after the attack, the stretcher-bearers arrived, did what they could at the time, and carried him away on a stretcher. He would have been taken to a base hospital and then back to 'Blighty' (England).

So the last I saw of him in wartime was when he was on a stretcher in a field in Normandy.

The next time I saw him, for I did see him quite often in subsequent years, was on another field. This one was quite different to the Bocage fringed field in France. This one had a goal at either end, and fifty-odd thousand people surrounding it.

This field was Old Trafford, home of Manchester United, and famous throughout the world. 'Allen' was centre half, and after a few minutes of the game I had an injury. As was our habit at West Bromwich, I went to centre forward for a while to recuperate, thus playing directly against my mate, whom I had last seen on a stretcher.

A nice little footnote is that we two DLI comrades both eventually played for England. Who could have expected this, had they seen us jumping into that slit trench?

However, there was not a happy ending to the story of another Manchester United player. You may remember that I wrote that it was difficult to get into the battalion team because of the number of professionals in our unit. I mentioned that Allenby Chilton was one of the United players. The other was a sergeant in a different company, his name unfortunately I have forgotten. I remember him well and I think that he played wing half. Regrettably, he was killed in action during the Normandy campaign.

Due to the battalion being split up, and the remnants being sent to various other regiments, I cannot record how many of the battalion team survived the war, but I do remember Joe Robinson, our right half, and his personal tragedy. Joe was captain of Norwich City and he used to go off most Saturdays to play for them, when we were stationed at nearby Thetford. He was a truly lovely fellow, with a kind winning smile that made you instantly like him, and he kindly invited me to play as a 'guest' for his club. I did not accept his invitation, because I lacked the confidence to go off and play for a League Club, where I was not known. Silly, I know, in retrospect, but that was how I was.

Dear Joe was blinded by a mine or an exploding shell. What a shame that was.

Every second an infantryman spends in the front line is fraught with danger. The slit trench gives some protection, but even then, there is always one of the two soldiers on the alert, with his head above the level of the trench, thus serving as a target for the enemy sniper, raking machine-gun fire, mortar bombs, or shells. His mate is relatively safe as he has his head down, except from a direct hit from mortars or shells, or from airburst shells.

Then the method of attack: going over the top and advancing towards an enemy position, be it a hedgerow, a building, or a fortified position, is extremely dangerous from all types of military hardware, and the nearer you get to the objective the more intense is the firing and thus the danger.

So these situations are the everyday lot of the infantry soldier. Could there be anything worse? Well yes, actually, there are two most disagreeable manoeuvres expected of you. Generally, you would take your turn as was necessary.

One was the reconnaissance patrol and the other was the fighting patrol. The former, often in daylight, was intended to pinpoint where the enemy was, and generally resulted in drawing fire. Such a patrol was often sent out after a retreat by the Germans. There is no need to elaborate on how dangerous was the procedure, and getting back to your own lines was the only pleasure involved.

However, the fighting patrol was the worst thing you could wish on anyone. Your intention was to capture a German soldier, so that he could be questioned to find out the strength of the immediate opposition, and which Divisions were in the line.

I was only involved in night patrols, and I recall one vividly, between Rauray and Tilly-sur-Seulles in Normandy. Our section was called to the platoon commander's dugout soon after dusk and we were instructed to wait until midnight, then to cross the field directly in front of us, in order to try to catch the occupants of a German forward position unawares, and then to take a prisoner.

Very often German trenches were quite comfortable compared to ours, thus making it possible for both occupants to nod off. The reason for the good construction of so many positions during the whole campaign was that the Germans had obviously prepared them ahead of time, in the event of having to retreat.

They were spacious compared to ours, all of which were dug hastily, invariably whilst under mortar bombing, and theirs were very strongly constructed, even sometimes having a roof of armour plate from a knocked out tank etc. Quite often there would be a mattress stolen from a French house, and other items of relative comfort. Every Allied infantryman who entered such a dugout will recall the odour left behind by the retreating Germans. I never found out what it was, but it could have been German army issue soap, or some kind of disinfectant to combat body lice. Invariably they would also leave a few of their stick grenades.

One day I picked up a 1945 official issue German soldier's diary. Obviously, they expected to see the year through all right, but the owner had made no entries at all. However, there was lots of interesting reading, such as Hitler's proclamations to the people, statistics relating to Jews around the world, and much more.

Now back to the fighting patrol. We set off in single file, a yard or two apart, and it was so quiet on the front that you could have heard a pin drop. The night was starlit, and as always in the Normandy countryside, the frogs were making croaking noises, which really got on my nerves during those warm 1944 nights.

After we had travelled about a hundred yards, we had left the bocage and were in the open field that separated the two forces. Suddenly it was as though it was years later when one was walking across a football pitch in the dark and someone switched on all of the floodlights, all at once; the Germans must have heard us and sent up some flares. Now here was a test of our training which demanded that for our personal and our comrades' safety, we stopped immediately and stood stock-still, until the flares burnt out. If anyone moved it would be seen, and a few bursts of Spandau fire would have sealed our fate.

No one did move, at least not sufficiently to be seen, although I do not think that I was the only one who was trembling. Our mission was not accomplished that night as we returned to our lines when the flares went out, but I do know more pleasant ways of spending summer evenings.

It was so very tiring in action. Apart from the danger, the incessant noise of whining bullets, screaming shells, and terrifying 'Moaning Minnies' mortars, fatigue was an ever present problem. The nights in June and July were so short, darkness not setting in until 11.00 pm and daylight appearing again by 5.00 am. With 'Stand to', one hour before sunset and one hour before dawn, little time was left for rest.

For the 11th Durham Light Infantry, a small Norman town called Rauray became a graveyard. One morning at dawn, we moved off to attack the enemy, who were in fact the feared 'Schutz-Staffel' (SS), known for their fanaticism and their willingness to die for their 'Führer' Aldolf Hitler.

Despite what was said to be one of the biggest barrages of World War II, as we crossed the first field we were decimated by Spandau machine-gun fire and mortar bombs.

We eventually captured the hamlet, but not before our biggest losses ever. The following day when we were relieved by the Tyneside Black Watch, I could easily see that we had lost a large number of killed or wounded. The battalion retired in the way we were trained, section by section on either side of the road, and spread out so that an exploding shell would have the least impact. Not as we now see in films where masses of soldiers march together, and where one shell could knock most of them out. On this day, many a section would have had only two or three men left, and some of them wounded, out of originally ten or twelve. I distinctly remember a pal of mine, a Lance Corporal, marching back on his own, having lost all of his section.

Tilly-sur-Seulles, our objective for the first few days, was not captured until 19 June.

Shortly afterwards we experienced an example of the Royal Air Force's might. They bombed the important road centre of Villers Bocage, dropping 1,300 tons of bombs one evening, and the result was that the town was flattened. To our amazement, we looked out of our slit trenches to see a cloud of dust approaching us, and we became covered in it. It continued for some time, and for a couple of hours we could not see a thing.

General Montgomery had a plan of drawing the German Armour to the British front, and he succeeded totally. We faced a large number of tanks, and in early July we certainly knew about it. At times, I would sit as best as I could in my slit trench and try to imagine how the war was going to end. The Tigers seemed so menacing that it was difficult to see how we could break through, despite the effectiveness of the Air Force's Typhoons. Progress seemed to be very slow and just capturing the next hedgerow was a major victory.

History shows that after many bitter battles we did break through. Many of our comrades were killed or wounded, and it was a great relief when we took to the roads to bite deep into France, making for the River Seine.

Looking back to the dreadful days of the Normandy campaign, I think of the lads in our battalion whom we left behind, and how we left them. The dead soldier would be wrapped in a groundsheet; placed in a slit trench; the hole filled in; a short service performed, by a steel helmeted army padre; the victim's rifle stuck into the impacted soil with the stock uppermost; and his tin helmet placed on top of his rifle. What a way to leave this life Later he would be gathered up and buried in a war graves cemetery with a stone cross and the appropriate name, rank and number. And to think that could have been my fate!

On a lighter note, I recall a Holy Communion service held in a cow byre. We left our slit trenches in a quiet period, those who wanted to, and head down hurried back to a barn. To start a hymn, the padre asked us for a note, and he was surprised at the response. A long plaintive 'moo' from a cow! We had to laugh!

CHAPTER TWELVE
THE BREAKOUT FROM NORMANDY

The first town of any size we liberated was Mezidon. We 'dug in' in the back garden of a modern house, in which we used to relax in between our 'two hours on and two hours off'. The town's inhabitants had gone to safer havens, although one day the neighbours turned up and immediately started to dig a hole in their garden. 'Funny' we thought, until it was explained that they had converted their savings into gold bars when the war started and they had buried them for the duration! When we left, I wrote a note in French to the absent owners of our billet, thanking them for the use of their house, and after the war Madame Vacher wrote me a very nice letter in response.

After leaving Normandy we crossed the River Seine – which of course, runs through Paris – at Vernon, and liberated several towns of First World War fame, including Amiens and Arras. En route we captured several V-bomb sites. This was a great thrill for us and gave us much satisfaction, as we had watched helplessly at one stage when we could see the bombs being fired, leaving their launching pads, and making for London and other targets in Britain.

We were surprised at the luxury enjoyed by the officers in charge of the V-bomb operations. They had beautifully furnished bedrooms made safe against attack from the air by reinforced concrete, whilst the other ranks had to make do with safe but Spartan conditions. From the items of clothing, perfumes, and toiletries we found, it was obvious that the Wehrmacht officers were not short of female company, in between pressing the buttons.

In Amiens and Arras, we met several members of the French underground movement. They seemed to have a motley collection of weapons. Having heard lots of stories of weapon and ammunition drops by the RAF, I thought that they would have been better armed than they were. For example, I did not see a Stengun, which was the weapon highlighted in most of the stories regarding dropping supplies over occupied territory.

What we did see, however, was quite disturbing. In the town centres large crowds gathered shortly after our arrival, their main purpose being obviously to welcome their liberators, but their second purpose was the antithesis of the first. Women, from teenagers to those much more mature, were having their heads shaved. There was much bitterness evident, and we were not short of people wanting to tell us the reason.

All of these females had been accused, and apparently found guilty, of fraternising with the enemy. It was rough justice and I thought that it was an opportunity for some people to settle old scores. I recalled stories of English girls being friendly with Italian prisoners of war, of British soldiers marrying thousands of German girls after the First World War. How can anyone legislate against the male/female attraction for one another? Unknown to us at that time, was the fact that enormous numbers of German girls and our servicemen were to fraternise and marry in less than two years from the Amiens/Arras incidents.

The plum target was Brussels, capital of Belgium, and there was much rivalry as to who would get there first. We were the infantry working with the Guards Armoured Division, and this partnership was to see plenty of excitement as time went on. The Welsh Guards reached the capital at 8.00 pm on 3rd September, exactly five years since the war began.

We arrived twelve hours later and we ran into an enormous roadblock, caused by the Belgian citizens leaping on to the tanks and other vehicles. It was an incredible, amazing welcome, but our joy was tinged with the worry that the Germans might counter attack, and we would be in real trouble.

This fear became much greater when the roar of guns, the whistle of shells, and the bark of airburst shells was heard. It certainly moved the Belgians and eventually we were able to get through the city, passing the Palais de Justice – which was a blazing inferno, torched by the enemy before they left – and setting up observation posts in the north side of the city. We 'dug in' in a park, and unfortunately we saw little more of the celebrations. I do recall seeing the Gestapo headquarters, which were in a commandeered hotel.

I fell in love with Brussels during that short, but happy and exciting visit. I made a mental note that I must come back one day and really see the sights. I was not to know that I was to spend the next Christmas there; that I was to play football at their main stadium, Heyschells, three times in the next ten years; and that I was to visit there two or three times on holiday with my wife Leni, and my daughter Margarete, twenty or so years later.

But the first time was the best. To see vast crowds of people so happy on the greatest day of their lives is something that could not be bettered.

After all of the celebrations in Brussels, accompanied by lots of rumours that the war was about to end, it came as an anti-climax to hear that we were to take part in the liberation of the great Belgian port of Antwerp. Obviously, if the war was to continue, it would be a great help to the Allies to take Antwerp, and so on the 5th of September, we entered the city.

It appeared that the Germans had retreated into the enormous docks area. It was like a rabbit warren of narrow streets and warehouses, and most difficult and dangerous to clean out the elusive enemy. Street fighting was not one of our more popular pursuits, and to be ordered to 'seek and destroy' in such an environment was not in the least bit welcome.

However, we had a pleasant surprise awaiting us. As mentioned previously, our experience of the French underground in places like Normandy, Amiens, and Arras was a non-event, but the Belgian White Army in Antwerp restored our faith in the European underground movements.

Sections of six or seven combed the streets and buildings, and were often easy targets for firmly ensconced Nazi snipers. We were expecting each day to join them in their task, but evidently they thought that their personal knowledge of the district gave them an advantage over their foes and us.

Therefore, we were deployed in observation posts and vantage points up above, so that our Bren guns could pick off the enemy as they were flushed out.

Our section was by far the luckiest. Indeed, what we looked upon as highly dangerous turned out to be almost relaxing. We placed our Bren in front of the window on the top floor of a three-storey building, the bottom floor of which was a cafe. There was also a cellar, so we borrowed the mattresses from the bedrooms, and took them down there. We had two at a time manning the gun, whilst the other six or seven indulged in the unusual luxury of sleeping in comfort.

I was the odd man out, but the rest of the lads were beer drinkers, and it is not difficult to imagine their delight when we found a large number of crates of the Belgians' favourite tipple, 'Stella Artois'. They demolished quite a quantity in the belief that as 'liberators', the cafe proprietors would not object to them doing the same to their bottles of beer as they were doing to their country.

Antwerp was eventually liberated and we were on our way again, crossing the Albert Canal being our objective. We had never ridden on the back of tanks before, presumably because of the design of the Shermans, but the Guards' new Cromwells, with their huge 17-pounder guns, were well suited to carrying infantry.

Previously we had walked behind the tanks, but on the cold bright morning of the attack on the canal, the warmth from the engines was welcome, as was the feeling of relative safety given by the armour plating.

I recalled that the last time we had operated with the American made Shermans had been a tragic occasion. As we neared a bend in the road, a camouflaged Tiger tank fired at and hit our lead tank, and then quickly did the same to the rear one, leaving the middle one a sitting target. They were all hit in the same place, just above the driver's visor. The result was generally that the tank was set on fire and, unfortunately, the driver was sometimes decapitated. On this occasion, the survivors from the three Shermans jumped out and ran back past us, for there was nothing they could do after an armour-piercing 88-millimetre shell got through the armour-plating.

The three tanks blocked the road, and we had to lie flat in a ditch running alongside it. In no time a Typhoon swooped out of the sky, its rockets knocked out the Tiger and the danger was removed. Then the Guards had to bring up more tanks to push the destroyed Shermans off the road, so that the advance could continue.

Passing 'brewed-up' tanks was a sickening business, because those killed inside were very often burnt, and the smell was ghastly.

Soon after we crossed the border from Belgium into Holland, we liberated the small town of Valkenswaard, which to this day is famous for its cigars.

As was our habit, we 'dug in' on the far side of the town from whence the Germans had just retreated. The peach trees were in fruit and I was able to eat a fresh peach for the first time in my life. They really tasted lovely and we did justice to them.

We had a tumultuous reception from the townspeople, and in beautiful weather, we thoroughly enjoyed it. Within hours of our arrival, streets and windows were decked in streamers and flags of orange, the Dutch national colour.

As we had previously experienced elsewhere, eventually resistance fighters started to appear, dressed in a motley array of military and semi-military uniforms, with the official armband on.

The war was over for the people of Valkenswaard. Or was it? No, there was a report received by the freedom fighters that Tiger tanks could be seen approaching the town (which was on a hill, enabling them to see several miles).

During the war the people had utilised some huge caves, which were at the back of the town, as air raid shelters, and it was to them that they flocked again. And so did the resistance fighters.

This latter rather disappointed us, but apart from Antwerp, we generally saw little of these civilian armies.

More disappointing was that the people had little faith in us. After crossing the Channel and fighting our way through France and Belgium, to in effect liberate the people of the Dutch town, they not only went back to the caves – this we could understand – but they took down all of their flags and bunting.

They must have felt a little ashamed when, after leaving us to it, the Tiger tanks turned around and disappeared in retreat. Later, our forward positions or OP's (observation posts), told us that it appeared that the German armour had got lost, and had not intended to return to Valkenswaard.

CHAPTER THIRTEEN
A BRIDGE TOO FAR

It was about this time that we were told about the 'master plan', for the operation that became one of the most spectacular of the war. The taking of Valkenswaard was just the beginning, and what happened, starting on 17th September, became immortalised in the film, 'A Bridge Too Far'. Our next target was the town of Eindhoven where the giant Phillips factories were situated. It was to be taken by the 101st American Airborne, whilst simultaneously the 82nd American Airborne was to capture the bridges at Grave and Nijmegen, over the rivers Maas and Waal, tributaries of the Rhine. The final piece of the jigsaw was at Arnhem, where the 1st British Airborne, aided by a Polish brigade, were to capture the bridge which became the 'bridge too far'.

Then the Guards Armoured, with supporting infantry, were to make a spectacular dash north into Holland to the Zuider Zee, so that the Germans in western Holland were cut off, and the British Second Army would get onto the North German Plain before winter. This was the master plan and it almost came off.

The people of Eindhoven gave us all a rapturous welcome, but none more so than a brigade of Dutch troops, who had been training in Britain. However, we were all brought back to our senses by an air raid, carried out by the Luftwaffe in the evening of the liberation. I remember it well. It was a real dampener and the euphoria soon evaporated. We were still at war.

Many years later I saw a film about the Dutch heroine, Corrie ten Boom, who was in a Gestapo prison in the town, and she told of the air raid in the film. It was a strange feeling as I watched the film to realise that I must have been just a few hundred yards from her. Shortly afterwards, she and the other prisoners were moved to a concentration camp in the Reich.

The next waterway was the Wilhelmina Canal and the bridge was blown up, but the Royal Engineers, the so often unsung heroes, erected a new one during the night. Then into Grave, where the Americans had encountered no opposition. My main memory, apart from the bridge itself, was seeing a large advertisement for Lux Soap Flakes on a wall in the town! 'So they even have Lux here', I thought.

The bridge had been damaged through bombing or shelling, and it had to be repaired. There was only one-way traffic but that was good enough. Although history tells of the American Airborne landing in Eindhoven, my memory does not, and my first recollection is of them at Grave, but there again, my memory plays tricks. I have vivid and gruesome memories of American paratroopers dead, and hanging in the trees by their parachutes near the Grave bridge, but the official history denies this. Certainly the memories are true, it is just the places my memory may have mixed up.

Also, I thought what great fellows they were, so friendly and cheerful, and quite different to the popular misconception. There is no doubt that their next operation was as good as any in the whole North-West European campaign. Their assault of the Nijmegen bridge, after clearing the town, was both brave and brilliant. Using British assault craft, which they were not used to, they crossed the Waal and secured the opposite bank.

Eventually, the Guards Armoured were able to cross the bridge whilst under considerable attack from artillery fire. We crossed shortly afterwards, when there were still dead German soldiers littering the roadway. It was a mystery that the Germans had not blown up this very important crossing over the Waal, for it was 400 yards long, and it would have taken the Royal Engineers a long time to build a new bridge.

The British Airborne were having a tough time at Arnhem and valiant efforts were made to link up with them, but the Germans fought very tenaciously, knowing that we were trying to find a quicker route into their homeland.

The weather broke about this time and our slit trenches became full of mud and water. Our fourth battalion performed valiantly, and they actually crossed the river at Arnhem and rescued a lot of paratroops. During this attack the battalion, whose strength at the time would have been seven or eight hundred, lost over 170 men.

The Germans were very determined and eventually it had to be accepted that operation 'Market Garden', for that was its name, had failed to reach its final objective, Arnhem, one bridge too far.

The remnants of the First British Airborne Division and the First Polish Brigade eventually passed through our positions on their way back to their bases, but we remained on what became known simply as 'The Island'.

We must have been there for at least a month conducting Normandy type attacks, generally with a dike as our objective instead of the French Bocage hedgerow. This island was the area, roughly triangular, formed by the Dutch coast and the main two Rhine tributaries, the Rivers Waal and Neder Rhine.

I have known a number of islands in my life including, for example, the Isle of Wight, Singapore, Gibraltar, Cyprus, Elcho, Croker, Goulburn and Millingimbi, and the word 'island' conjures up pretty pictures of lovely beaches, waving palm trees, gin and tonics and all things beautiful; but this one in Holland fell into a totally different category.

One of the main small towns was called Elst, about which I will write later, only to mention at this time that years after the war I saw some beautiful apples in Stockton market and on the box was printed 'Grown and packed in Elst'. I bought some. They were sweet and juicy, but they do not make up for my first encounter with the island.

It could only happen in the British Army. We were in our slit trenches just outside of Elst, when a 'runner' from Battalion HQ crept along a path towards us. He wanted me to go with him back to 'B' Echelon, as there was a message for me. This was most unusual, in fact unique, and I could not imagine what I was wanted for.

As I crawled the first few yards along on my stomach, being in view of the enemy positions, and continuing to be so until I was behind the shelter of a row of trees, I just could not think why I should be drawn out of the front line. If it was going to be permanent, of course I would not argue. I was soaking wet from days in the pouring rain, and there was about a foot of water in the bottom of the trench, so if I never saw it again, I would not have been the least bit bothered.

'You have to go back to Nijmegen as you are playing in a Divisional practice football match', was the extraordinary message awaiting me. I was amazed, but I did not know whether to be pleased or not, because my water logged slit trench was safer than going back to Nijmegen.

There was only one way to get there, and that was back over the bridge. That same bridge which we had crossed, as we fought to get up to Arnhem to link up with our airborne troops. Although now in our hands, it was shelled day and night by heavy enemy artillery, and the odd fighter-bomber tried to blow holes in it.

The British believe that sport is of great importance and seem to have invented most of it, but this was ridiculous!

A 15 cwt truck took me back. The driver was terrified. HQ drivers had about the best jobs in the battalion. Not for them the trench, and the 'over boys and at 'em' of the infantry attack. It was even said that they slept in pyjamas.

When we got to the bridge environs, a Military Policeman, who must have had the worst job in the CMP (Corps of Military Police), hurried out of his all steel 'sentry box', and told us that on his signal we must 'go like the clappers of hell', as we were under enemy observation as soon as we passed his post.

Was it really worth it? I liked playing football, but did I like it as much as this? Was it worth getting killed for? I suppose English pukka sahibs took chances playing a chukka of polo, as there could have always been a tiger or a rebel about.

Many years later, it was to become dangerous to play soccer due to hooliganism and the throwing of fireworks – but modern footballers' wages are thousands of pounds a week, whereas I got 3/6d a day. Oh well, it would not be something to be proud of in the future, to admit that the Germans had done to me what the Spanish had failed to do to Drake, so off we went.

A Bedford 15 cwt never went as fast, and in seconds we were clear of the enemy gunners' range.

Next we had to find the stadium. With German aircraft making frequent sorties over the city, and British anti-aircraft batteries opening up on every such occasion, there were not too many people on the streets. However, we did find it, and I entered the dressing room to discover that the person who had arranged the game was none other than Cliff Britton, one of my heroes from the great pre-war Everton team.

He was a Company Sergeant-Major (CSM) in the Army Physical Training Corps, and in charge of sport for the Division. I remember little about the quality of the football, not even whether I was on the winning side or not, but I do remember the anti-aircraft fire which thundered and flashed throughout the ninety minutes.

Cliff wore a white trench coat, and he needed it as it poured down the whole time. Strangely, our paths never crossed again, not even to this day. I would have loved to have been able to discuss this, the most unique of football matches, with him. The drama of the race across the bridge had to be re-run, and I got back in the dark to spend the night, two hours on and two hours off, in my wet and muddy piece of Holland.

One moonlit night two of us were on patrol through the streets of Elst. All of the civilians had been evacuated for obvious reasons, so we were surprised to hear a noise in one of the terraced houses, whose front door opened right on to the street.

We decided to investigate, and we forced open the door. I stepped inside and for a second or two I did not know what was happening. Then bang; as I hit the ground. I got gingerly to my feet in the pitch-blackness – I seemed to be hurting all over, but particularly my right hand. I saw light above me, and I realised that it was coming through the front door, that it was in fact moonlight.

I had walked through the front door and dropped straight into the cellar. I had a terrible job getting out, and if my mate had not been on hand, I would have been there until someone happened to come near to the house and hear my calls. Incidentally, we never found out what had caused the noise we heard. The battering Elst had received, first by the British artillery, and then after its capture, by the Germans, resulted in very heavy damage being inflicted on most of the houses. The floorboards had been demolished in this particular house, resulting in my rapid descent.

Of course I could have been killed, or at least broken some bones, but my only significant injury was a badly cut finger. I guess that due to not knowing what was happening, I fell relaxed, and just rolled over, thus preventing serious injury.

The Elst church served as an observation post for first the Germans, and then for us, and it had suffered accordingly. It was shattered, and it got worse daily.

Strangely, when speaking to a German who surrendered to us at the end of the war, it transpired that he had been in charge of the batteries that were responsible for the bombardment.

After five years of war, death and all the carnage had become quite commonplace. As we were facing death by the minute around the dikes of Holland, our compatriots in London, including grandmothers and mums and children, were doing the same in their homes.

By this time we had captured the V1 bomb launching sites, but the ever more horrific V2's were blasting the peoples' houses without warning, travelling faster than the speed of sound, and killing indiscriminately.

But one morning, the awful tragedy of this senseless death clearly became once more poignant and transparent.

Early that day, before sunrise, we moved forward to take over some positions facing the German lines. As always, we kept as quiet as we could, not wanting to alert the enemy and thus invite a barrage of either mortar or artillery fire.

As often happened, the awaiting slit trenches were on the nearside of the dike, and we reached them whilst it was still dark. To our surprise and then horror, they were occupied. The soldiers were infantrymen of the Green Howards Regiment, a regiment I had known of for years, because it was from North

Yorkshire, and one battalion actually came from Middlesbrough, where their headquarters were. And they were all dead.

Obviously, they had been surprised during the night. Normally they would have followed the pattern of one man off and one man on the alert, in two hourly intervals, but perhaps they were all very tired.

The trench my colleague and I were to occupy had only one occupant. All we could do was lift him onto the parapet, until the tide of war rolled over, and he could be temporarily buried.

I opened a pocket in his battledress tunic and took out his 'paybook', which contained his personal details, and it was then that the feelings of hopelessness and poignancy swept over me. I have forgotten his name, but his address was Teesbridge Road, Middlesbrough, a road I knew so well.

So a Mum and Dad who would have had all kinds of hopes and dreams for their nineteen year old son, would shortly receive a telegram regretting that the subject of those dreams for 'when it was all over', had been killed in action.

I went cold. I felt helpless and hopeless. This was only one senseless death out of millions, but it was a boy from Teesbridge Road who had been killed, and the enormity of what was happening became more apparent than ever before.

The lives of boys were being snuffed out before they had had a chance to taste life. This was surely not how God meant it to be.

I pondered later whether I should write to the boy's parents, or better still, visit them if I got back home myself. For a few years, during which I remembered his name and the house number, I considered the effect my appearance would have on his loved ones.

I always came to the same conclusions; that it would re-open the wounds caused by their vicious loss, and healed by time as much as they ever could be healed; and that I would be loath to describe the pathetic lifeless body as it lay, useless and inert, on the ground in front of our slit trench.

Even today, I mourn for that boy. I write with tears in my eyes. He was only one of millions who died because of the greed for power of heads of nations; one of thousands in the North-West European campaign who gave their all: but for me he will forever be the one who personified the utter futility of war.

We were in the trench for two days, during which we were under almost constant bombardment from a variety of artillery, including the dreaded 88-millimetre self-propelled guns, and airburst shells, which spattered their shrapnel all around us – and him.

His body probably lies in the War Graves Cemetery, at a place near where he fell; and no doubt his loved ones have made heartbreaking journeys to view that small cross on which is his name, regiment, and army number, standing in that part 'of a foreign field that is forever England'.

Around the same time, our platoon was involved in an attack during which we had the greatest losses we ever suffered.

Lieutenant Black, a tall, athletic, and brave platoon commander, led the attack. The platoon sergeant had visited all of our slit trenches before 'stand to', to describe what we were to do. We were to capture the higher ground a couple of hundred yards away where the Germans were 'dug in'.

This meant that on a signal just before dawn, we would get out of our trenches and move across the field, and up the slope where the German positions were. Hopefully there would be little opposition, because prior to our attack, our artillery and mortars would put down a carpet of shells and bombs which should knock out most of the enemy.

The barrage roared over our heads, with the accompanying whistles of shells and the ground shaking caused by the explosions. It was a hell of man's making, and when considering its objective, to blow our fellow man to pieces, just because he happened to be born in Germany, it seemed bizarre: then and as it still does now.

As soon as it ceased, the word spread rapidly from trench to trench, and we were up, 'over the top', and on our way. I was carrying a Bren gun, which is perfectly portable, with a carrying handle attached to the barrel. It is also not heavy, as heavy things go, but the further you run in full battle order, steel helmet, and carrying ammunition, the heavier it gets.

The first fifty yards or so seemed to confirm the planners' opinions, that the barrage had done its job. Then to our surprise and chagrin, we were fired on, not from in front of us, but from our left flank where there were knocked out Tiger tanks. It transpired that the fusillades came from Spandau machine-guns, whose firers were under the tanks for shelter.

The buzz, buzz, buzz of the machine-gun bullets wreaked a heavy toll. I was just about exhausted, and the shelter of a shell hole looked inviting. I jumped in for a few moments to get my breath back, then I carried on, with hundreds of rounds of machine-gun fire whizzing all around me.

I realised that our numbers had decreased, that colleagues had fallen, but I did not realise just how bad the situation was. We took the strongpoint, when the German occupants who had survived the onslaught, surrendered with hands held high, and it was then that we were able to count the cost.

Lieutenant Black, with his .38 Service revolver in his hand, was one of the first to be killed, and of the 29 in the platoon who had started out, only 13 had survived unscathed.

Many Germans had died too, and many were lying wounded in their trenches. Once more the stupidity of war was apparent, as despite our own losses, my heart went out to their killed and wounded. I remember, in particular, one young German lying huddled up in deep mud. It was freezing cold and he looked so helpless. Man's inhumanity to man was so evident. He was bleeding and probably expected little mercy. The fact that our stretcher-bearers saved his life, and carried him back to the warmth and comfort of a base hospital, just made the whole situation more ludicrous than ever. You let loose a hail of bullets and shells in another attempt to kill the enemy, then as though it were just a game, you pick up the wounded, you smile on them, you truly pity them, you tend to their wounds, and you carefully remove them to a hospital where kind and caring doctors and nurses make them better. How obscene.

It was about this time that XXX corps took two American Airborne Divisions, the 82nd and 101st, under its command. They were the paratroops who captured the bridges at Grave and Nijmegen, and for some time they operated as infantry. We would relieve them after they had been some time 'in the line', and they would do the same for us, only with a difference.

However, let me first reiterate that these Yanks were great soldiers, and we truly admired them. They were not as they were painted in some quarters. The only fault we found with them was when we were relieving each other. When we relieved them, we would use our skills and work our way to the American slit trenches – although whilst they were in residence they were called 'foxholes' – as quietly as possible, so that the enemy would not know, because if they knew that there were troops above ground they would fire on them.

Our stealth would result in a nil response from the Germans, but when our allies took over from us, they would make such a noise, shouting to one another and to us, that we used to have to scurry back to our base as quickly as possible. This was always at night, but it was just as bad in the day when they sent a few NCOs (Non-Commissioned Officers) and officers to reconnoitre our positions ready for the takeover. They would shout and bawl to one another such as 'We'll put a sniper up here' (this from up a tree – often an apple tree for this was a prolific fruit growing area), or 'We'll have a machine-gun there'.

Invariably, after they had left we would be rewarded with a few mortars or 88-millimetre shells fired by self-propelled guns over open sights.

It was very interesting to be in such close co-operation and proximity to our transatlantic mates! Many years later in 1991 to be exact, I felt a deep sense of pride and the warmth of comradeship, when in the Gulf War two American Airborne Divisions performed superbly – yes, they were the 82nd and 101st.

I had a particular pal from the South Coast resort town of Brighton, and one day when we were 'dug in' on the side of a Dutch dike, he was ordered to take a message to company headquarters, which was a few hundred yards behind the line. And that was the last I saw of him, for he was killed by a shell whilst doing his duty. Nineteen years old and lying dead; all of his hopes and aspirations dashed by a self-propelled gun. I have forgotten his name now, but I did remember it for years, including on two occasions when I was in Brighton in later years. The first occasion was whilst I was staying at the 'Grand Hotel', with West Bromwich Albion football team, prior to playing an important FA Cup game. The second, fifteen years later, was whilst I stayed at the 'Metropole' – where Mrs Thatcher was nearly killed by an IRA bomb – on business. On both occasions I toyed with the idea of looking up my old pal's relations, but I decided that I might just have brought back sad memories, as in the case of the Middlesbrough lad.

When you consider the complex problems of organising such an enormous venture as an invasion of Europe, you can rightly think that the planners must have been incredibly brilliant. To have the right men in the right place at the right time, and simultaneously to have all the equipment, ammunition, and other supplies including food, is surely remarkable. And right throughout the campaign this happened, to suggest that everything was thought-out like a game of chess, but when you are in the thick of it, it seemed that no one knew what was happening. And yet it always worked out in the end.

However, it did not always work out for our foes. Whilst we were very mobile in September 1944, the front changing all the time due to the thrusting of our Armoured Divisions, a German quartermaster got something of a shock. As he had been used to doing, he arrived at his food supplies depot early one morning to collect food for his battalion, but unfortunately for him, he was himself collected by the British soldiers who had just captured the food store. Incidentally, due to this we ate quite a lot of German food for the next few weeks, and we liked it. In the main, it was tinned pork and vegetables, and tins of jam.

Around about the same time, we were ourselves cut off for a few days due to our quick progress, and we ate American rations. The main food was also pork and vegetables, but it was so heavily spiced that I just could not eat it. They say that you will eat anything if you are hungry enough, but for me not spiced pork!

They even organised rest periods when we were sent back to a rear area for a couple of days or more. Our first such time in Normandy was welcome but slightly disappointing to say the least. I thought that all was not well when our rest areas were in effect shallow trenches, large enough to stretch out and sleep, with a raised tarpaulin cover to protect us from the hot sun or rain, if it came.

But why the 'trenches'? We soon found out. All of a sudden, whistle, bang, the earth shook, and then the curious 'zing' noise of the shell splinters as they sprayed around our positions. These were really big ones, fired from a long distance by the enemy heavy artillery.

I would not say that I was glad to get back to the front line, but at least you expected such things to happen 'up there', but not way back. This was an occasion when a few at a time from each company had a 'rest', and we left our equipment at what was known as 'B' echelon, the battalion's rear base.

On my way back to my platoon, I picked up my gear. Now next to an infantryman's weapon the next most important piece of equipment was his army issue enamel mug, and I saw immediately that it was missing because it was always carried attached to my 'small pack', which I carried on my back.

It was amazing how we seemed to manage to 'brew up' (our term for making tea). Hot tinned food was our staple diet, sent up from 'A' echelon, and tea would emanate from the same place, but a common method of brewing up was via petrol when we could get hold of some. We would fill a square tin with sand, pour in the petrol, and then light it, or if a tin were not available, we would loosen up some soil and pour in the petrol, to get the same result.

After my arrival back in the line, I had to borrow a mug after someone had drunk their 'char', to use the army expression (which originated in India). Whilst waiting one day, I noticed that Private Coxon had my mug. It was easily recognisable by the dents. We all knew the idiosyncrasies of our own mugs!

Private Coxon was a Durham miner from, I think, Houghton le Spring. He was built like an ox and immensely strong. I thought that we were friends. I said to him, 'You have got my mug'.

He replied, 'Yes, I know, what are you going to do about it?' Well you could always get a new mug, but not so easily a new face, so I let him keep it. But it was depressing to think that 'comrades in arms' could do such a dirty trick in the shared environment of constant danger.

My next rest of any consequence was after I had been transferred to the first battalion, the Dorsetshire Regiment, in 50 Div. After the long campaign from Normandy up to the Arnhem battles, we were sent back many miles, into Belgium in fact.

It was one of the most pleasant journeys of my life. Imagine sitting or lying on the bare boards of a three-ton army lorry, as it bumped along for a hundred miles in the dark, and in freezing temperatures, for it was early December. Does that 'grab you'? No? Well just suppose that you were being taken out of the front line, and that after six months of perpetual danger you were for the first time out of range of everything. Every mile was a mile further from danger, and in the early morning we arrived at our destination, Neuve Eglise, a small village near Ypres.

It had an interesting history, because during the First World War it served as a rest village for the British troops, in action near there. The people were more than just normally helpful, because they felt a camaraderie towards us that went back thirty years, reinforced by the holiday visits backwards and forwards by village girls who married 'Tommies' after the war.

An unusual situation prevailed between Neuve Eglise and another village a few miles away, which was similar in function to the Anglophiles. However, there was a difference. It was the village that the first war Germans had used for rest and recreation, and there remained an enmity between the respective villagers. Several people told me about it.

We played our village at football. We were far too good for them, but it was enjoyable and our host played centre forward, wearing a hair net! He and his wife ran a café, which was also the place where they cured the locally grown tobacco, and Lance Corporal Robb (a Scot from Edinburgh) and I, slept in the bedroom above the cafe. It was situated opposite the church and churchyard in the main street, which was cobbled.

Whilst there we had a wonderful rest and we really appreciated what was done for us. To conclude this anecdote, I would just add that Neuve Eglise figured again in my life, not just once but twice. Stay tuned!

One day (back in the war) when we were in Neuve Eglise, our platoon had to attend a very pleasant ceremony. In the vicinity, our C in C (Commander in Chief), Field Marshal Montgomery, held an investiture, and many Military Crosses and Military Medals were presented, the former to officers who had performed specific acts of outstanding bravery, and the latter similarly to other ranks.

Sadly, I was involved next in something which was as demotivating as the former was motivating. I was ordered to do guard duty at a field court-martial.

It was held in a monastery of all places, and the soldier I was in charge of was a Corporal from the Anti-Tank Platoon from one of the Durham Light Infantry battalions. He was accused of deserting his gun in the face of the enemy. Maybe the charge was cowardice. I cannot remember exactly, but I recall everything else vividly. He was small and stocky and had been in action since the Normandy beaches, but in the most recent action, his nerve had gone, and he had run away from his anti-tank gun when faced with the German Panzers.

I felt sincerely sorry for him. There is no worse job than being up in the front of the battalion, awaiting an onslaught from German armour. He had done this on many occasions with success. Millions of his fellow Britons were in the rear echelons or back in Britain, or Brussels, never having to face the 'ultimate test'.

I realised that something would have to be done, but his sentence of four years' imprisonment was brutal. His face is forever etched in my memory, and he had, and still has, my sympathy.

Another significant event took place whilst resting in Belgium. Our battalion, the first Dorsetshire Regiment, was converted to a training battalion, taken out of the line, and was to return to England to commence its training role.

You can imagine my feelings – home for Christmas ... but ... only the lads who had been through the Middle East campaign and North-Western Europe were to be kept as trainers, the remainder, including me, were to stay in the Dorsets, but be transferred to the 5th battalion.

CHAPTER FOURTEEN

THE 5TH BN DORSETSHIRE REGIMENT

I had gone to Normandy as a member of the Carrier Platoon, but we had no opportunity to ride in the Bren gun carriers, as on landing, the action was all purely infantry attacking and capturing Bocages. In effect, we were another rifle company, and when I was transferred to the 1st Battalion of the Dorsets, I went straight into D Company, a rifle company. However, when transferred to the 5th Battalion, I was pleased to be put into their Carrier Platoon; if pleasure can be derived from anything when in action.

It was in this battalion that I made some life-long friends, and 'Busty' Villis, Bob Rigler, and Reg Cobb correspond with me still.

'Busty' (called such due to his rotund build as a baby, apparently), real name Cyril, was a stretcher-bearer and medical orderly, later a sergeant, and he was one of the greatest guys I have met in my life. Born and bred in Swanage, Dorset, where he has lived his whole life, Busty was noted for his humanity and caring. In action, the stretcher-bearer had the worst job. He was unarmed and had to go out, often in front of and in the full view of the enemy, to bring back and tend to the wounded.

The Geneva Convention said that they should wear a white armband with a red cross on it and that, as such, they were sacrosanct from enemy action. This meant nothing to some of the SS – the 'Herman Goering' Division for example – whom we faced in Normandy and later, and there was always the chance that they would shoot the wounded and the stretcher-bearers. I saw this happen in Normandy: it was always a possibility.

What happened in Normandy was this. We had suffered several casualties due to snipers, and then when one of them was being stretchered away, the bearers had needed to dash for cover. Eventually, it was realised that the shots were coming from the nearby hedgerow of tall, bushy, well-leafed trees, but it was impossible to spot the culprits. So a troop of tanks were called up and they raked the trees with machine-gun fire. The snipers had deliberately stayed up there when the rest of their battalion had retreated, knowing that there was little chance of survival. They were fastened to branches by their belts. A macabre type of suicide.

Away from the front line, in the UK for instance, the stretcher-bearers were the medical orderlies running the sick bay, and this Busty did after the war was over, until his demobilisation.

Bob Rigler was the salt of the earth. Whoever loved a sergeant major? Well we loved Bob. A carpenter in civilian life, he was in 'S' or 'Specialist' Company, the same as the Carrier Platoon and the Mortar Platoon, but tradesmen like Bob were in the Pioneer Platoon.

In England the Pioneers had performed two functions. One was to work at their trades doing building and maintenance work, and the other was to train for war. This involved a variety of things including mine laying, mine sweeping, erecting barbed wire fences, breaking through the latter, defusing boobytraps, etc, etc. It really was a difficult assignment.

In action, Bob Rigler was platoon sergeant and to Bob that really meant leading. Before every attack, Bob would go out about dawn with his mine-detector and comb the battalion's attack path for anti-personnel mines. What a job! But Bob did it systematically and fearlessly.

After the war he was made our sergeant major, and later he managed to get a plum job in Brussels. He certainly deserved it and it was to change his life, for bachelor Bob met Belgian girl Louise, married, and came back home to Poole to resume his trade. He worked for his brother, and in 1955 when we moved to Poole, Bob was a frequent visitor, often popping in on his way home, always by bicycle.

Since then he has kept us informed about the regimental reunions, which he attends every year at Dorchester, and of the old comrades who have gone to their rest above, since the previous get-together.

Reg Cobb was not the smartest soldier in the British Army, in fact, he could have been the least smart, but he was a great bloke to be with. I had the exalted title of 'Carrier Commander', and Reg was 'my' driver. This was when we were mobile, chasing after the retreating foe. When static, we shared a slit trench, but static or mobile, Reg was always cheerful, a grin seemingly permanently on his face. He was always talking about his girl, Audrey, back in Poole, and it was wonderful to meet the one about whom I had heard so much when we went to live in Poole. And in 1986 when we were back in England on holiday, there they were, still lovebirds, but with photographs of grandchildren around the living room to remind us all of the years that have passed inexorably.

When it appeared that we were steamrolling the Germans back into their 'Heimatland', it was decided that front line troops would be given two days leave in Brussels. Some kind of lottery was used, and I could not hide my delight when I qualified for Christmas. Christmas in Brussels. What a prospect!

A few days before Christmas however, Von Runstedt's offensive frightened the Allies to bits, and I fully expected my trip to be called off.

However, once the bureaucrats formulate a plan, nothing can stop it, and so it was with my leave in Brussels. We were freezing in our snow-covered slit trenches, and fog swirled around the bridge which we were guarding. Fortunately, we had our snowsuits on top of our uniforms, and they served two purposes; for camouflage and for added warmth.

It would not be difficult to imagine how I felt when, on the morning of the 24th December 1944, I had to report back to A 'Echelon' for transport to the Belgian capital. It took about six hours to get there in the snow covered icy roads. It was great to go back again to the scene of our greatest triumph, and I was taken to the Rue de la Loi and given a room on my own with a bed and white sheets, the first for the nine months since my embarkation leave at home.

I had a marvellous time and everything was laid on for us, from the turkey and plum pudding to the theatre and carols, and many other leisure activities. I still have the programme, and it brings back quite unique memories of this most unusual Christmas, the first free Yuletide for the Belgians since 1939. The only adverse note was my observation of a certain amount of panic that existed in these echelons, which were so very far from the action. It was obvious that our hierarchy were ready to leave their lives of luxury, as the Germans drove further onwards through the Ardennes. Seeing so much packed and ready to move, where to I would not know, did nothing for my confidence.

In the three months since liberation, the city had not only returned to its former state as a pleasure centre, but the British Army's HQ had even improved on that.

The Officers Clubs were out of my reach, but the '21' Club, being the 21st Army Group's, was something to behold.

Everything comes to an end, good and bad, and soon I was in the back of an army three-ton lorry, on my way back to my cosy little slit trench somewhere by a bridge, in the Ardennes Forest, unless my battalion had moved on.

They hadn't, and I rejoined Reg Cobb and co, and swapped my Belgian bed for a Belgian slit trench. The weather was still terrible with fog, snow, and heavy frosts, and we were thankful for our white snowsuits, which kept us warm to the extent that I do not know how we would have got on without them.

We were not in action in the Ardennes, as the Germans did not attack our part of the front, but we were on tenterhooks in case they did, and on our guard all of the time. The story of the battle was well related in the film 'The Battle of the Bulge'. One incident I do remember was when we saw and heard our first German jet aeroplane. A salvo of bombs dropped nearby, and it was frightening because we did not know from whence they came, until we heard the engine noise. Looking up we then saw the plane disappearing, and realised that it must have been faster than the speed of sound. It was quite worrying.

The first time we set foot in Germany was a great thrill. Before the war started, Germany and France had built 'impregnable' defences, which would prevent either one of them entering one another's territory, if there was a war. France's 'Maginot Line' was easily taken care of. The Germans just entered France by going around the wall, through their attacks on Holland and Belgium. Germany's 'Siegfried Line' played little part in the war either, because by the time we reached it, the enemy had retreated from it. Of course, it was exciting passing through the famous fortifications, and it was near the Siegfried Line that we crossed the Dutch/German border. We could see a village across the fields, and unlike in Britain, there were no hedgerows, it was extremely visible. We approached it in the best infantry manner, one section covering another as we leapfrogged the last few hundred yards.

On the corner of the first street was a 'deli' type of shop with an upper storey, and steps running down by the side to a cellar below. Some of our lads went upstairs to find it deserted. So the rest of us descended the cellar stairs and it was then that we heard voices. House to house fighting was the worst of all. Always ready for anything, we kicked the door open. It was quite scary as our eyes had to become accustomed to the darkness, and during that time, anything could have happened.

The hubbub of voices continued and became louder. As our vision became clearer, we could see that the room contained about twenty people sitting on the ground around the walls. They were mostly women and children, plus a few old men, and they were all praying.

Apparently Catholics, the noise we could hear was of them saying the Rosary, with Rosary beads in their hands.

A lady stood up and I spoke to her, saying that we were just looking for German soldiers. As was our habit, we gave sweets to the children, but she forbade them to eat them, saying that they would be poisoned.

You see, it transpired that the Propaganda Minister, Dr Goebels, had told all Germans that they must resist to the last, as the Allies would kill them all. When we gave the kids sweets, she was sure that this was our intention.

What they were really doing was praying whilst waiting to die. There was absolutely no panic, no fear evident as they calmly prayed to their Lord, not for deliverance, but for salvation. They were sure they were going to die. Part of their Rosary is a prayer asking the Virgin Mary to 'pray for us sinners, now and at the hour of our death. Amen.' Never was it more appropriate, I should imagine they thought.

For me it was a shining example of faith, and something that I could never forget.

I can imagine how their prayers changed as we left, thanking God for their deliverance.

The next few weeks were tough, as we battled to gain a foothold into the Reich. Cleve and Goch, two ancient towns, were flattened first by British gunfire and then, after their capture, by their own artillery. To get at the two important towns we had first to get through the Reichwald Forest, and this was difficult as there were no roads running west to east. We had to stick to paths that were probably fire breaks. I recall spending one night in a vacated German trench. It had been well made, with a piece of armour plating for a roof, and a mattress on the floor. We were pleased to borrow it. There were several pieces of equipment left behind, suggesting that the original occupants had left in a hurry.

Unfortunately, a Sherman tank had been knocked out nearby. It burned all night, with the ammunition going off continuously.

During the Reichwald Forest battle, the British artillery put down what was the biggest artillery barrage of the whole war, some 11,000 tons of ammunition being fired from 1,200 guns. It was pandemonium as this huge volume of shells screamed over our heads, exploded and reverberated as they struck home.

The fourteenth of February 1945, was the least romantic St Valentine's Day I ever experienced, seeing that I spent the whole day in a slit trench in Germany.

Leni and I were not yet engaged at that time, although we had agreed that this would be accomplished whenever I got home again.

Being in constant danger, I found that I dared not think too much of 'when it's all over', as it was easy to fall into a state of depression, due to considering the possibility of the next shell falling into your trench.

Despite the fact that the Allies were winning on all fronts, the Germans were still conducting their propaganda campaign against us in the hope of breaking our spirits.

Part of this campaign was via leaflets, which were contained in airburst shells. They burst in the air above our trenches, and instead of the deadly shrapnel powering down on us, we were bombarded with paper. Of course, we much preferred it as can be imagined, but what showered down on us on St Valentine's Day was totally unexpected.

Who would have thought that the Nazi propaganda machine would have been aware of the day of the patron saint of lovers? Was Dr Goebels, the German Propaganda Minister, really a romantic at heart?

Out of the sky descended Valentine cards. I still have one. On the fortieth anniversary of the event, I sent a photocopy of it to Channel 9 TV in Perth, but they ignored it. So much for their penchant for news.

It was made of paper, in two colours blue and red, and on the front was a picture of a bunch of flowers and the words, 'Valentine's Greetings'.

The words inside were intended to upset us all, and there were drawings of everyone's girl or wife speaking to four different suitors. The first in evening dress, asking her, 'Would you like to go to a dance?' The next in tennis gear, asking in rhyme, 'Don't I have a little chance?' Number three, offering her a gift asking, 'Will you be my Valentine?' And, finally, casually dressed and offering a bunch of flowers, number four was saying, 'I am yours and you are mine.'
In the middle of the inside pages is a circle enclosing a picture of a British soldier with one arm in a sling, lying on the ground with shells exploding all around him, and completing the scenario, a row of gravestones and a German plane dropping bombs.

Finally, on the right hand inside page is the following:

You remember Valentine's Day
When your sweetheart was so gay
And you wrote each other cards
With wishes coming from your hearts?
Guess who is her Valentine
Now that you fight near the Rhine?
To her another sends his greetings
And asks her for more frequent meetings.

Who said that the Nazis had no romance in their souls?

A little later, our lot responded with leaflets that granted safe conduct through our lines the following night, for any German soldier who was prepared to risk the wrath of his comrades. I recall two who ran towards us just as dawn appeared. They got through safely.

It was the day after Valentine's Day that the next big attack started. Our division, the 43rd Wessex, was chosen to spearhead the breakout from the Cleve area. Our brigade led, and there was severe fighting. I remember well that morning, as it was so foggy that, eventually, the big push was put off until the following day. Names of towns like Xanthen, Werth, and Wesel, live in my memory as places we were involved in capturing, but after 45 years it is difficult to remember all the details.

At about this time I had some almost incredible news. I was to go on leave! How marvellous. I was to leave the front on the first and to be in England until the 10th of March. Of course, the ever-present concern about whether or not I would survive the war became accentuated. So near to seeing Mam and Dad, John, and Leni. How awful if anything went awry in the next two weeks.

Fortunately, I survived and the great day arrived. With others, I went back to B Echelon, picked up my greatcoat and clean suit of battledress etc, and then off to Bourg Leopold in Belgium, where I joined hundreds of troops from other units for the trip to Calais.

Calais to Dover was not far and would only take a couple of hours, but just suppose the ship hit a mine? Well, it didn't, and on 4th March I caught the train to London, then to Kings Cross station for an LNER train to Darlington, via York.

I could hardly believe it. I got out of the train about midnight, incredibly to the whine of the air raid siren! It was the first for some time and it turned out that it was the last of the war! Just to welcome me. There was some anti-aircraft fire, which made me kind of feel at home; home being the battlefield.

I walked home to Norton, about two miles away, to be welcomed by Mam and Dad, and John. After a good night's sleep, I set about making the most of seven days leave, visiting Dad's sisters, Auntie Nan and Auntie Edie, and then of course, Leni.

I had written to her as often as I could since leaving England, and when it was not possible I had sent the small 'on active service' postcards issued by the army. There were different messages on the card and you crossed out those that did not apply, leaving those that did, e.g. 'I have not received a letter for three weeks', or 'I am fit and well'. Conversely, if you were unfortunate you would be leaving, 'I have been wounded', or 'I have been taken to base hospital' etc, for your folks to decipher.

We had a lovely week and the culmination was with us getting engaged to be married. I bought a beautiful ring at the jewellers near the Royal Hotel in Stockton High Street. It was Friday, the 9th of March 1945, and it was the best decision I ever made. Of course, when the time came to leave, it was very traumatic. I had been following the progress of the war in the 'Daily Mail' each day. Cologne had fallen to the Americans, and the British Second Army was moving towards the Rhine, which was the biggest obstacle ahead of them.

I must confess that, having had a taste of civilian life, and having been so happy with Leni, I did not relish the thought of taking part in the Rhine crossing. Every day I hoped that it would have been achieved, but it did not happen. As I said a tearful goodbye to Leni at her home, for she did not want to come to the railway station, as she was too upset, I just prayed that soon the war would end, and that we could be reunited forever.

There was another reason for the sadness at our parting. I left home on 10th March, and I was on a Dover–Calais troopship on the twelfth. As I sat on a seat on the top deck, feeling sick partly due to the overwhelming oil smell and partly to the motion of the ship in the Straits of Dover, I had to feel sorry for myself.

It was my twenty-first birthday! What a way to spend it! So I was 21 on 12345, i.e. 12-3-45, numbers which only crop up every hundred years.

We landed at Calais and were soon on a truck to the Transit Camp at Bourg Leopold. Still they had not crossed the Rhine. Surely they were not waiting for me? Could they not do it without me? I was actually in the Belgian camp about three days. We used to parade every morning and it depended on the available transport as to how many could be returned to their units that day.

My number came up on 16th March and I was off to the front. When I eventually rejoined my unit they were 'dug in'. They were close to the bank of the River Rhine, and waiting for the order to cross. Just prior to this happening, we witnessed a most impressive and confidence building sight. The 18th Airborne Corps were given the job of securing a bridgehead over the next major river, the Ijsell, and four thousand planes, including 1,200 fighter aircraft, took part. They all flew over our positions, creating a pandemonium of sound.

We crossed in 'Buffaloes' – the only time we ever used them. They were tracked vehicles, like hollowed out tanks. We sat below the Buffalo walls, protected against small arms fire, but being open topped, shells, mortars, airburst shells and bombs could still reach us.

The river was 500 yards wide, and it only took a few minutes to get across. Dismounting on the far bank was exciting, as it had been often said that the great river was the last major natural obstacle. The Germans were fighting desperately, trying to dislodge us from our growing bridgehead.

The following day, to our amazement, Winston Churchill, our Prime Minister, actually crossed the Rhine, also in a Buffalo. It certainly gave us a boost of confidence.

We advanced towards our next objective, which was to cross a smaller river and clear out the enemy on the far bank. En route we passed through a number of hamlets and farms, where most of the buildings were shattered or on fire. A number of farm buildings had provided shelter for animals, and the smell of burnt flesh permeated the area.

We also came across the first Russian soldiers we had seen. They were living on farms and presumably, they were being forced to work on them as Prisoners of War.

Eventually, the time came for us to effect our first river crossing under our own steam, or rather under our own oars. And thereby hangs a tale or, to be honest, a fiasco.

It was explained to us how to find the right spot on the river to launch our boat, which was to have two oarsmen and a further six or seven soldiers. We were then to row across under cover of darkness, and attack the Germans in their trenches, hoping to catch them unawares, even asleep.

Two of us were lance corporals, so apparently it was logical that we should do the rowing! The other chap, whose name was Lampe, was from a farming community and probably had not even had a holiday at the seaside in his life.

There are not too many boats on a farm. Now I had had a good deal more experience than my fellow rower had. I had been out with fishermen, two or three times; and from Redcar, collecting the lobsters from the lobster pots. Although I never rowed. I also went out into the bay at Dunoon in Scotland, rowed by a friend, when on holiday. However, I never actually took the oars!

But we were lance corporals, leaders of men. Weren't we?

Either the Royal Engineers or our Pioneer Platoon, I cannot remember which, laid white tapes along the ground from our positions to the water's edge. We were allocated a tape, and as soon as it was dark, we set off. It was a simple, but clever method, of making sure that we all launched our boats at the right spot, so that theoretically, as long as we rowed straight, we would reach our objective.

We did a great job following the tape, and the launching was not too bad either, so that the first two tasks were accomplished successfully.

It was just the rowing that was not so good; well, not good; well, bad actually. In fact, it was not the rowing that was no good, it was the lack of rowing that caused the problems.

We started off all right, for we did remember where to put the oars, even to remember that the name of where they fitted in, was the oarlocks, I think. But what do you do after you have put the oars in the oarlocks? That was where we fell down. No one told us that this wide flat bottomed boat, when it hit the water, would be affected by what even I knew was a current; or what to do when the boat is spinning round and around midstream, and going further and further away from your objective?

We did have a lot of advice from the 'crew', most of it unprintable. We must have drifted three or four hundred yards, before we got a grasp of how to operate the oars, or 'row' I suppose you could call it.

Then with the boat steadied, we rowed back upstream. Progress was slow for we were now against the current. When we got to where we should have been an hour before, there was a bit of shouting but no shooting. The shouting was in English, so it looked as if we had won.

Most embarrassed, we lifted our boat out of the water, put it on the riverbank, and melted into what was going on, the collecting up of lots of Germans. They had all been caught asleep, and had given up without a fight.

So we really hadn't been needed.

We now had the bit between our teeth, and we knew that the end of the war was in sight. We were in the area of Anholt, a small German town near the Dutch border, when we started another push. At first it seemed a disappointment, because our two objectives were two Dutch towns, Enschede (pronounced enskhudA), and Hengelo. No doubt the High Command knew better than us, but we thought that once in Germany, we would keep on until victory.

Enschede was soon liberated to the delight of the Dutch townspeople, who seemed to be all in situ. There was a little excitement in the evening when a Messerschmidt fighter-bomber flew low over the town, but we did not stay long, and the next day we set off for Hengelo. An interesting postscript to the Enschede episode was when I received a letter late in April from an H J W Levers, to whom I had spoken in that town. His English was quite good, and he told me how he and his wife were well, but that, '...last night there has been a German bomber above our town and he has thrown five bombs on the town. Three persons are killed. That is no good. We shall hope it is the last time.' And so it was.

For the burghers it proved to be a wonderful day for three reasons. One, it was a beautiful sunny day; two, they were liberated after being under the heel of the Nazis for five years; and three, it was the Christians' greatest day. Yes, Hengelo was liberated on Easter Sunday, when the church bells rang, and the worshippers thanked God for Christ's resurrection, and for their own liberation. And, incidentally, I am actually writing this on Easter Sunday 1990, forty-five years later.

On Easter Monday we were asked if we could raise a football team to play Hengelo SV. This we did and we played them in the town's stadium. I was captain of the battalion's team, the first time I had played for them, and after the game I was made a life member of the Dutch club. However, I felt disappointed in 1985, on the fortieth anniversary, when I wrote to them and they did not reply.

We knew Hengelo was very important to the Germans, because it was on the main line from Hannover to Amsterdam, and was used as a supply route for the 'V2', which was the second of Hitler's secret weapons. The V2 was faster than sound, and the British cities against which it was being used had no protection against it.

The next and final objective was Bremen, the great German port. Cloppenburg had been captured and the plan was then to drive to the North Sea coast. We crossed the river Weser and moved into the area of Verden, to prepare to attack Bremen from the east. We were told that the people of Bremen were to be given the choice of surrender, or to suffer bombing by the Royal Air Force, and shelling by the army. The message was delivered to them by airburst shells containing leaflets.

They did not accept, and our brigade was involved in the mopping up operations, but not our battalion. However, our war was still not over.

We captured the villages of Whelkhorn, Wilstedt, and Tarmstedt, and between the latter two, the Germans reacted with Nebelwerfer (six-barrelled artillery guns) and heavy artillery, a final unpleasant reminder of our days in Normandy.

The saddest incident of all happened just three or four days before the German surrender. Our infantry companies were travelling in 'Kangaroos' (armoured troop carriers), and one went over what was in fact a magnetic sea mine, buried in the road between Wilstedt and Tarmstedt, killing the whole section of about twelve men. A crater about thirty yards wide was created, and the Royal Engineers had to bridge it.

On 4th May, we captured Kustedt, and we dug in by the side of the road, which led out the other side of the town. It was a beautiful day and it was one when rumours of a complete German surrender were rife. We were in the foremost line of trenches and our CO (Commanding Officer), Lt Col 'Speedy' Bredin DSOMC, visited us. He came marching down the road, boots highly polished, wearing a soft beret, just as though he was on the barrack square back home in Dorchester. He gave us the latest news, but we were glad to see him go, as we were expecting his presence to attract a barrage of shells and bullets from the enemy trenches on the other side of the valley, only about four hundred yards away.

I had often wondered how the war would end. I had hoped that the bombing of their homeland would persuade the Germans to surrender, but this had not eventuated. Even at this late stage, just make a bit of noise or stick your head up, and you would find that there was still a war on. We had survived all the way from the beaches of Arromanches, and we did not want to spoil our record now.

CHAPTER FIFTEEN
THE WAR ENDS

It was May 4th and about 8.30 pm. It was a beautiful evening, still broad daylight, and as always our section radio operator was fiddling about with his field radio, trying to pick up news, any news, when he suddenly shrieked, 'It's over!' As I write this in 1990, I am overcome at the recalling of the memory.

Yes, he was sure. It was all quite definite. What a moment. Messages started to arrive from the rear echelons, confirming that Admiral Doenitz, as German Commander-in-Chief, had surrendered, but the great news was tinged with a warning. Be careful. Watch out for mines; still keep your heads down. Take no chances.

Later, when it was dark, HQ sent us up double rum rations, but as I detest the taste of the stuff, others had triple rations.

This was our last night in a slit trench. As the hours slipped away, we did not even try to sleep. We just talked and talked, illuminated as we were by Very lights fired by any who had the wherewithal. When did we think that we would get home? Various forecasts were made, none of them accurate, for who would have guessed that for me it was to be another two years before I would be handing in my kit? I think that we assumed that the lads who had done the fighting, would be leaving to others whatever else had to be done.

However, none of our deliberations could alter the wonderful feeling of relief that at last the war in Europe was over. In the morning there was more excitement. Of all the troops along our front, our section of Bren gun carriers had been chosen to escort and guard our army's top brass, as they took surrender terms to the commander of the German Army facing us.

We were puzzled at first, because had not Doenitz already given in? However, it was explained to us that every commander of an army would have to surrender his particular command. This meant that individual Generals could in fact carry on fighting if they decided to ignore the surrender.

Later in the morning, we set off with a cavalcade of jeeps, tanks, and our three Bren gun carriers. It was the most exciting and the most interesting journey of my life.

Our slit trench had been sited by the side of a narrow country road, and it was along this road that we travelled.

For nearly six years, we were used to Allied and German soldiers firing at one another on sight, and yet after two minutes we came across a row of enemy trenches, their former occupants stretched out on the grass, enjoying the sunshine with their Spandaus perched on the parapets.

It went through my mind that it was possible that a fanatic, an SS man for instance, could decide to go on fighting, and it was going to be difficult to keep a lookout for such a person.

There was little response from these forward troops, but our interpreter did get out of them the directions to their battalion HQ. All we had to do was follow the road. We continued, to find a mortar battery about 200 yards further on. These were the Germans' 'Moaning Minnies', which had struck fear in our hearts ever since we got off the beaches.

It was becoming obvious that the only people who were even happier than us that the war was over were these battle weary members of the Wehrmacht. After a few more minutes, we came to a small village where the HQ was situated. The amazing thing was that everything was so similar to the British Army.

As we passed one house, the company barber was cutting hair, whilst a German sergeant was crossing the garden to go inside. To our surprise, he had a red sash across his chest, and carried a cane, the same accoutrements as our orderly sergeants. He seemed to be checking numbers and calling the roll.

I was a lance corporal at the time, and when our officers went into the headquarters, I started a conversation with a private soldier who was on guard. He was standing at ease, holding his rifle in much the same way as our sentries did, when all of a sudden one of his superiors arrived. He bellowed at the poor chap, pointing to my stripe and at the private's feet, which being 'at ease' were apart, obviously giving him a proper dressing down.

This was the discipline of the German Army. The war was over, but still the private must stand to attention when addressed by a non-commissioned officer, even if he were in a different army!

We got on the road once more, our objective being a large country house that was the Germans Army HQ. It was all tremendously interesting, for as we progressed deeper into 'enemy' territory, we passed the light artillery, then the heavies, and finally we came to a tank park. Here were the dreadful Tiger tanks with their fearsome 88-millimetre guns, some Panthers, and other various types of tracked vehicles.

Beyond was the country house, our objective. The officers went in, and we had to wait some considerable time, so I walked up to a Tiger tank commander and we had a discussion that made me realise the utter futility of war.

He was a schoolteacher from Dresden. He had a wife and three children, and he seemed to be as pleasant a person as one would wish to meet. Like me, all he wanted to do was to get home to his family, and we ended our chat by agreeing that it must never happen again.

We returned to our battalion area, and with that most important duty out of the way, wondered what we would have to do next, to grease the wheels of the 'machine that would take us home'.

As we had witnessed on our unique journey through the German lines, they were still heavily armed. Now to this time we had never given any thought as to how we would treat the defeated foe, but it soon transpired that the planners had been looking ahead in this regard.

The Royal Army Service Corps (RASC), the Royal Army Ordnance Corps (RAOC), and the Royal Engineers played major parts in what was the disarming of the Wehrmacht. The Service Corps' vehicles were fully employed, picking up weapons and ammunition and taking them to dumps. The Royal Engineers (RE) were the experts with the Ordnance Corps in destroying these enormous amounts of shells, bombs, etc.

We, the infantry, had to do much of the physical work of actually collecting weapons from the Division that had been facing us at the war's end.

Obviously, it was considered that we could have been in grave danger, being in such close contact with the defeated soldiers. It only needed one of them to lose control.

A particularly hazardous task was allocated to us, of getting rid of large quantities of the missiles or bombs, which were fired by what was known as the 'panzerfaust'. Apparently, the RE were not able to destroy them in quantity. According to our information, they could connect together lots of artillery shells, and blow them up together, but not these anti-tank missiles.

It was decided that the only way to destroy them was to fire them, thus exploding them, and who better to do this than the German Infantry who used to use them against us?

On being told that I was to be involved in this exercise, I could not help considering the dangers. I had experienced the effect of this weapon in action, and now I was to be in charge of a platoon of Germans armed to the teeth with this deadly weapon.

How could I forget an incident in Holland that illustrated the danger?

The enemy had retreated and we were trying to make contact again. As always, we were the infantry supporting the Guards Armoured Division. Walking in single file behind the tanks, ears always straining to hear any sound that could indicate enemy action, suddenly there was a flash and then the kind of bang we had heard many times before.

It was the particular explosion that told us that a tank had been hit. We had been following a troop, which means three tanks, and the front one was stopped in its tracks, literally. Smoke was emitting from the front, and as what had happened dawned on us, there was a second flash and bang, this time from the 17lb gun of the second tank.

We all took cover in a ditch by the side of the road. After a few minutes, our platoon sergeant called on us to proceed. There was a bend in the road and the lead tank had been negotiating it, when it was hit by a missile from a panzerfaust. It was knocked out, and the second tank had spotted a German soldier around the corner, only his head and his weapon above the ground, and the gunner had fired immediately and made a terrible mess of the German, as one would expect when hit with a 17lb shell.

He was a young SS man and he obviously knew he was committing suicide when he dropped into that hole. There was no way he was going to escape. There was something terrifying about an enemy, who elected to die rather than surrender, even when the war was plainly lost.

The German Army's engineers must have had a vehicle which operated a giant circular drill, because we had seen many of these holes in recent weeks. They were perfectly round and all about five feet deep.

So the news, that despite the war being finished I was to be involved with enemy soldiers armed to the teeth with these horrific weapons, was not the best.

We made many trips to a nearby forest, and as all of my colleagues were doing the same, we eventually finished our onerous task.

The first of these episodes is worthy of fuller description. A German sergeant got his platoon together, issued them with panzerfausts, and I believe it was three missiles each. He drilled them as though they were in the barrack square, and then told me that they were ready to move off.

I told him where we were going and that he should carry on. I walked along with him, and I was armed with a Sten gun, which was of the sub-machine-gun type.

In German, he asked me what it was for! This rather surprised me, so I told him it should be obvious. His platoon was armed to the teeth, so surely it was understandable that I should have protection.

It was then that I had a further example of the German mind in defeat. He told me that there would be no trouble at all. The war was over, Germany had lost, and that was that.

It was as though it had been an international soccer match; we had won, they had lost, and that was the end of it. I still kept a wary eye on the proceedings, but he was absolutely correct.

In the ensuing months we had no trouble at all, neither did I hear of the least disturbance. Intelligence had been telling us of terrorist groups, and we were very alert in case they were right, but nothing untoward ever happened.

A terrible thing did happen, however, on our first trip to the forest. A young lad fired his anti-tank weapon and the missile exploded whilst still in the panzerfaust. He was in an awful state, and in great pain. I had been given a first aid kit, but when we opened it, with the intention of giving him an injection to knock him out, there was no needle. We got him back to our first aid centre, but I should not think he would have survived.

This disarming of the German Army was a huge task, and there were enormous vehicle parks created and dumps made. It must have taken years to dispose of everything. Similarly, there were hundreds of thousands of the Reich's Armed Forces to be disposed of, but apart from seeing lots of them trudging along the roads, I was not involved.

During this period some bright spark in the headquarters of the British Army of the Rhine (BAOR), decided that we should all be in a Victory Parade. Now the idea of us all going off to London was certainly appealing, but the logistics dictated that this could not happen. Every battalion did send a few representatives to the big parade in the capital, and obviously those with the most active service were selected to go.

No, what the hierarchy had planned was for a number of these parades to be held in various cities around the western zone of Germany and everyone would take part. The cost in fuel alone should have made it prohibitive, but in typical army style this was ignored.

Hadn't we used millions of gallons of petrol to wash down vehicles and engines, when caked with oil; and hadn't other large quantities been poured into a large tin of soil, or straight into the ground, to heat water for a cup of tea? So what were a few million more?

Our fiasco was at the port of Bremerhaven, where thousands of soldiers and their vehicles, including tanks, were paraded down the main streets. What for I could not say. Certainly the German civilians were not remotely interested, having seen sufficient such displays for several lifetimes, and we found it a bore. I travelled in a Bren gun carrier, which had been polished to the 'n'th' degree, and I felt distinctly embarrassed as we drove slowly around the town.

Another edict, which probably emanated from Field Marshal Montgomery, was that of non-fraternisation. In other words, we were not to enter a German house unless on military business, nor were we to be friendly with the populace at large.

To many people, both Allied and German, the language barrier made communication difficult in the early days, but despite the 'non-frat' rule, most people learnt sufficient of the other's language to get by, as time went on.

Of course, the rule was impossible to police, and as has happened in all theatres of war since the Romans invaded Britain, and no doubt before that, liaisons between male and female were very common. I am sure that today there are many thousands of Germans who unknowingly are half British, and many German girls later married Brits and came to live in the United Kingdom. As the Holy Bible says, 'He made them male and female'.

We were also well known for our generosity, and 'chocolate', sounding so much like 'Schokolade' , was the first English a German child learned.

Looking back it is difficult to understand how the German civilians survived. They certainly earned my respect for their industriousness. With the country in ruins, cities decimated, river, road, and rail bridges blown up, rolling stock destroyed, trams unable to run because of streets being blocked and no electricity – they just got their heads down and started again.

Most houses had a cellar, which proved to be a Godsend as protection from the elements, but with most of the men in POW camps all over Europe, it was the 'Frauen' who had to get on with the work. And how they worked. Chains of weary women passed bricks from hand to hand to clear bombsites, and similarly the only way people in the cities could get water, was to find a tap somewhere that worked, and pass bucket after bucket until all of the street or district had got some.

Perhaps the most inspiring event in this context occurred in Berlin. On my first trip there, I was surprised to see the 'Strassenbahn' working with young women acting as conductors and drivers. This may not seem earth shattering, but one has to consider the options that were available to these girls. Just by fraternising with a soldier, they would have been able to obtain cigarettes and sometimes coffee, both of which were of greater value than their currency. The Mark could buy very little and the 'Schaffnerins' wages would have been just a few of them. That they preferred to work a long day, with the streetcars packed with people, did them great credit and earned my personal everlasting homage.

Soon after the end of the war in Europe, I received a sweet loving letter from Grandma and Granddad. I still have it, and whenever I read it tears come to my eyes. Grandma wrote it. She did not have the best of educations, but no letter ever had so much love and caring as this one. She told me that her two sons, three of her four grandsons, and her two son-in-laws had all survived the war. They had all been in action, and George, in Burma, was now the only one at risk. Grandma said she hoped and prayed he was all right and would soon be home. She said that we had all done our bit, that 'VE Day' had been quiet 'because there were still so many lads in Burma', and that 'it was very nice to go to bed and not think about air raid sirens'.

Dear Grandma. How she must have worried, dreading bad news about Alan on the high seas, Frankie in the Artillery, John, George, Bob, Oliver, Olive's husband, and me in the infantry, whilst she and Granddad had to suffer many air raids.

Once the German Army had been disarmed, and the search for caches of arms completed as far as was possible, the problem for the army hierarchy was that of keeping the enormous numbers of troops occupied.

There were obvious tasks such as the refurbishing of vehicles and equipment, and all military installations, which included the billets in which the troops were living, and their protection against possible terrorists.

In our particular case, our CO was very keen to show the locals just how disciplined and smart we were. Because of this we had lots of drill, which was not very pleasing to us, as we thought that with the war over, such activities would be dispensed with. Saturday mornings were particularly annoying, as we used to have a full battalion drill parade and march past, with the CO and his adjutant on horseback. The latter had done little riding, and the only satisfaction we experienced was when his horse bolted down the main street of Tostedt. As the idea was to impress the villagers, it was quite hilarious.

My company was housed in the very small village of Todtlüsingen, and it was even worse for us on Saturdays, because we had to march the two or three miles to Tostedt to take part in the parade.

Lieutenant Colonel Bredin had developed a hatred of all things German during his very arduous war, and another cross we had to bear because of this, was that he would not use German labour for anything. Most other units used the locals for potato peeling, washing pots and pans, cleaning the billets, and other either heavy or mundane tasks, but not us. This was a bone of contention all the time we were there.

Sport has always been an important component of army activity, and it now became even more important. The troops had to be occupied, and what better way than with sport, which offered both enjoyment and a means of maintaining fitness?

It was about this time that we were informed of the methods that were to be employed to demobilise the millions in the Armed Forces. In the main, it was to be via a formula, which included the two factors, age and length of service, with an acceleration in the case of the Royal Navy.

I had been a soldier for a little over two and a half years, and I was just twenty-one. This put me in 49 Group, and the projected date for my 'demob' was about the end of 1946. This seemed catastrophic at the time, but little did I know that, in fact, it was to be still several months later than that.

There was nothing I could do, so I decided that as I intended to try to get to the top in football, the best thing was to get as fit as I could, by training and playing as much sport as possible.

It was then that I decided to stop smoking. I was walking back to the old rural cottage, which was home to about two dozen of us, all sleeping on the floor. Of course, when I realised that if I was to get fully fit I could not delay stopping smoking any further, I threw away the cigarette I had just lit, and when I got back 'home' I gave the tin of cigarettes I had in my pocket to a mate. Ironically, when the mail came that day there were two hundred cigarettes in a parcel from Leni!

It took me two or three weeks of desperate self-denial before I felt that I had really kicked the habit. One evening I relented, and opened one of the packets from Leni and lit a cigarette, but fortunately it tasted terrible, and I dispensed with it straight away.

Athletic activities included a battalion and then a brigade sports meeting, and I was quite successful winning the 100 yards, the high jump, and the mile at both meetings.

Much more in my line was a Divisional Football Championship. We had been playing a lot of inter-platoon and inter-company games on the village pitch, which was quite a good one. During these games several good players surfaced, and we put together a good battalion team. Four of us, Jimmy Hall, Dennis Howe, Dennis Wade and I, all played League football after our demobilisation, for Port Vale, Derby County, West Ham United and Middlesbrough in that order.

We four in particular trained a tremendous amount, and became extremely fit. We fancied our chances in the championship and in fact, we got to the final where we beat the Wiltshire Regiment. This turned out to be a very important game. I was captain and at the end I went to shake hands with my opposite number.

He was attached to the Wilts as a CSM Physical Training Instructor and his name was Jimmy Hagan. He was a Sheffield United player, who had played several games for England during the war, and who at about that time was flown back to the UK, to play in an international match.

He genuinely congratulated me on my game and that of the team. This pleased me greatly, but I did not know at the time just how important his admiration of my ability was to be.

As a lance corporal, I was also involved in guard duties, but despite this and the training, time passed slowly. Church parade was still a must for all C of E's on Sundays, and, of course, I was very happy to be able to go. It was held in the Protestant church at Tostedt and it was one of the highlights of my week. I remember to this day the inscription above the altar. It made me think deeply about Jesus in those far off days, and it still does today. It went, 'ich bin der Alpha und das Omega, der Anfang and das Ende', or in English, 'I am the A and the Z, the beginning and the end.'

Another day when I was walking back to the billet, a message came for me to go to HQ as there was a 'signal' for me. I could not believe my luck when I heard the news. 'You are to report to the Hindenburg Stadium at Hannover next Wednesday at 12.00 noon to play football against Liverpool.' Incredible. What did this mean? It was another way army HQ had thought of, to entertain the troops.

I knew no more than this, and on the day, our football officer drove me to Hannover in his jeep. When I went into the dressing room, who was there but Jimmy Hagan! He had been asked if he knew of any good players and he recommended me!

It is not difficult to imagine how thrilled I was, particularly as we drew 3–3 against a team that was full of great players, players who were heroes of mine six years before. Then I was at school and people like Billy Liddell, Don Welsh, Matt Busby, Joe Balmer, and the South African, Nieuwehuys, I held on a pedestal. And here I was playing against them.

I could not have played better, and after the game we had dinner in an officers' hotel. My companion for the evening was Matt Busby, later to be Sir Matt, manager of the great Manchester United teams, which ruled football for many years after the war, and a survivor of the terrible air tragedy at Munich Airport in 1956.

All good things come to an end, and after saying our goodbyes, we were on the road again bound for Tostedt.

Nothing had been said about the possibility of playing any more games, but if nothing more had happened, I would have been happy, as I had proved to myself that I could play well in the very best of company.

I had no option but to get back into the routine of the occupation forces, and got involved in any activity that would help to speed on the time. One such thing was hockey. I knew all about it through watching it at Norton-on-Tees in the thirties, and when a chap called Brookes, who played for one of the Midland Counties, asked me to play in a battalion trial match, I was delighted. I was a good cricketer, and hockey from a tactical viewpoint was similar to football, so I had the attributes.

I thoroughly enjoyed the game and I was asked to play for our battalion, but the one thing that put me off was the possibility of injury, which could have ruined my football aspirations. Quite a few times the hard ball flew menacingly near my head, so I declined future invitations to play.

It was starting to be a bit cold at nights, so we decided that we should start looking for wood, as fuel for the open fires in our respective billets. All we needed was a truck, two or three axes or saws, and a forest of trees. None presented much of a problem, and on a crisp autumn afternoon, three of us set forth for the woods which were just outside the village.

Germany was in ruins. Cities were decimated. What difference did chopping a few trees make? Not much? This was not what the German forest ranger thought. There was no need to be able to understand German. It was quite obvious that he definitely objected to what we were doing. I could not help but admire the man as he stood there in his green uniform, gesticulating vigorously. Unfortunately for him, my colleagues were not in the mood to be ordered about by a uniformed German, and the chopping continued, but I thought that there was hope for the world when there were still people like him around.

Now we are in the 2000's, there are millions of similar 'greenies' around the world, all trying to do as he did, and prevent further damage to the planet.

CHAPTER SIXTEEN
FOOTBALL FOR THE COMBINED SERVICES GERMANY

Just when I was thinking that the Liverpool game was to be der Anfang und das Ende, the first and the last, a signal was received at Battalion HQ. It said, 'Lance Corporal Rickaby is to report to the Army Physical Training Corps Training Centre at Paderborn for a football tour. Best battledress and football boots, all the kit that is necessary.'

What news! How envious were the lads. Transport was organised and off I went to Paderborn, which was about two hundred miles away.

When I got there, I reported to the guardroom to be escorted to our quarters. There were three players there already, but they did not know what was going on. Every morning we went training. Two of the players, Dennis Westcott and Tom Galley, of Wolverhampton Wanderers, had played in the 1939 Cup Final at Wembley, and we became firm friends due to our being together for some time before the rest of the players appeared.

Eventually, more and more players arrived, and just about everyone was a household name back in the UK. At first they were all soldiers, but it transpired that this was to be a Combined Services team. One day we had a signal that a coach would arrive on the following day, and we were looking forward to seeing who it was.

Can you imagine our surprise when the coach turned out to be a red single-decker London Transport bus, advertisements and all! This was to be our means of getting around Germany.

Our next game was a marvellous occasion. It was the King of Denmark's 75th birthday, and as part of the celebrations, and in recognition of Britain's role in the defeat of Germany, who had occupied the Scandinavian State, we were invited to play a Danish Representative XI. Some RAF players joined in and our captain was none other than England's captain, Eddie Hapgood, of the Arsenal. Other players included Jimmy Hagan, Bernard Joy of Arsenal, Aubrey Powell of Leeds United, Billy Hughes of Birmingham, Tommy Pearson of Newcastle United and Tom Galley again, all internationals of England, Scotland or Wales. We flew from the RAF's airfield at Buckeburg in an Avro-Anson bomber. I had never flown before, so I was very excited at this new experience. Having flown a lot since, in the enormous and very comfortable Jumbo Jets, with inflight meals, drinks, and movies, I realise that in comparison the Anson was primitive.

You could see daylight everywhere between the panels, and the cold wind whistled through. Our seats were not even padded, and backed on to the side of the plane, so that we were all looking inwards.

During air raids, I had always thought that with German bombers travelling at two or three hundred miles an hour, little me would not be visible from a height. To my amazement, I found that this was not true. When I looked down out of a window, I could see that we were approaching a football pitch where a game was being played, and I was able to follow the play for several seconds. I could pick out players, and this made me think that I was glad that I was not aware of this during the war. The partial security I had felt would not have existed, and this would also have been true in action, when Messerschmidts strafed us.

Landing at Copenhagen Airport was terrific, and we had a good view of the city as we flew over the water, which must have been the Ovesund. Someone pointed out to me the mermaid statue, which is one of the city's landmarks, and is sited in the water close to the shore.

The game itself was an anti-climax, as we were well beaten. This was surprising and disappointing, but we had not even trained together, let alone played together. My position was left half, wearing number six, thus playing directly in front of and with the England skipper. This was a real thrill for me, but the rapport built up during the game, was to be tarnished in a very few hours.

At 8.00 pm. we crossed the main square of the Danish capital to attend a banquet given by the Danish Government, to celebrate the King's birthday.

If this had happened today, the occasion would have been outstanding, but as it was after six years of rationing and deprivation, it was just out of this world. The banqueting hall was dressed in the Danish National Colours: red and white. There were flags, bunting, and table decorations in these colours, and the tablecloths were a glistening white with red serviettes. Of course, there were red and white wines and as far as possible, the food was also red and white, from the lobster main course, to the white sorbet, which was the twelfth and final course.

There seemed to be a waiter to each diner, and every dish was brought into the room with military precision, as the waiters entered in line.

The only problem was the liquor. I was determined not to drink much, as was my habit, but there was a different wine with every course, it seemed. This was bad enough, but the worst was that the wine waiters kept on topping up the glasses before you had finished them, thus I had no idea how much I was drinking.

Stanley Rous, the secretary of the Football Association, spoke in reply to the Danes' toasting of Britain. I felt in control of myself at that stage, for I was able to follow the proceedings all right, but not all of the players were.

Tom Galley was one of the greatest players I ever saw, and I felt it a privilege to play with him. I saw him play in four different positions, and he was equally as commanding in each of them. He was elegant, a beautiful mover, and a class above most of his contemporaries, and when comparing him with modern players with a hundred or so international caps, I am forced to say that Tom was worth two hundred. In fact, I would prefer him in my team to just about any other player except for Ray Barlow at WBA, with whom he was on a par. I am convinced that his International career died in that banqueting room. During the game he had been injured and uniquely for those days, on his leaving the field a substitute replaced him. Apparently, Tom considered that this happened with undue haste, thus making his reappearance impossible.

This had rankled the normally urbane Wolves star, and to the horror of everyone present, he interrupted Stanley (later Sir Stanley) Rous' speech, insisting that he should have been allowed to come back on; that there was more interest in the substitute than there was in him!

He was probably right, but the old school at the FA would not forgive such a breach of etiquette, and I am sure that they never did.

So that was our Tom's gaffe: mine was still to come.

Eventually, I felt terribly sick, and tried to leave the room unobtrusively, but as soon as I got through the door I hurried to the men's room. I was violently sick.

Suddenly a knock on the door aroused me from a deep sleep. It was six o'clock in the morning, and the cleaners almost threw me out. Gone was the Danish/British rapport.

I crossed the square to our hotel, and later when I met Eddie Hapgood, he told me off in no uncertain manner. I have never been under the influence of alcohol since!

They say that necessity is the mother of invention, and during our stay in Copenhagen I saw a good example of this principle. There were few cars on the roads, but there were some taxis, and I was surprised at their means of locomotion. They had a kind of furnace on top of the car, fired by coal of some type, and although aesthetically they looked awful, they certainly did the job. It was relatively easy to spot one, as you just had to look for a column of smoke moving along the street.

We met an English jockey who had been riding in Denmark before they were invaded. He had been interned for the duration, but was by this time back in racing action. He knew where you could get good quality clothing, and he was able to get me some beautiful lingerie for Leni. After the war years of scarcity, they were most appreciated.

The excitement generated in me by these exhilarating events, playing top class football and flying as a means of transport, was intense. What was ahead of us after Denmark? Something even more exciting!

I had been trying to get to Cologne since hostilities ceased, but under normal circumstances soldiers were not allowed to travel very far, and you had to be back in your billet by lights out.

As already described, it was the opposite for us. Travel was part of the routine of entertaining the Forces in the main centres of the British Zone.

I was thrilled when I learnt that our next game was to be at Cologne FC Stadium, against Notts County. At that time, we were selected to play by a system of rotation, playing a couple of games and then missing one, as we had about eighteen players on strength. It was my turn not to play, so I asked permission to go to Porz-Urbach, which is the first steamer-stop down the Rhine, about eight miles from the ancient Rhineland City of Cologne.

Permission was granted, and I travelled with the team then left them at their hotel. I was to be at the match the following day, and if I was able to stay in Porz, I could report back to Paderborn the day after the game.

I was both happy and nervous. For this was it. Previously we were living in hope that Leni's Oma (grandmother), and Tante Maria, and their families would be all right, but now we were going to know the truth.

I hitched a couple of lifts from Cologne and arrived at last at Porz and then Urbach, which was a suburb. I saw some children playing on slides and roundabouts in a playground. I asked them if they knew where the Wilhelmstrasse was. They pointed to a street that led off from the park, and I was very worried at once.

You see, along the left side of the street all was rubble for at least four hundred yards, and on the right there were a number of gaps carved out by the Allied bombing.

I approached with diffidence and soon established that the even numbers were on the left. I was looking for number four.

I hurried along and as I got nearer to the far end, I could see that there were buildings standing up, seemingly growing out of the rubble.

The first house standing was number four! I pressed the bell and said a little prayer. A lady came to the door and I said, 'Hallo ich bin von die Leni in England!' To my surprise she turned and dashed down the passage leaving me on the doorstep. Then I heard a loud hum of conversation culminating in the lady returning and saying, 'Komm, komm herein', I followed her in and entered what I came to know well as 'die Küche' (the kitchen).

A number of people were in there, including Oma. I will never forget the emotion that was generated when I told them that all their family in England were well.

Their vital news for me was that Onkel Peter had been in a camp because he had not shared the Nazi view of things; Onkel Theo had been away working most of the war; Leni's cousin, Hans, had been in hiding with friends near Koblenz, to avoid being called-up; and cousin Peter was there in the kitchen, as was Gisela, his sister.

Out of all the family, only another cousin, Peter, Uncle Peter's son, had been killed in action, whilst fighting in the SS against the Americans at Nuremburg after being wounded in Russia.

He was an example of the Nazi methods of taking twelve and thirteen year olds off to the mountains to train in all of the pursuits which boys enjoy. They were only allowed to come home when they were sufficiently indoctrinated in Nazism, so that if they were to hear even their mother or father criticizing Hitler or the system, they would report them to the authorities.

Hans had been able to avoid all of this, but his cousin Peter gave his life for it.

Oma was well, as was Tante Maria. They asked me many questions about Leni and her family, and it was a very joyful meeting. There was this rule or law at the time forbidding fraternisation with Germans, and I was obviously contravening it, but the law was quite inhumane, particularly in my case.

I could not write home quickly enough to let the English family know all the news about their German relatives. The joy in Thornaby-on-Tees must have only been equalled by that in Porz-am Rhein.

From then on, I called as often as I could. On one visit Tante Maria told me that they had all been made to see the official film of the Concentration Camp atrocities. She was crying as she told me, saying that it was terrible that Germans could commit such crimes, and she told me a story, which could never be as shocking as the attempted extermination of the Jews, but was bad enough.

It was the Americans who crossed the Rhine in that area, and who captured Porz. The German soldiers who had been 'dug in' on the east bank of the river, had retreated through the town and had looted houses and shops as they went. Leni's Aunt was ashamed and horrified by this dreadful act too.

Incidentally, I created a bit of a stir on my first visit to Porz, because to that date I was the first British soldier they had seen from the Second World War. Up to that time they had only seen Americans, but later the British took over the town, and I was able to get cousin Hans a job as a mechanic with them.

Hans came with me to see the Notts County game in Cologne. I told the then officer commanding about my trip to Porz, and he said that I could stay a further night and return on the Thursday, by a rather superb executive train, which ran to Paderborn. This was a real piece of luck for me, because there was a severe snowstorm on the day, and although I had a slight problem getting from the station to the camp, my team mates got stuck in a snowdrift and were delayed for about twelve hours! There was no heating in the coach, and when they got back 'frozen to the bone', I was tucked up warm in bed!

It was five months since my last leave and, therefore, time for another. Much had happened since those happy days in March. The war in Europe had ended. I had been lucky and had become virtually a full-time footballer. Perhaps the only disappointment had been the way that we were to be demobilised, meaning that I still had at least another year to do, according to the predictions at the time.

There was another possible 'fly in the ointment' that I became aware of during May, and it was always in the back of my mind. My army pay book, which was also a book of record, had been marked cryptically 'Far East 1'. It turned out to mean that I was on the first list of soldiers to be transferred to Burma. This was due to my comparative youth, and it was quite worrying.

However, I was not called for before August, when I was to start on my trip to England. The news during that leave period was the most dramatic the world had ever known. Something called an 'atom bomb' had destroyed Hiroshima, a major Japanese city, and the Japs had been called upon to surrender. They had not responded, so a second was dropped on Nagasaki. Surely this would mean the end of the Japanese war, and the cancellation of 'Far East 1'.

As everyone knows, they did give in, in August, and the date has gone down in history, 'VJ Day'. And I was on leave with Leni! What a glorious day. A day of celebration. A day of thanks to God, and a day of hope. Hope for the future, and a day when planning our lives, for the first time, did not end with 'when it is all over'. It was all over and we had survived. Millions had died. Many more millions were homeless, or sick, or wounded, or even stateless. Displaced persons camps overflowed with refugees. Cities had been reduced to ruins.

But Leni and I were alive and well with a whole lifetime ahead of us. To share our joy we visited our parents, Auntie Nan and Auntie Edie, Grandma and Granddad, and finally the home where we had met each other nearly two years previously. Annie, Bella, and Katie Ward, plus Grandma Ward, and of course, Rosie, always had a special interest in us, and we often called on them.

'VJ Day' was special and they were delighted to see us. So special that we toasted the end of both wars with a 'cocktail'. A cocktail. How posh. We had only ever seen them in films. I thought it very pleasant, and so did Leni, but whereas it had little effect on me, I could not say the same about my fiancee. She introduced a word into our joint vocabulary that day and we have used it ever since. She said, 'I feel tiddly'. No, my Leni would never be classed as a habitual inebriate or, to use the phrase I think Harry Lauder used to use, 'never under the affluence of incohol' [sic].

It was a great time, made even greater by an announcement on the BBC news that all troops on leave from the British Army of the Rhine should take a further seven days, so I had three wonderful weeks.

On my return to Germany, I spent a very pleasant week at the beautiful country home of the great pre-war German Davis Cup tennis player, Baron Gottfried von Cramm. I must add that he did not know about it, as his home had been requisitioned by the army for courses of various kinds. I was there for a retreat of the religious kind. Taken by army padres of the Church of England, it served as preparation for being confirmed. Yes, at last I was going to be able to take Holy Communion.

We were up at the crack of dawn, and we observed all of the church services every day including compline. In between, we studied various books of the Bible and learned, or in my case, re-learned the catechism. It was the most peaceful week of my life, in exquisite surroundings and perfect weather.

The only blot in the week was when I mentioned to a padre that I was going to wed a Catholic girl. He was so bigoted that he quite upset me. Incredible. The culmination of the week was our confirmation and first Communion, by the Bishop of Winchester.

Every now and again players were needed to play for their other units, such as their Corps or Divisions. One such occasion was when I was required to play for the Corps at 's-Hertogenbosch in Holland.

It was to celebrate the first anniversary of the liberation of the town from German occupation, 27th October 1945. We played a Holland XI and we were billeted with some of the townspeople. The game was part of many celebrations the people enjoyed, and no doubt the date has been revered ever since.

Although the game itself has faded from my memory, only a photograph of our team taken before the game and the result, a 6–0 win to us, reminds me of it at all. I do recall the home in which we stayed for something like a week. The family was named Hendriks, and Mr Hendriks was a director of the well known department store empire C & A Ltd.

I believe that the family consisted of Mr and Mrs, a young son, daughter Pia, who was probably about twenty at the time, and an aunt who I think was Mrs H's sister. They lived in a very comfortable home, in a garden suburb.

Our goalkeeper, George Swindin, and I, lived with them, and the remainder of the team were distributed in different homes around the area.

Obviously, there had been food shortages throughout Europe, and this must have been so in Holland, especially in the bigger cities such as Rotterdam and Amsterdam, but we had quite a surprise, indeed a shock, whilst staying with our hosts.

We had been there a few days, and Geroge and I kept commenting to one another about the quantity and the variety of food we were eating. Perhaps it was rude of us, but we were amazed by how much the old aunt tucked away, as it was certainly a lot more than George and me.

So it came as a shock when, in an after supper conversation, our host said that, with the war only five months over, most things had returned to normal, except for food, and they were looking forward to the day when there would be plenty to eat. We could hardly believe our ears!

In another chat we were told of the Fifth Column, which had operated in Holland before and during the War. One glaring example that sticks in my mind, was of someone they knew who worked in a bank in The Hague. He had worked with a particular colleague for two or three years, and never had any doubt as to where his loyalties lay, but on the day after the German invasion, this fellow turned up in a German SS uniform.

I used to smile to myself every time George and I were introduced to the family's friends. I was introduced as just Stan, but George was always 'George Swindin the famous Arsenal goalkeeper'. This happened very often and on one occasion, George, who was not one to hide his light under a bushel, actually added the 'famous Arsenal goalkeeper' himself!

In those days, the two most famous teams in Europe were Schalke 04 in Germany, and Arsenal in England, and to the Dutch, having George play on their ground was deemed quite an honour. And he revelled in it.

Another one of these one-off trips occurred shortly after our return. The army in the North of Germany played the touring 'Army in Italy XI', at the Schleswig-Holstein City of Lübeck, on the Baltic Sea, and I travelled to the ancient port. It was felt that the team from Italy was too good for the team chosen from the army units stationed in the North of Germany, and I went up to strengthen it.

I stayed at a very nice hotel, but found it to be quite cold. Up on the Baltic, it was many degrees cooler than further south, and due to the lack of fuel in immediate post war Germany, there was no heating.

It was marvellous to be able to travel around playing football and seeing more of the Continent. The game attracted a big crowd and the result was a draw. I played centre half, and the centre forward directly opposing me was Willie Thornton, a very famous player from Glasgow Rangers and Scotland. I felt terrific when he shook my hand and said, 'Well played, son'. Of even more interest was their inside left, Bryn Jones by name. Bryn played for Wales and Arsenal, and they bought him from Wolverhampton Wanderers for 14,000 pounds, a world record transfer fee.

Shortly after this match, I had arranged a match of a different kind. On 20th November I arrived home for 21 days leave, and the match was to be at St Patrick's Catholic Church at Thornaby-on-Tees, between Leni and me on the following day. Nervous as a kitten, I could hardly make the promises and say the responses. Leni was disappointed that we were not allowed on the main altar, but being a Protestant I was relegated to the side altar. But this did not worry us, and we have not had a cross word about religion before or since.

I was in such a state that my main memory is not of the all-important ceremony, but of my dad sitting next to me and saying, as people entered the church, that 'the turnstiles were ticking merrily'. We had a lovely reception, Johnny French was best man, Leni's Corporation bus pals bombarded us with confetti, my new father-in-law, and Uncles Rob and Oliver, newly home from Italy, went down the pub, and frankly, I was very glad when it was all over. It was the best thing I ever did, and we have been madly in love now for more than 45 years. After my leave, it was back to Germany and the Combined Services Football team.

It must have been about mid-May 1946 when we had great news. The English football season had just finished, and for the first full post-war season there had been just two divisions, or sections, the Football League South and the Football League North. Sheffield United had won the latter, and the news was that we were to play them just a week after they had completed their great feat.

And we were to play them in Berlin, of all places, and on the Olympic Stadium where only ten years previously, Adolf Hitler had opened the 1936 Olympic Games. The last British team to play in Berlin had been England, when they beat Germany 6–3, and when the English team raised their arms to Hitler in the Nazi salute.

Of course, being able to see the German capital, for so many years the centre of world affairs, which Germany had dictated, was so very exciting.

We travelled up the autobahn in our coach, and we were stopped by Russian troops at the border of the Russian Zone of divided Germany. They were the first Soviet soldiers we had seen on duty, the only ones I had seen before had been the prisoners of war we had released somewhere in Germany before VE-Day.

The game was on a Saturday afternoon, and before a huge crowd we actually beat the English Northern Champions 5–0, but unfortunately I was not in the team that day.

However, we were there a few days and I was able to explore with the rest of the lads, the places and buildings which we had read about in the previous years. The Reichstag, the Brandenburg Gate, the Reich Chancellery, The Tiergarten, and the Kurfurstendamm, which although bomb damaged, were fascinating as they came into sight. Who would have thought that one day we would be able to do this, when only a few years previously it appeared that Germany could have been victorious?

Of course, the main place of interest was 'Der Bunker'. Yes, we went down into the Führer's bunker, by permission of the Russians in whose zone it was situated. They pointed out to us the spot in the garden where Hitler, along with Goebels and his wife and children, were incinerated, and they showed us the entry to Hitler's High Command headquarters of the last days. We went down fifteen to twenty steps and entered the living area, which was below a huge mass of reinforced concrete, secure against air attack or artillery shelling. They had been kept as they were at the time of Hitler's demise. There were chairs and communication equipment in the office rooms and the beds and drawers etc, still in the bedrooms. It was quite awesome, almost frightening to think of what had gone on in that bunker. Orders had been given from there, the consequences of which were death to thousands of people, including Germans who Hitler thought had been disloyal in the final weeks.

We came out and looked through the badly damaged Chancellery and walked around the shell-scarred gardens, just as Hitler used to do.

The Russian soldiers were quite friendly, although language was a barrier. The quality of their uniforms was poor, as obviously were the clothes of their girls and wives back home, because we were astounded to see the awful shoes and clothing they bought from the Germans in the 'Schwarzmarkt' (Black Market) in the Tiergarten, to send back to Russia. They would walk off beaming whilst carrying something, which if we were to have sent to our females, would have caused them to leave us.

By this time the British demobilisation was developing fast, and we knew what happened when a soldier left his unit to go home. His passage was free, and in England he went to a centre where he was issued with a full set of civilian clothes, even to a trilby hat.

The Russian system was somewhat different. They were given a few roubles and sent on their way, having to find their way home over vast distances. They would climb aboard goods trains, or get lifts on trucks. We felt very sorry for them.

Walking down what had been the great fashion centre of Germany, the Kurfurstendamm, but was then badly bombed, I saw a business being carried on down a cellar, below what had been a large fashion shop for ladies. I went in and introduced myself to the haute couturier, Frau Dorothea Schurger. A relationship developed that lasted for many years. Dorothea had lots of beautiful fabrics, which had been stored in the cellar, safe from the air raids, and she agreed that if I were to send her Leni's measurements and requirements, with a photograph to give an idea of the garment she wanted, she would make it up. I would pay her in the only hard currency of the day, cigarettes.

Leni was eventually one of the best-dressed girls in England, with her shoes from Brussels, watch from Switzerland, and clothes from Berlin!

It was an exciting trip, that first one to the German post-war capital and, although badly mauled, I fell in love with it.

We were becoming seasoned travellers and soon another very exciting trip was mooted. We had played Poland twice in Germany, at Brunswick and Hamburg, and had played very well and won both games. Possibly to get their own back, they invited us to play them at Katowice and Cracow!

This was great, and we flew from Buckeburg to Warsaw, but not without a few problems. There was something strange going on when we boarded our plane at the RAF base, for there were two RAF officers, or at least two men in officers' uniforms, aboard. When we got to Warsaw we were all taken off the plane, under guard, and escorted into a room in the airport. The guards had large capes over their uniforms, and as we walked over the tarmac, the wind blew aside one of the capes and I saw that the wearer was carrying a gun similar to a 'Tommy Gun'. Hardly the way to greet friends!

By chance, also in the airport at the time, was Sir Hartley Shawcross, the chief prosecutor at the Nuremburg War Crimes Trials, and we were told that he had interceded in the airport proceedings, and actually prevented us being sent back to Germany. Apparently, the two surplus officers were said to be spies, and we did not see them again.

We flew from Warsaw to Katowice, and marvelled how we just cleared the treetops of a huge forest for the last few miles, to drop straight into the airport at the end of the forest. Our first morning was a surprising pleasure. Poland had had a terrible war, and we were prepared for economies in eating, but our first breakfast was and is to this day, the biggest I have ever eaten.

The tables in the centre of the Bagatelle Restaurant were full of many different cooked meats, cheeses and a selection of breads, the like of which we had never seen before. Silver pots of steaming coffee added to the tempting aroma that pervaded the room. Sparking white tablecloths embroidered in a Polish way covered the tables, and the cutlery glistened.

We thought that we could not possibly eat and do justice to it all, but being fourteen healthy lads, we would give it a good try. We did do justice to it and left very little.

As we sat talking about how much we had enjoyed it, and sipping more coffee, we had a tremendous shock.

Three waitresses entered the room, each bearing an enormous tray. The whole of the surfaces were covered in fried ham, very thick, and covering it was a large quantity of fried eggs. In addition, we were served with some particularly tasty fried bread.

'English breakfast' they said, with huge smiles on their faces! Oh dear, how can you disappoint such generous and cheerful hosts? We just had to take a breath and start all over again. I have eaten in almost all of the countries in Europe, but Poland was the best. It was not sophisticated like the French, but was pure, excellent, magnificent tasting food.

It seemed to me that the Polish women did most of the work. Certainly in the fields men were conspicuous by their absence. In Katowice we saw our first ever women police, and they were on point duty at busy intersections. I took photographs of them specifically, as they were unique, but the developer back in Germany exposed the whole roll!

The game was played on a Sunday in great heat, a strange experience for us, as we had never heard of Sunday football. We played the Polish National team and, although we beat them 9–3, it was not without controversy.

The first problem was the ball, which was underinflated, in fact, soft. They said that that was how it always was, but of course, they were absolutely wrong according to the rules. It made it difficult for us, although the score would suggest that we overcame it.

The second was much worse. We were amazed to see the perimeter of the ground had high steel mesh fences erected. This suggested that they were to stop the crowd getting on to the pitch. At that time in the UK, nothing like that existed, and crowds were noted for their bonhomie rather than their aggression.

We soon discovered that there were hooligan elements in the crowd. The fences were really high, suggesting that it was pointless trying to throw stones at players, but we were wrong. Eddie Hodgkinson of Leeds United, one of our players, was struck on the leg with the sharp edge of a piece of slate, similar to a roof tile. It was rather a nasty incident, but it transpired that it was the only untoward event of an otherwise very enjoyable ten days.

That night the Polish Football Association hosted dinner, and after the meal and the speeches, we sat talking, and those who liked a drink, drinking. The Poles said that they would pay for everything up till midnight.

However, the party went on well into the night, although I had gone to bed earlier, and at about 4.00 am a waiter brought in a bill and gave it to Leslie Compton, our captain. He signed it Ernest Bevin, British Embassy and, apparently, the waiter was quite happy. Bevin was the British Foreign Secretary at the time! We never heard any more about it, so they must have sorted it out somehow.

We then went by coach to Cracow, passing en route a Nazi concentration camp. Of course, it was empty, but the barbed wire and the machine-gun towers were mute testimony to the horrible crimes recently committed there, in the cause of Aryan supremacy.

It seems that I have several photographs of the game at Katowice, and of the hotel where we stayed, but very little of our stay at Cracow. I know that we won, but memories of the game have dimmed to near oblivion.

Cracow was not damaged during the war or, if it was, it was not in the central city areas. A city of beautiful churches, its cathedral was the jewel in the centre. The present Pope (John Paul II) was archbishop there, and I like to think that he saw me play in that game, for it is well known that he played football and was, indeed, a goalkeeper. Consequently, he could hardly have missed such an attractive game, for we were the first British team to play there since before the war.

We played in Czechoslovakia later, during the short period when they were between the Nazi and the Communist yokes, but Poland was already under Communist oppression. And oppression it was, as many Poles risked their liberty to tell us. I remember walking down a street in Cracow with the rest of the team, when in true spy or secret service fashion, a man walked by my side and whispered, 'you think the Polish officials are from the Football Association, but they are not, they are secret police', and then he sidled off.

Another sign of the totalitarian state was at the cathedral. Down in the vaults was the tomb of Marshal Pilsudski, the great Polish hero but, although foreign visitors could visit it, as we did, the Poles themselves were not allowed to.

There was little to buy in the Polish shops, and so I bought Leni just one present, but it was particularly beautiful. It was a silver bracelet, each link being an engraving of a different church, and was quite different to anything I had seen before. Unfortunately, a few months later Leni lost it, or had it stolen, when at the doctors in Newcastle upon Tyne.

May 1946 was a busy football month for us, as we played Dundee United in Hamburg; Hearts of Midlothian in Celle; Poland in Hannover and in Brunswick; and Sheffield United in Berlin. Other games we played, the dates of which I cannot remember, were against Partick Thistle at Krefeld; Glasgow Rangers at Hamburg; West Ham United at Celle; Wolverhampton Wanderers at Cologne; plus Glasgow Celtic and Everton at venues which have gone from my memory. I do have a photograph of me tossing a coin with the Nottingham Forest captain at Hamburg, and I am sure that there were many more.

Certainly there was Hibernians at Celle, and I remember Captain Brent, our Aussie officer in charge, asking me, 'Who are these Hiberanians?' It sounded more like a flower and supporters of the famous Edinburgh club would not be flattered.

We were very fortunate to be able to serve out our time playing football, travelling all over Europe, and staying in the best hotels. And yet, through it all I was longing to return home to my Leni.

Although we were all quite happy at Paderborn, for some reason or other we were transferred to Wuppertal, and when we saw the facilities provided for us, we could hardly believe our luck.

We lived in what had been a restaurant, part of the facilities offered to the German spectators in earlier days, who would have watched a variety of sporting events in this excellent stadium.

There was a football field surrounded by a running track, which itself was encircled by a banked bicycle racetrack. In addition, there was a well-equipped gymnasium.

We had our own German chef, and women to clean the place. This really was 'living it up', and we thoroughly enjoyed ourselves.

Around about 1920 I believe, the city fathers created a means of transport which was not bettered anywhere in the world for many years. They built a monorail from the suburbs right through the main street, and up above it. It was very fast, extremely comfortable, and being above the streets did not interfere with traffic. Today, as I write, it will obviously be of greater significance, as the volume of motor traffic has increased dramatically everywhere. There were frequent stopping places with steps leading down to the street.

It was about then that I had a pleasant surprise. The strength of the squad of players was very high, as the forces in Germany had been combed for professional footballers. We had many top players, and as older players were being demobbed, younger ones were being found to take their places.

One day one of the latter category walked into our bedroom, and I was delighted to see that it was Eric Parsons, a team-mate from my Colchester days. It was great to know that, like me, he had survived the war.

We spent many happy hours chatting about what had happened to us between April 1943 and 1945. However, our stay at Wuppertal was not to be very long, and soon we were on the move again, this time to the ancient and historic city of Hannover. This was to be our permanent headquarters and it was ideal.

The 125 Transit Camp was created to handle the thousands of troops who were going on leave, or returning, or were on the way to the UK to be demobbed. It was in a modern German army cavalry barracks. The dormitories were very comfortable, with excellent bathrooms attached.

The facilities for football and for training were fabulous. We had a football pitch within the camp and it was in excellent condition, but the feature which was the most exciting was the indoor cavalry training ground, which had been built as an all weather facility. It was all grassed and was about the same size as a football pitch, but had a roof that could be opened to let in the sun and rain. What a boon it proved to be. I can remember training in there when there was deep snow outside.

We were all members of the Sergeants' Mess, with all of its creature comforts and benefits. This included a table tennis table, and a bar with drinks at very cheap prices. Cigarettes too were readily available, and as they were the barter currency in Germany, we were comfortably off. We were also able to buy boxes of chocolates containing two dozen bars, and the facilities became even more plentiful when they made my pal, Eddie Baily, Sergeants' Mess caterer. It really was the 'life of Riley'.

Switzerland had remained neutral during the war, and always a rich country, it must have been by far the most prosperous in Europe in 1946, if not in the World. We had survived nearly six years of war, of privation and of danger. What a contrast.

So we could not believe our luck when we were told that we had been invited by the Swiss Football Association to tour their country for two weeks in June 1946.

We were so excited, and even more so when we were told that we were to get two pounds per day spending money! We went by coach down the autobahn, and by the time we were nearing the German/Swiss border, it was dark. And dark was the operative word, because electricity was a scarce resource in postwar Germany.

We had not seen a street light or a lighted shop window since 2nd September 1939. When we suddenly started to go down a hill with the city of Basle (Basel) at the bottom, it was like Blackpool illuminations – a mass of twinkling light. A sight to be remembered for always. With eager anticipation, we crowded the front of the coach as we tried to see more of this fantastic panorama.

When we reached the streets of this Rhine-city, we could hardly believe the beauty of the shops, their windows containing displays of goods that we could only dimly recall.

The coach stopped at 'Die Drei Konigin' (The Three Kings), a beautiful luxury hotel on the banks of the River Rhine, which flows there from its source in Lake Constance. My bedroom was at the back of the hotel, facing directly on to the famous river. After a wash and tidy up we went down to the opulent dining-room for dinner, even though it was about eleven o'clock. An orchestra was playing and it transpired that it was broadcasting on Swiss National Radio. What a great start to what proved to be a magnificent tour of beautiful Switzerland.

Walking around the Basle shops the following day was tantamount to 'Alice in Wonderland'. Goods that we had either not seen at all, or which had been rationed in the UK for years, were there in profusion. I bought Leni a beautiful pair of red leather shoes in the latest wedged-heel style.

The food, of course, was superb, and we were very lucky with the weather, which was glorious throughout our stay. We trained on the local football field wherever we were staying and as we were travelling in our own coach, we were able to go off on trips to explore beautiful Helvetia.

We had two Royal Army Service Corps drivers allocated to us. They had two of the best jobs in the army, as one always travelled with us, either driving the coach or in charge of the kit, if we were flying or travelling by rail, whilst the other, although missing a trip, stayed back in camp with nothing to do.

One was Irish, and went under the unusual name of Paddy, and the other was from Newcastle upon Tyne who we called Geordie. We were so original.

Well, Geordie was our driver on the Swiss tour. He had a predisposition for drinking beer and, at receptions and in hotels, we tried to keep our eyes on him to make sure he remained sober, as he was a real nuisance when he was under the influence.

One day we went for a trip over the Alps, and we stopped for lunch on the top of a mountain road at a lovely chalet hotel. We all understood that alcohol had a greater effect the higher you were, and we were really at a high altitude this day. We were all careful to drink very little, as the British soldier abroad in uniform, stood out and was greatly respected, Britain having recently won the war with its Allies. We did not want to do anything to mar our reputation.

After lunch we continued our journey, and driving on the right, à la Continental, the side of the mountain dropped away to our right, the drop being many thousands of feet. Looking out of the window we could see how near we were to the edge, and this was scary, as hadn't we only just survived a war? But then we were even nearer the edge, in fact, it looked as though we were going over. This made Billy Steel, one of our number, shout, 'Stop the coach!' We were going uphill and therefore not very fast, so he jumped out whilst we were still moving. The vehicle swung towards the edge of the drop again, and at this I jumped out, followed by several others. I will never forget Billy Steel's face as he ran beside the coach telling everyone to get off. He was terrified and so was I.

Everyone was stone cold sober, except Geordie, who was drunk and incapable, and getting worse as the altitude took effect.

Leslie Compton had done a bit of bus driving as a wartime occupation before he joined the army, and he took over and got us safely back to our hotel.

Les was a genial giant, being about six feet four inches, and fourteen stone. He played football for the Arsenal and England, and he was Middlesex's wicketkeeper for many years – perhaps the tallest player ever to be behind the stumps in first-class cricket. His brother, Dennis Compton, played for the same two clubs, and was, of course, the great unorthodox England batsman of the forties and fifties.

Derrick Williams, still a bosom friend forty-five years later, was our only player from the Royal Navy. His job in the senior service was as a swimming instructor. I told him of my 'swimming' days with Peter O'Brien and how I was a complete failure. Unwisely, Derrick said that he had never had a failure, and that I would be no exception.

We used to go in a pool most days, and Derrick felt sure that by the end of the fortnight, I would be swimming. How wrong can you get? That was 1946. In fact, I did learn to swim eventually. About 1959 we were on the beach at Branksome Dene Chine, near Poole in Dorset, and I watched a young girl swimming. I said to myself that surely if she could swim, I could. At that, I went in the sea, took my feet off the bottom and actually swam!

The most important game was in Berne, the Swiss capital. Our opposition was the Swiss National team. Unfortunately, I did not play in the match, which we won 2–0, but I did play in the other two games which we also won.

All of us were presented with a beautiful, very modern Swiss watch, and I noticed that on the box was the name and address of the shop from which it had been bought. It was from Basle and we were going back there prior to returning to Germany.

Also, it was Leni's birthday the following month, and I intended to get her something extra special. Would the Basle shop do a swap, a lady's watch in exchange for a man's? Well, I could only try and this I did. To my great pleasure, they agreed immediately, and I got for Leni a type of watch that was absolutely new and had not yet been exported. It was called a 'cocktail watch', gold plated with a pink face, and the bracelet was very chic, being 'rope' with gold clasps. It was a magnificent present and Leni wore it for many years, until the gold plate wore and became scratched. She still has it, and its sentimental value is incalculable.

One of the highlights of our Swiss tour really was a 'highlight', as we stayed in a fabulous hotel in Interlaken, and the tremendous view from our window was of the Jungfrau, an ice-capped mountain that reflected the sunlight. It was particularly beautiful when the sun went down behind it, and we were able to see all of the colours of the rainbow through the ice-cap, which acted as a prism.

We stayed also in a hotel on the lake at Lugano and, similarly, at Lausanne. After six years of the greyness of war, and for me four years in barracks or slit trenches, the luxury and the bright lights of Switzerland were such marvellous antitheses. It was certainly a fortnight I will never forget.

Sometime during the summer of 1946, the Allies decided to organise sporting championships between the victorious nations, and the most important event was the football, or as the organisers called it, the Soccer Championship. In the immediate postwar euphoria it was said that this would be a regular event, perhaps even annual, and it was great news for us that the British powers that be had decided that we should represent Great Britain. We were always referred to as 'Great Britain' and then, in smaller print and in brackets, 'Combined Services Germany'.

There were four groups to start with. The first consisted of Russia, Poland and Czechoslovakia; the second Denmark, Great Britain and Norway; the third Belgium, USA and Luxembourg; and the fourth France and Holland (Netherlands). Excepting group four, which had only two teams, we all had to play the other two teams in the group and the group winners went into the semi-finals.

The USA fared terribly, as was expected, and lost by 12 goals to Luxembourg and by 18 to Belgium!

The four semi-finalists were the Czechs, the Dutch, the Belgians, and ourselves, having beaten Denmark 5–0, and Norway 6–0 (the other game in the group resulted in Denmark beating Norway 2–1).

In that penultimate game we drew Holland, and surprisingly but pleasingly, we had to play them in Lyon (Lyons) in the South of France. We could not understand why it was not played in Holland, but who was to complain about a train journey to Lyon, via Paris, especially in those days in 1946?

We stayed at a beautiful old hotel which was very comfortable and where the food was magnificent. The area being one where grapes grew in abundance, both green and black varieties were always in baskets on the tables. I had never known such a thing before, as grapes had not been available since 1939 in the UK, and even then they were a luxury fruit, beyond the reach of my family.

By this time I was team captain and, before the game, I had to introduce the French President's representative to our team. We actually won 8–0, as by this time we had developed wonderful teamwork, and so our goals total in the championship was 19, from only three games. I loved Lyon, and a highlight of the visit was being asked to dinner at the home of a director of the French tyre manufacturer, Michelin. I found it quite remarkable, the difference between a French family meal and ours back home.

Mam and Dad always laid the table properly, and I recall that Dad was always in charge of the bread. The homemade loaf would be on the circular bread board at Dad's elbow, and after asking us how many slices we wanted, he would slice the requisite number. So often today, people eat a quick meal, before the television, and there is no sense of occasion. In our house we had to be properly seated, hands washed and all of us there before the meal commenced.

But in France! Eating dinner was an event that lasted most of the evening. It was a combination of eating a number of courses, drinking, and talking, the latter being as important as the former. My most vivid memory was of a course that consisted of a large partly hollowed out tomato, stuffed with a deliciously flavoured minced beef.

We left Lyon with great anticipation, as we knew that we had actually made the final. Our train journey back to Germany was punctuated by two quite different occurrences, which are still vivid in my memory. One was almost laughable in retrospect, and the other was sombre and chilling.

We were in a closed compartment, as the train had no corridors, so we could not escape when an archetypal Frenchman, 'avec' navy blue beret and small black moustache, and sitting next to me, pulled out of a canvas bag, which he had on his lap, a small round wooden box and a knife.

It was Camembert cheese of a very ripe variety and, although it was October, it was a hot day, making the atmosphere very stuffy. 'Pierre' proceeded to stick the knife in the cheese. The smell all of the way to Paris was appalling.

We were so glad to get off the train, but the pleasant feeling of relief soon evaporated. Newspaper sellers were screaming the headline news of their newspapers, and their bundles were disappearing so quickly that one would have thought that they were giving them away. Something very dramatic had happened, that was obvious.

FOOTBALL FOR THE COMBINED SERVICES GERMANY

Having just survived the war and its many threats to life and limb, one always feared the worst where news was concerned, and this was my feeling as I bought a 'Paris Soir'. On the front page were photographs of some of the main Nazi war criminals hanging on the gallows at Nuremburg. They were lurid, explicit, and omitted nothing, and sent a shiver down my spine. I remember that one was Foreign Minister Von Ribbentrop; another Julius Streicher, the infamous Jew baiter; and a third deceased was Reichsmarschal Hermann Goering, but his death was self-inflicted by swallowing a cyanide capsule.

We stayed the night in Paris and, after seeing a few of the sights, including the Notre Dame, we set off for Hannover. In my case were a few unique presents for Leni, including, of course, French perfume, and a particularly beautiful pure silk scarf, which she still treasures.

Arriving back at the end of October we immediately started training, ready for the final. We learned that our opponents were to be Czechoslovakia, but with a wonderful team spirit, and a record of three games, three wins, nineteen goals scored and none conceded, we felt that we could take on just about any team in the world. We knew we were taking part in a unique occasion and that we had to represent Great Britain in this great final confrontation.

How excited we were to learn that the final of the Inter Allied Soccer Championships was to be played on the Olympic Stadium in Berlin. What a thrilling prospect that was and, although no doubt richly deserved, it all seemed like a dream when I contemplated that only a little over a year ago, most of the team were in action on the battlefield, with the same city as the ultimate objective.

So, although the big military prize was won by the Russians – and perhaps this was a mistake by the Western Allies, not to press on to the German capital themselves – here we were with just one more hurdle to overcome to be Allied Soccer Champions.

It seemed very symbolic that the victors of war should hold the final of the world's most popular game, soccer, in the heart of the enemy's country.

We were allowed to train on the pitch for a couple of days before the match, as were our opponents, Czechoslovakia.

One day when we were en route to the stadium for practice, Captain Brent kept giving our driver instructions, which surprised us because, as far as we knew, he had no knowledge of Berlin, and to our utter amazement he told him to stop outside a particular house. We watched as, incredibly, he ran up the garden path, knocked on the door and when it opened, in he went!

Everyone in the coach was taken aback. We were all discussing what Gerry's secret could possibly be. How could a 'Sydneysider', on his first trip to Berlin, know someone in this house?

After waiting for about an hour, we were to discover what the mystery was all about. 'Who was that?', 'How did you know the house?', 'A bit of a dark horse aren't you?' These were some of the questions which were thrown at our boss. There was a hush as he began to explain. 'I went to Berlin University in the 1930's' he said, 'and that was where I lived.'

We were astounded. Not particularly because a person attended the university, many thousands more did, nor because the house was still standing and his landlady had survived the air raids, shelling, and the Russian invaders, although all of these things were catastrophic. No, it was because our commanding officer had never intimated in any way that he had ever even set foot in Germany previously. The revelation probably had an even greater effect on me than on anyone else, because whenever we needed directions or information from a German, he would always get me to speak to the locals in my halting German – and all of the time Gerry was fluent in the language!

He never commented on this again, although it seemed to have given him a lot of pleasure. However, he had, as yet unknown to him, to face a very tragic situation during this his second stay in Germany. He was out hunting wild pig with his girlfriend, when he saw a movement in a bush. Thinking it was a pig he fired, but when he went to examine his target, he was horrified to find that he had hit his girlfriend, and she died from her wounds.

On the great day, 3rd November 1946, the excitement was intense as we left our hotel to travel the few kilometres to the Olympic Stadium, to play in this unique match. We were not to know that it was to be totally unique, that this was to be the one and only such final.

We arrived at the ground about an hour before kick off, and already there were hordes of spectators queuing at the turnstiles. Straightaway we went to the dressing room, and thence out on to the pitch to absorb the scene, and I could picture Adolf Hitler on the podium opening the 1936 Olympics.

By the time we left the field, there was a huge crowd building up in that magnificent stadium. Suddenly things had changed so much for all of us. A little over a year ago we were insignificant soldiers, just army numbers, but now we represented that two million army, and our numbers were on our shirts from one to eleven. All these thoughts flashed through my mind as I got ready in the dressing room. Whereas most players took a long time to bandage their ankles, and took great care in putting on their boots etc, I could get ready in a couple of minutes. It was better for them because it took their minds off what lay ahead, that they had been chosen to represent Great Britain in the first Inter-Allied Soccer Championship final. I just used to sit around, trying to get into conversation with anyone who was willing. This was always so, from playing as a child, right through my career.

Players who had not made the team were assisting their mates by massaging their legs, and the dressing room smelt of the liniment used. However, I never bothered to have massages.

We were to be presented to the British Commander-in-Chief, Air Marshal Sir Sholto Douglas, and this served to heighten the tension, for although soccer players, we were still all members of His Majesty's Forces.

The same as anyone interested in sport in those days, I was a great admirer of the incomparable Jesse Owens, winner of three gold medals in the last Olympic Games, and as we hurried through the tunnel, out on to the running track that surrounded the pitch, it was as though the colossus was watching us. It was awe-inspiring.

There was a great roar as the 100,000 strong crowd saw us enter the magnificent arena. As Berlin was split into four zones, British, French, Russian, and American, the vast majority of the spectators came from those countries. No doubt most of them supported us, and this was evident by the nature of our welcome.

It appeared to us that the various nationalities were kept in specific sections of the arena, and so we were very surprised to see a photograph in an English newspaper showing how friendly the Russians and British were. The photograph was an obvious fraud. Two photos had been 'welded' together, and it could be seen quite easily. This is not to suggest that we were anything else but friendly with one another, just to show how silly propaganda could be.

Both teams were presented to the Commander-in-Chief of the British Zone of Germany and, as captain, it was my duty to introduce each player to him. The two National Anthems were then played, after which we were pleased to be able to run off to one of the goal areas to warm up on what was a cold, crisp November afternoon.

Then the Czech captain and I shook hands, I spun a coin and it fell to my opponent to choose which goal to defend. The referee was a British Army officer, Captain Howlett, of the Military Police.

We got off to a good start, urged on by the vociferous British Forces contingent in the crowd, and at half-time we appeared to be in a virtually unbeatable position, as we were leading by three clear goals. However, the Czechs fought back very skilfully and, at one stage, appeared to be in with a chance when the score was 3–2, but we recovered and ran out worthy winners 6–3.

Since its inception, the Combined Services XI had been composed of mainly army and air force personnel, with a single exception, my good friend Derrick Williams, who was in the Royal Navy and who came to us from his base at Flensburg, on the Danish border. But on this great day it transpired that we were all soldiers. It is interesting to recall something about some of the players. Our goalkeeper, Jimmy Cowan, was a Greenock Morton player and he was to become a legend in Scottish football, when in 1948 he played at Wembley Stadium, the great home of English football, against England. It has been remembered as 'Cowan's match' as he kept out the marauding Sassenach forwards almost on his own.

One of his colleagues, both in Berlin and London, was Billy Steel, who was also to play for Great Britain against the Rest of Europe, and who is remembered today as one of the all-time greats. Another Scottish International was our right half, Willie Mills, our oldest player, but one of immense class and ability. Our number eight was Eddy Baily and he had a whole lifetime in the game ahead of him. He was an illustrious inside right with Tottenham Hotspur and England, when the 'Spurs' were the best team in England. Later he was assistant manager for them for many years during their most glorious era, when they were the first team to win the 'double', winning both the First Division and the FA Cup in the same season,

Eddy's wing partner, Eric Parsons, was to enjoy a career in the First Division with Chelsea, and he also earned representative honours with England. I was to play for England and the Football League, and our outside left, George Lee, and I were to team up again four years later, for West Bromwich Albion, when they had their best team in their history.

There was great jubilation at the end of the game, and Sir Sholto presented us with our winners' medals, which are absolutely unique, as this was the only Allied Soccer Championship ever played.

I have previously referred to my shyness, and to how introverted I was, and as we left the Stadium to go back to our quarters, everyone but I was excited at the prospect of the banquet to be given by the Commander-in-Chief. Realising that, as captain, I would be very much in the forefront of the social activities, and obviously I would have to make a speech of acclamation or in response to a toast, I became very nervous.

Our coach transported us to the hotel where the ceremony was to be held, and there were lots of people there, including all of the top brass, civil and military.

Quickly I decided that I could not face such an imposing audience and I became quite neurotic. I made an excuse to leave the room, I said nothing to anybody, and when no one was looking, I walked briskly down the steps in front of the building, and I disappeared into the streets of Berlin.

I spent the whole evening trudging around in the dark, and eventually I decided that the best thing was for me to find my way to where we were staying. This I did and later I was able to make what seemed to be acceptable excuses, to do with not feeling well.

Certainly it was one of the most miserable evenings of my life, as I walked alone in the bitter cold November night, with the remains of bombed buildings silhouetting the skyline.

Ever since, I have wracked my brains wondering why I did what I did, but I have always come to the same conclusion, that I am such an emotional person that if I was to live my life over again, I would still absent myself from those celebrations. This extreme emotionalism was to surface many more times in my life to spoil similar occasions, which should have been enjoyed, and also to prevent me succeeding in other situations.

The following day we returned to Hannover as Allied Soccer Champions, and naturally I was proud to have been Great Britain's captain in this great success. A further bonus awaited us when we got back, the news that we had been invited to play a return game against the Czechs in Prague, a city that appeared to me to be one of the truly historic capitals of Europe. It had for me an aura that other European cities did not have, and the ancient kingdoms of Bohemia, Moravia, Slovakia, and Silesia, which made up Czechoslovakia, had always appealed to me. In addition, I think that most of we British had a bit of a guilt complex about not declaring war on Germany when they annexed the Czech state in 1938, and we were very happy to know that they were free again. Another attraction was to visit the land where 'Good King Wenceslas looked out'!

It was decided that we should go by coach and it was a most enjoyable journey through some spectacular countryside, where the beauty of the scenery often took my breath away. We left Hannover on 14th November 1946 and travelled to Prague via Göttingen, Fulda, Würzburg, and into Nuremburg, where the Nazi War Crimes Tribunals had been held, and near which we stayed the night at an American camp. I can remember little about the accommodation, but much about the breakfasts. We ate with our allies and were amazed to see the type of food they started their day with. It may be well known today, but it was a surprise to us then, to see them eat mountains of sweet pancakes swamped in maple syrup. Of course, we had to follow suit and I must say that my sweet tooth did not object at all.

After saying thanks and goodbye, we travelled east and passed through Pilsen, where the lager comes from, and then we were well on our way to our destination, Prague. Coming down from the mountains, we could see the ancient city ahead of us, and we entered it with great anticipation. Our hotel was old but was full of character, and I cannot describe adequately the feeling of antiquity, history, and old-world charm which it had for me.

The atmosphere wherever we went was tremendous. Although historians are apt to say that Britain let the Czechs down by doing nothing when Hitler invaded the small Central European state, this was not the attitude of their people. We were lauded everywhere and made so very welcome.

In November 1946 they were free. The feeling of freedom pervaded the place. They had been freed from the Nazi jackboot, although they did not know that this was to be short-lived, that Stalin was waiting, ready to pounce, to replace Hitler.

There was a British Club in the city, and we were invited to meet some of the Brits who lived there, and to have tea. One had the feeling that this was indeed a 'corner of a foreign field which is forever England'.

The most interesting feature for me came when I signed the visitors' book. Earlier on that very day a Captain Rickaby had signed the book. I could not find anything else about him, but my family name is most uncommon and it was quite a coincidence.

We had a very enjoyable time and one of the most interesting events was our visit to the open-air skating rink. It was to see an ice hockey match between Sweden and the home country. Most of the crowd were wrapped up and wearing fur caps and ear-muffs, because they were in the open and in freezing air, but we were most fortunate. As guests of the Government, we sat at tables in a dining-room above the standing accommodation. We had a beautiful meal and then we watched the game through windows, in the warmth and comfort of the enclosed room.

It was magical and I found the game fast and entertaining. Another evening we were taken to the cinema to see 'Anthony and Cleopatra', the sound being in English with Czech subtitles. It was most enjoyable, but the most surprising thing about it was that it started at 11.00 pm.

We came out at about 2.00 am and, by this time, a few of us were feeling hungry, so we decided to see if we could get something to eat, although anticipating that it was too late.

To our surprise and pleasure, restaurants were still open, and we did something we have never done before, by starting dinner at 3.00 am. Food was magnificent in Prague and the bread was the best I ever tasted, except for some which was covered in caraway seeds.

Another terrific excursion was to the grounds of Sparta Football Club, on a Sunday afternoon. They were playing Dukla and it was an absorbing game. We were able to see the different styles, the strengths and the weaknesses of the game in Central Europe, at our leisure. Two facets of the European game were well known, but only one proved to be correct in this instance. The first was that goalkeepers were very spectacular and were, therefore, not too reliable, believing in last second dives to save the ball going into the net, rather than the safer but less exciting method of good positional play. Done properly, the latter way gives the impression that the shot has been hit directly at the goalkeeper. We certainly agreed that this was a valid criticism, as both goalkeepers were bringing off breathtaking saves, due really to bad positional play. The other then current criticism was that the Continentals could not shoot well, but that day we thought that they were quite good in this respect.

Whenever we went anywhere in our coach, it would be recognised as carrying what was billed as the Great Britain team, and we were shown great friendship. When we left the stadium on this Sunday afternoon, we had to have police to clear a way through the crowd for us, as they were pressing up against the coach, waving and calling to us.

Shopping was exciting too, as the shops had plenty of goods on sale, and they had lots of things unique to Czechoslovakia. I bought Leni several gifts, but the most spectacular was a beautiful white blouse with puffed sleeves and typical Czech embroidery. There was a fine selection of Bohemian glass, but the thought of it getting broken on the way to England put me off buying it.

Wherever I went, I would try to make sure that I found time to visit the cathedrals, and Prague's Saint Vitus was magnificent. There had been four kings named Wenceslas in the thirteenth and fourteenth centuries, I discovered, but strangely it was a Saint Wenceslas who is remembered in the carol as a king. He was Duke of Bohemia and he died around 836AD, having been reared a Christian by his grandmother. He promoted Christianity and was also remembered for having made peace with Henry I of Germany. Sadly, he was killed by his brother, Boleslav, and his Saint's Feast Day is on 28th September. From information received, it would appear that this good Christian man was also known as a King, being the 'Good King Wenceslas' referred to in the carol.

However, we had come to Prague primarily to play football, and to give our hosts the chance to get even with us after their 6–3 defeat in Berlin.

They certainly got their own back, beating us 5–0, but unfortunately the game was spoilt by bad refereeing. It is now 56 years since that game, and misinterpretations of the laws of the game have been ironed out during that time, but in the forties there were some tactics used by the Continentals that could be very frustrating for British players.

One tactic they employed was body checking, deliberately getting between one of us and the ball, but not trying to play the ball. Another was 'late tackling', which resulted in us being tripped up. Both of these happened over and over again, and our appeals to the referee were in vain, as he spoke no English.

We were very frustrated and it badly affected our game. They also did not really understand tackling. Often we would get a free kick awarded against us, for a perfectly fair tackle.

As captain, I spent a lot of time and energy telling players not to retaliate as it would make things worse, but eventually the worst thing possible happened. Billy Steel who was, as I have already mentioned, a brilliant player and who went on to be one of the world's outstanding players in the late forties and fifties, was tripped for the nth time. To our horror, he got back on his feet, and went and kicked the player who had fouled him. He was sent off the field, and this really affected us. We were upset and with ten dejected men, we just collapsed.

Worse was to come. At the end of the game, we walked down the corridor to our dressing room, passing the Czechs' room on the way. What had been a glass panel in their door was shattered with jagged glass sticking out of the frame. Billy had put his foot through it. He never played for us again, and he was returned to his Corps of Signals unit.

Thus ended what had been a wonderful holiday. We went to a reception in the Town Hall that night, and left for Germany the following morning.

Around about December 1946, we were all sent back to our units, as it was considered that there was to be a hard winter ahead. There was also always the chance that teams from Britain might not be able to fly over, or worse still, that they could make it to Germany, but could not get back for their Saturday matches. European teams would not be available, as most Leagues closed down for the mid-winter period. My battalion was stationed at Brunswick, having just returned from a period in Berlin.

I was entitled to some leave, so I arranged to be home for New Year. The New Year was 1947 and of all the years of my life, unbeknown to me on that New Year's Eve, it was probably the happiest that my life had in store for me.

FOOTBALL FOR THE COMBINED SERVICES GERMANY

Before I went to England, I heard of a three-month language course to be held at the University of Göttingen, starting in January 1947. The two subjects were German and French, both advanced. I had studied French at school, and since meeting Leni, I had been learning German. Her mother had given me a German grammar book entitled, 'Heute Abend' (This Evening). I had found it very useful and, having lived in Germany at that time for more than a year and a half, I had had plenty of opportunities to practise speaking the language.

Göttingen is an ancient town with a charter dated 1220, and by the middle of the fourteenth century it had become a walled and moated stronghold, necessary in those days to keep out bandits and ambitious lords. It has had its ups and downs, and it was taken by storm twice in the Middle Ages. The town is linked to England through the Hannover Kings, who were responsible for much of its restoration.

When I arrived in this lovely old town, there was deep snow and this, apparently, was quite normal in mid-winter. Our dormitories were quite ancient, with a wood burning stove in the middle, and we seemed to spend a lot of time sitting around it to try to keep warm.

Our class was small with about seven or eight soldiers and three ATS girls. It was an enormous change to be back in a classroom for the first time for seven years, and it was difficult to be so immobile.

I became friendly with a very tall lance corporal from the Household Cavalry, whose name was the antithesis of the person. It was Lance Corporal Small. A Londoner, he had a tremendous sense of humour, he was the comedian of the class, and he stood about six and a half feet tall. During the week we had periods of German and French, with homework to do in the evenings. Some were written translations and some were conversational.

On Saturday mornings, we had two periods, the first being the learning of German songs. I thoroughly enjoyed this, and to prove how successful those lessons were, I can still remember many songs word for word. I could never sing in tune, but I used to love to sing the lieder. As related previously, both of my primary schools discovered that by asking me to desist from singing, the performance of the remainder improved dramatically. Presumably, I was just as flat and out of tune on these Göttingen Saturday mornings, but no one was sufficiently impolite to tell me.

An old German professor took the period, and for musical accompaniment he played a little accordion. This was fine, and he was obviously an accomplished musician.

So far so good. However, he had a habit that caused me an enormous amount of trouble. He had few teeth in his head, and he kept time by opening and closing his toothless gums. He looked so funny, and this did not escape my friend Small.

We used to sit in a semi-circle with 'Herr Professor' in the centre. Our class comic knew that I had great trouble in restraining from laughing, and he used to sit on the edge of the semi-circle in a position where our teacher could not see him, but where he could see me. Somehow I used to feel my friend's eyes on me, and I could not avoid looking at him, and whenever I did, he would imitate the Prof's champing gums.

I would then break up. I felt awful because I respected the old man and I would have hated him to think me impolite.

After this ordeal, we would then go to the main hall of the university to listen to a lecture. This could be on any subject – historical, political, or scientific, etc. The seating was raised up theatre fashion. I used to avoid the lance corporal and I made sure that he did not sit near me. This was because he always tried to make me laugh whenever we should have been serious.

Sitting in raised up seats gave me the feeling that everyone on the hall platform could see me, so it was vital that I should not be seen to be laughing.

I always managed to lose my comrade en route, and I would take my seat in the middle of the audience. However, I fell into the same trap every time, and I found myself looking for him. I could not resist it somehow or other, and there he would be opening and closing his mouth like the professor. The people amongst whom I was sitting must have thought I was an idiot. How could, for instance, a lecture on the changing political systems in Eastern Europe, be considered funny?

Lance Corporal Small was a good friend, despite the aforementioned, but as happened many times with army mates, I never saw or heard of him again. He has never been forgotten, nor has the learned professor, not least because I have many German gramophone records containing the songs he taught us, and because he taught us a good pronunciation of German sounds.

He said that it was all to do with the positioning of the tongue and the shape of the mouth. For example, when speaking English, we do not have a sound that is created by rounding the mouth as though we are going to say 'O', but where we try to say 'ee'. However, as our tutor taught us, this is necessary to say 'Früh', the German word for 'early', for instance.

He was so emphatic about speaking with the correct accent, that all he taught us has stayed with me all of these years. For those who are interested in German songs, some of them were as follows, 'Die Lorelei' (my favourite), 'Hans und Liesel', 'Lilli Marlene', 'Caprifischer', 'Roslein auf der Heiden', etc.

Certainly the Herr Professor was responsible for thousands of happy hours which I have enjoyed through listening to German songs on gramophone records.

This also reminds me of another three incidents which happened during my sojourn in Germany, and which were to do with music. I had never been interested in music, even though I had been to a church school where most of the boys played an instrument, generally a violin or piano, and where we sang the canticles every morning. We also sang pieces from opera such as the 'Anvil Chorus' from Verdi's 'Il Trovatore', but that was the limit of my musical experience.

My father used to play some light music on his gramophone, mostly such as Peter Dawson, a fine tenor in his day, and the Austrian, Richard Tauber, but it must have gone over my head as I took no interest.

I was introduced to classical music and the opera during my stay at the 125 Transit Camp in Hannover.

Somehow or other we met the manager of the Deutsche Gramophon Gesellshaft, something I had never heard of at the time, but which I realised in later years was one of the premier gramophone record producers in the world. 'We' means Eddie Baily, Eric Parsons, and I, who shared a bedroom in the barracks.

In 1946 we were invited to the factory, which was closed down, presumably through the record market not having yet recovered from its demise during the war. They had no stock either, but they had all of the master copies in wax. The manager showed us a catalogue of literally thousands of records, and said that we could buy anything we wanted.

I remember getting a Grace Moore song for my dad, as I knew he liked her singing, and I decided to write to him to ask him if there were any pieces he would like. The list he sent escapes me, but it did include songs from 'Barber of Seville', which he had to have in German via 'Der Barber von Sevilla'! 'Liebestraum' and the 'Barcarolle' were two others I now recall.

That was one musical incident; the second was a consequence of the first. Eric chose several records, including 'Symphonie aus der neuen Welt' (New World Symphony), by Dvorak, and he kept playing it over and over again. It sounded awful to Ed and me, and we harangued him not to play it anymore, but to no avail.

In fact, the only 'avail' was that to our utter amazement, we found that there were some bits that we liked, and then later we actually liked it so much to the extent that we often asked Eric to play it!

Then the same thing happened with Sibelius', 'Finlandia', and another piece by the same composer, the name of which I have forgotten.

At about this time we went back to the factory and bought a few more records, and I discovered a new pleasure in life, that providing I played a classical piece a few times, I found great joy in listening to it.

This second experience led to the third, because now that my interest was aroused, I was looking for opportunities to enlarge my musical arena. The Hannover State Opera House, had escaped the ravaging of Allied bombs and began to produce opera again. The first I saw was a double bill, 'Pagliacci' and 'Cavallaria Rusticana'. This was a magical evening for me, and I have been haunted by the music ever since. The 'Easter Hymn' from the latter, gives me goose pimples as I think of the beautiful meaning of the words, whilst listening to the ethereally haunting music, and recalling that evening in the summer of 1946.

I can still see the inside of the theatre in my mind, with the British Royal Coat of Arms of the House of Hannover above the stage.

I saw 'Der Fliegende Hollander' (the Flying Dutchman) there too, and who could forget the haunting music when the apparition of the boat, 'The Flying Dutchman' was approaching?

So for the gift of the love of good music, thank you the manager of the German Gramophone Company, and thank you Eric Parsons, for doing me such an enormous favour.

During 1946 there was a period of a couple of months when we did not have a match, so most of the players were sent back to their units, but somehow or other the three of us managed to stay on at the Transit Camp. We must have had a bit of influence somewhere!

However, it was not for us to be idle, as we were seconded to the Regimental Police, of all people. So here we were, all police sergeants! It just shows how easy it was.

Our main duties were to hang around the Guardroom and take turns on traffic duty on the main gate. The most important facet of this job was to give the CO a particularly smart salute whenever he left or entered the barracks. 'Do that and you will be all right', the RSM (Regimental Sergeant-Major) told us.

One day we came close to performing a proper policeman's job, but good sense prevailed. To our horror, we had a phone call to say that there was a riot at the 'cafe down the street'. This was a place we knew we must beware of, as it was quite normal to have a glass shoved in your face.

This occasion was a definite 'no, no'. The information was that the Argyle and Sutherland Highlanders were involved in a drunken brawl. Eric, Ed, and I discussed the matter and, having taken everything into consideration, such as that we were cowards, and that we did not want our lives shortened, we elected to leave them to their fates.

One of the perks of being on the staff of the Transit Camp was that if we felt like a trip to Berlin, all we had to do was volunteer to act as guard commanders on the train to the old capital city. The difference between being part of the train guard, and being a normal passenger, as far as we were concerned, was that passengers were about twelve to a compartment, whilst the two sergeants of the guard had a compartment to themselves.

Eddie Baily and I went a couple of times. Our main objectives were to buy presents for Leni and Elsie, or 'Else' as Ed called his fiancée. Actually, 'buy' could sometimes mean 'trade', which sounds better than admitting to operating on the black market. We were able to spend our 'Occupation Marks', which were forty to a pound sterling at the NAAFI shop, and there was quite a variety of goods on display.

The Black Market currency was cigarettes, and as we did not smoke, but we had an allocation of fifty a week, we could soon save a large number. Another advantage of being on the train guard, was that being on the staff of the train, we did not have to queue to get onto the station platform on the return journey. Now this was very important because the Military Police on duty at the station were there to try to prevent soldiers taking part in the black market, and they used to examine kits and suitcases. Looking back, I do not really know why they bothered, as barter or exchange of goods has been a method of trading for thousands of years.

On one of our trips, Eddie was extremely embarrassed. We were issued with a rifle and a bandolier of ammunition, being train guards. We had to hand them in at Hannover on our return. Well this time he lost his weapon! Now this must be the worst military crime a soldier can commit, but being a footballer and a Regimental Police Sergeant, somehow or other it was smoothed over!

We saw a remarkable act in the theatre one night. It was really amazing. A gymnast balanced himself by standing on his hands. Then he took one hand away, thus he was standing on one hand. And then, unbelievably he took away the thumb and little finger, leaving the three middle fingers to balance on. Then he took away the two outside fingers of the three, thus balancing on one finger. People were saying that he probably had a splint on it to strengthen it, but irrespective it was the greatest feat of balancing I had ever seen.

However, apart from such rather rare trips to the theatre and the Opera, and our most enjoyable football encounters, there was really very little to do. When Derrick Williams was with us, he used to drag me out every day for a walk after lunch, but if it had not been for our football, time would have gone very slowly. There was also a rather unexpected situation that would have been deemed impossible a year or two earlier. I enjoyed a quite close friendship with Heinz Alter, an ex-German U-Boat officer, and we corresponded for many years after the war. Just another example of the stupidity of war, as given the opportunity, we could all have been friends instead of enemies.

On the Wednesday evening in the third week of April 1947, I played my last game for the Combined Services and somewhat appropriately, it was in Brussels, the scene of the British Liberation Army's greatest triumph. We played Belgium, known as 'les Diables Rouges' (the Red Devils), because of the colours they wore, at the Heysel Stadium, where I was to play again in later years, and where in the eighties a terrible tragedy occurred when many people were killed during the Liverpool versus Juventus match.

We played very well, but sadly for me as captain, and as it was my finale, we lost 2–0. One of their goals was most unfortunate. The game was played under floodlights, which lit the field of play but not the stands or the terraces. Consequently, it was pitch black behind the goal, where there were a number of Press photographers taking flash pictures. Every time they flashed, we were temporarily blinded and we complained without effect. Then a Belgian player had a shot at goal and Jimmy Cowan was about to move towards the ball, when flash went the camera and Jim lost sight of it.

It was a vital goal because at 1–0 we were confident that we could still win, but at 2–0 the Belgians played much better, and with more confidence.

So that was that, and I returned to Hannover to pick up my release papers, my gear and a Telefunken radiogram which I had bought in Berlin for fifty cigarettes, and after emotional goodbyes, for Eric, Eddie, and I had been together for much of two years, I was on my way. I travelled with the orderly room sergeant who was also 49 group, and who I have to admit put himself and me at the top of the 49 group release list! We fastened rope around the radiogram, with a handle on either side, and we carried it between us. I remember climbing up the narrow gangplank at Cuxhaven. It was a bit of a struggle for two, but we made it.

We travelled overnight and got to Hull in the early morning, to have really rough treatment from the Customs and Excise. I had boxes and a big case etc, and the first officer took it all apart. I had told him the things I had to declare, all presents for Leni, and he charged me ten pounds, which was a lot of money as I only got fifty pounds 'demob' pay for five years' service. I had the receipt in my hand, and after laboriously repacking everything, which took a long time, I struggled on. A few yards further another officer said, 'Sergeant, come over here.' So I showed him the receipt and told him my kit had all been taken apart. To my amazement he said, 'I don't care, open it up again.' And we went through the same procedure, to be told finally, 'You can go now.' I thought it was very bad.

However, nothing was going to spoil this day of all days. I got the train to York where the barracks served as a demob centre. To our surprise and disappointment we had to sleep there overnight. We handed in such as our belts and other 'webbing' and we kept all of the clothing. We then got our demob clothing, a grey or brown suit, I chose brown because whenever there were ex-soldiers in the British teams who played us in Germany, they always wore grey pinstripes; a raincoat, a trilby hat and maybe a pair of shoes from their demobilisation.

I sent Leni a telegram and her dad travelled to York Station to meet me, and to help me with the radiogram and the rest of my gear. It was great to see him, and to be going home with him, as for the previous four or five leaves he had accompanied me to the station, always with the soothing message that the time would soon pass, and I would be home again. As an old soldier who was also stationed in Germany, where he met Leni's mam, he knew how it felt to be saying goodbye to the one you love, for several months.

But this time there was no going back, and when we got to Thornaby Station, Leni was waiting to start our civilian lives together, full of hope and optimism. She looked beautiful wearing a light coat, which I had sent her from Berlin, and the red shoes from Basel! She was also a little less trim, as she was nearly four months' pregnant.

CHAPTER SEVENTEEN
I BECOME A CIVILIAN

We caught the bus to Leni's home, where she had prepared a sitting room for us, as every young married couple lived in 'rooms' (in one of their parents' homes) in those days. It was like heaven to sit in our little home and just feel wonderful that there were to be no more tearful partings, that at last we could get on with our lives.

I got the princely sum of fifty pounds on demobilisation, but it was still by far the largest sum of money I had ever possessed. I had always had a secret desire to own a brand new bike after the troubles I had had with my five bob Royal Enfield, so Leni and I went shopping one day and bought a new Rudge Whitworth. I could hardly believe it! It was to serve me well, and it became well known, even worthy of newspaper comment in later years. Of course, if I were playing today it would be a Jaguar, but who cares?

Normally the football season used to finish at the end of April, with the FA Cup Final on the first Saturday in May, but season 1946–47 was extended several weeks because of the hard winter, when lots of matches were cancelled due to heavy snowfalls.

Because of this, Middlesbrough still had several First Division matches to play when I got home. The club knew when I was arriving and I had said that I wanted to play on the first Saturday, as I was obviously very fit.

I went to the ground on the Friday morning to train and to sign forms, only to be told that I was to play for the reserves at Blackhall Colliery Welfare. Brussels, on Wednesday, and a pit team on Saturday. What a comedown. The biggest mistake in my life was made when I signed for my favourite club.

The manager, who had signed me as an amateur in 1941, had died. He thought the world of me. His successor, David Jack, although he had been a great player, was hopeless as a manager as far as I was concerned. Although there were six more games to play, the season was nearly over, and the team could not win the championship, or be relegated, I did not get a game in the first team. I was a centre half and had played against many First Division teams and several international teams with great success, yet despite Middlesbrough having tried six different players at centre half that season, they still did not give me a chance.

During the ensuing summer they actually paid £16,000, an enormous fee at that time, for a centre half from a Third Division team. I could have cried when I read it in the newspaper.

Back to my first full day at home. I did not have any advice, or anybody at all to talk to, and I was not the most forceful type of person, rather one who hoped that others would do the right thing by me. I had to sign a contract and I wish that I hadn't, because it tied me up hand and foot. The maximum wage was eight pounds a week in the season and six in the summer. This I expected to get, as I knew that Everton and West Ham United had offered me such terms, and in the case of the former, they were going to let me rent a club house. I know that I was good enough, but Herbert Glasper, the secretary, offered me six in the season and four in the summer, and I had no option but to sign. You see, I had signed a contract whilst on leave a year previously and – even though they had never paid me a penny, and I knew Eric and Eddie (from the Combined Services IX) were having two pounds a week paid into a bank – I had to accept. The secretary said that Wilf Mannion (a star player) got eight pounds, so he could not pay me the same. What a fool I had been to sign when I was still in the army, just to be able to say that I was a professional. I did not even get the ten pounds signing-on fee until a year or two later, after much argument.

That first day I was very shy and nervous, as I did not know one player. They had either been signed since Jack became manager, or they had been away in the Forces when I played during the war. Naive me. At first I wore my 'demob' suit and my grey army socks and army underpants, and when I was in the bath after training, Wilf Mannion (who was one of the game's greatest players and also a wit), pretending to be a quartermaster sergeant in the army, held up my socks and pants and shouted to me, 'Bring them to me this afternoon and I'll change them for you!'

How embarrassing. You see, having been back playing for a year or two, they had all been able to afford proper socks, and such as 'Daks' slacks and fashionable underwear.

I could have gone back to my job at Head Wrightson & Co Ltd and I could have gone to university under the army scheme, but the thought of playing football for a living, after five years in khaki, was very appealing, especially after my tremendous experience of playing the game at its highest level in Europe.

I played several reserve matches, which I found to be rough, but very easy, and then I 'nearly' played in the first team at Huddersfield. It was rumoured that I would play, but in the end they played Jim McCabe, with whom I had played against Liverpool in Hannover. He was a wing half. I was a centre half, but David Jack was just not interested in me. However, I was 'twelfth man' and so I had my first trip with the first team.

I had to catch the train on the Saturday morning at Thornaby, whereas the rest of the party had already got on at Middlesbrough. I had to take my football boots just in case someone was sick and I had to play. Unsophisticated as I was, I got a paper carrier bag off Leni and put the boots in. As the train arrived, there I was in my 'demob' suit, 'demob' raincoat, and with my carrier bag in my hand. I soon saw the carriage where the team were, as Wilf, Mickey Fenton, and others were killing themselves with laughter at me and my carrier bag, as they looked through the window. They, of course, had swish leather bags.

Being the last match we had not to report for training again until early July, so it meant about six weeks holiday for Leni and me. Unfortunately, she suffered a lot from sickness due to the pregnancy, and she seemed to eat mainly fish, and that mostly halibut.

It was a beautiful summer, which we made the most of, and then it was back to football. As I expected, there was no place for me in the first team. The only satisfaction I had was that the three senior players, Mick Fenton, Wilf Mannion, and George Hardwick, all England Internationals, told me on a number of occasions that they thought that I was a much better player than the one who was playing at centre half. I also thought that I was a much better right back than the first team No 2, but my opinion counted for nothing.

It is never very pleasant thinking of my chequered career with my home club; I was very badly treated in every way. For example, they would buy players from other clubs and get them nice houses, which they rented, but for over two years we had to live in 'rooms' in our parents' homes. On the playing side, I was used as a mug. If someone was injured, I played left back, right back, centre half, and inside left; but however well I played, I was kicked out as soon as the player was fit again.

One highlight was a trip to Southern Ireland. I had played the last two or three games of the season at left back, as George Hardwick was unfit, and as he was still unavailable, to my surprise I went on the tour.

There was always a sting in the tail though, because for the first match of the following season, the right back was unfit, and I was the obvious choice to replace him, but to everyone's amazement, manager Jack chose a half back instead. I went to see him. He was always a bit bleary-eyed, and was known to be a drinker, and this particular time he was unable to command his thoughts.

He said he did not pick me, 'because you were not playing well at the time'. It was the first match of the season!

I had lost five of what should have been valuable seasons, whilst in the army, then I wasted almost another three seasons at Ayresome Park (the home of Middlesbrough FC). I was not demanding enough, and I just expected that my ability would do the talking, but it didn't. I knew that Sunderland wanted to buy me as I was told by one of the staff that Bill Murray, their manager, had been to see Jack on a number of occasions. Blackburn Rovers, a top First Division team then, sent one of their players to see me one Sunday, when we were living at Mam and Dad's, to ask if I would like to play for them. My Aunt Jessie and her son, my boyhood pal and cousin Frankie, also lived there, and I said 'yes' straight away, but when they asked Jack how much he wanted for me, he said that I was not for sale. This happened with Burnley too, who again were a top team at the time. Our vice chairman introduced me to their chairman after a reserve game I played in, and they said that a deal had been agreed if I also agreed. I was told to see Jack on the Monday. He bluntly told me that I could not go.

How many other teams wanted me I do not know, as mostly these things were kept secret, because the buying club would not want their own players to know that they were looking for a replacement. Once they had made the purchase, of course, it was different.

The most disappointing of these situations, of other clubs wanting to buy me, only came to my knowledge a few seasons later. I was with West Bromwich Albion by then, and we played Tottenham Hotspur at White Hart Lane, London. After the game, I was sitting in the dressing room when their manager, Arthur Rowe, came in and sat next to me. He congratulated me on how well I had played, and told me that he had tried to buy me, to play right back, for two years. First Eddie Baily – who by this time was playing regularly for England – had told him what a good player I was, and then he had watched me play. Jack had refused to sell me and had actually said that if I was good enough for Tottenham, I was good enough to stay at Middlesbrough!

So Arthur Rowe bought Alf Ramsey from Southampton, and Spurs went on to be the best team in England, and maybe in the world, whilst Ramsey played for England for years. I always played better than he did whenever we played against Spurs, and I always thought that all of the honours that came to Alf Ramsey would have come to me, if it had not been for David Jack.

So why did he eventually let me go to West Bromwich? Perhaps because he was sick of hearing me knocking at his door asking for a transfer, and certainly it was something to do with the club's assistant secretary, John Fairweather. John was friendly with Alan Everiss, West Brom's assistant secretary, and he thought a lot of me as a player. Somehow or other, when Alan told him Albion were keen to buy me, John was able to persuade Mr Jack and the board to sell me. One morning the coach, George Camsell, knocked at our door and said Jack wanted to see me. I went straightaway and he told me that he had agreed terms with Albion. As I knew that Sunderland wanted me, I said that I did not want to go to the Midlands, and that I wanted to stay in my native North-East. It was well known that Sunderland looked after their players better than any other club, and I knew nothing about West Brom. Jack just had to be horrible to me, even at the end, saying that if I did not go to West Bromwich Albion, I would finish up at Middlesbrough in the fourth team. He really was a swine to me. Perhaps it was also that I was always very polite to him. I always called him 'Mr Jack', when other players called him 'David' or 'boss', and maybe a psychologist could make something of that.

Of course, the greatest event that happened during my years with Middlesbrough was the birth of Margarete. She was born at home in Thornaby and I was so delighted. I loved little girls, and from day one I adored our little daughter. I was never happier than when taking her out in the pram or when, cradled in my arms, I used to take her on the bus on a Sunday morning to Mam's, much to their mutual delight. Leni had endured a rough time whilst carrying our baby, but it was all worth it.

The football side of life was frustrating, but I made up for it, at least financially, by working for Les Pinkney in his office in Middlesbrough, as a clerk. I used to train in the mornings and work in the office in the afternoons.

After living in 'rooms' for over two years, Middlesbrough let us rent one of their houses, albeit the worst one, the only one in a terrace without a garden. However, it was great to be on our own and use the furniture that we had bought, and had stored in various friends' houses. Also, it was near the ground, and I did not have to travel, merely walking about two hundred yards.

I can hardly believe the memory of how we moved our furniture from friends' houses to our new abode. Johnny French and I pushed a handcart for about six miles through many main streets! How ridiculous it sounds today, when players not even as good as we were, earn thousands of pounds per week. And we pushed a handcart to save paying for a removal van!

One thing I appreciated at the 'Boro', as the club is known, was the lunch we used to have after training. It was at a small private hotel. Food was still rationed and a three-course meal was very nice.

How different things are today. Players earn fortunes and I suppose a 'perk' is a BMW or a Mercedes Benz car. In those early postwar years, when a player's maximum wage was the same as pre-war, but when prices had doubled and income tax was astronomical (to pay for the war), a perk, believe it or not, was a quarter of a pound of butter. After lunch at the hotel, Laurie the owner used to hang about by the door and, as we left, he used to surreptitiously slip a packet of butter into the eager hands of the club's top players: Mick, Wilf, and George. And would you believe it, the rest of us used to envy them!

I must say, though, that the lads at the Boro' were a great bunch, and I would have much preferred to have been a regular first team player there, than at West Bromwich Albion.

CHAPTER EIGHTEEN
WEST BROMWICH ALBION

Leni and I realised that we had no option but to go to West Bromwich Albion (WBA), even though it meant leaving our parents, and therefore Margaret's grandparents, behind. I tried to get David Jack to make a definite promise about how much 'benefit' money I would get. I had been with them over eight years and they could have given me the full amount of 750 pounds, especially as they got me for nothing and they were getting ten or twelve thousand pounds for me. The amount is in doubt because both figures were quoted in different newspapers.

I went down to Birmingham on my own and I was picked up by Harry Ashley, one of the WBA staff, and taken to the Arden Hotel in New Street. The next day I went to the Albion's ground, 'The Hawthorns', which is in West Bromwich (but just over the boundary from Birmingham), to meet the manager, Jack Smith. He offered me the maximum wage for winter and summer whether I played in the first team or not, promised us a nice house to rent at a low rental, and said that I would soon be a regular First Division player.

He also told me that I would be fitted out with a club blazer and trousers. It shows how naive I was, because this really was fantastic to me, whose expectations had been dulled by Jack. And then he showed me 'the travelling bag'. The previous Christmas – it was now February – all senior players had received a large bag, plastic by the way, as a present. I plucked up courage and asked him if I would get one. He said no, because they had a lot made together thus lowering the cost, and it would be too expensive to have one individually made up. So I stuck my heels in. I would sign if I got a bag! Not a million dollars over five years, as I would get if I was playing now, but a plastic bag, oh, with my initials on by the way! Mr Jack Smith went next door to see club secretary Mr Ephraim Smith (no relation), as the latter controlled the cash. The manager was bubbling over with joy when he came back. Yes, I could have a bag, with my initials on. So I signed!

It was not long before I found that it had been remarkably generous of 'Eph' to let me have a bag, as he was so mean. I was to play a few games in the reserves, to settle down, whilst still training at Middlesbrough, and I had to ring every

Thursday to find out where I was playing. After only a couple of weeks, I rang and Jack Smith said that we should all come down to Birmingham and live in the Arden Hotel until a house was ready to move into.

We were happy to agree, as in those rather grey days of high income tax and food still being tightly rationed, the thought of 'living it up' in a hotel in the main street of Birmingham, seemed almost like heaven.

After saying all of our goodbyes, Leni and I, along with two-year-old Margarete, caught the train for 'Brum'. We thoroughly enjoyed the Arden. In the evenings, one of the chambermaids kept a watchful eye on our daughter, whilst Leni and I wandered around the streets window shopping, or even playing snooker in the hotel. Leni had never played before and she thoroughly enjoyed it, playing quite late at times. After about three weeks in the hotel, I was starting to feel despondent, as I still was not in the first team. I was doing what was required, I was training with the players, a supposed pre-requisite for first team selection, but I was still playing in what was known as the Central League.

Then something happened to make me wonder if I had walked under a ladder or broken a mirror. I was training on the pitch when the secretary came out on the terrace and shouted for me. He said that he had just received a bill for the first two weeks in the hotel and he asked how I was going to pay for it, all at once or would I like so much to be taken weekly out of my wages? What a joke! Of course, I said that the club had insisted on me staying there, and that I had no intention of paying anything. Then I saw the manager who said that they would pay it, and they did, but it did nothing for my morale.

One evening whilst at the hotel, Leni suggested that we should go to the Odeon Cinema next door, so we joined the queue, which those days, always seemed to precede a visit to the pictures. There were four young men standing and talking together immediately in front of us. Leni asked me what language they were speaking, as she could not understand them. I told her it was the Birmingham dialect! I had experienced all accents in the army, but 'Brummy' talk was foreign to her.

After I had been out of the army for a year or so, I made a big decision. I would buy a suit. I went to Burtons in Middlesbrough and chose a grey tweed one with thin blue stripes. I thought it was terrific until it rained! I got wet and the lapels curled up! Leni had to keep ironing it. When we knew I was going to Birmingham, we made a momentous decision. I had to look smart, for I was Albion's big new purchase, so I had my suit dyed navy blue! Oh dear, how naive we were.

We were lucky to find a house that we liked, almost immediately. We only looked at two, to fall in love with 54 Camp Lane, Handsworth, and it turned out to be the perfect choice. However, when I relate that it was opposite a cemetery, it suggests that our choosing was awry, but the fact was that all we could see was a magnificent, high holly hedgerow, which was always beautiful, and in the winter was red with berries.

Our lane was in fact the last row of houses in Birmingham and Warwickshire, and for several miles from the bottom of the lane there was lovely countryside, including Dartmouth Golf Club.

We inherited lots of very nice neighbours and soon we had many friends. Margarete was still in a pushchair and twins Pat and Pam Smart, about seven or eight at the time, used to take her for walks. Unlike today, this was perfectly safe and on Sundays they used to take her with their older sister Anne to the Methodist Church Sunday School. They used to all love the 'anniversaries', when they would sing children's hymns and all the parents used to go. They would practise in our house and that way Leni and I used to learn all the hymns too. I still know them. Favourites were 'We love our Sunday school', 'Remember the lilies of the fields, how they grow', and 'Now Lazarus was a very little man'. Oh happy days!

Leni went to her Catholic Church, where the Catholic priest, Father Canning, was an Albion supporter. He had bought a season ticket but his assistant, Father Brady, could not afford one, although he was just as keen, and so I always gave him one of my two complimentary tickets, Leni having the other one.

Father Canning made us laugh one day. We were talking about weddings at his church. Almost all were on Saturdays and I asked how he managed to see all of our matches. He said that he married them at any time on the Saturdays when we played away, but when we were at home, he would only hold weddings until 11.00 am, after which he said that he was otherwise engaged.

When the young Father Brady went back to Ireland, Father Canning called around our house to say that now that his assistant had gone, he, Father Canning, would be able to use the complimentary ticket and it would save him buying one!

One day during our first Birmingham summer, we were walking down New Street when we bumped into Alan Townsend, Warwickshire County Cricket Club's star all rounder. Alan worked at Head Wrightson when I did, as I have mentioned earlier. It was a happy occasion and it was the beginning of a lifelong friendship. I used to see him often at Edgbaston, the Warwickshire Cricket Club headquarters, and he introduced me to the other players, to the secretary, Les Deakins, and to various of his friends. He, Hilda his wife, and their daughter were living in Edgbaston, in what had been the live-in servants' side of a lovely mansion. It was owned by John and Margot Madden, who lived in the main part of the house with their two boys, Russell and John.

Alan invited us to their home and thus we meet John and Margot, who were to become dear friends also. Incidentally, their address was 52 Farquhar Road, Edgbaston, and Lady Chamberlain, widow of Neville Chamberlain, Britain's Prime Minister who announced the declaration of war in 1939, lived next door at 54.

We had many happy times at 52, and later when Alan and Hilda bought their own house, my mum and dad moved in and took over their place.

Dad used to tend to the garden of the house opposite, and the extra income was a good help in their retirement. John and Margot were very good to them. Living there, Dad was able to come to our matches at West Bromwich, and sometimes he was allowed to travel with us when we journeyed by coach.

We had many good times at Farquhar Road. John used to invite visiting county cricket teams to his home, and I remember Somerset playing Warwickshire at the time of the Queen's Coronation. We stayed at John's for a couple of nights and on one of them, almost the whole of the West Country team came to the house. Of course, cricketers were well known for their affinity to beer, and after a day's play, they used to imbibe freely of the amber fluid. This particular evening was no exception, and they went on until the early hours. I remember Harold Stephenson, the same one who was responsible for my split eyebrow when playing cricket as a boy, had 'had a few' to the extent that he was slurred of speech. The following day he actually kept wicket all day, bobbing up and down, concentrating on every ball bowled. How he did it on 'the day after the night before', I do not know. Incidentally, one of his opponents in this game was Dick Spooner, the Warwickshire wicketkeeper-batsman and fellow cricketer/footballer of my Norton-on-Tees days.

One weekend when staying there, the gardener told Margot not to forget to close the windows in the greenhouse at 4.30. Of course, he meant 4.30 pm. The party went on and on and Margot asked me the time. I looked at my watch and said, 'half past four'. 'Oh!' she said, 'that's the time we have to close the windows.' We went down the garden and did as the gardener requested, and it was 4.30 – am!

On the day of the coronation, we all went to John and Russell's school playing field to take part in various sports and festivities. It was a cold blustery day with rain squalls, but we had a good time.

Most footballers were very keen on cricket, and vice versa, cricketers loved football. Indeed, I found that many cricketers would rather have succeeded at football than cricket. Alan Townsend was certainly in this category, and he used to train with us when he could, as did Bert Wolton and others.

One of Warwickshire's all time greats was ace slow bowler Eric Hollies, who was also a native of the Black Country, and a red-hot WBA fan. I remember at the end of one football season, and thus the start of the cricket, when I was talking to Alan. I used to let him have complimentary tickets for games, and one Friday night he told me that he would not be able to make it to our match on the Saturday. Every year they used to play the Midland Cricket Conference in a two-day game, Friday and Saturday, and on the Friday night the position of play meant that there was no chance of them being able to finish in time to get to the Hawthorns for 3.00 pm.

So it was quite a shock when I got to the ground to find Alan and Eric waiting for me. I asked what had happened and Alan said that it was Eric, that he had bowled all of the opposition out in quick time.

That incident reminds me too of another meeting with Alan at the Players' Entrance. To give myself accounting and general business experience, I had got a job with Facchinos' Biscuits and Meddocream Ice Cream. I worked weekday afternoons at their offices and on a few occasions, such as stocktaking, I worked on Saturday mornings.

It was the beginning of season 1950–51 and one of our first games was against Middlesbrough, my old team, at the Hawthorns, West Bromwich, kick off 6.15 pm. – we did not have floodlights at that time. I went to the office in the morning and got back home at 1.30 pm, had some lunch and went to bed, asking Leni to wake me at 4.45 pm, to give me sufficient time to get ready, and to walk up to the ground.

Leni woke me and I started to get ready. I checked the time and was shocked to find that it was 5.45 pm. I was not ready. I had to walk to the ground as my bike was out of commission, and we kicked off at 6.15 pm. I said to Leni, 'I asked you to wake me at 4.45 pm.' She said, 'Yes, I know, but you looked so sound asleep I didn't think I should disturb you!' I do not recall my reply. I had a quick shave with my electric razor, and ran all of the way to the ground, the last few hundred yards, pushing through the hordes of spectators.

The previous evening I had been to Birmingham, to the hotel where Middlesbrough were staying, to have a chat with my old team mates, and also to ask some of them to give me their two free tickets, which all visiting players were given.

I had promised a number of Warwickshire cricketers tickets, and when I sprinted to the Players' Entrance, they were all waiting for me. I was in a real panic. I dashed up the passage which divided the home and visitors' dressing rooms, and turned right into the Boro's room. Jimmy Gordon was captain that night, and as I burst into their room, he was bouncing a ball and giving final instructions to the team, who were all dressed, on their feet, and ready to take the field.

They all asked if I was playing, I gasped, 'Yes', grabbed the tickets, ran down the passage, opened the door, shoved them into Alan Townsend's hands and ran back to the West Brom' dressing room. I opened the door and ran in to find the players all ready, including the twelfth man, who was to play in my place!

The manager told me what he thought of me, but he knew I could get ready in two minutes, which I did, and there I was trotting out just a few seconds after the rest of the team.

I could not expect a happy ending, and there was not one. We lost 3–2, Alec McRae scored the winner, and to lose to your old team was just the worst thing that could happen to any player. As I walked home with Leni and Margarete, who had turned up late, I had never felt quite as miserable.

The summer of 1951 was unusual because we actually played two matches out of season. This normally was forbidden, but the occasion that caused the relaxation of the rules was the Festival of Britain. There were many celebrations going on around the country, not the least being the opening of the Festival Hall in London. It was to be the venue for an important meeting for me, many years later, but in 1951 it was built primarily for the playing of music.

We played a team from Vienna, 'Sportklub Wacker', and one from Valetta in Malta, 'Floriana FC'. We lost 4-3 to "Wacker" but beat Floriang 2-0. There were matches being played all over the British Isles against teams from all over the world.

Our part of the celebrations ended with our club giving a dinner at the Grand Hotel, Birmingham, for us and our guests. It was a most enjoyable conclusion to the festivities.

However, whilst the details of the games and of the dinner have passed from my memory, one occurrence never will. As right back I had played against the Floriana outside left. As the game ended, we shook hands and walked off the field together. He told me that he had a sister in England and on this, his first visit to England, he was going to go and see her.

I asked him where she lived and I was astounded when he said Norton-on-Tees! You see, I knew only one Maltese and she lived in the same street we used to live in. Norton was 190 miles away. I asked her name and it was she! What an amazing coincidence, but I had several more to come in my life, and some even more amazing.

I always enjoyed my journeys to the North-East to Middlesbrough, Sunderland, and Newcastle United, three great teams in those earlier post-war years. One reason was that my friends from home could come to the games, and being the only 'Geordie' in the Albion's team, I was always given lots of complimentary tickets by my team mates. Another, was that the club kindly allowed me to take Margarete and Leni with me, and I would drop them off on Stockton station where Dad would be waiting. This was prior to their move to live in Birmingham. Then I would be allowed to stay over until the Wednesday, if it was a Saturday game, and I would train with my old pals at Middlesbrough.

It also gave me great pleasure to play well up there, to emphasize to my old club that they had made a bad mistake in not making the most of me when I was there. We had a great success record too, with lots of terrific victories, including beating Newcastle at St James' Park 4-1, 5-3, and 7-3, in successive years, when they were one of the great 'glamour' clubs of that era.

But earlier in this book I mentioned a surprise event connected with us playing at St James' Park. It was a Wednesday evening game and we stayed at the Rex Hotel at Whitley Bay on the night before. In the morning, we went to see a cricket match at Jesmond, as it was early September. It was between Northumberland and Yorkshire, and not far away at Ashbrook, Sunderland, there was to be a game between the Canadian Cricket Touring Team and County Durham.

That was the scenario as we entered the Jesmond cricket pavilion. Immediately it was obvious that we were not the only sports team in attendance, as it was not difficult to recognise the group of athletic, suntanned, and blazer-clad men already seated, as a cricket team. In fact, they were the Canadians whose game had been abandoned due to overnight rain.

Shortly after sitting down I felt a tap on the shoulder and heard a transatlantic voice saying, 'Hello, I was hoping that I might meet you, as I know your brother in Canada.' Not having a brother in Canada, I said that I was sorry, but that he had got hold of the wrong person, to which he responded, 'No, surely you are Stan Rickaby aren't you?' 'Yes,' I said, 'but I do not have a brother in Canada.'

The Canadian cricketer was shocked and said that surely I had a brother George. Of course I had, I told him, but I did not know he was in Canada.

It transpired that brother George – whom I had not seen since 1942, and our parents had not seen since he returned from the Far East in 1945, and went straight off to Durham University – was living in Niagara Falls and was general manager of North American Cyanamide's plant there.

Apparently they met every Sunday lunchtime at the local cricket club, and the surprising thing was that George would read the Sunday newspaper and show people any reference there may have been to me. And yet, at that time, he had not contacted Mam and Dad for about seven years.

His friend was amazed at all of this. He gave me the company's address and later I wrote to my brother, asking him to at least send our parents a Christmas card, but the Company Secretary wrote to say that George was no longer employed there. This I found impossible to believe, but that was the end of the trail.

Being a parent myself, I realise the sadness Mum and Dad must have felt about George opting out of a happy family. They had so many reasons to be proud of him. He was said by Mr Coward, our English master, to be the best scholar in both English grammar and literature that the school had produced. He became a major at the tender age of twenty-one, and he served his country well in the Burma campaign, where he was wounded. He did not let them know, so that they did not worry; he arranged for food parcels to be sent to them; he gave them a good allowance from his officer's pay; and came 'home' to them on his demobilisation.

This was some of the good side of George. There was always another side to him as he could be quite cruel to me as boys, when he was always much stronger than me. Similarly, he was cruel to Dad and Leni. Dad said to him that he could get me special leave, because anyone who had been in the Far East could apply to their brother's commanding officer for two weeks' leave. George had replied that if he were my CO, he would not give me leave, as they got too much leave in Germany as it was. Dad's hurt reply was that fortunately he was not my CO.

The final reason for Mam and Dad to be proud of their eldest son was kept from them, and that was being General Manager of North American Cyanamide's plant at Niagara Falls.

They died not hearing a word from him and not knowing if he was alive or dead. We were brothers, and yet we were so different. I loved sport and he didn't, and Mam and Dad were an integral part of my life always. Even though we had to live away from them sometimes, they were always in our thoughts and as in Poole and Birmingham, we got them to live near us.

Now a little detail about our progress as a football team in 1951–52. I thoroughly enjoyed playing as we had got together a classy eleven which was improving rapidly, and being sixteenth in the First Division one season, thirteenth the next, followed by fourth and then second, is concrete evidence. The Albion at that time could be said to have had one of the best FA Cup records of all the clubs, having played in several Cup Finals and in more semi-finals than any other club. In season 1951–52, it seemed as though we were going to add to those laurels. First Division clubs start their Cup quest in the third round of the competition, and we were drawn against Bolton Wanderers, a tough prospect as Bolton had four English Internationals in their team, including Nat Lofthouse, their prolific goal scoring centre forward. We beat them 4-0, an emphatic victory, and next we played Gateshead, a Third Division North team.

Although we were expected to win against such a team, it was always a risk because some of our players were unhappy against less cultured opposition. We won 2–0 and there were three items of note, which I remember from this game. It was played at St James' Park, Newcastle United's ground, as being a Tyneside club it was obvious that supporters of both Newcastle and Gateshead would want to see the game and Gateshead could not house them. I recall three points: It was played on the day King George VI died, we wore black armbands, and the third memory was of Norman Fowler. Do you remember how he was my hero when I was a little boy at Oxbridge Lane School and he played for England Boys and then Middlesbrough? Well for the first time we played against one another in a professional game, he was Gateshead's left back and I was WBA's right back! It was quite nostalgic.

Things were going well and we were not unhappy when we were told that Blackburn Rovers were to be our Fifth Round opponents at Ewood Park. Incidentally, my cousin and pal of childhood days, Frankie, lived in Ewood and of course came to the game. Win this and the next round and we would be in yet another semi-final. Then the blow fell. We had a flu epidemic! Most of us were in bed for a few days, including me, but whereas I managed to recover before the weekend, five of our regular players were unable to play. This of course was catastrophic. Since then games have been postponed because of such happenings, but we had to make changes and Jimmy Nicholls made his debut..

However, the patchwork team did far better than could have been expected and with five minutes to go, and the score 0-0, Len Millard our left back handled the ball; Bill Eckersley scored from the penalty and we were down 1-0. We pressed hard for an equaliser, I hit the post but the ball bounced out, and that was that. Ironically, on the following Wednesday, when the game would have been replayed had we drawn, every player was fit and free of the flu bug. It was a bitter disappointment. Frankie did not know whether to be pleased or disappointed, being a Rovers supporter!

Maybe at this point the reader may be interested in our training methods and whether they have changed today, and if so, in what way. 'Things are not what they used to be,' and 'they are not as good as the old days,' and 'when I played, we ...' etc, etc, are oft heard sayings, so what do I think? Are players fitter today than they were in my day? We played with a leather ball, which got very heavy due to water absorption, whilst wet pitches do not affect the modern plastic covered ball. Therefore, it was much harder on our legs and our stamina. Yet I and others played many a season without missing a game, so we just had to be fit. Are players faster today? Possibly slightly, but only due to the lightweight boots to go with the much lighter ball. Some wingers I played against were very, very fast, and I believe our method of wing play contributed to a faster game. Do they train harder today than we did? Well, we certainly did not do all of this ridiculous weight training, and I cannot see why a soccer player needs large biceps. Maybe Rugby players do, maybe even goalkeepers, but our captain, Len Millard, who played twenty years for his club, had thin arms, a slim chest, but magnificent legs, and he played more than 600 first-team games.

One of the best teams of the 1970's/80's was undoubtedly Liverpool, and I know that their method of training – when my old friend, Bill Shankly, became manager – was to play six-a-side games, concentrating on developing the skills, the teamwork, and the muscles, which are needed on a Saturday. Not for them the complicated manoeuvres of the textbook coach. And that was how we trained – with a ball. At the beginning of the season, we trained morning and afternoons, Monday to Friday, but after the first three or four matches, when we became match fit, we only trained on Monday, Tuesday, Thursday, and Friday mornings.

We were one of the most attractive teams of the fifties, playing before huge crowds, with lots of goals scored, and sometimes conceded, but we never felt safe in a game until we were three goals ahead. Today, a team will often defend a one goal advantage by defensive tactics.

Comparisons are invidious, and I would rather be playing today for the incredible pay the players get, but for the enjoyment, the crowds and their behaviour, and the way we played, give me the forties and the fifties anytime.

Here is a brief account of season 1952–53, taken from 'West Bromwich Albion – The first hundred years' by G A Willmore, and first published by Robert Hale Limited.

'August 1952 and the parched football grounds of England were ablaze with sunshine, and Albion began in similar dazzling fashion, with a famous odd goal of seven win over Tottenham at White Hart Lane. Such high form, whilst not quite at the level required to lift a major trophy, was certainly sufficient to carry the team into the higher reaches of the First Division and, with a series of powerful displays, particularly away from home, by Christmas, the Albion were well placed in second position, one point behind the Wolves. By this time, good away performances had done their job, with wins at Cardiff, Manchester City, Chelsea, Portsmouth, Newcastle (5–3) and a freak game at Sheffield Wednesday, in which Albion sneaked home by the odd goal in nine, being credited with two own-goals by the luckless Wednesday defence. Yet the Christmas tussles with the Wednesday illustrated the factor which was still lacking from the team – consistency. Following this great win, in which, in all honesty, Sheffield were completely outplayed in every department despite the closeness of the result, Albion entertained the same team the following day and were beaten by the only goal, from Britain's newest scoring sensation, Derek Dooley, who was later so tragically to lose a leg after an innocuous on-field collision.

However, despite this, and two five-goal lapses at Burnley and Stoke, the Albion looked odds-on bets for a piece of silverware – until, that is, their season was destroyed by an unfortunate Cup-run. It began innocently enough, with an easy win at West Ham, but in the fourth round, it took four meetings and seven hours of stamina-sapping football on heavy spring pitches, to be eliminated, eventually, by Chelsea. A good 1-1 draw in London was followed by a goalless draw, after extra time, at the Hawthorns. The next replay merely prolonged the stalemate, with another 1-1 draw, Jimmy Dudley scoring a rare goal, at Villa Park. The tie was settled decisively to the tune of four goals to nil at Highbury, where, ironically, new manager Buckingham watched his team in action for the first time; there was even more irony in the fact that, after the cup elimination, Albion, for the first time that season, were standing proudly at the top of the league table :

		Won	Points
1	ALBION	16	35
2	Burnley	12	34
3	Wolves	13	34
4	Arsenal	13	33

However, four crucial defeats followed, at Liverpool, immediately after the Cup defeat, at Wolves (disastrous!), at Blackpool and finally, worst of all, at home, to the team in twenty-first position: yes, Chelsea again. Still, three points were taken from the Villa over Easter, and the club finished respectably in fourth position, after a season which had promised so much until that fateful Cup marathon in February.'

Despite the fact that, as far as playing football was concerned, the bigger the crowds the better and more motivated I felt, I still found it difficult to handle adulation close at hand. I avoided fans as much as I could, and sometimes it was to my cost. For example, I always turned down personal invitations to appear at functions. If the team was all there, then I would be too. For two or three years I had been asked to spend the whole summer coaching youngsters at Butlins' Holiday Camp at Skegness, but I had always refused, even though the wages were ten pounds a week for five hours coaching, a fortune in those days. It was just that I could not face the personal publicity. In 1953 I agreed to go for four weeks, but even then I had cold feet and asked team-mate Ronnie Allen to do the first two. However, I was committed and Leni, Margarete, and I, arrived on a Saturday in 1953 to be more than pleasantly surprised at what we found. Our chalet was very nice, and we proceeded to enjoy all aspects of life there, including the food, entertainment, and would you believe it, the coaching? Of course, then I wished that I had not turned it down in previous years, but it was too late – and as fate would have it, I was unable to go the following summer.

CHAPTER NINETEEN

WBA, THE BEST TEAM IN ENGLAND

After the huge improvement by the team in 1952–53, we approached the new season with great enthusiasm and optimism. Many sports journalists predicted us winning the First Division and others made us favourites for the FA Cup. Some even went as far as to say that we could be the first team since 1897 to win both, known as 'the double'. I was beginning the season with a total of 125 First Division games in succession, not having missed one since August 1950.

It was great to be one of the glamour teams and we were featured in many newspapers and magazines. Pre-season training was a joy and we could not wait to get started. Before the season we trained morning and afternoon, Monday to Friday, we played two public practice matches plus several private, and then we opened the season by beating Arsenal 2–0. We then went ten games before we lost, and in fact lost only one in the first fifteen. Once the season was under way and we were match fit, we only trained on four mornings, Wednesday being a day off, although during August and September we played every Wednesday evening.

We were top of the League for many weeks and as such we played before huge crowds home and away, to the extent that a million people had watched us by December, before the season was half over. Being on the top, every club wanted to knock us off, so every match was a big occasion.

Our success brought us to the attention of the England team selectors and I was the first Albion player for many years to be selected for the national side. I knew that I had been playing well and I had always considered myself better than Alf Ramsey, later Sir Alf, who held the England right back position for several seasons. We had played at Blackpool and were staying over for a couple of days, when my selection was announced. I was to play against Ireland at Everton's ground on 11 November 1953. We won 3-0 and I played as well as possible, considering that I had never appeared with any of the other players before, and our method of playing at West Bromwich Albion was so different, and so much better.

It was a thrilling occasion and, although I was a little nervous at first, as soon as I got involved I felt confident. The National Press all wrote well of me and said that I should make the position my own for a long time to come.

How wrong they all were. Shortly afterwards, England played Hungary at Wembley, when the Magyars were looked upon as world champions, and Ramsey was back in, because of experience it was said. Anyway, England lost 6–3 and Ramsey was baffled by two of the Magyar stars, Puskas and Czibor.

The next representative game was the Football League versus the Football League of Ireland, at Maine Road, Manchester, on 10th February 1954. Ramsey was dropped and I took his place, proving, in my opinion, that they had made an error in their team selection for that most important game versus Hungary. In addition, colleague Ray Barlow, who should also have played against the Magyars, as he was indisputably the best wing half in Britain, also played. Neither of us put a foot wrong and we won 9–1. The captain, Billy Wright, told me that he thought that I had made the right back position my own.

The season had continued successfully and at Christmas we were still on top of the League, with our next door neighbours, Wolverhampton Wanderers, second. In January 1954, our FA Cup campaign began. We had been knocked out of 'the Cup' the previous year by Chelsea after four games, the first three being drawn, and we looked upon them as our bogey team. Consequently, when we were drawn to play them again, we were quite worried.

There were over 35,000 spectators present on the afternoon of 9th January. We had Chelsea already beaten 5-2 in the League, and the atmosphere was tense as we ran out on a miserable, wet winter's afternoon.

The game went very much like our four cup games of 1952–53, with us attacking all of the time, but the ball would just not go into their goal, until with a few minutes remaining, I took the ball up the field and, when I got near to their penalty area, I unleashed a terrific shot with my right foot. The ball was flying into the top right corner of the goal when one of their players, Ron Greenwood, dived across to try to head the ball out. It just skimmed off his head and continued on its way to the net. I had scored. But for an unknown reason history shows it as an own goal, scored by Ron Greenwood. So often today on television, I have seen blatant own goals marked down for the player of the scoring team, who played the ball last. Ah well!

With Chelsea out of the way, we felt that we could not go wrong. Most Saturday nights we sat on the top of the First Division, with Wolves pipping us on the odd occasion, and we were happy to read in many newspaper articles that the Cup and League 'double' was on. In the fourth round of the Cup we easily accounted for Rotherham United (4–0), and in the next we played our favourite opponents, Newcastle United. This was the great Geordie cup-winning side of the early fifties; a team that played pure football and one with whom we enjoyed great camaraderie. Ron Allen scored three goals and we seemed to be home and dry at 3–1 in the second half, but when the great Jackie Milburn scored five minutes from the end to make it 3–2, we had to struggle to prevent them equalising.

The sixth round was against Tottenham Hotspur. We were undoubtedly the two most attractive teams of the day, so a classic was anticipated, and no one was disappointed. We won 3–0, which was a tremendous victory, but little did I know that it was the match which was to change my life. With about ten minutes to go, my direct opponent, George Robb, an excellent player and an English international, accidentally put his knee into my right thigh. I went down as though poleaxed and my thigh seemed to be paralysed. The trainer rubbed it and got some feeling back into it, and eventually I was able to continue.

By Monday, I could hardly walk and I had to have intensive treatment from Fred Pedley, our physiotherapist. I had missed only one First Division game since August 1950 against Cardiff City in November 1953, and this was April 1954. Fred was partly responsible for this fine run of League games, but this time I had to miss out again, sidelined for a game against Blackpool. By the time the semi-final came round, I was much improved. We were to play Port Vale at Villa Park, Birmingham, so on the Friday I was given a fitness test, and it was left to me to decide if I should play. Bearing in mind that the club chairman was never friendly towards me and that if I did not play, he would probably keep me out of the team which would play in the Cup Final, were we to win the semi-final. I decided to play, despite lingering doubts still in my mind about my complete fitness.

We won 2–1, though it was a hard game as 'the Vale' were tough, yet lacking in skill, and although I got through it, I limped off at the end. The legend is that I had a 'mystery' injury in the semi-final, but the truth is that it occurred in the sixth round. I went to see the specialist on the Monday to be told that I had myositis ossifican (a sliver of bone in the thigh muscle). It was very painful and took six months to clear up.

My disappointment, and that of Leni and our family, was intense. I had been hoping to be picked to play for England against Scotland in April, to play in the Cup Final, and then to play in the World Cup in Switzerland in the summer. I was included in the World Cup squad, but of course, all of my hopes were dashed. And all due to a knock in the thigh by one of football's gentlemen, schoolmaster George Robb.

So my season was over. Just as bad as that, was the dreadful results suffered by the team subsequent to my injury. I played in 33 First Division games that great season, and we only lost six. In the final seven games, when I did not play, they lost five, and so ended our quest for immortality! The double, which seemed so very attainable on the night of the semi-final, when we were top of the League and in the FA Cup Final, had gone forever. It was left to Tottenham Hotspur in the early sixties to accomplish this seemingly impossible feat, followed of course by Arsenal, then Liverpool and Manchester United.

It was strange that a Tottenham player was responsible for my injury, which kept me out of seven vital League matches, and deprived us of the 'double', and then it was the same club that did what we had so narrowly failed to do. However, I was pleased for my old pal, Eddie Baily, who was by then assistant manager of the Spurs.

On the Wednesday following the semi-final against Port Vale, we played Sunderland, away at Roker Park. This was an important game as we were still hoping to win the First Division. Tragically, Norman Heath, our goalkeeper, with whom I had played well over a hundred times, was badly injured. There were no substitutes in those days and we were reduced to ten men, Ray Barlow going in goal. We lost 2-1, dropped two vital points, but much worse, Norman's injuries were terribly serious.

He was paralysed from the neck downwards, and was lucky not to have been killed. He never played again and, although he recovered the use of much of his body, he could not write, wore callipers to keep one foot parallel with the ground (thus he limped badly), and he had to wear a thick collar to keep his head up. We were permanencies together for several seasons, and within four days we became casualties. The team was never to recover from the dual tragedy.

But worse was to follow, as Norman died at the age of 59 in 1983.

We were all allocated 64 tickets for the Final. We paid for them, and we were all besieged by friends, relatives, and acquaintances. Today, they seem to make money out of the tickets, but I actually lost, with two people not paying. Perhaps they forgot!

At last we came to the week of the FA Cup Final. For me it was an anti-climax. The season had seen so many hopes realised, so many impossible dreams become realities, but the most impossible of all for the team, the FA Cup and Football League double, had remained unachievable as it had for all other teams in the twentieth century.

And the ambition of every red-blooded footballer, that of climbing those steps at Wembley Stadium at the end of the Final, to receive a winner's medal, was still a possibility for the rest of my colleagues, but it had been denied me.

As we got on the bus, which was to take us to our hideaway in the country, I realised the full impact of what I had experienced. Until my injury, winning the League had been a foregone conclusion, I had played for England and the Football League, and the Cup Final was to be the thrilling and rewarding finale of a wonderful season, but I had to accept that fate had stepped in to deprive me of the ultimate accolade.

Crowds of our supporters had come to see us off, and with lots of good wishes from them all, we left the Hawthorns to travel to a lovely country hotel at Twyford, on the river Thames.

Of course, I also realised that, compared to Norman Heath who was still in hospital and facing a very uncertain future, I was fortunate. I was limping with pain in my right thigh, but there was hope of a good recovery. However, none of this could take away the actual physical ache which I felt in my stomach all of the time.

The hotel was old fashioned but very comfortable and, despite attempts at secrecy, every newspaper had at least one reporter waiting for us. Very quickly I realised that no one was interested in me. Although our reserves had not played in one cup-tie, it was they who were important, not me. Of course, this is how I knew it would be. It was the first cup-tie I had missed that season. What a one to miss!

The team trained every day and I was asked to stand and watch, to allow photographers to take a picture to illustrate a 'hard luck' story about me. The 'lads' did not train too hard, just enough to keep in trim for the last game of the season.

One day they went for a trip on the Thames, so I took the opportunity of being picked up and taken to High Wycombe to consider a business opportunity. Ernie Rixon was a keen football supporter, and also managing director of a firm called Firview Furniture and Sales Co Ltd. He had heard of my interest in furniture and, in particular, the gramophone record cabinet, which I had invented and which I was in the process of patenting.

We came to an agreement whereby I would sell their range of products, some of which they made at High Wycombe and others they handled for other manufacturers. Most exciting of all for me was that they would make and market my record cabinet.

On the Friday before the great day, we were taken to Wembley Stadium, to examine the pitch and generally familiarise ourselves with the environment. Photographers had a great day, and I appeared in two or three of their pictures. We were all dressed in our club blazers and slacks.

On the following day, the players slept late and had breakfast at about ten o'clock. The mood was one of optimism. Although they had gone through this bad patch, they seemed to have put it behind them.

The time came for us to leave on our journey to the stadium and we stopped at Hendon for lunch. Footballers' lunches varied according to personal tastes, but whereas if we ate at home before a game I would have two 'Shredded Wheat', the club would generally give us a choice of chicken, boiled fish or poached eggs on toast. Quite often I chose the latter as did most of the players on this pre-Final lunch.

We got to the ground at 2.00 pm, having spent the last half an hour ploughing a way through the enormous crowds making for Wembley. On the clothes pegs around the dressing room were the beautiful specially designed shirts with the club badge, and crisp white shorts. Navy blue and white hooped stockings, completed their outfits. Typical of WBA, there was not a spare one for me, to be kept as a souvenir, although those who played were able to do so.

Probably to relieve the tension felt before a big match, we all went through the famous tunnel, which led to the magnificent green manicured turf. This was our normal practice, as it was of most teams.

For the first time since I limped off Villa Park after the semi-final, our supporters had the opportunity to see me, and I must say that their welcome for me as I stepped out of the shadows into the sunlight brought tears to my eyes. Officials of the club seemed almost annoyed with me, that I got myself injured, but there was no doubt of my popularity with the fans.

Whereas I always felt that the 'bench' where the trainers sat to attend to injuries, was a poor spot from which to view the game, I expected to be seated there, as was the habit of other clubs, to be near the action and to be as involved as possible. But not WBA. I had served my purpose, and I had a seat in the stand with the wives. This meant that I was not allowed in the dressing room at half-time, and I really felt as though I were an outsider.

It was a beautiful May day as I sat with Leni to watch the match. If I were to say that I did not feel envious as I watched the teams come on the field, I would not be truthful. I felt my bad luck more keenly than ever before. The occasion, which I was to miss, was now happening before my eyes. Six weeks previously I had expected two successes: the winning of the First Division Championship and winning the FA Cup. Now it was a fact that I would miss both.

It was a good game and there were moments of high drama. Preston North End scored a goal through Charlie Wayman that seemed blatantly offside; we were awarded a penalty, which was only given, in my opinion, to make up for the offside error; and Frank Griffin, not a scorer of many goals, did what all players dream of - he scored the winning goal to make it 3-2. The penalty was taken by Ronnie Allen who was the right man for such a pressurised situation. He had won us the semi-final with a successful penalty kick, and he levelled the scores at 2–2 for us this time.

Frank's goal was only three minutes from time, and we held out until the uproar that came with the final whistle. Tears came to my eyes. Tears of emotion at winning, but surely mixed with those of disappointment and self-pity.

The presentation ceremonies by the Queen Mother were like a dream, and then it was back to the dressing room.

I have always been very emotional, as I have observed before, but life has had fewer moments, if any at all, as emotional as when I stood with 100,000 others before the game to sing 'Abide with Me'. All of the disappointment, allied to the normal reaction to a vast crowd singing this great hymn, welled up inside of me, and in addition there was the thought of my dad, so proud of his son, but unable to see him receiving the ultimate accolade. I knew the praise was for the victors, those who did it on the day. This did not include me, but not one single person, be him player, director, trainer or manager, thought to say a word to me. I should have been included in the adulation, but I was not. After all, anyone can play in the final, but five games had to be played and won to get there. This was the contribution made by Norman Heath and me.

We were booked in at the Grosvenor House Hotel, to which we repaired after the game, and after fixing up our rooms, we all went to a reception and dinner at the 'Cafe Royal'. This was a splendid affair, attended by our wives, a large body of officials and their families, members of the Football Association, and a few invited members of the Press.

After the dinner there were a number of speeches, most of which were predictable considering the reason for us all being there, and passing mention was made of Norman Heath and me. The most memorable was by a 'Times' sports correspondent who injected a lot of humour into a vote of thanks made to their hosts, West Bromwich Albion Football Club, on behalf of the guests.

Entertainment followed, principally by David Nixon, a kindly person who was a well-known television personality of the day, but whose original art was prestidigitatious. Some of his conjuring was totally brilliant and mystifying.

Whenever I had seen tricks performed on the stage or on television, I had always believed that those who helped the performer were planted and instructed beforehand. David's best trick would have been in that category – had it not been that this was an impossibility.

None of us had even seen him in person until he appeared on the little circular stage set up for the purpose. He asked for volunteers to help him play a game of cards, and he chose four of the team. I can only remember the captain, Len Millard, and Ronnie Allen specifically, but the game was 'Solo' and each player was dealt five cards. Then as is the system, they were each asked what they intended to do, that is how many 'tricks' could they get, or when appropriate they could say that they would win no tricks, called a 'misere'.

Len Millard who had shuffled the cards, so they were not pre-set, dealt them. I cannot remember the others' 'calls', but Len said that he could only get one trick. David told him to go 'solo', that is try to get five tricks, to which he replied that it was not possible.

However, our conjurer announced that he would tell each player which cards to play. It was wonderful to see the players' faces when they were, in fact, told which cards to play, even though they had carefully shielded their 'hands' from everyone else's view. Len won the first trick, and then right through to the fifth.

It was the kind of performance, which if I had been told about it, I would not have believed for a moment. But I was there, and I was completely baffled.

We returned to Grosvenor House, but no one was keen for this great day to end, so we all made for the lounge and sat in groups recounting the triumph.

The day ended very pleasantly for me. One of the greatest goalkeepers of all time, Frank Swift, was writing for one of the national newspapers and he chose to sit and chat with me. This was a great pleasure, as I had never met him before. He was a giant of a man, and when we shook hands mine disappeared into his. He was known to be able to pick up a football as though it were an apple. Both northerners, we got on very well and he was so genuinely sympathetic about my bad luck. It was heartening to be praised as I was, by this quite legendary figure. Sadly he was to die just four years later at Munich Airport, when the plane carrying Manchester United, with whom he was travelling, crashed on take off. He truly lived and died the great game of Association Football.

After a lazy Sunday, we went in the evening to two events that were very interesting. First we went to the BBC studios to take part in 'What's My Line', which was the most popular panel TV show of its day, and we met the celebrity participants. We were photographed with them and I still have a copy from the 'Daily Mail' with Barbra Kelly, Lady Isabel Barnett, Gilbert Harding, Bernard Braden, and Eamonn Andrews.

Following this we went to a party given for the FA Cup winners by the 'Variety Club' and it was our pleasure to meet many of the top stars of stage and screen. This included my sitting on the ample knee of singer/comedienne Tessy O'Shea.

Our generation of footballers, being of meagre expectations, had a magnificent surprise to cap off the evening. A London tailor must have won a fortune on our winning the Cup, because he came to the 'Variety Club's' party to throw us an invitation that was to us, in those times, unbelievable.

He had a large top class tailor's shop by the 'Elephant and Castle' pub in London and he invited us to go there on the following morning, so we could choose any garment we liked. We could have a suit, or a sports coat and slacks, or an overcoat, or a raincoat; and it could be 'off the peg' or it could be made up for us!

Now to put this into perspective, all we were given from elsewhere – which of course included the town of West Bromwich, the football club and the directors – was the grand total of three white handkerchieves from a gents' outfitters, and a silver plated table cigarette lighter from our favourite director, Tommy Glidden (who had captained WBA when they last won the Cup in 1931).

Today they get motor cars and immense rewards from sponsorship, but compared to three hankies, albeit with an initial on them, and a cigarette lighter, although much appreciated, choosing a garment from a top tailor's shop was manna from heaven indeed.

The shop was spacious, and the walls were from top to bottom and from side to side, full of 'bolts of cloth', to use their expression, on wooden rollers. I had decided that I would have a suit made to measure, and this I told one of the shop staff. 'Which suit length would you like?' he asked. 'Which are the best?' I enquired rather timidly. 'Ah! now that is your problem,' he responded. There were no prices at all on any of the material. I could have the very best provided I chose it! What a predicament. I shall never know if the powder blue with the tiny navy blue spots was the dearest, or the cheapest or whatever, in the shop!

Irrespective of this, I was delighted with the suit when it arrived by parcel post a few weeks later.

We were due to travel back by train from Euston to Birmingham New Street station in mid afternoon, and this gave me the opportunity to buy Leni a beautiful tea service, which we had seen in a shop window whilst walking down Oxford Street on the Sunday morning.

It had become the practice for winning teams to parade the Cup through the streets of their respective towns, on the upper deck of an open double-decker bus, and we were informed that this was to be the case with us. The bus would pick us up at Birmingham Snow Hill station and take us to West Bromwich.

We duly caught the train and stopped briefly at Coventry and then we were off to Snow Hill.

The road to West Bromwich Town Hall was, in fact, the one that led from the side of the station and carried on to the boundary of the two municipalities, where we passed our ground, The Hawthorns.

Navy blue and white was everywhere. Enormous crowds lined the streets and as we entered the High Street we had difficulty in moving at all. At the Town Hall, we all went on to the balcony to show the Cup to the assembled populace.

It was a magical time and it was enjoyed by all. The crowd's obvious respect for my contribution lifted my spirits tremendously. There was no doubt in their minds that I had made a large contribution to the team's success, and that if Norman and I had kept playing we would have been celebrating the Cup and League double.

This euphoria had about another fifteen or sixteen hours to last. After the Town Hall celebrations, trainer Arthur Fitton, told me to report at the ground on the morrow, for photographs.

This I did, and he gave me a nice new outfit. We all went on to the pitch where two forms had been placed for half the team to sit on, with the rest standing behind, as was the norm. As usual I stood at the back with Ray Barlow.

The manager came out, saw me, and said, 'You are not in this!' I was shattered. This was the official photograph to hang in the boardroom for as long as the game would be played, and contrary to the habit of all other winning clubs, who always included an injured player such as me, I would not be on it.

Writing almost fifty years later, that which I predicted has come true. The team photograph of 1954 is there in all its glory. I had played 159 First Division games until my injury, and that season I had appeared in five of the six Cup games; but the photograph seems to refute all of this.

Of course, at the time everyone knew how hard it was for me, missing out on the Cup Final and the World Cup in Switzerland, but few knew of the cruel treatment meted out to me by the club. Winning the Cup and being runners-up in the League was still a fine achievement, so Ronnie Allen initiated a request to Major Keys, the chairman, for the board to have made a memento, such as a medal or a cup, recording our little piece of club history.

The answer was 'no, it is not allowed,' yet our achievement was greater than anything a WBA team had done before, and as time has told, greater than anything since.

To conclude the 1953–54 story, although the Football Association presented us with winners' medals (incidentally, this was the first time they had done so); Norman and I gained nothing by winning the Cup. Not one pound, but we would not have expected it, as was it not just a year previously that the same chairman was quoted as saying that if the Football League were to put our wages up from 13 pounds a week in the season to 14 pounds, it would be the end of football?

I think that time has proven him wrong. Today they earn £6-8,000 per week, and the record is apparently £23,000!

So it was all over and I was getting the feeling that the club was not too interested in my recovery.

But I was. I was limping rather badly, with a nasty pain in the right thigh, and a stiffness which would not go away. I decided that I had three months to get fit, although the specialist had said six months and perhaps not even then.

My favourite exercise, tennis, seemed to me to be the best way to achieve this fitness, and I played almost every day, mostly with a young lady whose name I have forgotten, but who was a club supporter.

She was a very good player, and gradually the pain and stiffness decreased, although in the early days it limited my movements.

I also got plenty of exercise through one of my part-time jobs. My representative work for Repton Engineering was mostly in the office, and whenever I needed to visit a customer, John Madden would usually take me. However, I used to sell Firview's furniture by taking a Birmingham Corporation bus to a suburban shopping centre, and then walking all the way down one side of the main shopping street and back up the other.

In this way, I called on every possible outlet. I carried a folder of photographs, a price list, and a selection of fabrics relating to the fireside chairs, which were one of our best selling products. Almost always I could get at least a small trial order, and this was all I needed for the shop's manager or buyer to see the very good quality of our products.

Two incidents are worthy of recording. One day I went to Worcester, and had a wonderful experience, selling a wide variety of goods to all and sundry. But the previous week I had called on a wholesaler just a few miles away and, due to the range and quality of our goods, I had taken one of the biggest orders ever.

Being new to this side of commerce, it had not occurred to me that the wholesaler had to sell to the retail trade, and in this case, some of the prospects were in Worcester!

You can imagine his chagrin, when his representative called on these people who were already his customers, full of enthusiasm, telling them about this new range of products, to be told that they had ordered something very similar from a firm called Firview Furniture and Sales!

Our terms used to be: for the retailer, the retail price less thirty-three and one third per cent and a further two and a half per cent for payment within a week; and to the wholesaler less thirty-three and one third per cent, less a further thirty per cent, provided the order totalled a hundred pounds or more. The idea being that we made a bigger profit selling to the retailer (although transport costs were greater), but bigger drops were cheaper re the freight – and other economies of scale came into effect.

I had learnt one lesson. However, I still had one more to learn, and that was to do with commission.

Firview added another great seller to its portfolio. In those days, most houses had in their kitchens some kind of free-standing furniture, whereas today the 'fitted kitchen' is the vogue. The new article was a free-standing kitchen cabinet in four two-colour combinations, blue and cream, green and cream, red and cream, and yellow and cream, and also in plain cream.

It was particularly well designed and was most competitively priced, and this was going to be a big seller for these reasons.

I had quite recently opened an account with Cheshires of Nottingham, who claimed to be Britain's biggest furniture wholesalers. There were two or three brothers, and I had met the one who ran their very large wholesale warehouse in Birmingham.

He was so pleased with the new cabinet that he thought it best for me to take it to his brother, Jack Cheshire, in their head office in Nottingham. Jack would be in a position to place a large order for all of their branches.

Now, apart from the virtues already mentioned, there was another terrific advantage for both the wholesaler and the retailer, apart from greatly reduced freight charges. Up till then furniture was made, shipped, and stored in warehouses and shops, fully erected, taking up large volumes of space. Our new kitchen cabinet was delivered and stored collapsed in a box. This does not seem very exciting now, but in the early nineteen fifties it was.

The eventual householder could erect it or the retailer could. The wholesaler would save many cubic feet of valuable storage space, similarly the retailer.

And this was of great interest to Jack Cheshire, so on the day appointed, I had a cabinet delivered in its box and later in the day I arrived to demonstrate how quick and easy it was to put together. I had had plenty of practice, so this would not be a problem.

After the usual pleasantries, I emptied the box, which was waiting for me in Mr Cheshire's office. Everything was there, and it was only a matter of sliding horizontal shelves into the appropriate grooves, and fitting the protruding dowels into the accommodating round holes.

Or that is how it should have been, but supposing the holes are not concentric, what happens then? Put simply, panic and chaos.

After a few minutes of embarrassment and perspiration, when it was obvious that this marvellous system of saving space, by storing it flat, and re-erecting it in moments, was not working, Mr Cheshire kindly smiled and said, 'Stan, do not worry. It's not your fault. Your factory has let you down. Get them to send another one, and let them make sure it is correct this time.'

What a relief to hear that, after the poignant silence.

They did send another up to Nottingham the following week. It was right this time. It did go together easily and quickly. And I got the biggest order so far – 108 cabinets, two dozen of each of the four colour combinations and one dozen of plain cream.

I was their best salesman, but the gremlin which seemed to be always waiting for me to get to the top, ready to knock me off, as many instances in the years to come were to prove, was sharpening his claws just around the corner.

The agreement I had was that I got a small wage as a retainer, and 2 per cent commission on all sales. No mention was made of a lesser percentage for sales to wholesalers. I was paid after the customer had taken delivery.

I had already sold a few kitchen cabinets prior to the Cheshire sale, and, as agreed, I had got my 2 per cent; the next month I got one and three quarter per cent, the next one and a half per cent, the next one per cent – and I decided that I no longer wanted to work for Firview. I had no contract. I had been asked if I wanted one, but I had refused, naively saying that I relied on trust and good faith.

Whilst I was losing my respect for the firm, I was told that they were closing down temporarily, that the Customs and Excise were suspending them over the cabinets. The story went that they were being bought from 'the Everest organisation in Holland', but that it had been discovered that their country of origin was East Germany, and it was illegal to import from behind the Iron Curtain.

Just another of life's surprises! I carried on with Repton, although I regretted very much losing the furniture contract, as I found it most interesting and so much more aesthetically pleasing than nuts, bolts, and turned parts.

I have gone on somewhat, so I must return to my football world, and my battle to get fit enough to start the 1954–55 season in the WBA first team.

I had thought for some time that I was not the most popular person with the chairman. If you were an intelligent, educated and articulate person, the chairman would put up with you as long as you were playing very well, but he did not like people who could speak up, such as Ronnie Allen and me. This had been amply demonstrated to me in the 1952–53 season when I missed my first games for three years, two drawn cup-ties on Saturdays and the following Wednesday, against Chelsea.

I had had influenza, and I was fit to play the following Saturday against Manchester City, but despite having played 110 First Division games in succession, at that time, the manager told me that I was not in the team. My deputy was a player whose father was chairman of another Football League Club, and it was obvious to me that his two games were more important than my 110, due to the 'Old Pals' Act'.

I was aghast and I demanded to see the chairman immediately. I would not leave the ground until I had seen him. He came and I told him that if I did not play on Saturday, I would leave the club. I was a very consistent player, popular with the Press and the club's supporters, and he knew that there would be a furore.

At this I was picked to play and I never missed another game until November 1953 when I was absent from the league match v Cardiff City.

As the date for our returning for pre-season training approached, I knew that, given the slightest opportunity, 'the Major' would have me out. In fact, rumours abounded that I was finished. The knives were sharpened.

It must have been galling when I turned up hale, hearty, and as fit as any other player. I remember going to the club doctor for our pre-season medical examination and he was delighted. The six months' lay off he had predicted, I had shortened to three months.

A little anecdote to do with that visit to the surgery. I must have been the first player to be medically examined, because as I entered, the receptionist, recognising me, said, 'Oh! footballers and chrysanthemums, how sad, the summer must be over!' Ever since, every time I have seen a chrysanthemum, I have recalled that scene, and those words, and as I write I have that picture of the lady sitting there, with a surprised and sad look on her face.

As always at the start of training for a new season, I was half a stone overweight. After two or three weeks, I shed the extra pounds, and a few more as well. This was also normal, as I eventually built more muscle and returned to my best weight of 13 stone 6 pounds.

We played several practice matches, including two what were called 'public practice matches', and I was pleased with my progress. Apart from a slight ache, and a more severe pain when Margarete sat on my knee, I was returning to normal.

The first League game was to be at Sunderland on 21st August, and I was more than surprised to be selected without any argument. With the end of the previous season's bitterness still in mind, I thought that I would be receiving short shrift. I knew that the knives had been sharpened and that they would be plunged in my back at the first opportunity.

The team got off to a poor start losing our first two games, both in my native North-East, 4–2 to Sunderland on the Saturday, and 3–0 to Newcastle United on the following Wednesday. Then it seemed that the magic had returned, because we played the next 9 games without defeat. The crowds were back and all was well again. In one of these 9 we beat Leicester City 6–4, and later in the season we lost to them 6–3, a remarkable 19 goals scored in our two games against each other.

It transpired that the two greatest games of that 1954–55 season, my last with WBA, were against our neighbours, Wolverhampton Wanderers, and against the Hungarian champions, Honved.

Every year the First Division Champions and the FA Cup winners of the previous season, play each other in what was known as the FA Charity Shield. I am not sure who gets the money, but presumably charitable causes. In recent years the game has been played at Wembley and at the Millennium Stadium on the Saturday before the season starts, but our game was on a Wednesday evening in September, at the Wolves ground.

In recent years the Press seem to downgrade the match to some extent, by writing that it is like an exhibition game. I cannot believe that because professional footballers do not like to lose.

Certainly our Charity Shield encounter was as competitive as any Cup Final. In 1988 I wrote an article for the 'British Soccer Weekly' in Australia, and it included this story of our Charity Shield encounter.

'My favourite football trophy is the FA Charity Shield replica which is a solid silver copy of the shield, set on a plaque which looks very smart sitting on the sideboard or mantelpiece.

Readers, whose memories of soccer go back to the early and mid 50s, will remember that two of the great sides in those days were Wolverhampton Wanderers and West Bromwich Albion. Although most would know that they are both from the West Midlands, not all would know that they are, in fact, neighbours.

You can imagine the rivalry between supporters of the two clubs. In the great industrial factories and installations, workmates would often be at variance regarding the team they supported.

Gold and black or blue and white scarves indicated their choice, and Monday mornings during the season must have seen a lot of leg pulling, dependent on how their respective teams had performed on the Saturday.

A lot more could be written about this subject, but for the moment, back to the FA Charity Shield.

It is normally played for between the winners of the FA Cup and the winners of Division One, although when the double has been achieved, obviously this is not possible. In any event, I think that it is by invitation and not necessarily between the winners of the premier trophies.

At the end of the 1953–54 season the honours list showed Wolverhampton Wanderers top of Division One and West Bromwich Albion FA Cup winners. A sharing of the spoils between the two arch Black Country rivals, one could say. So the stage was set for a kind of decider between these two great teams. Many things were being said of the events of that wonderful season; most started with "if only", but here was the ultimate. Here we had the chance to prove once and for all who was the best team.

In those days the game was not played at Wembley and in this case it was staged at Molineux, the home of the Wolves.

Floodlighting was still rather a novel idea, and very few grounds were so equipped, but the Wanderers were very enthusiastic exponents of this relatively new medium.

They established a great reputation for their ability to play under lights and they remained unbeaten for a very long time in these night matches, which were attracting maximum attendances.

Readers can imagine the enormous interest that there was in this game of games.

Both teams had around 50,000 supporters who came to the matches and hundreds of thousands more who claimed allegiance to one or other Midland giant.

The capacity of Molineux at that time, was 56,500. Both teams were sprinkled with internationals, more than half the players on view being of that stature.

It is hardly necessary to add that the demand for tickets was extraordinary.

Came the night and for the Albion this was their first real game under floodlights. We had played in one or two friendly matches for old players' benefits etc, but this was the first game for real.

Floodlighting is now old hat, but on that autumn night, 29 September 1954, we felt that we were stepping out onto a stage.

We could hear the expectant hum of the packed crowd but due to the lights focussing on the playing pitch, we could not see them. For us this was the ideal setting for the meeting of the gladiators.

After a truly titanic struggle we drew 4-4. Can you imagine - eight goals going in on that night of nights?

I would imagine that there must have been a few near heart attacks as the game ebbed and flowed.

Certainly my most vivid memory was of a personal nature. At 4–4 with a couple of minutes to go, we were throwing everything into trying to get the winner and I hit one from about 20 yards.

With that brilliant England goalkeeper, Bert Williams, beaten, the ball hit the post to Bert's left and came out again.

So a lifetime of glory was denied me by about one inch of woodwork! Instead of the memory of Stan scoring the winner in the last two minutes to make it 5–4, all that is now on record is that Wolverhampton Wanderers and West Bromwich Albion shared the FA Charity Shield in 1954.'

The adrenalin was really flowing again, and then we had wonderful news. And this news forms part of another article I wrote in 1988. Here again is a reprint (from Issue 131, Column 1 Para 7):

'Then we had this wonderful news. We were invited to play Honved, the top Hungarian side in a Festival of Football in Brussels in mid-October.

We were to represent British football and that made us very proud. As a Belgian newspaper put it, West Bromwich Albion and Wolves had carried on the exciting type of football which had typified the Spurs' style of a couple of years earlier.

So after all the talking, we were to be given the opportunity to test out our theories!

The match was to be played under floodlights at the Heysel Stadium, Brussels on 13th October and it was to be a double header, Austria FC and the Belgian champions, Anderlecht. The four teams were thought by many to be the best club teams in Europe.

Interestingly Honved was the Hungarian Army team, which doesn't sound so hot, but eight of them were the mighty internationals of Wembley and Budapest.

I used to write a column in a monthly soccer magazine in those days, and I wrote that Walter Winterbottom, the England manager, sat next to me on our way to the stadium, and told me that in his opinion, Hideguti, the centre forward, was the only important player missing from the full international side.

Our team had not had much experience under the floodlights, having only played once previously against Wolverhampton Wanderers in the FA Charity Shield and we welcomed the news that we were to be allowed to train on Heysel Stadium the night before the match. However, I had actually played there under lights against Belgium for the Combined Services and thereby hangs a tale.

Jimmy Cowan our goalkeeper, about whom I wrote recently, was moving to catch the ball, when a Press photographer took a flashlight photograph, temporarily blinding him and the ball finished up in the net. Despite protests, the goal was allowed.

Back to the story.

It had often been said that the only team likely to give the Hungarians a run for their money was a good English club side, so here we were with the opportunity of backing those words with action.

Our manager, Vic Buckingham, was most anxious that we should win and he believed sincerely that we could. He had developed us from being a bunch of good players, but who were without a method, to a team that played football which was exciting and ultra-active. This was his moment.

We had played together a lot, and the only players missing from the team which had done so well for the two previous seasons were Norman Heath the goalkeeper, and Jimmy Dugdale at centre half.

Poor Norman was injured the previous April and never played again, and Jim had been injured in the first game of the season, but their places were filled by Jim Sanders and Joe Kennedy, who had both played a lot of first team games.

The England international teams of those days only met one or two days before a game and their instructions were "good luck and do your best" kind of style, but the club sides, used to playing and training together, obviously had more chance of beating sides such as Honved.

Only the previous season had not Wolves beaten an Argentinian side which provided many of that country's national XI.

With all of the Argentines' brilliant ball control and pattern weaving, the well-drilled Wolves had still beaten them easily. So if our local rivals could do it ... well!

We flew from Birmingham airport and we were accompanied by a large body of supporters. This was the first time for may years WBA had been abroad, except to Ireland, and quite a few players had never flown before.

How different to today. Our goalkeeper Jim Sanders had been wounded whilst flying with the RAF in the war, but for most it was all excitement. I was pleased to be going back to Brussels, a city which I had visited several times, the first as an infantryman when we liberated the city 10 years previously.

We trained on the Tuesday evening, then on the Wednesday afternoon had a team talk and it was an occasion I will never forget. Our manager had always maintained that we should not change our method whatever the opposition, and we agreed. Why worry about what they might do? If we stick to a proven, successful system it would be our opponents who would do the worrying.

But Honved?

So how did it go, you must be wondering. Honved included Grosics, Lorant, Kocsis, Puskas and Czibor who were all looked upon as truly great players, and the remainder were all pretty good too!

My most lasting memory was when I looked at the giant clock behind one of the goals, and it said 25 minutes of the match remained, and the scoreboard said WBA 3, Honved 1.

But as we left the field disconsolately, it read WBA 3, Honved 5. Yes, we conceded four goals in the last 25 minutes. How did it happen?

Writing in November 1954, I said, and I quote, "I have been asked that somewhere before! If I give no reason, the worst is thought, whilst if I say what I think is true, it seems as though I am just making excuses." But without bias it is true that Ray Barlow was injured after giving a great performance against possibly the greatest inside forward in the game, Kocsis.

It happened with 25 minutes to go and it did most certainly affect us. Secondly, one of Honved's goals was, in my opinion, definitely off-side.

"We upset the Magyars in the first hour of the game. They were arguing amongst themselves, and I'm sure in some pretty choice Hungarian language," etc, etc. However, we struck a blow for English club football, and we were not afraid of the Hungarians.

Until next time ......

I felt that I was playing really well and several leading football writers were saying that I should be back in the England team. I think that I was always intelligent enough to know how I was playing. After all, my job was to stop the opposing outside left getting the ball, and if he did, to take it off him. Then having got the ball, I had to start an attack by accurate passing, and clever use of the ball. Now I was back at my best, I didn't miss a game, I was very fit, and I was succeeding in what I had to do in the team. Another task was to cover the centre half, so that if he was beaten, I was there to take up the challenge. I was also an attacking full back and many of my sorties upfield brought danger to the opposition goal.

In short I was enjoying playing and was so pleased that I had got over my injury. In the New Year of 1955 we struck a bad patch and, although still well up in the First Division, the team seemed to lose confidence. The goalkeeping position was uncertain and a young lad, Reg Davies, who had just finished his National Service was introduced into the team. We played Charlton Athletic at home in the 4th round of the FA Cup, and were beaten 4–2. This was a real blow, for after some excellent performances in the autumn and early winter, hopes of retaining the Cup were entertained.

I was very confident in myself and I had forgotten the concern I had felt in the close of the 1954 season.

Then we played Sheffield United on a cold March afternoon, and after leading I think 3–0, we finally only drew 3–3. Again the goalkeeper was badly at fault, although he was not the only player to be below par. Jimmy Dudley who played in front of me, and with whom I had a great understanding, could do little right. I felt sorry for him and as we were walking off the field he said how poorly he had played, but added that I was about the only one who had played really well. This was the feeling of the team as expressed by several of them. There were genuine fears by some of them that they would be out of the team for Saturday's match.

But there was only one player dropped. That was me. I was shocked. And I was never picked again. I was finished. I was the only player ever in nearly six years at West Bromwich Albion to be only dropped once, and never to be given another chance. It was unbelievable, but the Major had his pound of flesh – but not his many thousands of pounds in transfer fee, which he placed on my head.

I was put on the transfer list, told to get out of the house as soon as possible, and it was then that I decided that I would not go to another League club. I knew that if I went to a club outside of the Football League, they did not have to pay the fee. This, of course, was exactly the thing WBA did not expect. They actually had the nerve to say that they only wanted the money back that they had paid for me; this after more first team games than any other player during the period I was with the club.

I was treated like a leper, and I was deeply hurt. I will never know why the manager, Vic Buckingham, whom I had always greatly respected, allowed me to be so miserably treated.

I made no attempt to go to another League club, and I let it be known that I wanted to go 'non-League'. There was a rush of clubs all over the country, so Leni and I decided that I would go to a club in a nice part of England, play part-time and work as well.

The football world was shocked that I was treated so badly, and Maurice Smith of 'The People' newspaper asked me to write a few articles on 'Soccer Slaves', a term that was being bandied about a lot at the time. This certainly highlighted the problem of a professional being tied to an organisation by a contract which had no term of years to it. We were guaranteed a certain wage for a year, but after that we were still the property of the club.

I am sure that the publicity I created in those days was a stepping-stone towards the eventual destruction of such 'term-less' contracts, and the players of today have reaped the benefits.

We were so stupid, and I was guilty of this naivety when at Middlesbrough. At the end of April 1949, I played at Hartlepool for the reserve team and after the match Harold Shephardson, the trainer, said to me, 'Oh Stan, you are retained for next season.' I suppose I was probably pleased, having got used to small mercies by that time.

During the following week, I was talking to two other players, Cecil McCormack and my friend, John Spuhler. Somehow or other one of us brought up the subject of being 'retained according to rule.' We found that the rules of the Football League said that for the retention to be valid a specific wage had to be offered by, I think, the first Saturday in June. Now none of us had been offered anything, so we decided to wait until after the first June Saturday to see if the club complied. Well we heard nothing, and the rule concluded with the words, 'shall be deemed to have a free transfer'. This meant that we could go to any club who wanted us without them paying a fee, and we were all worth quite a lot of money.

Should we go 'non-League', we asked ourselves? Cecil said that he had been in touch with Jack Tresadern, the manager of Chelmsford City in the Southern League, and that he would like to meet all of us at a hotel in Darlington the following Saturday. As all expenses were to be paid, we hired a taxi. En route we talked of our plans and decided that we wanted a 500 pounds lump sum, the same wages as the maximum in the Football League, and a rent free house.

Mr Tresadern agreed and we shook hands on it, but we were tied to Middlesbrough until 30 June, so we went back to wait for the contract to expire.

The manager, Jack, sent for me the week after the meeting at Darlington and told me that I was a 'barrack room lawyer' and that he knew all of our plans. The taxi driver had dropped us off home, and had gone to see the manager and had told him everything!

We then made a ridiculous move. We wrote to the Football League, claiming free transfers. They immediately refused us them, and terrified in case we were put on the transfer list at too high a fee, thus putting us out of the game, John and I signed again for the 'Boro. What we should have done was to write to the Football Association who would have found for us. Cecil went to Chelmsford somehow or other, then got himself transferred to Barnsley and made money out of both deals, but I cannot remember how he managed it!

To cut a long story short, I settled on Poole Town, who were in the Western League at the time. Leni, Margarete, and I, loved Poole when we visited it. The club was to provide us with a beautiful rent-free house, and I was to get the same pay as in the First Division in the winter and a lot more than they got in the summer. I was also to manage the team on a part-time basis, and 'work' as well during the week.

CHAPTER TWENTY
I LEAVE THE FIRST DIVISION

We went to Poole in early July and I signed a five-year contract, giving me five years of security whether I played or not. In the First Division, one year was the maximum period! We loved the beaches and the beautiful Dorset countryside, and we settled very quickly. I met several of my old Dorset Regiment pals, including Reg Cobb and Bob Rigler, and, of course, they were keen Poole Town supporters.

Shortly before we left Birmingham my brother, John, finished his National Service, and he asked if he could come with us to Poole. We agreed and as an electrical engineer, he soon got a job with a company manufacturing lifts.

One evening when we were playing away, Leni arranged to meet John in the cinema, and whilst she was watching a film, a girl next to her lit a cigarette and held it in such a way that the smoke went into Leni's eyes, so she asked her if she minded holding it in her other hand. The young lady was so embarrassed that she put it out! Leni was so embarrassed now that she offered the ex-smoker a sweet. They got talking. When the lights went up, John came in and Leni introduced them.

The Poole and Dorset Herald was the local weekly paper and they gave the club a great deal of space. There was always an account of the previous match, and columns on what was going on during the week, plus comments on the forthcoming matches.

The reporter who covered our affairs was a good looking, hirsute young man, always smartly dressed in checked sports coat and slacks, and Ian Wooldridge by name. Ian used to call at our house every Monday and we would discuss current soccer events over a cup of tea or coffee.

He did not know too much about the game in those far off days, all of 40 years, but he was a good listener, very enthusiastic, and a quick learner.

I followed his career with great interest when he left the local paper and went first to a well-known Sunday national, 'The Empire News'. I believe he then went on to the 'Daily Herald', a daily paper, and then perhaps another Sunday national before joining the 'Daily Mail', with whom he has had enormous success.

He has reported all of the popular sports at their highest levels, such as world championships; Olympic Games; Wimbledon; the FA Cup Final; the Ashes, at home and in Australia; and even the America's Cup, when he also produced the official film for the BBC. He has appeared often on television, has been 'Sporting Journalist of the Year' at least twice, and Leni and I were delighted to read that he was awarded the OBE in the 1991 New Year's Honours List.

The last time I saw him was when he came to Fremantle for the Australian defence of the America's Cup in 1987, when the Aussies lost.

During our early years in Poole we were minor celebrities and, as such, we were invited to various functions, such as dinners and dances. One of the most enjoyable was the Bournemouth Bookmakers Association Annual Dinner, where we sat at the top table with other sportsmen, including Peter Allis, the golfer, and Colin Ingleby-MacKenzie, the then Hampshire cricket captain. It was a very pleasant evening and I still have a souvenir of it. It was held at the 'Pavilion', Bournemouth, and I have a silver teaspoon to prove it. Someone put it in my pocket and I was always going to take it back... Another memorable evening was a Freemason's Ladies Night to which Leni and I were invited, and the 'memorable' bit came at the end of a response to a toast to the Borough of Poole, given by the Sheriff, when he chose this unlikely occasion to regale us with the Council's achievements of the previous year, commencing with, inappropriately, the new sewerage system, and ending with an account of the improvements in the local schools and in education generally. His final remarks I will never forget. He said, 'So in the field of education we can 'old our 'eads 'igh.' It seemed that he had not had the opportunity of taking advantage of a similar level of education.

Poole Harbour has at least two claims to fame. It is the second biggest natural harbour in the world to Sydney, and it was where King Alfred built the first English Navy in the 9th century. However, due to it being too shallow it has ceased to be used for making ships of any size.

We played in some delightful places, including Weymouth, Dorchester, Trowbridge, Salisbury, Glastonbury, Yeovil, Chippenham, Portland, and Street. The football was better than I anticipated and we did quite well in our first season. In the summer of 1957 we applied to get into the Southern League which, at that time, was very strong, and included several clubs which are now in the Football League. Wimbledon, Oxford United (then known as Headington) and Hereford United, are examples.

Due to the publicity I gained for Poole Town, we were accepted immediately, although the club had tried for years to be admitted. We had a tremendous start to the season, going ten games without a defeat, and several grounds on which we played had record crowds to see this new team. I had got together a team, partly consisting of experienced players and partly of some young ones. We also played several friendly games against League clubs under our floodlights, with great success. When we played Fulham, I remember Johnnie Haynes, the England captain, asking me why I was not still in the First Division, as I was playing so well.

At Poole I discovered again that nothing should be taken for granted. As we won our first ten matches, the directors seemed to think that it was a catastrophe when we lost. I tried for hundreds of jobs outside of football, but nothing any good materialised. What I had not appreciated was that there was little interest in the game down there on the South Coast. We had far better crowds than ever before, even reaching 6,000, but the directors were not employers of labour, with one exception. Mr Matchan, the chairman, was also chairman of Cope Allman, which was to become a public company, but he never used his influence to get me work of any importance. I helped his wife on their mink farm for a few weeks, and it was nine months before I received all of my wages, after many attempts.

Margarete went to a lovely private school; I got Mam and Dad a very nice flat in a house overlooking Brownsea Island; Dad worked at the club, looking after the dressing rooms and marking the pitch. Brother John lived with us for a while until Mam and Dad moved down, and from the point of view of enjoying life, I suppose being down in Poole was a pleasant interlude.

Our first summer was one of glorious sunshine and we were able to spend a lot of time at the beach. Branksome Dene Chine was our favourite spot and not having a car, we used to go by bus, and walk down through the chine to the beach. The chine could be best described as a valley leading down to the beach through an avenue of pine trees. It was equally lovely in all four seasons. The golden hues of the trees in autumn, the freshness of the atmosphere in the spring, when all of the trees were green with new shoots, and the spectacular sight of the pine branches bedecked with hoar frost in the winter, made the trip down through the chine ever changing and always enjoyable.

In the November of 1955 I had quite a serious injury. I was struck in the back, and rarely for me, I had to have attention from the trainer. I felt unwell when I got home, but I did not worry about it. We watched television, drank orange squash, and ate chocolate all evening. This was our idea of supreme relaxation, which we practised every Saturday evening when we played at home.

But this particular Saturday night ended in high drama. I had gone up to bed first as I felt out of sorts. Suddenly Leni came dashing in the bedroom telling me that I was bleeding; that there was blood in the bathroom and a trail of it into the bedroom. Denying that it was anything to do with me, I got out of bed to prove it, but Leni was right, my pyjama trousers were badly bloodstained. I was bleeding internally.

Not wanting to cause panic, I said that I would ring the doctor. The telephone was by the front door. I was just telling the doctor who I was when I found myself lying on the bare wooden floor, and I noticed that the phone was swinging backwards and forwards against the wall. Unknown to me, I was lapsing into unconsciousness and back again into consciousness. Leni was very distressed, and was even more so when I summoned my calmest voice to tell her that I was all right, that she was not to worry, and if she could just put my head on the roll of carpet behind the front door, and put a blanket over me, I would sleep there the night! The carpet was there awaiting to be laid.

Brother John and Leni got me into the dining-room, laid me on the settee, and then I asked them to put the kettle off, as I could not stand the whistling. As the kettle was not on, and I was the only one who could hear the whistling, it was obvious to them that it was to do with my condition. At that the doctor arrived and immediately diagnosed internal bleeding as being the cause of the whistling I could hear. The ambulance arrived, and I was taken to Poole General Hospital only half a mile away, but I did not remember the journey or my admission.

What I do remember was the Sunday morning. I must have been unconscious all night. Then I found myself lying there thinking and wondering where I was. What was the sacred music? Who was singing hymns? Truly, for a few moments I thought that I was in heaven.

The reality was more mundane, but still surprising. It turned out to be Mr Spinney, our next door neighbour, playing the organ, and he and other people in the ward singing. It transpired that he brought his portable organ every Sunday to play for the patients. We knew him to be an ardent Methodist, but did not know of his good works.

It was diagnosed that I had a lacerated kidney. This was serious, but it was healed by the use of drugs, and it was nine weeks before I was fit to play again.

The most enjoyable football we played were the floodlit games we played against Football League clubs, when I was able to gauge how well I was playing.

At the end of my first season at Poole Town, I had a phone call from Fred Cox, who was the manager of Bournemouth and Boscombe FC (now AFC Bournemouth), telling me that West Bromwich Albion had failed to include my name on their transfer list through error, and that consequently I could go to a Football League club without a transfer fee.

I cannot remember the sequence of events, but I do remember a phone call from Mr Halliday, the manager of Leicester City, who had just been promoted to the First Division. He wanted me to come up to Filbert Street to see him. I said that I would want £2,000 signing-on fee, and he agreed. This, of course, was illegal, although it sounds paltry by the levels of today's game, but it went on quite a lot.

I went to Bournemouth West railway station to set off for Leicester, and I bought a Daily Mail at the kiosk. I sat waiting for the train and turned to the back page first, as do all sports enthusiasts. The headline said that Sunderland FC were to be accused of 'under the counter' payments to players! Immediately, I realised that this would ruin my plans.

I carried on to Leicester, met the manager and his first words were, 'Have you seen this morning's paper?'

He still wanted to sign me, on the promise that I would get the £2,000 sometime in the future. I am sure that he meant it, but if WBA could treat me as they did after playing more games than any other player during the five and a half years I was there, why should I expect better from a club for whom I had not played at all?

I was always very popular with the supporters at Poole, and for about three years after my kidney injury I did not miss a game and in season 1956–57 I actually played 56 games. The last week of the season, I must have created a world record by playing on every night, Monday to Saturday inclusive, and again on the Saturday afternoon – seven games in six days. Some were for the first team, the rest for the reserves. We had done so well in the various cup competitions that we had a backlog of games in the last week.

But what of the future? I could not find a job in Poole, and I could not play forever.

Something was telling me that I was not getting very far in football. I had the experience. I was better educated than the vast majority of players and managers, and I knew that I could improve a team by a combination of tactics and methods of training. I was annoyed at some of the people who got the job, got the sack, and then walked into another post straightaway.

The Press were doing their best, linking me with vacant positions, but nothing was materialising. Then there was a big piece by the 'Daily Express', saying that I was going to New Zealand to coach, and what a loss that would be to English football. Now whereas I would agree with the latter sentiment, I must say that I had no intention of going to New Zealand.

CHAPTER TWENTY ONE

WORKING FOR A LIVING IN DEVON AND CAMBRIDGE

However, it is strange how one's life-plan seems to be preordained. Havard Knowles, who had been sales manager at Meddocreem and Facchino's Biscuits, read the 'Express' article, and thought, 'I wonder if Stan really wants to go to New Zealand, or would he prefer a job outside of football?'

Consequently, I received a letter from him on 'Neilson's Ice Cream' paper, asking me that question, and suggesting that I should come to his office at Keynsham to see him. He was Divisional Manager for the South-West of England, and he had a vacancy for a depot manager at Newton Abbot in Devon.

It was a great opportunity for it meant of course living in glorious Devon and virtually running a large business. I also had a depot in Plymouth, and I was responsible for hiring and firing, merchandising, increasing the business, selling deep-freezers, supplying ice cream to such as Newton Abbot Races, etc, stock control, accounting, banking, and everything necessary in running a big business.

The products were a wide range of Neilson's ice cream which won the 'Dairy Show's' first prize for its Cornish ice cream, and a full range of frozen foods both retail packs and catering packs. Most of the frozen food was from 'Eskimo Foods', but I was able to buy such as meats and poultry from wherever I wished.

I was to have comprehensive training at the Bristol depot, but things got desperate at Newton Abbot, due apparently to bad management, and I was asked to take over after only one week's training.

During my short stay in Bristol, an amazing thing happened. I knew one person only in that city, his name was Peter (I have forgotten his surname) and he was the reporter who followed Ian Wooldridge on the 'Poole and Dorset Herald'. He had got a good job with a Bristol evening paper, reporting football. It was a very dark night and I went for a walk away from the city centre. It was black except for a pool of light shed by a tall lamppost. As I approached it, three people stepped into the circle of light and one was Peter. Out of a population of a million I knew one person, and I met him on a dark night!

Until then I had not owned a car, although on occasions I had borrowed one, but Leni and I decided that with a secure job we could afford to buy one on hire purchase. We bought a three-year-old Hillman Minx, and it was in this that I drove one Monday morning in January 1960, to Newton Abbot.

I had never been there before, I did not know how long it would take, and I had only driven the car a few miles. On top of that, I was to take over two depots, where all of the staff knew much more about the business than me. I must admit that I was visibly nervous, and when I found the depot, I parked the car outside of the front entrance, took a deep breath and walked down the steps into the offices.

The company's chief auditor, Mr I O B Carlson, was awaiting me to introduce me to the staff, and then later to do a full 'stocktake', as from that moment the stock was my responsibility. There were 164 different frozen food lines, plus about sixty of ice cream, so I had to take the word of the chief 'cold-storeman', Dennis Williams, not that I had any doubts about his ability or honesty.

I lodged in a terraced house near the depot, and I travelled home on Friday nights and returned first thing on Monday mornings. Leni made a few visits through the kindness of Poole friends, Harvey and Win Buckmaster, giving her a lift, and we settled on a lovely three bedroomed bungalow on a hillside, with magnificent views of Haytor, a favourite rock for climbers on Dartmoor.

Margarete went to Newton Abbot Grammar School and quickly settled down. Leni was in her element organising our first home of our own, and I absolutely loved my job. I had very little interference from Mr Knowles, and our depots seemed to win just about every competition the company promoted.

Soon I got a good name as a manager, and our managing director, Mr H Gyle-Thompson, mentioned our successes often in his 'news flashes', which went to every depot in Britain.

I got together a good team and it really was a happy ship. Our sales grew rapidly and I felt that I had found my metier for life. I played for Poole Town for the rest of the season, although it was mostly in the reserve team, and I still got paid the same amount as I did when I was manager. My contract ended on 30 June, and I was delighted when the manager of Weymouth Football Club offered me a good salary for the next season.

I enjoyed my first summer in the ice cream and frozen food business. When the sun shone we all worked until 9.00 pm, but everyone expected this to happen. It could almost be said that our life in Devon was idyllic. We had a lovely home, I enjoyed my work, Margarete liked her school, and Leni made some good friends.

The only criticism that could be made was that the Devonians were very insular people, and you could not get to know them. All of our friends, with the exceptions of June and Gordon Battshill, were from other parts. Arthur and Connie Woods were from Yorkshire, to where they returned and we still write to one another. We knew lots of people who came from the North, but could not settle and returned. After a lifetime in one place they found that, although Devon was beautiful, they missed their friends.

Gordon and June were good fun and we had some nice times together. Leni, Margarete, and June, used to run our ice cream kiosks at the races, and other outside events, and as they were paid 10% of the takings, they used to do quite well.

We were invited to June's parents' at Exeter for tea one Sunday, and we were on the Exeter By-Pass when Leni noticed a lamb on the verge. I stopped the car and she chased the lamb. She slipped and slithered in the wet grass, got covered in mud, and eventually caught the frightened animal. She took off her gloves and carried the lamb to the farm gate, let the lamb in, and got back in the car. When we were having tea, she suddenly realised that she had left her gloves on the grass verge. We looked for them without success on our way home, so Leni's good turn cost her a pair of expensive gloves!

We used to go to the morning service at St Peter and St Paul's in Newton Abbot, when we first went to live there. We enjoyed the services, but the vicar and his congregation did not practise their Christianity. As we came out of the church we always hoped for a smile and a chat with someone, but it never happened. Like many priests, he gave us a frozen smile, asked how we were, but did not wait for a reply before 'helloing' the next person.

We stopped going after several months and tried the little Norman church at Combeinteignhead on the road to Teignmouth. That was much better, although not as good as the churches we knew in the North of England.

In my job it was necessary for me to know the geography of the South-West. I visited customers whenever I had time and Leni sometimes came with me. This, of course, was wonderful. We were there four summers and every July we used to go to the famous Widdecombe Fair. We used to take a load of Cornish ice cream, as the sales for the day were immense. A cafe customer made the best Devonshire cream teas ever, and we used to look forward to that.

A very nice perk of the job was our invitations to dinner. We used to supply most of the best restaurants and hotels in Devon with both ice cream and frozen foods, and in appreciation of our summer service, a lot of them used to ask us to come out to dinner in the autumn and winter. This was most enjoyable, and enhanced our relationship.

Christmas was a busy time as we sold enormous quantities of turkeys, ducks, legs of pork, etc, and the week – and particularly, a couple of days – before Christmas Day, were incredible. I used to be delivering in my car to make sure that everyone was supplied. And then there were crackers. Yes, we also sold Christmas crackers, and in fact we had to take orders every January for the next Yuletide.

Although it was more than four hundred miles, we used to go home to Mam and Dad's for Christmas, and the driving after such a busy time at work was very tiring. One year we had planned to return on 3rd January, but it started snowing on New Year's Day and by the third, the whole country was white. We decided to wait one more day in the hope that things would improve, but it didn't so at 8.00 am on the fourth we set off.

Our journey through the Northern counties was not too bad as they were well practised in the art of snow clearing. We had fish and chips at quaintly named Ashby de la Zouch at about 1.00 pm. By this time all of the car windows were covered in ice except for semi-circles made by the windscreen wipers, and inside, the heater manfully melted a small area. I had a stiff neck by this time, because of the angle of my back and neck, necessary for me to see through the windscreen.

We were frightened at this stage. We had just heard on the car radio that an old couple had been found suffocated in their car, which was caught in a snowdrift, just as we turned left. Prior to that, we had had the wind behind us, but as we turned, the snow in the field to our left started to blow onto the road and we could see it piling up. We managed to get through but when we got to Bridgwater at 4.00 pm the road to Taunton had been blocked all day. Dozens of vehicles, almost all trucks, because car drivers had been advised to stay at home, were stuck. Just as we got there, a snow plough got through to Bridgwater and the truck drivers waved us through. When we got to Taunton it was dark, and it looked like a village up in the Alps in winter, with all of the house lights reflecting in the snow.

It was obvious that they had not been used to heavy snow in the South-Western counties, because they had done little to clear it, and in Taunton we were told that the council workers had gone home at 4.00 pm as normal, whereas up North they were used to working all night if necessary.

What was generally a two-hour journey from Taunton, took us eight hours and we went off the road four times. On one occasion a truck had to pull us back on. When we got to our house after midnight, we found the drive full of snow. The garage was down the drive below the level of the road, and the snow reached up to the top of the door. We left our car in the road, and the next morning it was the only one driveable, because those in their garages were snowed in. Our water pipes were frozen, but a nearby plumber fixed them and I was back at work the next day.

Our cat, Fluffy, had been in a cat home for a couple of weeks in 'Sunny Devon' but it could have been better described as 'Snowy Devon', for they had recorded the biggest snowfall ever. We could not get through to the cat home until several days later as the road was blocked. When we were able to go to collect him, we saw the most amazing sight. Outside the building was a huge pile of empty cat food tins. It was enormous. Normally they would use a lot of fresh meat etc, but they had used up what they had, and were unable to get out. Fortunately they had always kept a large stock of tins for just such an emergency.

At the end of football season 1960–61, I had decided to hang up my boots even though it would have been easy to carry on. I started to watch the game at Exeter, Torquay, or Plymouth, dependent on who they were playing.

Gordon Battishill and I joined the Teignmouth Golf Club. We had several lessons from a professional and played two or three times a week. One winter I played indoor tennis in Torquay, and another badminton at Teignmouth. I also kept up my training by running to the Combe Cellars Inn at Combeinteignhead, on Tuesday and Thursday evenings. There were steep hills en route and I often thought of turning round halfway. To make sure this did not happen, I disciplined myself by touching the sign on the wall of the pub, before running back home.

So I kept pretty fit down in Devon, and we all enjoyed life. We settled down to thinking that this was where we would spend the rest of our lives. Margarete was in the school netball, tennis, and hockey teams, and she was a member of the Newton Abbot Repertory Company, where she played in 'Ann Veronica'. She also produced a play at school and we often laugh about something that happened at a rehearsal. Rehearsals were always a problem and I always asked her how things had gone. I did on this particular occasion and she said, 'Oh that Trout, he wouldn't exit!' Firstly, we could not help laughing at his name. I knew that we shouldn't, but I think particularly in the context of what Margarete said, it really sounded funny. She had been directing them, and came to a part where the character young Trout was playing had to leave the stage. 'Exit, Trout' said Margarete. 'I'm not going to exit' said Trout. I'll bet this never happened at the Old Vic.

One summer, Mam and Dad came for 'two or three weeks' in August, and stayed so long that Mam said one day, 'I'm the only person in Newton Abbot who is wearing a straw hat in November!' Dad did his usual gardening stint and made a great job behind the bungalow. I had transformed the front from a heap of weeds to a neat lawn, surrounded by flowerbeds, and the way I did it is worthy of record. A firm advertised in the 'Sunday Express', just above the 'Skeleton Crossword', I recollect, and they offered something that must have been a commercial failure as I have not seen it since, but I certainly took advantage of it. At a very reasonable price and delivered to your house, they marketed a lawn rolled up like a carpet. In fact, it was a carpet made of a substance similar to cotton wool, and you flattened the surface on which the lawn was to be laid, and then rolled it out, covered it with lawn sand, soaked it for a few hours, and then left it, except for keeping it watered.

The material contained lawn seed and fertiliser, and eventually the 'cotton wool' rotted into mulch which, kept wet, aided the growth of the lawn. In addition, the existing weeds were killed by the blanketing effect.

And the borders were made the same, with tall flowers at the back and the smallest at the front. I have never been able to understand why such a brilliant idea could not have been made viable.

Yes, we have lots of happy reminiscences of Devon until one day... It just had to happen. One Saturday morning in August or September 1962, Leni brought in the 'Daily Mail' to me. There were two headlines, one on the left and one on the right. The former was political; the latter was shattering. 'Giant Ice Cream Merger', it said. Lyons Maid, Eldorado, and Neilsons, had merged, and the senior partner was Lyons, who had bought the other two companies. We knew all about the two 'enemies' because hadn't we taken a lot of their business from them, along with that of the biggest competitor Walls? So Lyons was going to get it all back, and lots more.

We had not heard a word, not a single rumour. Garfield Weston had obviously made another fortune. We had worked long hours, more than twelve on many a day, including Saturdays, without extra pay, to establish Neilsons Ice Cream. Our signs were everywhere and we were proud of our product and our company. And the people who had achieved it all, had been ignored and sold out without even a thank you.

On the Monday we found that Havard Knowles did not know either. Eventually news started to leak through. All of our customers were perplexed. Were they still going to be able to get their favourite ice creams and frozen foods? Of course, we could not tell them, so it just produced more trauma and hours of work for Gordon and me.

We all had mortgages and families, and we also had got to thinking that we had a good future ahead of us, but multi-millionaires do not concern themselves with such trivia.

It was obvious to us that there were three managers, three lots of sales representatives, three fleets of refrigerated vehicles, three depots, office staff, van salesmen and cold-storemen, and both Eldorado and Lyons were based in Exeter, twenty odd miles away. There was going to be a big sort out and heads would roll.

In the fullness of time, as they say, we were all interviewed by several Lyons people. At last we had some good news. Havard Knowles was to be Divisional Manager of the South-West, and then I was appointed as the Devon manager for the new company, Lyons Maid Eldorado Neilsons Ltd.

My first job was to arrange the sacking of every one of our staff. I felt dreadful. There was no leeway. The operation was to be centred in Exeter and all of our people lived in Newton Abbot or Torquay. I was asked by one of the many Lyons managers, if I could recommend anyone to run the beach franchise, which Lyons had just got at Dawlish Warren. It was a good job, needing a manager and his wife to live in very nice accommodation on the beachfront, and there was to be quite a large staff for the beach kiosks.

I recommended Gordon, he happily accepted, and I do not know if he is still there, but he certainly was there for a number of years.

I have never known a company with so many managers at their head office as had Lyons. They had a manager for everything, and they all found plenty of excuses to come down to Devon and to stay at one of the best hotels. As soon as I took up my position at Exeter, an avalanche of them arrived.

Incidentally, all of the Eldorado staff were sacked, including the manager, whilst all of the Lyons staff were kept on, including the manager, who was made my assistant, although he eventually worked as chief clerk.

The merger plan was that all customers of all three firms would continue to get the same ice cream as they had always had, a matter of one vehicle going down a street and servicing all of the Lyons, Eldorado and Neilson's customers. Thus it was said there would be a big cost saving which would be beneficial to all.

And this is what happened – for a few weeks, and then the bomb dropped. We had an innocuous looking low key letter merely saying that as of a certain date there would be no more Neilson's or Eldorado's Choc Ices, that all customers would change to Lyons. Of course, the balloon went up and hundreds of Neilsonites and Eldoradoites wanted to see the manager – me.

I could see it was a big con-trick, and gradually the catalogue, as they called it, was put together. It was not all Lyons that remained, and, for example, the second item on the sleight of hand – 'now you see it, now you don't' – was all dairy ice cream had to be Neilson's Cornish. At least they knew what they were doing then.

I had to learn Lyons methods. For example, they worked a tele-order sales system, where a team rang all of the customers to be serviced the next day, made out the invoice, and raised an order on the cold stores. Now our Neilson customers had always been used to van sales, where the driver was not just a driver, but he was also a salesman. With a comprehensive stock aboard, he would go to the customer and sell to him on the spot. This our customers preferred, but they just had to change.

I had a rugged time and we obviously lost customers, but after several months it seemed to settle down.

When I started, I was given a contract and it seemed very good. I kept the company car, and my basic salary was equal to what I had at Neilson's, plus the commissions I had earned through selling freezers to customers. Also, I retained the perks of petrol, and an amount for garaging and washing the car. All of these were positive. The negative aspect was having to drive backwards and forwards to Exeter. The icing on the cake, though, was the commission I was to get for 'outside events'. We were to supply ice cream at the Paignton Dog Show, Exeter Races, Newton Abbot Races, numerous Point to Point meetings, etc, and I was to get a percentage (I have forgotten the figure) on all such sales.

The contract was signed in the September after all of the outside events had finished, but next year it would be really big and, of course, I would be looking for more such events.

My job satisfaction was nowhere as good as at Neilson's, as I could not do anything without asking some manager or other. Everything was governed by a printed instruction. Everything had to balance to a penny, that is the value of every line taken from the invoices, similarly with the orders on the cold stores, and the receipts and cash brought back by the drivers. And I mean a penny. I remember once when two clerks had to come in on a Sunday, for which they got double pay, to look for something like two pence, not for the cash itself, but for a perfect balance!

After several months of turmoil, hard work, and stress, we managers received letters acknowledging that the merger was complete, we had done a good job, and now we did not need our company cars anymore, so could we please return them to London by a certain date! I rang head office and I asked what compensation we were to get. 'Nothing,' they said, 'if you need to visit a customer still, borrow one of the reps' cars!'

So that was our reward for putting the merger together, for it was only in the field that it could be accomplished. All the directors did was talk. It was in the depots and in the customers' premises, that the merger really took place.

I was still working out whether it was worth me staying on. I now had to buy a car and drive it forty miles per day just to get to work and back again. I was beginning to think that it was time to look for a new job, when another letter to all managers solved my problem. It said that from a certain date there would be no commissions for outside events. We had not yet earned one penny from them, and now we never would.

I was, by this time, much worse off than I was at Neilson's. In effect I had the Neilson's' wage plus their commission, but not their car, their petrol, their garage allowance, nor their car-washing fee. In the days when twenty pounds a week was a top income, I lost the equivalent of about eight pounds.

I decided to look for another job, but there were none available in Devon, as most national companies transfer their own people to 'Sunny Devon'. Eventually, I had three offers. One in London for the now-defunct Rolls Washing Machine Company, another in Tonbridge, Kent, with a company I had been doing business with, Cherry Valley Duckling, and the third with a Cambridge company which was over one hundred years old, and was famous for its meat pies and cooked meats.

I was to start with Rolls on one Monday, and start with the two others on the following Monday! Quite difficult to do, and Gordon and I spent all of the Saturday night prior to the Rolls starting date, talking it through and through. We decided against London and left the final decision for a few days. I was working two weeks notice by the way. I told Rolls I was not coming.

They were all Sales Managers' jobs. We now had to decide finally where I was going. We chose Cambridge because of the company's long life and, therefore, it was very well known and respected in East Anglia and the East Midlands. The rewards were good, and it was very similar in method to Neilson's, I would be very much my own boss.

Leni and I liked the Tonbridge people very much. We went there for a weekend and liked everything about it, but we had to choose. Incidentally, Cherry Valley went on to be Europe's biggest producers of duckling; so much for my perspicacity!

And we chose Cambridge, partly because of the age of the firm and the quality of its products, and partly because of lovely Cambridge.

I went on ahead of Leni and Margarete and stayed in rooms at a boarding house. There was a great opportunity to get on and make money. I had a good salary, and a bonus worked on the increase in sales of each of the numerous vans. I could see ways and means of achieving this, and for the umpteenth time I thought that this was where my long term future lay.

We opened a depot in Norwich and one in Colchester. We already had one in North Walsham, and we started to expand rapidly. Initially, I was also involved in the winding up of a chain of retail grocers' shops belonging to the firm, but which had not moved with the times and were losing money.

I started just before Christmas when sales of hams, sausages, pork pies, and fruit mince pies, were enormous. I went home to Newton Abbot for Christmas, and took a selection of our foods and everyone thought them tremendous.

The firm let us have a nice flat above one of the retail shops until we bought a house, and so Leni and Margarete joined me. Our daughter was accepted by Cambridge High School, and things were looking rosy.

We got to love East Anglia, and we explored it most weekends. Thetford Chase was our favourite haunt. We loved the forest and we used to take our 'Fluffy' with us in the car. He used to give the impression that he was hunting as he roamed around, his nose to the ground sniffing away. But we called his bluff when we did what we did at home at mealtimes. We tapped on his tin of cat food with a spoon, and he soon threw off his pretence and came running.

Cambridge was a superb place in which to live, and the environment of the colleges and the undergraduates on their bikes, their academic gowns blowing in the breeze, was invigorating. There was always something exciting happening to do with the university. I was also able to watch some first class cricket at Fenners.

We went to Great St Mary's Church on Sunday evenings, when up to 1,200 'undergrads' attended Evening Prayer. The music and singing was superb and the whole thing was stimulating. The vicar, Reverend Hugh Montefiore, who was initially a Jew, was a very interesting preacher, and his church was very well organised. We filled in a pew card and very soon we had a visit from a curate, and the fellowship helped us to settle in for hopefully a long stay.

Margarete made friends and one summer evening she went off with them to go on a punt to Grantchester, made famous in Rupert Brooke's poem. Unfortunately, due no doubt to lack of experience, the punt turned over and in the river they all went. She was soaked, but worst of all her new and expensive portable radio, quite a rarity in those days, went to the bottom and was lost. However, it was just looked upon as a bit of a lark.

She excelled at sport as usual and was in the school teams at netball, tennis, and hockey. The Lawn Tennis Association coaching, which she received at Torquay, because of the promise she showed, had been a great help to her. She had all the strokes, but I felt about this time that she was a bit too slow to get to the top. She had started playing golf at Teignmouth in Devon, and showed great promise, and I took her to the Gog Magog Golf Club at Cambridge. The 'pro' was very impressed and said that if she were his daughter, he would make her a champion, as she was a natural with a beautiful swing.

Leni and I went to the course one summer evening and unseen by Margarete, we watched her driving balls at a target. When she had finished, almost all of the balls were in a small circle, showing her accuracy and the smoothness of her swing.

We had talked about visiting Leni's Tante Maria, Onkel Peter, and their families in the Rhineland, for some time, and we decided to go in August. This was 1964, I had been away from Germany for seventeen years, and Leni had not been there since 1938, so it was very exciting for us.

We went for a month, and it was quite definitely the most magical month of my life. To see Leni revisiting her birthplace and meeting her aunts, uncles, and cousins, was wonderful. Tante Maria was a kind, smiling 'Hausfrau', who was so thrilled to see us, to talk to Leni, to fill in the intervening years since they had been together, and to meet Margarete.

Onkel Theo was so good to Margarete and bought her lots of Schockolade, and Tante Maria took us to meet friends and relations, proudly showing us off. I renewed lots of friendships I had made in the forties, and I was pleased to find Leni's cousin Hans doing well in his own business as a metalworker, specialising in making security proof counters for banks.

Cousin Gisela was married to Lothar, who was from the East and who worked in the local glassworks, and they had a son, Wolfgang. We stayed with them a few days and I could never have been happier than when I was observing the two girls watching German television together. Leni's German was very rusty and in fact hardly existent on arrival, but in a very few days she could follow all the TV, including American cowboy pictures, with them all speaking German. She and Gisela would sit and laugh at the funny scenes and 'oh, ah' together when danger loomed. None of Leni's relations could speak English, so it was better for us practising our German.

Onkel Peter, who had been a political prisoner, lived with his wife, Martha, in a beautiful country area with much woodland, and we were given a great reception at his house. His children were also Leni's cousins and some were married with children, and they were all at his house waiting for us. It was heavenly seeing my Leni being welcomed with so much love.

Cousin Peter, who was the youngest of Maria's three children, had married another Gisela, and they had two children, both girls. Now Gisela is my very favourite girl's name, but the two girls' names almost equalled Gisela in my appreciation, Petra and Gabi (Gabriella), and they were beautiful. They lived in Neukirch, a village beyond Marburg an die Lahn, a small university town. To get there we used to drive along the magnificent Rhine valley to Siegburg, and then through the Westerwald forest via Siegen.

There was a lot of history to be experienced in Marburg. It is the home of the great German family the Hindenburgs, and their tombs are all in the parish church there, along with those of Frederick William I, and Frederick II of Prussia.

However, the main attraction for tourists is the Schloss Marburg (Marburg Castle), which is famous as being the place where ex-Catholic priest, the great Martin Luther, met the Protestant Zwingli. They hoped to be able to come to an agreement about such as the celebration of the Holy Communion, but they failed to do so.

The room where the meeting took place has been faithfully maintained, even to the extent that the documents involved are now encased in glass, but still lying on the table used at the meeting.

This part of the State of Hesse seems not to be on the tourist track, as we saw hardly any foreign number plates, and yet it is really picturesque. Even in the early seventies, the women working in the fields wore full-length Hessen peasant dresses.

We loved Cologne too and we often had a trip on the Strassenbahn (the street railway), which gave an excellent service to and from the city. They have dispensed with conductors there, and you buy your ticket from a slot machine at the train stop, and woe betide you if the Inspector catches you without one. The fines are horrendous.

Out of all the beautiful places in the world I have visited, if I had the choice of where to live, I would choose the Rhineland. But for the moment we had to go back to Cambridge, with the expressed hope that we would go again to Porz one day, and that Leni's relations might visit us.

WORKING FOR A LIVING IN DEVON AND CAMBRIDGE

We caught the ferry at night and we intended to drive from Dover to Cambridge in the dark, but after a couple hours of driving, I decided that for safety's sake I had better stop in a lay-by and have a sleep. This we did, and when I awoke, I drove off with my two passengers still asleep. When Leni awoke, it was with a shock and she actually asked what time it was – in German! She had got so used to it because of her relatives' lack of English, that she automatically continued with her German. Learning it as a child, she had learned the Cologne dialect and she had often had to translate for me.

Malcolm Fraser, the Liberal Party Prime Minister of the 1970's here in Australia, was famous for a phrase he coined. That was, 'Life was not meant to be easy'. He did not need to tell me that.
When I got back to Winton Smiths it was to find that this century old company had been bought by a 'Smithfield Meat Marketing Company', but that I was to continue as General Sales Manager. So far so good, but when I met the new Managing Director, I felt that I would not last long. His attitude to me told me that this was a temporary arrangement, and so it proved.

He sent for me one day and said that they were bringing their Marketing Director from London, and that I had a month's notice, during which time I could have as much time off as I needed to find a new job. Fortunately, we had not as yet bought a house. We had had a rent free flat and had looked at lots of houses, old and new, and we had just decided to buy a particular bungalow when the blow fell.

During our searching we visited one of the villages near Cambridge, I think it was called Cottenham, and liking it, we wondered what kind of a bus service it had into the city. We asked at the village shop and the proprietor enthusiastically replied, 'Oh it's much better now. At one time we just used to have one bus on a Wednesday, but now we also have one on a Saturday!' Terrific, a 100% increase.

Now a few lines about football to keep the reader up to date. I kept myself very fit during my short sojourn in the university city. I had played for Newton Abbot Spurs up till December 1963, after being persuaded to put on my football boots again. I had been invited by their manager, Bill Anderson, to join them from the July, when they started pre-season training. The idea was for me to help in any way I could, but definitely not to play. However, I did play in practice matches, and of course, I loved it. On the Thursday night after training, I read the notice board to see my name on the team sheet! I protested loudly and refused to even consider it. But Bill said that all of the players wanted me to play. Faced with this I said that I would play as long as they did not inform the press, to which Bill agreed. The game was at Newquay. When I turned to the back page of the 'Daily Mail' on Saturday morning, the headline said, 'Two Stanleys in the news.'

It went on to say that Stanley Matthews was starting a new season despite it being his 50th year, and that I was making a comeback! It was August and holiday time, and when we got to Newquay we found that the ground was packed. As I ran onto the field, up went the cry, 'Come on the Albion!' It seemed that half of the Midlands were there. I felt exhausted by the end of the game, but after a few games I was thoroughly enjoying my football, and we hardly lost a game up until the time I had to leave to go to Cambridge. As soon as I arrived in Cambridge, I started training two nights a week with Ely City and thus retained my fitness.

Back to the job saga. So it was once more into the breach! Twice in a year big business had thwarted me, without compensation, no tribunals to appeal to; just get out and find another job. That was not going to be easy as they were scarce in Cambridge, so a further move was on the cards. The 'Daily Telegraph' was, as always, best for jobs, and soon I saw an advertisement that intrigued me. It said little, but mentioned working in Germany as a possibility. As we had recently caught up with Leni's family, the thought of working there was attractive.

Whilst looking into this possibility I applied for other jobs, and I was offered a sales manager's position with another pie and cooked meats manufacturer in Burton upon Trent. Normally, this would have been very acceptable, as it was better paid than my previous jobs, but the other avenue I was exploring seemed to offer greater rewards, opportunities for promotion, and job satisfaction.

After the two previous disappointments, Leni was looking for security, and she felt that the Burton job would supply it. On the other hand, I pointed out, that Lyons and Winton Smiths were supposed to be secure, and look what happened. The other post I was looking at made a lot of the point that you could make your own security. I said that I would work part-time during my month's notice, to prove to her that I could do it. She was horrified that it was commission and not a salary, but I tried to get her to understand that it was like going into your own business, where there was no guaranteed income.

CHAPTER TWENTY TWO
THE INTERNATIONAL LIFE INSURANCE CO. (UK) LTD

Commission was looked down upon by most people, but the company's President said that where a salary was paid, either the employer or the employee was being exploited, and after my experiences, I could not but agree with him.

Everything about the company's products and it's own philosophy appealed to me. The only problem was going to be getting over the fact that the UK company was a life insurance company known as 'The International Life Insurance Company (UK) Ltd.' and it was registered in Luxembourg.

For some reason, life insurance had a poor image in Britain, even though it was always, and always would be, a valuable financial contract. Basically, it meant that a person paid a premium on a regular basis, and if he lived for the term of years stipulated, he received the amounts he had contributed, plus the profits that had accumulated through investment; if he died, even in the first year, the stated amount of life cover was paid to the estate, and of course, if the client died in the early years much more was paid out than had been contributed.

Also, via a formula, there was a tax relief dependent on the amount of the premium (contributions). The type of contract referred to above is known as 'endowment insurance'. There were other features available such as double the amount was paid in the event of accidental death, for a small extra premium, etc. Another policy very much in vogue in those days was 'Whole of Life', which paid out on death only, but it could last for the whole of the client's life. 'Term insurance' was also available if you happened to know about it, but it was almost unheard of because, due to the premiums being small, the consultant made very little commission out of it.

I could go on, but the above was true of lots of well-known companies such as the Prudential, Sun Life of Canada, Royal, and many more.

So why was I so excited that I should enter a market which was already very competitive, with salesmen everywhere? Incidentally, I never liked the word, 'salesmen', as, if it aptly described the function of such an operative, then a doctor or accountant, both of whom 'sold' their services, could also be called salesmen.

There were many reasons for my belief that I could succeed in this already overcrowded environment. One very important feature of the company's philosophy was that we looked upon the insurance funds, that is the accumulation of their clients' contributions, plus the earnings made through investments, as belonging to the clients. All other companies at that time looked upon these moneys as their own. There was no way you could find out how or where the funds were invested, and the bonuses were at the whim of the company.

Similarly, it is obvious that you have to pay for everything you buy, whether it be a car or an insurance policy, but no way could you find what was being taken out of your contributions by these various companies.

Some of the bonuses declared generally annually were poor, and this was a reason that a section of the public looked askance upon life insurance policies.

There was just no interest in what your policy was all about, because all you ever knew was how much was the premium, for how many years did you pay it, how much would be paid to your estate if you died during the term of the policy, and how much you would get if you survived. The answer to the latter was the sum assured (the same as would be paid on death), plus bonuses if it was a 'with profit' policy.

Although over the years I have realised more and more the importance of being insured – any company's policy is better than no policy – in those days I would have found it difficult to earn a living introducing people to these policies, when I had so little to talk about.

So again, what was so different? Before I answer that question fully, herewith is a short history of the company. The International Life Insurance Company (UK) Ltd started operations in April 1963. It was an offshoot of the International Life Insurance Company (SA) Ltd of Luxembourg, which in turn was owned by Investors Overseas Services Ltd (IOS), registered in Panama.

Bernard Cornfeld was the President and founder. He was an American who originally was a social worker, but who turned to the financial world, on the basis that to make a lot of money you have to be where the money is.

He became a salesman for a Mutual Fund known as Fidelity. A Mutual Fund being a fund of money contributed by clients who invested with them either on an agreed contractual basis, so much a month or a year, or by a lump sum. The fund was divided into units or shares, which fluctuated in value according to the fluctuations of the total fund. The units always had a declared price, published in the financial pages of newspapers daily, so that clients could always calculate their holdings by multiplying the daily price by the number of units they owned. Similarly, when they invested they knew how many units they had bought. There was a charge to the client when he invested and again when he cashed in his holdings, and there was generally an annual service charge. What they were paying for was management of their investment by professional fund managers, who bought and sold shares on a daily basis. Millions of Americans had made a lot of money in this way.

Bernie Cornfeld looked around for a bigger market in which to operate, and it occurred to him that there were large numbers of US Servicemen around the world who were earning plenty of money and, perhaps, they had nowhere to invest it. He decided to go to Paris around 1955. He was so successful offering the Fidelity Mutual Fund as managers of servicemen's savings, that he soon needed more people to help him service this burgeoning market.

More about that later, but to get back to the UK. One of Bernie Cornfeld's great ambitions was to operate in Britain with British people, not only with US servicemen. However, when he had his attorney look at the UK's laws regarding offering investments, he found that this was illegal except through stockbrokers. The problem there, was that they only dealt in relatively large sums of money.

This was against Bernie's philosophy, which was what he called 'people's capitalism', and as he explained it, it gave the 'little people' around the world the opportunity to share in the growth of the world's economy.

One of the greatest innovators in the financial world, the IOS President, was not to be defeated. How could he get over this problem? Through life insurance. After all, every insurance company had a fund, so why not create a life insurance policy, whereby part of the contributions paid for life insurance, in the event of early death, and the balance less charges, bought units in the life fund?

IOS and all of its companies always had the very best advice. In the UK their solicitors were Freshfields, who were solicitors to the Bank of England; their accountants were world famous Arthur Andersen and Co; and their investment advisers were the best available in the centre of the world's investment scene, the

City of London. Later I will explain the brilliant concept that was employed to get the best financial returns.

Thus the stage was set for the launching of International Life Insurance Company (UK) Ltd. As always the Board of Directors consisted of some international executives, including Bernie Cornfeld, and some well-known Britons, notably the Earl of Lonsdale, Sir Eric Wyndham White, Mr A A D Montague Brown CBE, and later Sir Harmer Nichols.

The company's chairman was Richard Hammerman, an American insurance executive of impeccable background, and the managing director was Roy Kirkdorffer, another American, who had been part of the Mutual Fund sales force. The first company office was in Dover Street, London, and because of this, the first company product was called the Dover Equity Plan Policy. This was a brilliant concept and it turned the investment and insurance world in Great Britain upside down.

You had to have complete faith in the company and the concept, because there were knockers everywhere. The Sunday Times used to delight in having a go, for reasons we could only guess at. 'The parent company is a Panamanian company' was the favourite weapon and anyone using it seemed to consider that this was the coup de grâce, totally ignoring the fact that we had the top solicitors, the top accountants, top investment advisers, and most important, the British Life Insurance industry was policed by the Board of Trade.

The company worked on the basis that it would be in the UK forever, not a fly-by-night institution, and as time went on it attracted many top people to its ranks, particularly in marketing and public relations.

To get back to me and how I began. I saw the advertisement which asked anyone interested to ring a Philip Bell in London. He took my name, address, and work telephone number and said that a Douglas Clarke, who lived in Cambridge, would contact me. This he did, and in my initial interview he outlined the company's commission and promotion structure. He also showed me his previous month's commission cheque, which was 760 pounds, a large amount for 1964. Now Douglas went to the right school, he had many contacts after a lifetime in Cambridge, and he was comfortably off, but my final motivation for agreeing to go on a short training course was that if Douglas could do it, I could do it better.

I did not realise what a dramatic step I was taking, for it was to see me one day earn more than the Prime Minister, and yet finally it left me in financial and emotional tatters, as will be seen in the ensuing pages.

Douglas had recruited a few part-time consultants and we all took part in a five night training course at a hotel in Bury St Edmunds. Then on the Saturday morning, Roy Kirbendorffer came up from London and told of his vision for the company in future years.

The week truly motivated me, as I learnt a lot more about the Dover Plan, and I could see how it was suitable for just about anyone up to the age of 55, and that a fully paid policy was suitable for older clients who needed income. The group were all professional types, and we were all to become good friends and, eventually, managers for the company, covering offices in Birmingham, Wolverhampton, Chester, Liverpool, Leicester, Nottingham, and Coventry.

The company's training was first class, and to make sure that the product was presented to the public in a proper and unambiguous manner, consultants had to learn a presentation script. The Dover Plan was a ten-year policy, which was guaranteed renewable without medical evidence, in ten-year periods. The only difference being that the term life insurance portion of the premium increased on each renewal, according to age.

The presentation started 'Suppose that we had met ten years ago, and I had outlined a method of saving money which you had found to be attractive, and you started to save money regularly. If you had invested a 1,000 pounds in total over that time, and it had been worth, say, 1,200 pounds today, would you have been satisfied with that result?' and went on to explain just how it worked. (That was very attractive back in 1964).

The main points were that the client could have any amount of death cover he needed, in the way of cheap term insurance, so that if he did not live long enough to accumulate a large sum of money, insurance provided it for his beneficiaries, and if he lived, his savings – instead of being in such as Building Societies which at that time paid two and a half per cent – were invested in funds managed on a daily basis by professional money managers. Every ten years he could renew if he wished. He could leave his money in and still continue to contribute, and still have his cover renewed at the rate which was determined by his age.

Then one huge difference with the other company's endowment policies was that we told the client how much of his contributions went to pay for the life insurance (although in many cases the tax relief in effect paid for the life cover) and how much were our charges.

There was a cash value in the first year, whereas other companies had no value after two years and some after three years. Furthermore, clients could withdraw money up to the cash value at any time for a small charge (one shilling and sixpence), and if they wished they could put it back in. For remember, we looked upon the money in the fund as their money, not ours.

As they made contributions, they bought 'Equity Units', at the price they were on the day, so the units could rise and fall according to the Stock Market, and the managers' expertise. This had two positive effects. One was that if you had cashed in Units at a price and then put the cash back in when the Units' value dropped, you bought more Units. So clients could 'play the market' if they wished.

Another very positive and attractive feature of a regular savings programme was that 'pound cost averaging' could be dynamic. If a ten-year graph showed values of units going down for some long time, it meant that you bought more units for your contribution during that time; and then if the graph showed an upward movement at the end, then all of the units were worth the higher price.

This also made the Dover Plan very interesting, as well as having a much greater potential for profits.

The philosophy of the Equity Fund was innovative as well. A few hand picked managers were allocated a certain amount of cash, and their performance was monitored. Those who did the best got more, and so there was a lot of competition, which produced excellent results. In 1963 the Equity Unit was One pound, nineteen shillings and sixpence, and today as I write it is 179 pounds.

So much innovation created a lot of worry for the life insurance industry, and they were constantly trying to get us a bad name. They would get financial journalists to write, as an example, that our charges were high. But they never said what the other companies' charges were, the fact being that they never told even their salesmen.

The whole thing excited me and I could see myself doing a lot of business with, for example, professional footballers, whose high earnings time span was generally about ten years.

The week at Bury St Edmunds and my study of the technical details of the Dover Plan, convinced me that this was the career I should follow. Douglas was supposed to go on three appointments with me to show how to present the Plan to a prospective client, but he only made one presentation for me, to a person he knew. I did not think much of it, and a sale was not made.

I decided to go ahead without his help, and I went off in my car one day and drove to a village called Cottenham, outside of Cambridge. I must admit that I was nervous as I parked the car and wondered on whom I should call.

There was a smart looking village store, which looked quite prosperous, and I decided to go and talk to the proprietor. I waited. I kept telling myself not to be nervous, as I firmly believed that I was going to do him a favour.

I introduced myself and said that I wanted to talk to him about a method of saving money that I thought he would find attractive, so was there a table or desk at which we could sit?

He asked me into a storeroom at the back of the shop, and we sat at a table. I went through the presentation and asked the appropriate questions, which gave me an idea what he was doing with his savings, and whether or not he had sufficient life insurance.

At the end I asked him how much he could save and he said about 2 pounds a week. I worked out that including death cover, it came to 110 pounds per year. To my amazement and delight, he got out his cheque book and asked to whom should he make out the cheque!

This certainly confirmed what I thought about the Dover Plan, that it was an opportunity for anyone to take part in the growth of the economy. I stopped at the first phone box I came to and I rang Doug Clark. He was out so I left a message with his wife, Vicky, and then I went home to tell Leni the good news. I earned a little over half of what I had been earning as sales manager at Winton Smiths – for a week.

The next day I called in at Burton's the Tailors in the main street and one of the salesmen from whom I had recently bought a suit, became my second client.

I had finished my notice by now, and I had to buy a car as I had handed in my company owned vehicle. I bought a dark green Singer Chamois, and it was to do excellent service for me, until the day when, for prestige purposes, I bought a Volkswagen Fastback, my first 1,000 pound car.

I decided that the world, or at least England, was my oyster, and that with five consultants other than me living in Cambridge, it was time for me to move. The house that we had been interested in, and for which we had been offered a mortgage, we decided to bid goodbye to, and Douglas Clarke was happy to hear that I wanted to work down in Poole in Dorset, as it enlarged his supervisory area.

Before going down there, I arranged to talk to the players of Peterborough United Football Club. Anticipating that when explaining the Plan to twenty or more people, there were bound to be a few questions that I may not be able to answer, I asked Douglas to accompany me. Nothing could be worse than being caught out in such a situation, as it could result in the rest of the prospective clients losing confidence.

I asked Douglas to give the presentation, and he took me in his new Rover 2000, which was the 'in' car in 1964, to the football ground. The players were assembled and we had a little chat about football as I was still well-known as an ex-player at that time. Then when I turned to my supervisor to take over he declined! I think he was more afraid than I was! So he never did as was required of him, that is to give three presentations for me.

My talk was a great success and I signed up several players on the spot, and I arranged to go back later. We drove back to Cambridge, and Douglas worked out that his overriding commission for listening to me and driving back and forth was 95 pounds. Now few people were getting 40 pounds per week at that time, so this was a princely sum.

These successes pleased Leni, and proved to her that I could make a good career of it. The following Saturday after the Peterborough trip, there was a company sales meeting in London, in the Dover Street offices. I was delighted to have the opportunity to meet more people, to learn more, and to see the offices.

One of my new colleagues, David Parfrey, and I, went with Doug Clarke in his car, and it did not take us long to get to London. However, there was one hitch. Just after we got onto the London Road, we were pulled up by police, and kept waiting whilst they asked questions of the car drivers in front of us.

We were most annoyed to find that the 'police' were, in fact, Cambridge undergraduates dressed in police uniforms, and they were asking for money. It was the University Rag Week, but I was not amused. I thought that the students had a cheek to do this, and during the time we lived in Cambridge I often considered that many of their antics were puerile, and that they could be arrogant and consider themselves above the law.

I was not disappointed by what I experienced at my first company meeting. There were only about twenty to thirty people there, but there was a nerve tingling air of excitement. A competition was launched, whereby on your first sale you got a company tie, and as you made your fifth sale, tenth sale, etc, you won further and more expensive prizes up till the end of the competition, when there were several prizes to be won. I was most impressed.

With so few at the meeting, I could see that there really was a great opportunity to grow with the company. Perhaps this was that chance of a lifetime, which it is said we have to look out for.

Me at 6 months!

I needed two carrier bags to take my winner's prizes home from the athletics meeting

Me as a new soldier

Picture courtesy of © Colorsport

West Bromwich Albion's greatest ever team. 1953-54
We won the FA Cup and were second in the league.

I am off to play for England. Leni saying goodbye.

WBA group examining the beautiful Wembley turf before the Cup final in 1954.

Picture courtesy of © Colorsport

I challenge Edward McMorran (Northern Ireland) with Gill Merrick the England goalkeeper looking on at Goodison Park. By winning this game, England duly qualifed for the World Cup Finals. 11/11/53.

Captain of Great Britain XI in the final of the Inter-Allied Soccer Championship. Meeting Sir Sholto Douglas at Berlin Olympic Stadium. We beat Czechoslovakia 6-3.

Playing 'Head Tennis' at Middlesboro'

Captain of great Britain XI and Czech Captain 'spinning up' at Prague

I am studying Accountancy

I am lecturing an IOS group

Our daughter Margaret and grandchildren outside of Buckingham Palace.

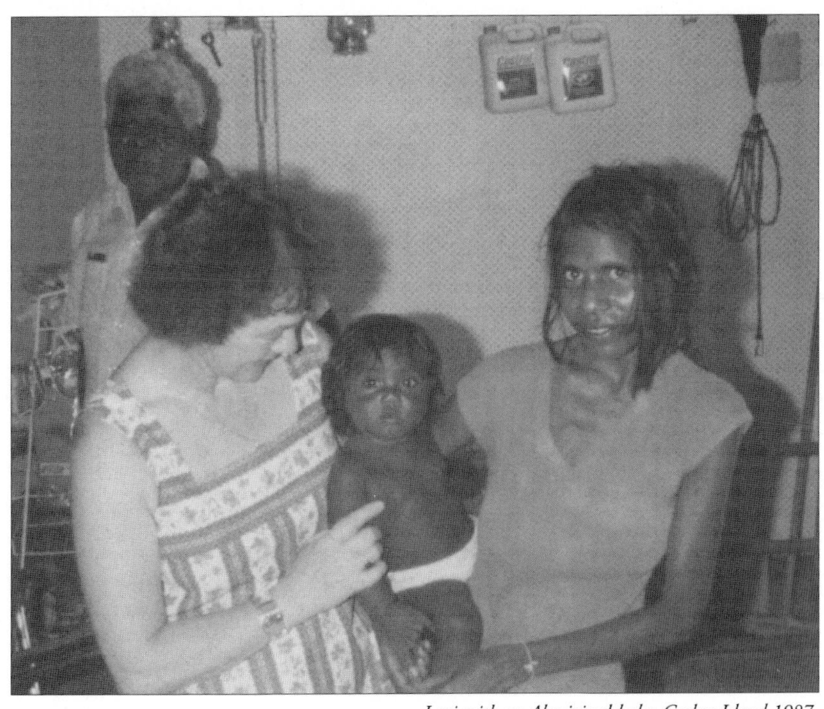

Leni with an Aboriginal baby. Croker Island 1987.

Bamyili Football team. I was President.

Leni and I 2003.

We were still in the flat above the shop, and we arranged to store our furniture down in Poole, and to move into a furnished house there.

Our cat, Fluffy, aged about fourteen, had died in the Blue Cross Cat home when we were in Germany, and the proprietors had kindly kept for us a kitten, which had almost the same markings as Fluffy. When I took it home, I went into the flat leaving the kitten in the car. Leni and Margarete ran down the passage when they heard me come in and, of course, they knew that Fluffy must have died as I was empty-handed. They both broke down and wept. It was sad to see, so after a while I said that I did have some good news, I had a kitten just like Fluffy. 'I don't want another cat,' they both shrieked. I decided that the best thing to do was to bring in the kitten immediately.

As soon as they saw it they both told me to take it away. They were never going to have another cat. No cat could replace Fluffy. I said nothing. The kitten ran around and then played with a bit of cotton hanging down from the sofa. It did all kinds of tricks and suddenly they both witnessed its antics. And that was it. Although tears continued to flow whenever Fluffy was mentioned, or thought about, the kitten won our hearts and his predecessor's name. Yes, we had a Fluffy again.

Next door to us in Cambridge lived three nurses and they too had a kitten, 'Benjy' by name. Our new Fluffy soon made friends with him and they played together, but Leni observed over a long period that the nurses did not look after their pussy. She could not face leaving Benjy behind when we went to Poole, as 'he would miss Fluffy and the food and milk he had got used to in our place.' So she asked the nurses if they would like her to find a new home for Benjy, and to prove that they did not want him, they straightaway agreed.

I got the job of finding a new home and I was lucky first time. I asked the girl on the telephone switchboard at Winton Smith if she could spread the word around, but this was not necessary as, incredibly, her grandmother's cat had just died, and she wanted another. And thereby hangs a tale.

The furniture lorry had just gone, and all that was left were a few cases of clothes etc, and Fluffy, and a cat basket, Leni, Margarete, me, and Benjy. I put him in the basket, slid the bolt across to fasten him in and I left for the address in Cherry Hinton, the same Cherry Hinton as I had stayed at when a fifteen-year-old footballer in 1939.

I found the house, knocked at the door, put the basket on the step and, as I did this the bolt slid out and so did Benjy. It was about 4.30 pm on a pitch dark November afternoon, and pouring down. Benjy shot around the back of the house. I raced after him, but lost him in the dark. I had to give up the search.

There was nothing else I could do, so I told the lady and she said that she would keep looking for him. When I told Leni she cried her eyes out saying that he would starve etc, etc, and that she was not leaving unless we found him. I tried to dissuade her, but no, that was her decision.

She had a torch and we went back. Leni was wearing her best clothes, including high heels and a fur coat. She went straight around the back of the house on arrival and she ploughed through the November vegetable patch mud, torch in hand, crying out 'Benjy, Benjy'. I said that I had done that for half an hour, but at that, we heard a distant 'Meow, meow'. Following the sound and shining the torch, Leni decided that it was coming from the shed we could see at the end of the beam. 'But it is in next door's garden,' I said. This did not deter her, for she climbed over the railings, by this time up to her ankles in mud and entered the neighbour's shed to find dear Benjy cowering in the corner, but delighted to see Leni. She picked him up, climbed back over the fence, and gave him to the lady with lots of instructions on how to feed him, how to keep him warm, and so on.

Only then did we start off for Poole! On arrival we stayed the night in a hotel and on the morrow found a really nice bungalow in Panorama Road, down by the beach at Sandbanks, a peninsula with the English Channel on one side and Poole Harbour, with its glorious views, on the other. A few doors away lived Beatle John Lennon's aunt, and next door by absolute coincidence, lived friends from Birmingham. We just happened to knock at their door to seek some information, and to our amazement there stood Irene Allen. Her husband, Geoff, used to work for Facchinos Biscuits when I worked in the office.

I soon got started introducing people to the Dover Plan, and shortly after my arrival, the company had a national contest, with the person making the most sales the winner, first prize a suit, or a blazer and slacks at Regent Street's Austin Reeds. David Parfrey, up in Birmingham by this time, and myself in Poole, both sold twenty-six Dover Plans in a month, and so the company had to give two first prizes.

Having been a professional footballer, and knowing that it was a relatively short life, it was obvious that a ten-year investment plan was a terrific idea, so I contacted a few clubs whose managers I knew. I had great success by giving a talk to groups of players and in this way players from the Arsenal, Aston Villa, West Ham United, Nottingham Forest, Newcastle United, Middlesbrough, Sunderland, Southampton, Fulham, West Bromwich Albion, Coventry City, Norwich City, etc, became clients.

I could see that the key to long-term success was in management, and I soon qualified to be a supervisor, the first step. It was at this time I also realised that I should be making long-term plans, that we were a long way from Mam and

Dad, and that the populous North-East was as good a place as any. We decided to stay with Mam and Dad for a while to see how things went.

It was then that I did a lot of business with the North-Eastern football clubs. I also trained two players and thus got started in supervision. I decided to go down to London to see the managing director, but he would not allow me to supervise or manage up there. However, they had just opened new offices in Birmingham, and I could supervise there along with David Parfrey, Douglas Clark being the Branch Manager.

CHAPTER TWENTY THREE
BACK TO THE MIDLANDS

Mam and Dad were disappointed, but there was no more I could do. We moved down, stayed with Edith and Jack Geary, old friends, in Harborne, whilst a house we had selected was being built in West Hagley. It was a confirmation of our friendship that after staying with them five months, when our house was ready to move into, Edith persuaded Leni to stay for a further two weeks.

It was a lovely house in a pretty little village, with beautiful views of the Clent Hills from our dining-room windows. The back garden was small but very private, a very high holly hedge was on two sides, a high wooden fence was on a third, and the fourth side of the rectangle was an attractive small stream which flowed through many gardens and under roadways. The local vet's house was on the stream and they had a pet duck that stayed put most of the time, but occasionally went exploring. It used to come to our lounge window and knock on the glass with its beak, knowing that Leni would give it a few titbits. We also had a large variety of birds that visited us, attracted by the variety of food she used to put on the bird table.

Sadly, shortly after we had moved in, I had a phone call from cousin Jessie, who was very kind and caring to Mam and Dad, to say that Dad was ill in hospital and she thought that we should come home straightaway. Because Dad looked after Mam, whose Multiple Sclerosis had worsened, she had been taken to Stockton and Thornaby Hospital as well.

We got to Dad's bedside at about 6.30 pm and he died just as we arrived. I had then to go up to the ward above to tell Mam. When I told her she said something which I will remember until I join them in Heaven. 'Your dad was a Saint,' Mam said. And there could have been no more fitting epitaph than that.

The funeral was so traumatic for me that my memory of it is very sketchy. Mam never came home again, but was moved to two different hospitals, before she too died, in 1967. We often went up to Teesside to see her. We wanted to have her near us, but we were persuaded that she would miss Jessie, and her friends who often visited her.

Another sad trip awaited us when she passed away, and we had the heartrending task of disposing of the home which had been my home too, for so long. The home that Margarete had come to love and know so well, and that which had been a home of peace where never a voice was raised, never a word was spoken of criticism one for the other, and where Meg and Tom were idyllically happy. No need for them to have a car, no four bedroom and two bathroom detached. Just a home built on love.

By the time Mam died, I had progressed rapidly with the International Life Insurance Company (UK) Ltd. I had been a successful supervisor due to my enthusiasm and my ability at recruiting good people. Eventually, Investors Overseas Services, the parent company in Geneva, decided it was time to open more offices. I was interviewed in London and the result was that I was told to find offices, for which the rent would be paid, a full-time secretary would be employed, an advertising budget provided, plus telephones, typewriter, duplicating machine, etc. Everything that was necessary to create a new Branch Office. Margarete became my secretary, working at home at first.

We soon found excellent accommodation, and head office sent us all of the equipment and furniture we needed. Margarete carried on as secretary and we were ready to take-off.

The office was in Wolverhampton, and to get there we used to drive through some of the most beautiful countryside. I ran a number of training courses, and we held monthly meetings on the first Saturday of the month at the Connaught Hotel. These were instructive and inspirational, and we invited associates' wives as well, so that they knew fully the opportunities available to their husbands.

Head office could see that my success was due partly to abilities in recruiting, and the type of meetings I ran, so I was invited to lecture on these two subjects at supervisors' conferences, which were held at different Universities during the vacations. Just after Mam died, I had to attend such an event at Queens College, Belfast, and I found it very difficult to get through it.

Another reason for my success was our sending of sales bulletins and information every Monday. Margarete and I would never leave the office until we had finished the job, whatever the time might be.

However, in the year prior to the above, two exciting events had occurred. The first was via a letter from Gisela, Leni's cousin in Germany, that she, her husband Lothar and their son, Wolfgang, were coming to England in the summer of 1966 to see the World Cup Finals. They had never been to England before, and knowing that Lothar was a keen football fan, we looked forward to their arrival immensely.

I had bought tickets at the Aston Villa ground for all of the First Round games in which either England or West Germany were involved. Wolfgang and Gisela would stay with Leni and Margarete, whilst Lothar and I would go to the matches.

If England were playing we both supported England, and we did the same for West Germany when they were involved. We did this right through, including the quarter and semi-finals. Lothar saw all of the games, but I missed one at Sheffield Wednesday's ground when Germany were playing there.

We were all so pleased, so happy. England was doing well. Germany was doing well. And then... they both got to the final! What would we do now? Could the camaraderie continue?

The game was to be at Wembley and, although I could have got tickets, I did not relish the prospect of getting there, or the crowds getting back, etc, so we decided to watch it on television.

Six of us watched it. Margarete and I definitely pro-England; Lothar, Gisela and Wolfgang definitely pro-West Germany; Leni pro-England but not wanting the country in which she was born to lose!

So the moment arrived. The game started. It is now well recorded in the game's history. I was extremely polite when England got in front, articulating how well the Germans were playing, and longing for the final whistle, and an England victory.

With two minutes to go and having dispensed much largesse concerning how well our opponents had played, to my horror, it happened! West Germany equalised! And incredibly the scorer was Franz Weber. On a recent holiday I had been introduced to his father, by Lothar. Weber was from Porz, just like Leni and our visitors!

'Ein Porzer! Ein Porzer!' shrieked Lothar as he cavorted exultantly around the room. Now did he need to do that? After all, I only did it inside my head when we went into the lead!

But it is only a game isn't it? Is it? Ah! well, we will sort them out in the extra half hour they have to play, I thought. And we did! But how about that goal which England scored, or did they? Did the ball really go over the line? Strangely, England supporters saw clearly that it did, but German fans saw equally clearly that it did not. But it is only a game, although there was no point telling West German football supporters that!

The World Cup Final, result apart, Leni's relations had a great time, and went back to the Rhineland with many stories of how friendly were the English, just as we had found the Germans on our holiday trips. So why the two World Wars? It was obviously nothing to do with the ordinary people.

Writing about football brings back memories of games and players, and one story I have yet to record is about Sir Stanley Mathews and the last time I spoke to the legendary figure. I had been to a managers' meeting at Upper Brook Street, off Park Lane, which runs next to Hyde Park in London, and I had stayed at the Cumberland Hotel, by Hyde Park corner. On the morning I was leaving to go home, I went downstairs to pay my bill. There was a queue at the office, and I was standing behind a slim smallish man whose hair was thinning at the back of his head, when I realised that I knew that head from somewhere.

I stood to one side so that I could see the person's face. Of course, I had seen it before, as had countless millions of people around the world, for it was Stanley Matthews. For readers uninitiated in football's (soccer's) Hall of Fame, Stan was probably the greatest player who had ever played. His body swerve, speed off the mark, and ball control, left all of his adversaries behind him, and come to think of it, they would all have recognised that back view of Stan's head, as they vainly tried to catch up with him.

I said, 'Hello Stan, what are you doing up in London?' He was pleased to see me and after asking one another how we were, he answered my question. 'Oh,' he said, 'I am going to Queens Club to see my son play tennis this afternoon.' The Queens Club tournament is a top championship and at that time Stanley Matthews junior was a top British tennis player. Then we talked about Stan's new job as manager of Port Vale and he asked me to pop in the next time I was in the Potteries. He paid his bill, I paid mine, and we said our goodbyes.

Now this had been witnessed by Peter Mowatt, a friend of mine, who was sitting in the foyer. 'That was Stanley Matthews wasn't it?' asked Peter. 'Yes,' I said, 'he is in London to see his son play tennis.' 'Maybe he is,' said Peter, 'but haven't you seen this?', showing me the front page of the 'Daily Telegraph' where there was a large photograph with the caption, 'Sir Stanley Matthews is knighted by the Queen.' I felt awful. Of course, I then recalled that he had appeared in the recent Honours List. How had I forgotten? However, it did illustrate the modesty of the man, something everyone who knows him is aware of, and it has been my experience that the greatest are often the most modest.

CHAPTER TWENTY FOUR
WE START TO TRAVEL

The second exciting occurrence of 1966, after the visit of the German side of our family, was to do with Investors Overseas Services Ltd (IOS). Later in the summer, Leni and I were invited to a conference in Geneva, and as Margarete was branch secretary, I got her an invitation too. This was really an exciting prospect. We had read and heard so much about IOS, and its growth all over the world, and we looked forward to meeting and talking to our opposite numbers in other countries. We decided to go by car, get the ferry from Dover to Calais, then drive through France to the Jura Mountains and on to Geneva.

We stayed the first night at Ardres, a village about two hours from Calais, and we then took our time driving across France to stay at a delightful chalet hotel in the Jura Mountains, overlooking the city of Geneva and the lake.

The Company had virtually taken over the Hotel Intercontinental for the conference, and for accommodation. On arrival, we had our photographs taken and in a matter of minutes we were issued with official badges containing our photographs and a copy of our signatures. We marvelled at some of the IOS secretaries who were on duty to book us all in, as their language skills were tremendous. Most of them could speak English, French, Italian, Spanish, and German, and switched quickly from one to the other as required. During the conference sessions in the main hall, we all had earphones, which we used if the speaker used other than our own tongue. The interpreters were housed in small cubicles looking down on the speakers' platform, and their translations were immediate and continuous. For someone like me, with some knowledge of French and German, and an interest in languages, it was awesome.

It was interesting to compare our experiences with those of colleagues in other countries and continents. Strangely, there was little difference. People are the same everywhere, as we found that the problems we faced in persuading people to invest money and insure themselves, were the same in Brazil as in Italy or Canada, or in any of the many lands in which we operated.

The German firm, IOS Deutschland, was the frontrunner, and with Dr Erich Mende, ex-Vice-Chancellor of West Germany as President, they went from strength to strength. The Honourable James Roosevelt, son of the United States President, and recently Ambassador to the United Nations, was introduced to us as a new director of the parent IOS company, and of the UK company.

We came away knowing that we were part of the most vibrant and exciting organisation in the world. Record sales were reported from everywhere and we were very motivated. Most people went straight back home at the end of the fortnight as they felt that they should impart the news and knowledge that they had acquired, as quickly as possible. We felt, however, that it would keep, and that we had earned a holiday after a hard year of long hours.

The ladies had enjoyed themselves. They attended the main conferences, so that they could understand the IOS philosophy and objectives, and they also took part in seminars with the IOS Foundation, which was a charity run by the ladies. It was very successful, their method being to raise money which was to provide the seeds for various philanthropic enterprises. The 'Cambridge Associates', as an example, created the Cambridge Association of Drug Addiction, which helped the many people who were addicted. The ladies also went on trips to places like Montreux and Mont Blanc, and we joined them in the evenings for dinner, and often for parties put on by IOS at their villa on Lake Geneva.

Altogether, a most exciting, rewarding, and motivating time, much enjoyed by all. We left Geneva on a Saturday morning and did a little touring, with our final objective Tante Maria's at Porz-am-Rhein. We crossed over the bridge, which connected Liechtenstein to Switzerland, and stayed the first night at the 'Goldenen Adler' (Golden Eagle) in Vaduz, probably the smallest capital in the world, with its ancient castle at the top of the mountain – a castle well-known to British Royalty.

Then into Austria, and some shopping. At that time it was extremely cheap there, and Leni bought attractive Austrian clothes and various things for the house. Next we went into Bavaria, staying odd nights in small hotels, and then a few days in Garmisch Partenkirchen where, surprisingly, we came across a bar selling the best Irish Coffee I have ever tasted. The weather was magnificent all the time, and we had a wonderful holiday. Finally, we set off for our beloved Rhineland, for me the most romantic place in the world.

On arrival, Tante Maria nipped out for 'Ein paar Minuten', which meant two things: a 'short while', and some gorgeous mouth-watering German cheesecake and Black Forest Gateau. There is nothing in the world to beat proper German 'Kasekuchen'. They use something called Quark for the cheese filling, and it tastes superb.

Onkel Theo was always so pleased to see us and to please him we went to the local pub, where we were remembered from our 1964 visit. We always felt very nostalgic when we went there, as it had existed for many years, including when Leni's mam and Dad were young. They went there when they were courting, and I am sure that nothing had changed in the interim.

I believe that it was during the 1966 visit that Leni went to a funeral with her Aunt and Uncle. The deceased was someone Leni's mam had known, so it seemed right for Leni to represent her mother.

The hearse was drawn by four horses, which were clothed in black and were quite splendid. There were many mourners walking slowly behind, so different to the fast cars we see today. After the internment, we were all invited to the pub for a drink. It seemed that a Porz-am-Rhein funeral was somewhat similar to an Irish one, and the departed was remembered through a haze of cigarette smoke and alcohol.

On a brighter note, one Friday evening Lothar was to play for the local glassworks at 'kegelin' (I am sure that I have spelt it wrongly), a form of skittles, similar in some ways to the tenpin bowling which is so popular these days. Leni decided that she would like to go and watch, so off we went to the 'kegelbahn' which was in the cellars of a well-known local hostelry. On arrival, although it was after the 6.00 pm starting time, they were still just practising, and this was because one of the 'glasfabrik's' team had not turned up.

After a while, I heard the team captain ask Lothar if he thought I would like to take the absentee's place. I knew nothing about the game, but 'in for a pfennig in for a mark', and so I agreed.

The 'bahn', or alley or whatever we might call it in English, was slightly shorter and narrower than a tenpin one, and there were nine skittles, I think. I soon discovered that there was quite an art to it, for when I aimed the ball directly at the first skittle, which was in effect the point of a diamond, it completely missed, although it knocked down some of the other skittles. There was a bias, which had to be taken into account. To some extent I mastered this, and the team were quite happy with my debut performance.

However, the most difficult part was still to come. Apparently, it was not just a matter of scoring as many as possible in a specified number of strikes, but it was also necessary to finish on an exact number. A few of the Kerls (chaps) had tried to score the required final number, but all had exceeded it, so it came to my turn.

I was not absolutely certain what was required, and even less sure how I could achieve it. So I took my courage in both hands, and a ball in my right hand, knelt as though I knew what I was doing, and delivered what transpired to be the coup de grâce. Well, I guess it was, as when the ball struck the skittles and came to rest, there was an eruption. All of 'mein Mannschaft' jumped in the air and all seemed to land on my back, as they yelled 'Holz, Holz, Holz!', obviously meaning more than the literal 'Wood, Wood, Wood!'

I was then transported by 'meinen Kamaraden' up the stairs into the bar, where I was given a much too large glass of Schnappes as they sang their victory song. I guessed that we had won. I was told what 'ein gut Kerl' I was, and jokingly asked could I fly over to Porz every Friday night to play in the team!

The following evening was also very enjoyable. Lothar and Gisela took Leni, Margarete, and me, to a restaurant that was built right on the bank of the Rhine. Its name was 'Vater Rhein' (Father Rhine), and after a meal, a delightful German band provided the music for dancing. This pleased my two ladies, as they liked nothing better than to pirouette on the dance floor.

Nothing very exciting about that, you may say, and you would be right, but there were happenings that made it into a unique event. A young man who wished to dance with our daughter, actually asked Leni and me if he could approach Margarete. Of course, we agreed, and the young German courteously took her hand and led her to the floor. They danced beautifully; he had a hand around her waist and the other holding her hand. When they finished he brought her back, bowed to all three of us, and thanked us. It was a revelation, and we realised that what we considered 'old-world charm', was alive and well on the banks of the Rhine.

I may have written this elsewhere, but to me it is worthy of repetition, that my idea of 'heaven on earth' is sitting on a bench on the Rheinterrasse at Porz, watching the Rhine barges and passenger steamers going up and down the great river, especially on a warm August day. As I write this in Western Australia, I look forward to the day, God willing, when Leni and I revisit that romantic place again, this time with our Toby and Elizabeth, who have Rhineland blood in their veins.

In May 1967, Leni, Margarete, and I, had a really wonderful holiday in Gibraltar and the Costa del Sol in the South of Spain. It was our first experience of really hot weather. We arrived at Gibraltar airport late in the evening, and as we walked away from the plane I felt quite an intense heat, which I thought was from the engines, but as we got further away I realised that it was that of a Gibraltar evening. I must say that I loved it. We were taken to the 'Rock Hotel', a really classy place, and we stayed there for a few days whilst we had a conference. It was so exciting to learn of the progress of IOS worldwide, and even in the tiny British dependent territory of Gibraltar.

We found it remarkable that so much could be packed on to an oddly shaped rock attached to the end of Spain. Then we moved to a new hotel, the 'Catalina

Bay', and from our bedroom we could see one of the wonders of 'Gib', the rain catchment area. Fresh water on the rock was obtained from it by a series of troughs inter-connected and leading to large storage tanks.

A reception was held by the company where various local dignitaries were invited. Leni and I were talking to an extremely smart and dignified gentleman of military bearing, but who was dressed in civilian clothes. During the conversation, I asked him if he lived in Gibraltar. When he replied in the affirmative, I asked him what he did for a living. He said, 'I am the Admiral of the Fleet!'

The main reason for our Iberian sojourn was to visit the IOS Development Corporation's (Indevco) villas and skyscraper blocks of units at Torremolinos and El Rosario. This was another example of the innovative power of IOS. All of the accommodation was superb, and it strengthened our resolve to go back to the UK, and promote a company that could achieve so much. The units were right on the Torremolinos beachfront, and the villas were spread over some hills at El Rosario. Margarete was with us and we decided to stay longer and have a holiday. We had to return to Gibraltar, where most of the party flew off to London, and a few of us returned to Spain.

To get there we had to go through the border at La Linea. It was at the time that General Franco's air force was patrolling the airspace with their fighter planes, and vehicles were not allowed through the border. Thus, we had to walk with all of our suitcases from the 'Gib' customs to those of Spain, a distance of about a quarter of a mile. We did get some satisfaction as Brits, because they held a referendum in Gibraltar during our visit, when the people were asked if they wanted to be ruled by Spain. More than 99% said, 'No!'

The Spanish were quite silly to their own people, because whereas prior to the 'troubles' large numbers of Spaniards crossed the border daily to go to work, when the border was closed to them, as it was, all of their jobs went to people from North Africa, who came across the narrow Straits of Gibraltar by ferry.

We went up the Spanish coast by taxi and passed through what were then tiny villages such as Fuengirola and Estartit. We decided to stay in Marbella and we found a charming old-world hotel known as 'Pension Mena', in the General Franco Platz, would you believe? We certainly chose correctly. The food was truly excellent and the idea of the 'siesta' appealed to us, whereby in the heat of the day everything closed down, to open again in the early evening. We loved dressing up in light clothing and walking through the streets, which were perfumed by tropical flowers and shrubs. Dancing was in the open air and we generally got back to the Pension at about 2.00 am.

One day on television there was a football match from Madrid between England and Spain, and it was most interesting being the only Englishman amongst Spaniards and Germans (the latter incidentally all cheered for us, surprisingly).

The family Mena were so unbelievably kind to us that on our last day we went out and bought them a large bouquet of flowers. When Leni went to present them to the family, they had a bottle of brandy all gift-wrapped to give to us! They were beautiful people and so were the guests. We made lots of friends and, in particular, a German couple on their honeymoon. In 1970 Margarete was invited by them to stay with them at their home in Siegen am Westerwald – to be Godmother to their newly born son! How we would love to see them all again!

To be a successful manager in our company there were various necessary attributes. One was a total belief in the philosophy of investing in equities, and also very important was recruiting. One of my best recruits was Fred Pearce, whom I had known at both Facchinos Biscuits and then at Neilsons, for whom he managed the marketing of Meddocream, an ice cream powder we sold to soft ice cream vendors. He took to selling Dover Plans as quickly as I had, and he was soon full-time with us. He became a supervisor and he and I enjoyed a close relationship, helping one another most successfully. His wife, Cherry, was a real enthusiast too, and we all enjoyed life in those exciting 1960's.

Fred had a great sense of humour, and he was one of those people who could remember every joke he heard. One night we went to Stoke to take a course, and all of the way he regaled me with the whole of a comedy programme, which he had heard on the radio the previous evening.

But one thing Fred had never done was to travel abroad, and neither had Cherry. They gave us a few hints that they would like to come with us when we were planning our 1967 trip. So we asked them and they jumped at the chance, even though after the holiday they confessed that they had always looked down on all things European and, particularly, those that were German, even though the war had been over for twenty-two years. The holiday radically changed their perspectives.

So back to the beginning. We planned very loosely to visit France, Germany, Switzerland, and Spain, so we caught the ferry at Dover and got off at Calais, staying the first night at our favourite pension at Ardres. Neither of them spoke any French, and this lack of foreign languages may have contributed to their anti-European stance. They were happy that Margarete and I could act as liaison.

I had my new BMW 1800 and Fred his beloved Jaguar, so we were well equipped to do the journey, which would be several thousand miles. After a typical French breakfast of croissants, farm butter, conserve, and lots of delicious coffee, we set off for Aachen, intending to give our companions a look at the area in which Leni was born.

We passed through the outskirts of Cologne, then Bonn and Bad Godesberg, where Neville Chamberlain had first met Adolf Hitler. Next we made for the Eiffel, a particularly beautiful hilly area, and as it was the early evening we decided to start looking for a 'gasthaus' to stay the night. On enquiring at such a place, the owner apologised, saying that his establishment was full, but that he would ring his brother, who had a guest house in a village further on, to see if he had vacancies. Fortunately, he had, but we were implored not to go immediately, but first of all to spend the evening where we were, as it was the local church choir's annual outing and they would be singing German folk songs. Now there is absolutely nothing in music that I like better than the old German songs. I suppose that the combination of Leni being a Rheinlandmädchen (Rhineland-girl), and my time at Göttingen learning some of the songs, created this almost overwhelming nostalgia. I felt that we were very fortunate to take part in something so very German. What a night we had. We had to refuse the many offers of drinks as Fred and I were driving, and Cherry and Leni were not great drinkers, but it was marvellous to be part of the choir's annual celebration. They sang all the songs I asked them to sing, plus many others.

It got very late and we started to worry about the journey ahead, getting lost, etc, but we need not have worried for the proprietor had a plan. After our 'auf wiedersehens' he went before us in his car, and we followed. He was accompanied by a friend and in about half an hour we arrived at our destination. By this time it was 2.30 am and the place was in complete darkness. This worried us, but after a minute or two we heard some movement, a light went on, the door opened and a somewhat Dickensian figure appeared, dressed in a nightshirt down to his feet, and wearing a woollen knitted cap.

He welcomed us most warmly, beckoned us in, and with a lantern in his hand disappeared down some steps. When he reappeared it was obvious that he had been to the wine cellar, for he opened a bottle and filled the biggest glasses we had ever seen with a beautiful cold moselle. It took two bottles to fill all of the glasses. We were there until about 4 am, when our original host's friend said that he would have to get back as he was a forester and he started work at 6 am!

Fred and Cherry could not believe the friendliness and the generosity of our erstwhile enemies. We had a lovely breakfast, swearing that the huge cups of coffee were the best tasting that we had ever enjoyed.

We then made for the Black Forest, the very name of which creates magical pictures in my mind. Oh! How I loved the Rhineland, the Schwarzwald and

Bayern – Bavaria. How I would love to visit there regularly and spend a lot of time exploring it. But back to 1967. We eventually got onto the 'autobahn' (motorway), the one that runs from Cologne to Frankfurt. What a joy this was for Fred to be able to drive his Jaguar at full speed on the no speed limit motorway, something the law prevented him doing in the UK. We got down to Osthofen, a distance of about 250 kilometres, in two hours. We broke our own rule for the second night, which was that we would find accommodation before 6.00 pm, a golden-rule whilst touring in Europe.

After trying two or three places without success, I saw the local shoemaker on the doorstep of his shop, and I asked him if he could suggest where we could try. To our most pleasurable surprise, he said that he would phone around a few people. After a few calls that produced no positive result, and after refusing point-blank to let me pay for the calls, despite my protests, he locked up the shoe shop door and got in his car, signalling us to follow. It was a steep hilly area, and after climbing quite high and trying a number of places all of which were full, we went full circle arriving back in the village.

Incredibly, when we got back he tried the very last place, the last place in the circle and actually nearest to him, and they said, 'Yes,' providing we did not mind sleeping in two rooms in the attic. They were full of apologies, but when we saw the rooms we could not understand the apologies, for they were spotlessly clean, although Spartan, and the beds were very comfortable. And cheap! We just could not believe the cost of bed and breakfast.

As we ate breakfast, Fred and Cherry articulated how amazed they had been at the heart-warming friendship they had been shown once again.

Then we were off once more, our next stop being Geneva, the home of IOS, and a city that Fred had longed to see. We visited the offices and I am sure that it did him a lot of good to see the places and people he had only read about.

Our next port of call was to be Lyons in France, where I had played football twenty-one years earlier. Back in France we got on to the autoroute, with the usual plan, Fred to go first so that we were always following, and without problems I renewed acquaintance with Lyons.

Shortly after leaving Lyons we were involved in what turned out to be a hilarious incident. For a change I went in front, as we were off the autoroute and on to narrow country roads, and we wanted to see a bit of the French countryside. We would drive relatively slowly until we rejoined the motorway, so there was little danger of Fred getting into any trouble.

As we drove sedately along, we saw a long steep hill ahead of us, with double white lines from bottom to top. A slow moving truck had just started to climb, and whilst knowing that I should not cross the double lines, particularly having been taught in England to treat such lines as a brick wall, I could not help thinking that it would take ages to follow the truck, and that we would be nauseated by the black smoke issuing from its exhausts. So with several hundred yards of clear vision ahead, I overtook the truck and resumed the sedate perambulation which we had been enjoying. Fred followed suit, and off we went.

Suddenly, forty or fifty yards further on, I saw a French gendarme (policeman) jump out into the middle of the road. His motor cycle was parked in a long lay-by, and before I reached him, I saw a second officer waiting for Fred!

Up went his hand and he motioned us into the lay-by. 'Leesornce', he said, 'leesornce'. 'Me Inglees,' I replied. 'Leesornce, leesornce,' he screamed. Pointing to my chest I repeated, 'Me Inglees.' After a few 'Sacre bleus' and other expletives, he gave up the interview and waved me on, and looking in my mirror I could see that the same was happening to Fred.

Further on we compared notes when we stopped for a drink. I told Fred what I had said, and he told me what had transpired between him and the other gendarme. He said, 'Me speak no French', then pointing to me, 'My friend, he speaks French!'

We then continued on, and got back on to the main autoroute for the Spanish border. The weather had been beautiful, and with Fred in the lead we kept a safe distance behind the Jaguar, but then it started to go dark, and worst of all it poured down. My windscreen wipers, although in perfect order, could not fully cope with the volume of water, so we had to slow down, and thus lost sight of our friends' car. Our reserve plan was that in the event of such a happening, we would stop at the next motorway cafe.

This we did, but no Fred. So the plan failed. After wasting some time, Leni suggested that we should go on to the Spanish border, as surely they would stop there. We looked in at the various cafes en route, but with no luck, and eventually we got to the border where they could have been in a cafe or, more likely, they would have left a message at the border office.

Neither eventuated and all of our plans had come to nought.

So we had to acknowledge that a minor catastrophe had occurred, not really for us, as we were used to Europe, although we had been looking forward to showing our friends around further, but certainly for them, as they would be quite lost. Our telephone call to the IOS office in Madrid had been our last hope, and it was fruitless.

We decided not to go down to the South on the Costa del Sol as it was a very long drive, and the whole idea had been to show our fellow travellers its attraction; but to go down the Costa Brava which is to the North of Spain.

Its reputation seemed to be marred by the behaviour of some British drunks, whose idea of Spain was one of cheap liquor and all night binges. But we wanted to see for ourselves, so we set off on the road which went left from the main road and which led to the well known resorts, such as Tossa Blanes and Playa del Mar.

We aimed for Sitges, but we had no idea of what we had taken on. There must have been more than a hundred sharp bends, and the road was too narrow for such a busy route. And when we got there we did not like it one bit. There were flashing neon signs advertising fish and chips, would you believe it? I mean, who wants 'real English fish and chips' on a Spanish holiday?

Then as we wound our way back to the main road to the border, we saw some of our compatriots, bottles in hand, staggering along the pavements. We had had our fill of the Costa Brava, so we decided to go back to Germany and another visit to Leni's relations.

It was evening, but still daylight, when we reached the main road. We were talking about where we should stay the night, when Margarete noticed a sign showing that a town called Rosas was not too far off to the right. She persuaded us to have one last look for a place where we might have a beach holiday, seeing that she was a good swimmer with beautiful new bathing costumes and desirous of a tan. Well who could blame her? So we duly followed the sign and an hour later we were driving around Rosas looking for a place to stay. It was the first week in August and there were no vacancies anywhere. However, we were lucky in the end, because one proprietor took pity on us. He said that, provided we would rise at 6.30 am, we could sleep on mattresses in the dining-room! Any port in a storm, so we accepted with alacrity, locked up the car, which was parked in the street, and gratefully had supper and went to bed.

We were awakened by kitchen workers very early, and we were soon ready, thanking our benefactor and intending to go to Germany, as we knew that there was no chance of accommodation in the quaint little seaside town, whose only two industries were tourism and fishing.

As we approached our car, I could see a piece of paper under a windscreen wiper. Fancy, a parking ticket on our holidays, I thought. I released the paper to read, 'We are staying in a caravan at the Almedraba Caravan Park a couple of miles up the coast. Cherry and Fred.'

The chance of us meeting up again was ten billion to one. There were so many reasons why this could not possibly happen and yet our friends had seen our car parked in the street of a town which none of us intended to visit!

We drove straight to the caravan park, found Fred and Cherry, and then spent the next hour or two telling one another what we had done since missing each other on the autoroute. Fred had done none of the things that we imagined he might have done, and they had decided to stay at the first coastal town they found. This was Rosas, but they could not find accommodation, so they had gone up the coast to tiny Almedraba.

We did not fancy a caravan, so we decided to see if there were any vacancies in a block of luxury units right on the beach. We were very lucky first time and we leased a magnificent three-bedroom unit, beautifully decorated and furnished with superb Spanish furniture. The crockery and cutlery were first class, and all of the floors were marble, which helped to keep the place cool, despite the Mediterranean sun. And the rent included a cleaner coming in every day. We put down a deposit and then I went to a mini-market, which I had noticed down the road. We only needed milk and coffee, for the time being, and I was short of pesetas anyway. To my surprise the shop sold just about every type of food, even Lipton's tea and Kellogg's Cornflakes, so I decided to load up my trolley and then go to the bank in Rosas to change some travellers cheques. When I got to the till, I explained with hand signs that I would leave the goods in the trolley, go to the bank and return to pay. To my amazement, the lady, who had never seen me before, said, 'Manana', which means 'tomorrow'!

We had a wonderful holiday with beautiful weather, and we all made the most of it. The bay was lovely and excellent for bathing. We found that the concierge supplied milk, bread, local wine, and Fanta soft drinks. The wine was perfectly enjoyable and it cost so little, a shilling in those days – cheaper than the Fanta.

When we went to see him at the end of four weeks to settle up the bill, we asked him what we owed him. We were able to work out the rent, deducting the deposit, but when we asked him what the bread and drinks had amounted to, he said he did not know, so what had we had?

We sorted it out to our mutual satisfaction, but what amazed me was the extraordinary trust we enjoyed from the Spanish people. We always found them so helpful, friendly, and trusting. I hope that we return to live in England and if so, I shall look forward to seeing whether or not mass tourism has affected this trust and generosity. Yes, a trip to Spain again will be very interesting.

When Margarete and I returned to the office to start a new business year, we were delighted to find that Barry Elwell, a supervisor whom we left in charge, had created a record amount of business. He had encouraged everyone to show that they could succeed without me! And whereas it was a common excuse for lack of business in August to blame it on lots of prospective clients being on holiday, Barry had told them all that because of the holidays there would be more people at home to see. This was, of course, true and was good thinking.

However, it was not all plain sailing or good news. One of our Wolverhampton supervisors named Don Winton, was a solid businessman of great integrity, and I felt that he had a very good future with us, so I could not believe it when he came to see me to say that he and one of the associates he had trained were leaving. Successful people just did not leave.

He convinced me that he was serious and that they were going into the lingerie business! This did not seem like Don, but he said that they were going to sell ladies underwear via 'Party Plan', a marketing device which was known only at that time as a means of selling plastic kitchenware, viz 'Tupperware'.

I tried to dissuade him, but when I read about 'Pippadee' two or three years later in the 'Financial Times', being probably the biggest lingerie retailer in Europe, with enormous sales in Scandinavia, I had to admit that he had been right! I am convinced that he learned a lot with us and that this put him in good stead. Later I read that he had sold his shares for more than half a million pounds! Ah well! Incidentally, the word Pippadee came from the two wives names, Pippa and Dee.

We were always thinking of new markets and it occurred to me that there must be a lot of business in the immigrant communities, as they were people who needed to save money to improve their status in society. West Indians, in the main, were not savers, nor did I think that they were workers, due to most of them being unskilled. The various groups from the sub-continent were the best prospects, in particular, the Sikh Indians, and the 'Patels' of whom there seemed to be a large number. Some Pakistanis were also of a saving nature, and I decided to look around for a few recruits in these ethnic groups.

I was introduced one day to a highly intelligent leader of the Sikh community in Birmingham, Jasmer Singh Rai. He was from a very good family, his brother was the United Nations' expert on tropical diseases, and he was working as an adviser to Indians in general. With so much influence in the community, he was obviously the man for the job, and it did not take me long to convince him.

I got on very well with all of the Indians and Pakistanis and I used to pull their legs and make them laugh. For example, Sikhs who wore turbans got used to my remarks whenever we parted company. I always said, 'Well, cheerio', Ranjit or Jasmer or whoever, 'and I hope that your head soon gets better!'.

Ranjit Singh Hans was a really fine fellow. From a very good family, he did some first class business for us, and we became good friends. He used to call at our house every Christmas, always bringing us presents. One day he told us that he was going to India for a few weeks as his parents had found him a bride – arranged marriages being still the norm in the sixties. Any man would agree with it, if it always produced a Pammy, for that was Ranjit's betrothed's name. She was truly beautiful, both in looks and in manner, and the gold earrings, bracelets and necklaces she wore, looked even more alluring against her dark skin.

They bought a house at the new town of Telford in Shropshire and they asked us to dinner, saying that we should let them know when it was convenient for us. I have to confess that the thought of eating in an Indian's house was less than attractive to me. I am a conservative eater, roast beef and Yorkshire pudding and the like, being my staple diet, and as for Eastern food, well I had heard all kinds of horror stories about that, and also the hygiene, or lack of it. However, this kind of open-ended invitation was easily put off by such replies as, 'Ah yes Ranjit, we must do that.'

Of course, after a large number of these answers, he started to try to pin us down to a date and eventually I succumbed. 'Alright,' I said, 'We'll come for dinner on Saturday evening,' and then I worried about it and dreaded it all the week.

Saturday arrived, as it was bound to do, and the hours crept by until it was 2.00 pm. 'I can't go,' I said to Leni, 'I just can't face that Indian food.' She said, 'Well, you will have to ring them, as they will be starting to prepare, but I don't know what you can say.'

Being the man in the family and the leader, the decision maker, I resolved to show my authority, so I dialled Ranjit's number. He answered quickly and the conversation went something like this, 'Ranjit .... I .. I .. I .. I am ss..sorry, b .. but we won't be able to come after all. You see, I don't feel well.' (What a fib). 'We'll have to come some other time, I'm so sorry.' 'Well, what about tomorrow?' he replied, without a trace of disappointment or anger. I don't know why, but this simple question floored me. Meekly, I said, 'Oh, oh alright then, we'll come on Sunday.'

Maybe it was because I had been to church and had said the 'General Confession' which included all my sins of omission and commission, and of telling Ranjit an awful fib, that when it got to about 5.30 pm we got into the car and set off for Telford.

Following our Sikh friend's instructions, we found his road and looked for his number. When we came to it, it was a new house with a fence around the garden, a path to the front door, and a button marked 'Bell'. I pressed it and Ranjit opened the door. We went in, and there was carpet on the floor, a lounge suite in the lounge, a set of dining furniture in the dining-room and by then I was ready to believe that there would be a bedroom suite in the bedroom! Just how wrong can one get? I felt quite ashamed, but of course no doubt the food would prove my point. The smell from the kitchen was nice, but that did not necessarily mean a lot.

Soon we sat down and the first course was served, and the 'waitress' was another very beautiful Indian lady, who was introduced to us as Pammy's sister. Surprisingly, it was a vegetable soup, served with something that looked like thin cold pancakes, called, I think, chapattis, and I actually liked both.

We had six courses in all and every time I kind of knew that the next one was going to be the one to prove my fears were not without foundation. But it was the sixth which had all the hallmarks. It was best described as three dirty looking potatoes in a pool of evil looking gravy.

It took a lot of courage, soul-searching, and time, before I dug my fork into one, sliced a small sliver and gently placed it in my mouth. I engaged it with my taste buds, after several seconds I might add, and... it tasted absolutely gorgeous. It was a coconut concoction in a sauce, which satisfied even my sweetest of sweet teeth.

As we drank percolated coffee in the lounge, I decided that it was time to come clean. After congratulating Pammy on her food, I said, 'There is something I have to tell you.' Then I bared my soul and told them everything about my fears regarding an Indian home and their cooking. I don't know if I felt better or worse, so mixed were my emotions when our host said simply, 'Don't you think I knew?'

The coup de grâce came when I said that so many delicious courses must have taken a long time to prepare. 'All day,' was Ranjit's reply. Hesitatingly I asked about the food they had cooked the day before, to be told, gently I must admit, that most of it had to be thrown out. After Pammy and her sister, who came purely to help, had taken so much time, had made such an effort, and had obviously produced a similar menu to that which we had just enjoyed, the guests had rung and told a big fib to renege on a kind and generous invitation. One lives and learns.

Another Indian 'food' story began when we took Jasmer and his wife out to dinner at the Queens Hotel in Birmingham. Whenever anyone performed especially well, Leni, Margarete (being my secretary), and I, had started a habit of taking the person and his wife out to the Queens. Apart from showing my appreciation of a job well done, it proved to be very motivating for all of our group. Going to the Queens with the manager was a kind of status symbol.

One thing it wasn't intended to be, was a precursor to a similar invitation to us from the recipient. But Jasmer insisted that he must return the compliment. Eventually, I realised that with him there was some sort of pride involved, that if it was all right for me to pay for him, he should be allowed to reciprocate.

Eventually, reluctantly I agreed, but I was amazed to learn that we were to dine at Knowle House. Now I had passed the entrance to this, perhaps the best and most expensive eating-place in the Birmingham area, but it horrified me to think of what it was going to cost Jas.

On the night, we put on our best bibs and tuckers and set off for Knowle House, which we found was at the end of a very long drive. It was brightly lit and as we started up the steps to the hotel, a liveried attendant welcomed us with, 'Good evening Mr and Mrs Rickaby and Margarete,' and conducted us to the foyer where Jasmer, his wife and family, and his most distinguished brother, were waiting for us. From thence we were conducted to a private dining-room where we were treated like royalty. There was a waiter to each one of us, and when we were eating, they stood behind us, backs to the wall, watching and waiting for an opportunity to do something for us. Incidentally, Jasmer's brother was a world authority on tropical diseases, working for the United Nations World Health Organisation, and also as a professor at a Californian University.

It was a truly regal evening and it transpired that Jasmer was a regular guest at Knowle. Whenever the Indian High Commissioner or other high official visited the Midlands, our Sikh friend was always invited to meet with them. Because of this, the manager of this august establishment fawned over him. You certainly learn something every day.

Another of my top performing associates was Ifor Evans, who supervised a group in the North-West for me.

After attending a Branch meeting at Chester, we decided to go across the country to see Leni's parents on Teesside. We had to cross the Pennines and our route included Blackburn, Skipton, and Ripon.

At first we spent a few hours with our friends Derrick and Vera at Little Sutton, and as often happened, we stayed longer than we had intended, setting off finally at 9.00 pm.

I knew that we would need petrol pretty soon, as we had to travel about 150 miles and the indicator said 'low'. At that time of night, we were surprised that so many filling stations were open, so we kept going, trying to make a dent in the 150 miles.

We decided that we would definitely stop at Blackburn and, as we entered the town, a garage was open and serving petrol, so we knew that we were going to be all right. We would stop at the next place, but we eventually became a little uneasy relying on the almost certainty that one would be open on the way out of the town.

It added to my uneasiness when I realised that we were then out of the town and on the open road across the moors, which were the foothills of the great Pennine Chain.

There was no point in worrying and Skipton, an important market town, was the next on the route, and there was sure to be at least one petrol station there, as long as we had sufficient fuel to get there.

At last we entered the outskirts, and it was nearing midnight, so we looked ahead for those welcoming lights which are so important when your petrol tank is almost empty. However, we had passed through the main part of the town, and we had started that long tortuous climb out of the town that takes you out on to the moors. Surely this is where we would be lucky? There could not be such a long way between filling stations.

To my horror, I realised that we were now out of the built up area altogether, and that our petrol prospects were as bleak as our surroundings. It was raining hard by now, and the prospect of spending a winter's night on the moors was less than appealing. Then what I dreaded happened. We stopped. To say that I was not popular with Leni and Margarete is an understatement. 'Didn't I tell you to get petrol when we started the journey?' 'You are always taking chances with petrol,' were typical comments. It was then that I recalled my army golden rule – if it stops suddenly it is electric. If it splutters before it stops, it is petrol...

The fact was, prior to that occasion on the moors, I had only ever run out of fuel once in my life, and that was on the M1 motorway going back to Cambridge from Birmingham one day!

Anyway, my mam had always said, when facing a minor catastrophe in life, that 'worse things happen at sea,' but this in no way helped my fellow travellers, and they decided to settle down for the night, excluding me from their deliberations.

I decided to try to forget my sorrows in sleep, but at first it was only the howling wind and belting rain which kept me awake. The worst precursor to somnolence arrived during the night, on four legs and with a woolly back. Sheep bleating two or three feet from you are definitely not the accompaniment you need to nod off.

What a night, but all things come to an end; all things come to him who waits. Such philosophy was wasted on my 'companions', but if we were to make progress, they would have to help me.

It was about 5.00 am and the dark grey clouds were lightening somewhat, although they were still causing rain squalls to scud across the moors and to hit our car. Leni and Margarete were eventually persuaded to get out of the car and to push me back on to the road, then a few more yards to the downward slope to Skipton. They got back in and off we rallied. Our luck was in. Coming up the hill was a postman pushing his bike, as it was far too steep to ride. We asked him where there was a garage, and when would it be open.

He directed us, adding that there was already someone working there, so our saga was nearly over. Or was it?

We coasted down the main street, turned left, as the postman had said, and there on the right was the filling station. It was for us, the equivalent of an oasis in the desert, for thirsty travellers.

There was a light on, but the door was locked. We knocked, the door opened, and out came a chap in slacks and short sleeved shirt, scratching his head, obviously just waking up. I asked him to fill the tank please, and he turned to go back in to 'switch on the pumps'.

The wind howled, the rain poured and the door slammed in his face. Oh! The language, just because he did not have a key to get back in with.

He lurched across the street to the owner's house, rang the bell, and suddenly the house lit up. A man in pyjamas appeared at a bedroom window and shouted, 'What's up?'

'I'm locked out, and it's pouring down,' was the reply. 'Can you loan me your key?'

The owner soon obliged, and we heard the gurgling noise of petrol being delivered, as he went back to bed.

The empty tank soon filled up. Gruffly the attendant said, 'Three pounds.' I only had a five-pound note. I gave it to him and he went inside, never to return. We took the hint and resumed our journey.

We were getting used to doing a lot of travelling as by this time I had offices in Wolverhampton, Chester, and Nottingham, and I was often asked to speak to other branch staff, including Croydon, Edinburgh, Bristol, Manchester, and Birmingham. In addition, I was a regular speaker at supervisors' and managers' conferences, particularly on the subjects of recruiting and the importance and purpose of meetings. I was also in the company's Executive Council, which always met in Upper Brook Street, in London.

We were very excited to learn that the next meeting was to be in Cyprus! We had a small but very successful company there, and it was thought a good idea to give our people some support.

Cyprus was magical. Having read of St Paul visiting the island, it meant a lot to me to follow in his footsteps, even though he got there in a small sailing boat and I by BOAC (now British Airways). It was by far our longest flight, being about 4,000 miles. The scheduled meetings were to be over five days, but David and Kathy Parfrey, and Leni and I, decided that we would stay a fortnight.

We stayed at the Cyprus Hilton, in the capital Nicosia, a fine hotel as good as any we had stayed at in London, and the weather was so beautiful that all of our Executive Council meetings were held in the open air. Something happened there that we had never experienced before or since. We celebrated two Holy Weeks, the first was the Western Easter, and the following week was the orthodox or Greek Easter. Apparently, the two ancient wings of the church have never been able to agree on how to set the date for Christ's Passion and Resurrection.

Our Easter was first and we had superb food to highlight the event, and everyone was given chocolate eggs. And what happened on the Orthodox Easter? Well, exactly the same, but with the extra feature of seeing Archbishop Makarios leading a candlelight procession into the hotel.

We visited the many very interesting places of antiquity including the ancient city of Salamis, where there is a perfectly preserved Greek amphitheatre and a Roman gymnasium. We saw marvellous displays of national dancing, and we attended a party that concluded with everyone throwing their glasses into a stone fireplace, thus smashing them into smithereens. A habit presumably invented by glass manufacturers.

At the end of the official business, our two ladies asked David and me if we could go for a week to Famagusta, on the coast, so we booked into the well known King George the Fifth hotel. As we were leaving, the concierge asked us where we were to be staying, and when we named the hotel he said, 'You'll be back!' And he was right. We entered the 'King George' and Kathy and Leni disliked it immediately, saying that they preferred the Hilton! Well who wouldn't? However, we now look back on the incident and feel ashamed at our attitude. We earned a lot of money at that time and it obviously had played havoc with our values. We wish now that we could afford the King George the Fifth!

As we left the troubled isle, which was ancient in St Paul's days, and was said to be the birth place of the Goddess Aphrodite, we said that we would return one day, as it was the most wonderful place to spend a holiday that we had experienced. This cannot happen now, as sweet Kathy has passed away and we have lost touch with David. However, if this book is successful, and God being willing, Leni and I would love to retrace our steps and also those of Saint Paul.

It was not long before we were packing to travel once more, as we were again invited to attend the annual IOS Geneva Conference. By then I was a Divisional Manager, and I had qualified via a very tough series of achievements which included a very large volume of business from my group, and a large number of 'associates', who themselves had attained management or supervisory goals.

On our previous visit to Switzerland, we had stopped at Dijon, known as the 'gastronomical centre' of France, and we had fallen in love with the Hotel Chapeau Rouge (Red Hat). We organised our journey so that on Leni's birthday, the last day of July, we could spend the night in that beautiful ancient hotel. We slept in a genuine four-poster bed in a lovely bedroom, and earlier we agreed with the town's boast regarding their food.

That particular conference was disappointing in one respect, as I felt sure that I would be promoted to General Manager. I wasn't, but there were many happy events and some good seminars. In one we were taught how to remember people's names, by creating a mental picture and then recalling it whenever possible. But I have forgotten how! The lecturer asked all twenty of us our names, not in seated order but at random, and at the end of the session, he rattled off all of our names in seated order without hesitation.

Another session was also memorable for a totally different reason. I have always 'sat at the back', or in photographs 'stood at the back', and I took up my usual position on this particular day. The chairs were not fixed, but free standing, and this clever chap came into the room, looked around, and with a cunning smile said, 'Please turn your chairs around,' thus leaving me feeling naked – in the front row!

On one of our sorties from West Hagley to Teesside was born the legend of the 'Black Chip'. 'What's that?' you say, well read on.

We were driving up the M1 motorway when Leni said that she felt hungry, and would I stop at the next restaurant. I knew that we were approaching the Selby turnoff and that there was a Forte's eatery, catering for quick snacks, along with a high class, well, expensive anyway, restaurant.

We decided to have a proper meal, so we stopped and entered what was a very comfortable, almost luxurious dining-room, and asked for the menu. A smartly dressed and courteous waiter took our order, and we had a glass of tomato juice to start with. This was followed by a tempting looking plate of ham, eggs, and chips, but it was not all that it appeared. The ham was just warm and the chips were not fully cooked. We decided to complain, but before we did so, I noticed that one of the chips was black. It must have been a bad or bruised potato and I realised that it could be our insurance policy.

We sent for the manager, but as often is the case when all trade is passing trade, he could not see too much wrong, and he said that he would take our food and heat it up. We disagreed, saying that we would have something different, but this was not acceptable to him.

You will recall that in the early fifties I worked for Facchinos Biscuits in the afternoons, after football training in the mornings. The Sales Director with whom we were very friendly was Mr Dominic Facchino, and since those days he had really prospered and was a director of Fortes, one of the biggest hotel and restaurant groups in the UK.

I had removed the black chip and put it in a serviette, which I held in my hand. I merely said, 'Alright then, I will send this black chip to my friend Dominic Facchino.' Oh dear! We had a specially cooked meal, and as we left the manager said that, of course, he did not want us to pay. The moral is that if you want a free meal, carry a black chip around with you, and threaten that you will send it to a director! Only joking!

This was now 1969, I had become a Divisional Manager and we were invited to Geneva again for the annual conference. I thought that maybe I would be promoted to General Manager, as I had qualified via a long list of credentials, but it was not automatic and in the event it did not happen. However, it was a wonderful week. We heard of the continuing great successes of our companies around the world, and we enjoyed the social events, which were really spectacular.

On the Saturday morning we said our goodbyes to our colleagues, most of whom were flying back to the UK, and we set off to drive to Leni's relations in Porz am Rhein.

It was a beautiful day and as always, we enjoyed wending our way along the Rue de Lausanne, which runs along the side of the Geneva lake, or Lac Leman as the Swiss know it. From there we drove to Berne, the capital, where we saw some of the sights, including the grotesque figure of the 'child eating ogre' on the fountain in the Kornhausplatz. Our next stop was at Basel, on the Rhine near the German border, which we crossed in late morning.

Eventually we joined the autobahn and an amazing site awaited us. As far as the eye could see, and that was a long way, both of the northbound lanes were jam-packed with traffic. It was only then we realised that it was the last Saturday in August, the day when hundreds of thousands of families return home after the August holidays. Early in the month they pour down the autobahns from Northern Europe en route for the sunshine shores of the Mediterranean Sea, and whereas the exodus might occur over a few days, the vast majority go back on the same day, in this case August 30th 1969. Hence the tremendous traffic jams.

Once we were on the great arterial road, there was no option but to have patience and do our best. One incredible situation helped us. I have driven in many countries and there are always some bad drivers, certainly those in Western Australia take some beating, but the Germans are for sure the most aggressive.

I love Germany and most things German, but it is true to say that the nation has had a history of aggression for a long time. Perhaps they may now get rid of some of their pent up feelings on the road. Whatever the reason, they do drive at tremendous speeds. Of course, there is no speed limit on the autobahns, and this is another obvious factor in their passion for driving fast. In Europe, the fast lane is the left and the slow on the right. I could see gaps in one lane and I realised what was happening. Most drivers counted themselves as of the speedy variety, and therefore they hugged the 'fast' lane. Consequently, there were far fewer vehicles in the 'slow' lane. So we stuck to the latter and passed literally thousands of vehicles, although we would slow down to a stop on occasions, especially where the feeder roads joined the main road. We could not believe either our luck or the stupidity of the left lane 'speedsters'.

If the situation were opportune, due to an infrequent gap on the left, we would nip in and take advantage of it. On one of these occasions, we slowed down to a snail's pace. Both columns were creeping along. Although my BMW was a German car, being bought in England it was a right hand drive vehicle. The vast majority were left hand drive, thus as driver I was close to the drivers in the right lane.

We were about 10 miles west of Frankfurt, and I noticed that we were slowly catching up a truck, which was registered in Marburg. It just could not be Leni's cousin Peter, could it? For we knew that he was a truck driver, and lived near Marburg.

As we drew alongside, I looked up into the open driver's window and called out 'Hello Peter!' He looked down and was as amazed as we were. Yes it was Peter all right. We were about 300 miles from Marburg and about 350 miles from Porz. We were going to his mother's, and we met on the autobahn!

We agreed to stop at the next parking area. This we did and to add to the incredibility, we opened the car boot and took out two already wrapped gifts, for Peter's two little daughters, Petra and Gabi.

We were still a long way from our Rhineland destination, so we bade Peter farewell, and went on our way to Porz Urbach. When we arrived at about 8.30 pm, Tante Maria was relieved to see us, as she had been very worried.

Naturally she wanted to know why we were so late, and we explained about the volume of traffic but added that we had spent time with her son, Peter. 'You haven't been to Neukirch have you?' she asked. When we said that we had met on the road, she could hardly believe it. Incidentally, Neukirch is a village near Marburg.

Of course, she had the usual treats awaiting us. A large cheesecake and Black Forest gateau were on the dining table, and the aroma of percolating German coffee issued from the Melita pot and filter. Onkel Theo was his usual happy and welcoming self, and he quickly gave Margarete the special German chocolate, which he knew she loved.

When the morning came I could not get down to the Rheinterrasse quickly enough. As I have written earlier, for me, sitting on the banks of that great river watching the steamers and barges going past, was as near to Heaven as I could get on earth.

It was then nearly twenty-five years since I had crossed the Rhine in a Buffalo troop carrier, not many miles upstream from Porz. The atmosphere was magical for me. I had photographs of Leni, when she was a little girl with her big bows in her hair, and the railings on which she perched were still there. In fact I found the exact spot where she had been so many years ago, by reference to the bend in the river opposite, and the railings themselves.

So much had happened during the period between the time of Leni's childhood snaps and the photographs I took on that 1969 visit. I have the two now, and they give me goose pimples as I look at them together. Just eight kilometres up the Rhine, Hitler ordered his troops to cross the river to take back the Rhineland. German bombers crossed it to bomb Britain in the early forties. Many divisions crossed the river bridges to man the Siegfried Line and then to attack Holland, Belgium, and France.

Retribution was meted out near here too, as Allied bombers pounded the industrial areas, but flattened thousands of houses in the process. Had not the Wilhelmstrasse, where I had found most of Leni's family, been almost totally destroyed? And Cologne was reduced to a pile of rubble, that beautiful ancient city which had been a cultural centre for centuries. However the cathedral with the twin spires, known to the Germans as 'der Dom' had survived, and I could see it from my seat on the 'terrasse'.

Later the Americans had got across the Hohenzollern bridge and they had managed to cross the bridge at Remagen, a few miles further downstream.

After the war, the West German capital became Bonn, which was just a few miles away. In addition, the 'Koln/Bonn' airport was situated at Porz Wahn, another Porz suburb.

So much had happened in what was, historically speaking, a few fleeting moments.

After such reflections, I would walk back to Tante Maria's through the main street of Porz, soaking in the 'Germanicness' of it all, and thinking romantically that as this was Leni's birthplace, it had a place in my métier as well.

Hansie had prospered. From the young lad who had worked for the British Army in 1946, he had become the owner of a metalwork business, which specialised in making beautiful metal fascias – which were very strong, and even then were anti-armed robbery devices – for banks. His wife, Betti, was very loving towards us, and it was a real disappointment when we heard in later years that they had been divorced.

Leni's cousin Gisela, and her husband Lothar, were as welcoming as ever. When we stayed with them, we particularly enjoyed their breakfasts, which consisted of a variety of cooked meats, delightful cheeses, German breads, and coffee. Lunch was never necessary after such a repast.

By this time the German miracle had well and truly happened. What I had first known as a wilderness of piles of broken bricks and rubble, was now rebuilt and extremely smart. One day we saw an example of how this incredible transformation had been effected. Just fifty metres from Gisela's they had been building a new road bridge and during our stay it was completed, several weeks ahead of time. On the last day of construction, the bridge was decked out with flags and bunting, and after the final nut or bolt or whatever was in place, a whistle blew and all of the workers ran to the end nearest Gisela's, where the employers had provided champagne and eats. They got a bonus for early completion and after the celebrations, they all went home for the day.

During this 1969 trip we took the opportunity of touring Bavaria and the Black Forest. The weather was wonderful and we were thrilled to see beautiful forests and inland lakes. There were huge areas of magnificent countryside and we hope one day to visit the area again. We called into Munich and stayed a night with an American colleague, who was married to a German girl, and I had a look at his office and saw how IOS's German company operated.

Then we made for Oberammergau, where the great Passion Play is performed every ten years. Being one year before 1970, when the play was to be on again, they were already working in the open-air theatre, getting it ready. We actually met the person who was to play the part of Jesus Christ and saw how he was growing a beard ready for the first performance. We promised ourselves to try to go in 1970, but we were not to know of IOS's impending eclipse. Then we were determined to make it in 1980, but we were on the other side of the world, and this year, 2000 (after starting to write this book in 1989), we are still in Australia.

Back to Porz though. The US Open tennis being on TV at the moment, reminds me of the difficulty Margarete and I had to play tennis in Europe. In Geneva there were no public courts, only private clubs, and this was the same around Porz. The surfacing of Steffi Graf and Boris Becker has made the game very popular in Germany, so maybe there are public courts now, but then we were only able to play through Hansie, who knew a person who was a member of a club.

However, it was quite an occasion and worth waiting for. The courts were in a forest clearing and the smell of the pine trees in late August lent something special to the atmosphere. We were made so very welcome and they told us that we should use the club as often as we wished. They would not take payment and we enjoyed a lovely meal afterwards, out on the balcony above the courts.

As on previous Rhineland visits, we went to see Onkel Peter and Tante Martha, and as ever they laid out the red carpet for us. Leni's many cousins and their children were waiting to meet us, and Martha had made her peach pastries which had no equal anywhere. The peaches were from their beautiful gardens. Again it was a very happy experience and we thought of how much Leni's mother had given up, when she had left behind such a large and close family.

An interesting feature of our German visits was to do with Leni's ability to speak and understand the language. Whenever we set foot in the land of her birth, she struggled with her German, but after a day or two she would be sitting with her cousin, Gisela, watching television programmes and understanding it all. Unlike me who, in effect, has to translate German into English, and generally not quickly enough to keep up, she merely accepted and understood the German as it was. I always thought it funny to see American cowboys on the screen and speaking German, dubbed of course.

Just a week before we left England, I had traded in my BMW 1800 for a new white BMW Tilux 2000, and so our first trip was to the IOS Conference at Geneva. This meant that the first service had to be done en route. We found a BMW agent in South-East France, prior to staying the night in a hotel in the Jura Mountains. The car was beautiful and we thoroughly enjoyed touring in it.

After the Geneva Conference, as I have mentioned, we went to Bavaria and one day we were driving in some high country when we saw a fairy-story kind of town on top of a mountain, ancient castle and all. We turned off the road, climbed up the winding hill and when we reached the small town, we found that cars had to be left in a car park on the perimeter.

We investigated all of the places of interest, which were many, finishing at the castle at the far end of the main street. Leni then decided that we should get a move on and return to the car, so we set off, but our 'boss' walked so quickly that she left us behind. We knew that she was a little annoyed that we had not kept up with her, so we were delighted with what happened next. She reached the car park and sat on the bonnet of the white BMW. We increased our pace, got to our car and jumped quickly in, started up and drove off, passing dear Leni sitting on the bonnet of a German registered BMW! Leni never could recognise one car from another. We all had a good laugh.

That white car was fated. On our way home, we were on the motorway from Aachen in Germany to Ostend in Belgium. It was 11.00 pm, pitch dark, and we had made such good time that we slowed considerably, as we were going to be far too early for the ferry. I saw a car in my mirror. It was coming very fast in the slow lane. Obviously, it would change lanes to overtake when, bang, it ran straight into the back of us, pushing us on at great speed. We finished up on the verge. We all got out. Leni fainted and I caught her. Margarete was rubbing a sore head, which had hit the car roof. Although it was dark, I could see that the back of the car was all badly damaged.

I went to the car that had hit us to find that the driver and his two British soldier passengers, were only shaken. It transpired that the driver was a Belgian who was very kindly giving a lift to the two lads, and it appeared that he had dropped off to sleep just as he should have been pulling out to overtake us.

The police appeared with a mobile office and we all had to enter it to make statements. I could not help but feel sorry for the Belgian who was doing a good turn. When dawn came we could see the extent of the damage. The back end was a real mess and the cases in the boot were all smashed, but they had probably given some protection to Margarete in the back seat. The most horrendous thing was when we examined the tyre marks on the road and verge made by me braking. We had missed a huge concrete bridge support by inches. A few inches to the right and we would have all been killed.

A mobile mechanic towed us back to his workshop, where he straightened out the rear end sufficiently to allow the wheels to turn etc, and we set off back to England. I was surprised to get a great deal from the dealer who sold me the car. He took it back as it was, and I bought a new BMW 2500, which was the first in England. Although it was dearer, the allowance on the 2000 made the deal very attractive. Later I was asked to go back to Belgium to act as a witness against the other driver, but I refused.

CHAPTER TWENTY FIVE

WE ARE NOW IOS (UK) LTD

By this time our company had reorganised. The International Life Insurance Co (UK) Ltd (ILI), for whom I had been working, changed to being the administrative arm only, and we of the sales arm joined the new company, IOS UK Ltd (Investors Overseas Services UK Ltd).

The first long trip I made in the new metallic green BMW was to Gleneagles, the famous hotel and golf course up in Scotland, North of Edinburgh. It was more to show the flag to our Scottish people than anything else, but it was a real thrill to stay at Gleneagles. I rated their dessert trolley equal to the Gresham in Dublin, and that was something. When asked what I would like, I replied, 'a piece of everything!' Leni actually had a golf lesson on the famous course. It can be said that she commenced and finished her golfing career at Gleneagles, because she has not had a golf club in her hands since.

Colleagues David Parfrey and Peter Grace, and their wives, had a bit of a fright getting to Scotland. They set off in David's aeroplane from Coventry airport, but got lost in heavy cloud in the area of Derby! Eventually, they made it back to their home airport and then travelled by car.

Shortly after our return from the far North, the company had a managers' conference at York, and it was particularly meaningful for me. It was announced that I had been promoted to General Manager. I had achieved this in exactly five years and I was very proud of what I had done. Only three others had qualified according to the laid down criteria, which was extremely difficult. Two Americans had been brought from the States and created GM's without having to qualify. When I rang Leni and Margarete, I could not help a few tears.

Leni's mam and dad had come down to York by train and they came back home with me and helped to celebrate the great event.

Christmas 1969 was the most prosperous we have ever known. My groups of consultants had expanded dramatically all over the Midlands and North-West

England, and amongst them were 64 with University degrees, a number of accountants, and two solicitors. We had a great Christmas party at the Connaught Hotel, Wolverhampton, and I was so proud of the quality of the people who attended.

Prior to Christmas we had a sales contest with beautiful clothes for the ladies in the winning consultants' lives. Margarete designed them, just another of her gifts. Another exciting event in our lives was a monthly dinner at the Bell Inn at Belbroughton. The Bell was centuries old and was one of the best eating-places in the Midlands. I formed a 20,000 Pound Club, for all those who had ever sold 20,000 pounds of Dover Plans in a month, and the dinner was for all who had achieved this, plus their wives of course. On reaching this target for the first time, I used to present a beautiful specially made silver bracelet to the lady. It was inscribed with her name and the words, '20,000 Pound Club'.

Oh happy days, and as the year 1970 dawned, I put on a great motivating one-day seminar on how to make the most of the 'Golden Seventies'. It was very stimulating and we started the decade in fine style, increasing our sales volume each of the first three months. Our product was the best on the market, and we had increased our portfolio with pension plans and sickness and accident policies.

The company's training programme was second to none. Annually in Geneva the training was conducted by the Harvard University Business School, and in the UK we used the Manchester University Business School. At the latter, in early 1970, all of our top managers took a special course in management. It was very stimulating and yet we still had a good laugh, particularly when I decided to play a trick on my colleagues. We all had our name in plastic letters in a frame, standing in front of us. Being a crossword fan and, therefore, interested in anagrams, I played around with their names on a sheet of paper, and then at lunchtime I altered all of the names. G Shelford became Fred Glosh and D Parfrey was Padre Fry, for example. I waited a while after we sat down again after lunch. Suddenly people noticed those opposite, because our tables formed a circle, and for a while it was quite hilarious.

Just a little footnote to the piece about Manchester Business School. The course was taken by Professor Roland Smith, and this week it was said in the 'West Australian' that he is to be the new chairman of Manchester United Football Club.

We had always had enemies. The banks did not like us, and the bank managers often persuaded their clients not to invest with us, despite the fact that they had little or no understanding of our policies. Often I would be asked to see one on behalf of a prospective client, and it was obvious that the 'BM' was ignorant of the Dover Plan by the tenor of the questions he asked.

Meanwhile, our parent company had expanded its administrative facility by creating new offices in Ferney Voltaire, which was just over the border in France, from Geneva. We visited the place in August '69, and I thought that it was far too large and lush, and that the directors had gone berserk. They were empire building. Then the UK company's Annual General Meetings were growing in size every year, and the euphoria was out of control for a company whose task was to look after the security of thousands of clients. Whereas the first meeting I attended in 1964 was in a small office with about twenty people present, the 1968 meeting was held in the Festival Hall, and that of '69 in the Royal Albert Hall – and it was packed. And I was a General Manager! But at the latter meeting I was not entirely happy because Bernie Cornfeld, our President, made a ludicrously dramatic entry, to a standing ovation, all engineered of course. I could not help feeling that he really thought that he was God. Certainly I felt that his antics would have had a bad effect on newcomers to IOS.

In '69 too, we had moved into some new offices in the Mander Centre in Wolverhampton. We had been doubling our sales volume every year and the signs were that even that would be exceeded in the seventies.

Sometime in the spring of 1970, the ICI raised many millions of pounds through the sale of debentures, a means of creating capital for expansion. At about the same time it was said that IOS were short of cash and, whereas they did not say the same for ICI, the positions were similar. IOS needed capital to expand, but the financial institutions and press were happy to merely report that we were short of cash. Now with millions of pounds, dollars, escudos, francs, pesetas, etc, around the world invested in our funds by many thousands of clients, our enemies did nothing to calm their fears, by saying that their monies were safe, that they were invested in stocks, shares, and property, etc. Instead they let them think that their headlines such as 'IOS short of cash', meant that something had happened to clients' monies.

Just prior to this I had been invited to speak at a quarterly meeting of a large IOS group in Croydon. It was held in the Town Hall. Another speaker was Lionel Schiff, an American IOS'er who explained the IOS Stock Option programme, and used my situation as an example of how it was possible to become very wealthy. My stock at that time was worth over half a million American dollars. You can imagine our fears when the financial world turned all of their big guns on us.

There was no doubt that the same people who had been responsible for the dynamic growth of IOS, now its directors, had been spending more than the company was earning. But they had realised it and were prepared to put things right — if given the chance.

By the end of 1970 it seemed certain that the company would never be the same again. A lot of very good people had left and all was gloom and doom. I never get depressed, being ever an optimist, but to say that I was disappointed is a great understatement. I had found the perfect job, which allowed me to use whatever talents I had, and which also was responsible for my learning new skills.

The idea of 'people's capitalism' had appealed to me more than anything I had known. Whether I was talking to a prospective client or to a group of fellow IOS'ers, that concept spurred me on, gave me confidence and helped to convince the listener. And compared to my early ILI days when the thought of speaking to a group frightened me, this confidence and the faith I had in what I was doing, drove me on to conquer my fallibilities. One day I spoke to over a thousand colleagues, on the same platform as ILI's chairman and IOS Germany's president, Dr Erich Mende, ex-vice-Chancellor of West Germany.

It was a job where I was always delighted when Monday morning came around. I loved the weekends, which always included a church service, and often a trip somewhere, but there was always something to look forward to on Mondays. I was motivated and it was transmitted to my colleagues.

But it looked as though it was all slipping away. There was 'in fighting' and various Americans were joining the very solid UK company, and I soon found myself being ruled by people who had done nothing to build the business.

I could not really face the idea of doing anything else, and to leave was to damn everything I had believed in, but things were out of my hands. For example, I had been senior to David Parfrey in every way; bigger group, bigger sales, I was a General Manager, he wasn't; and I had been a director of IOS UK which he hadn't. And yet a non-ILI American appointed him in a new position of Group Manager over me.

CHAPTER TWENTY SIX
I TRY TO RECOUP

Other companies who had followed our lead, and had produced investment-linked insurance policies, were grabbing some of our best people. Today many of them are leaders of these companies, but I was so committed to the Dover Plan that, as I had always maintained that ours was the best, in all honesty, I could not change sides.

So I started to look for something else whereby I could use the talents I had developed with IOS, and also their managerial and promotional structures. I saw something advertised in the 'Daily Telegraph' that I thought looked attractive. A Swiss company called Gerwi were wanting a few entrepreneurial people to market a product in the UK, that they said had been very successful in Europe. They were expanding worldwide and it all looked very promising.

What they actually did was to teach dressmaking in a unique way. People could always learn to sew at night schools, but it had been proven on the continent that learning at home had many advantages, particularly with the Gerwi system. It was more a dark night activity; light nights as in late spring, summer and early autumn being times when most people preferred to be outside, in the garden or elsewhere. And going out on the dark nights to night schools, when it might be raining, snowing, freezing, or foggy, was less than attractive.

So what could be different? There had always been books on dressmaking, even home correspondence courses, so what did this Swiss firm have that the others lacked? There were twelve lessons, from the use of a sewing machine to making tailored suits, with the whole gamut of female garments in between. For example, the first thing the student made was an attractive tea towel, and the first thing to wear, a simple but smart Dutch apron.

The system worked like this. On payment of a deposit, the student received their first parcel, which contained the first lesson, a tape measure, a pair of scissors, French chalk, cottons, materials for practising machine sewing, and the material to make the tea towel. Here was one of the advantages. We know that it is not impossible to go down town and buy all of these things, but being as we are, the easier things are for us, the better we like it. And then, after following the printed and illustrated instructions, the sewer sent their work back to a central point where a proficient dressmaker checked it, and returned it with the necessary comments and criticisms. Thus by post the clients had their own teacher.

There was no time limit to the course, as long as they worked regularly. After the satisfactory completion of the course, the student received a red bound book containing all of the lessons. From a selling point of view there were many appealing features, culminating with the fact that the value of the clothes when finished was far greater than the total cost of the course, materials having been provided for fourteen of the garments.

Leni and I met a representative of the Swiss company in Birmingham and we were very impressed, to the extent that we agreed to go to St Gallen, the home of Gerwi, to see the whole thing in operation. We chose to go over the Christmas holiday period in 1970, and in fact eventually flew off on New Years Day 1971, as London airport was fogbound for a few days prior. We landed in Zurich and the airport was covered in deep snow. We had never seen anything like it, nor had we experienced anything like what was waiting for us in the airport building. We were searched, not for the possibility of being smugglers but terrorists! There had just been a few bombs and hijack incidents, and the Swiss were not to be caught out.

Our journey by car along the side of Lake Zurich to St Gallen was exhilarating, the snow transforming the landscape into a spectacular 'Winterama'. A room had been booked for us in a lovely old timbered hotel in the town, which stood at the foot of the Appenzell mountains. After a beautiful dinner, we sampled a drink recommended by the barman, made of Rossi (red Vermouth), soda water, and a slice of lemon. It is still a favourite of ours. Then we went for a walk. Now, we had experienced freezing conditions in England and Germany, but never had we walked out of a building into such a temperature, that the inside of our noses iced up immediately.

The following day we were taken up the mountains to the small market town of Appenzell. Prior to going, we had heard that the people up there were very small, and a favourite joke was that when one died he was buried in a matchbox for a coffin! We went round a bend to enter the market place. It was market day and it seemed to have all finished, as people were standing around in groups chatting. They seemed to be all dressed the same, in thick grey suits, and most had knitted hats with tassels. Many smoked pipes, which were apparently permanently clasped between their teeth, and believe it or not, the pipes were all upside down. Incidentally, I nearly wrote 'they smoked them upside down,' thus giving the reader a picture of a Swiss farmer standing on his head, smoking a pipe. However, the most striking part of their appearance was their height, or lack of it. They were all tiny! So the stories were true.

When we got back to the hotel the receptionist asked us if we had had a nice trip and where had we been? I said to Appenzell, and I added that the stories were true, they were all small people! Oh dear! I had put my foot in it. She exclaimed indignantly, 'They are not small. They used to be, but they are not small now!'

We learnt later that she was 'eine Appenzeller Mädchen!' (an Appenzell girl)

Of course, we visited the headquarters of Gerwi and also the mills where the fabulous Swiss cottons and other fabrics were made for the sewing course. It was amusing and at the same time annoying that the directors all spoke English, but at times they broke off to discuss something in their Swiss German dialect; for Leni understood them. They were shocked when she told them what they had just said! It occurred to me that as St Gallen is at the end of Lake Constance, from which the great Rhine river flows, maybe all of the people who live along the Rhine banks speak a similar dialect.

We were satisfied with the arrangement and in effect bought a franchise for the Midlands and Wales. On our return to England, we opened an office and engaged a few canvassers to train to look for prospective students. Margarete and I made a number of improvements to the marketing literature, including a book for each canvasser that demonstrated each lesson by virtue of Margarete's excellent drawing. They also carried coloured pictures of all of the finished clothing. This was impressive, and consisted of the tea towel and the Dutch apron in lesson 1; 2 was a beautiful Swiss pinafore plus how to make buttonholes; 3 was zip fasteners and making a Dirndl skirt with patch pockets, plus an overall with zipper; 4 dealt with pressing clothes, and making a summer dress and a pinafore dress with lining; 5, a little girl's dress with an A line shape, and a beach dress; 6, child's play trousers, and a simple Empire line evening dress; 7, the student made her own patterns (up until now all patterns were provided) and then made a simple skirt with lining and a lined flared skirt, plus a wrap skirt; lessons 8 to 12 included making a skirt with front pleats, one with fancy seams, a maternity dress, a child's short trousers, a child's long trousers, a blouse, lady's pyjamas, lady's long trousers, a long tunic, a house coat, a button through dress, and then finally she made an evening dress, which she has herself designed.

In St Gallen we watched the garments coming in by post, we opened them for ourselves, and we saw the excellent quality of the work. There was no doubt that it worked well in Switzerland and had done so for many years, so it seemed to be just up to us.

Our accountant set up a system for the payment of the courses by monthly instalments, and he found a suitable person to examine the work and evaluate or criticise it, before returning it to the clients. We got started and the initial response was as good as hoped for, but it turned out that most of the early examples of work sent in, were from ladies who already had some idea of sewing.

We discovered this through a questionnaire. Soon we started to get complaints that some could not fully understand the printed word. When we were at Gerwi's, I criticised the many grammatical errors and spelling mistakes in what were new English translations from the original German. They promised me that this would be put right. Checking the first lesson, I complained that the mistakes were still there, but they once again reassured me.

However, it was a failure. I believe that the main reason was the very poor translation, but one of the commercial decisions was also awry. Clients were to pay off the capital sum by equal monthly instalments, but with hindsight, they should have paid a substantial deposit to commence. Instead, for a twelfth of the course cost, they got a parcel containing goods worth substantially more than the instalment. In fact the first two or three were like that, and it meant that lazy students could cease studying whilst being still in front financially. We could have sued them, but the legal costs made this prohibitive.

It was another of those things in life when we say, 'If only I had my time over again...'

There were two other people, in the South of England, who took out franchises, and I know that one was seeking damages from Gerwi via the Swiss Commercial Court, on the basis that the translation caused many clients to stop working and paying because they could not understand it. I met a Swiss lawyer in London and he said that if I sued I would win, but he wanted so much money up front that I could not afford it. I was in a 'cleft stick' and I had just got to accept my losses.

Another chapter of my life closed on the downside.

Whilst this was going on in 1971, I still had a tenuous grip on ILI, who had once more taken over the reins from IOS (UK) Ltd, but despite the efforts of many good people, it seemed impossible to avoid further bad publicity.

Whereas the funds belonging to our clients were safely invested, this bad publicity made creating new business very difficult, and it appeared to me that the new managers and directors did not want to know me. I was never one for creeping around people. I let my results do the talking, but a number of lesser lights managed to set themselves up in those UK offices that still remained open. My main offices in Wolverhampton, Liverpool, and latterly Leicester, all closed, and the future was bleak.

Lots of people joined other life insurance companies early on, but I was so enchanted with our philosophies that it was proving difficult for me to make advances. However, Marcus Begley-Clench, from our Birmingham office, had joined a firm known as Investment Annuity Life Assurance Ltd (IALA) and he had recommended me to his managing director, Bob Mueller. I met Bob, who made an offer to me that I could not resist. I was allocated their Darlington and Leeds offices to manage as a Regional Manager; I could live back on Teesside; I would get a car on the firm; a good salary, commission on group sales; they would pay for my removals; and many other perks.

We happily accepted and moved back home. Of course, Mam and Dad had died, George had disappeared, John lived in Poole, Dorset, but Leni's mam and dad, sister Marsha, brother Hansie, and favourite niece Eleanor, lived in Thornaby, which was where we bought a very nice detached house.

It was wonderful to renew friendships, and to rediscover the beauties of the North Yorkshire coastline, and the Cleveland National Park. Margarete stayed in West Hagley for a while, living in a caravan, kindly loaned by our friends and neighbours, Peter and Jessica Fallows. She and Timothy Gardner were courting and this was obviously why she chose to stay behind.

She had met Tim due to our Silver Wedding anniversary, when she went into the silver department of Beatties, where he was manager. She bought us a beautiful silver wine cooler, and Tim wrote to her using the address from Margarete's credit card!

However, caravan life was not really her bag, and she soon decided to join us. We had one of the bedrooms especially refurbished for her, and she moved in. She soon got a job as a secretary at the 'Evening Gazette' in Middlesbrough, working for the editor. It was not long before Tim asked if he could live with us, as they were getting engaged, and would be marrying in the foreseeable future.

Tim had the small bedroom. He soon got a rep's job with a scale company, and then applied to Binn's, the large department store in Middlesbrough, for an advertised position as personal assistant to the manager. He was quite young and I admired his courage for even applying, but he got the job, and within a few months he was appointed assistant General Manager! A real success story. Margarete got a better job with Barclaycard, and in June 1973 they married in the new Roman Catholic church, 'Christ the King', in Thornaby, with a Church of England priest helping in the ceremony.

It all seemed to augur well for the future. They had a lovely linked home in Marton, in Cleveland, where Captain Cook was born. It was nicely furnished, and they moved in on their return from a Majorcan honeymoon.

But in February 1974 they said that they were thinking of emigrating to Australia, and would we like to go as well. Leni's sister-in-law, Enid (whom I had known as Enid Fox at Head Wrightson in 1940–42 – she was the attractive girl down the corridor, but much older than me: she was 19 when I was 16!) had been to Adelaide on holiday, and suggested that we should go to the Middlesbrough Town Hall to see a film about emigrating 'down under'. It was at the time of the three-day week, when strikes closed down virtually everything, except for three days a week.

In addition, we were having freezing fog, and this, plus living by candlelight most evenings, helped to persuade us to look into this major move.

We all decided that Tim and I should look into jobs in Sydney. Within weeks, Tim had three appointments all on the same day in London, with three major Australian department store groups. They all offered him jobs and he chose Grace Bros in their store at Bondi Junction. So they were all fixed up. But how about us?

Bob Mueller had been very good to me, and he used me to chair meetings, and to speak at different venues around the country. I tried very hard to motivate myself to sell products, that is the company's life insurance and pension policies, in which I did not really believe. I constantly compared them with IOS's policies and found them wanting. The career I had to offer to prospective employees was not convincing, and in the North there was growing unemployment.

I had a few good people who made a living, but I never felt that I was really earning my salary. Bob tried to motivate me without too much success. Three features of my time with IALA were trips abroad. The first was a company conference in Granada in Spain, where we were intrigued by the buildings of medieval Spain, including the Alhambra and the beautiful Gothic Cathedral, where we were able to see the box which contained the jewels which Queen Isabella gave to Christopher Columbus, to finance his American adventures.

The following year we joined with our colleagues from the company's Dutch operations, in a conference in Palma, Majorca. At the last moment Bob Mueller could not make the trip, and he asked me to take his place. This I did, and I remember my opening remarks to the assembled throng from Britain and Holland. I welcomed everyone on behalf of the company, in English, and then I addressed a few words to the Dutchmen, in their own language. To this latter were two reactions. From the Brits was obvious amazement that I could communicate in Dutch, and from our European friends was a roar of laughter. Grandly I then translated the Dutch into English, and the latter joined in the merriment.

You see, when I was in Holland in the war, I had picked up a few words of their tongue, and I had spoken them in my opening address. They included the Dutch for eggs, potatoes, apples, peaches, and 'watch out the Germans are coming'. The latter was often heard, if we were speaking to the locals at such times as having just cleared the enemy from their locale.

Said with a serious demeanour, I straightaway had a relaxed audience, when they realised that I was pulling their legs.

I also spent a week in Amsterdam to indulge in some cross fertilisation of the two company's methods. This was very interesting and it was during tulip time. We all know the phrase from the song 'Tulips from Amsterdam', and I can tell you that if you have not seen such blooms, you have missed something that is quite remarkable. The flowers are massive and are truly beautiful.

During my time with IALA, I developed a very painful back. I could never discover the cause, but it became progressively worse. I had lots of advice from friends about various people who would cure my problem, but initially I did the obvious and saw my doctor. It was always pleasant to see Dr Donaldson, as he was a keen supporter of my old football team, Middlesbrough.

He sent me to a specialist at Stockton and Thornaby Hospital. He was a Sikh Indian, and our encounter was a debacle. A new treatment for some back problems was prescribed, and I had to go to the hospital every morning, or so he said. In the event, I only went once. I had to sit in a chair, which vibrated and nearly crucified me. The pain was dreadful and so I went straight to see the specialist again. On being told what had happened, he merely told me not to continue and that was that!

Then I started to listen to anyone who knew of 'this chap who will fix your back'. In total, I saw ten of them. And none were any good. When I rang number ten, I actually told him and called him 'number ten'. He was a highly qualified physiotherapist who said that he was so confident that he could cure me, that he would delay sending a bill until he had done so. Of course, he failed, but he still sent the bill. His predecessor, who practised in Newcastle upon Tyne, used to put me under a lamp, and then he would massage me gently, finally sticking some sticking plaster on my back. I felt no benefit whatsoever, and after paying many visits and even more pounds, number nine was done away with.

I went back to my doctor and told him my sad story. Incidentally, I had got much worse. I could do very little, and I had to tell Bob Mueller that I could not continue. He was very kind and let me keep the company car for quite a while, but eventually, we felt the financial strain of being without income. Leni decided that she would look for a job and she applied for a position as deputy head housekeeper at the 4-star Swallow Hotel at Stockton-on-Tees. She got the job and made a remarkable success of it, but I was not happy about her starting at 6.00 am, especially in the winter months.

We looked around to see if there were any more suitable positions available, and we had an amazing stroke of luck. Our house was next to a large hotel with a shop attached. The latter sold all types of drinks, confectionary, snack foods, and tobacco products.

We heard that they wanted a full-time manager and a part-time assistant manager. We applied for both jobs and we were accepted. Actually, Leni was the manager and I was her assistant, as I was still recovering from a back operation.

Earlier I referred to number ten in my search for a back cure. Fortunately, there was a number eleven. My doctor sent me to a neurosurgeon at Middlesbrough General Hospital. His name was Mr Moore-Robertson and he earned my lifelong gratitude. I walked into his consulting rooms and he asked me to take off my coat and jacket, and to get on the bed.

He watched me carefully as I did this, and he soon told me that he knew what was wrong with me. Just by watching my movements he knew my problem, and he said that I should come to the hospital on the following Wednesday for an operation. He said that first he would do a test, injecting the spine and then X-raying it, but this was just to confirm what he felt he already knew. This would be followed immediately by a laminectomy, which I believe means the removal of a disc, which in my case was towards the base of the spine. There was also some fusing of vertebrae.

It was a great success, and I was sent home after nineteen days of treatment. I was fitted with a corset with metal ribs, to give me support whilst my back was recovering from the operation.

After a day or two at home I started to feel the same symptoms I had felt prior to the operation, and this of course bitterly disappointed me. I went back to the neurosurgeon and he examined me and told me that there was nothing wrong, that the operation was a success.

Still I had the weakness and pain, and lying in bed I tried to understand what was happening to me. Suddenly, I realised that what was different to when I was in the hospital, was the corset. The following morning I decided to go to a surgical supplies shop and see if they could help me. Immediately, they knew what had happened – one of the metal ribs of the corset was pressing against a vein, I believe, and affecting the blood supply. Anyway, I was fitted with an all-elastic corset, and I never had any more trouble. A couple of months later I took it off and I have never had any back trouble since. I told Mr Moore-Robertson and he was very annoyed that the hospital corset fitter could spoil all of his good work, by doing such a poor job.

It was about this time that Margarete and Tim left for Sydney. We dreaded the day, but it had to be, and in November 1974 we were separated by 12,000 miles. We drove them to Darlington station and bade them farewell, and then we cried our eyes out.

Leni and I made a wonderful job of the shop, increasing the sales dramatically. One simple improvement we effected was to price every bottle and every other article we sold. Previously customers had to ask the prices, and I know that I am not happy to have to do that.

We thoroughly enjoyed our work and, despite our wish to join Margarete in Australia, we were sorry when we had to give the owners notice that we were to leave.

Once more, we need to go back in time a little. What a dreadful birthday present I had on 12th March 1975. We had fully expected that we would be accepted for emigration to Australia, and we would not contemplate rejection, for was not our only child living in Sydney? But the letter I received amongst my birthday cards said that they were 'sorry, but…'.

Leni was shattered. All our plans were in ashes around our feet. That new start in a new country was denied us. All the correspondence about jobs had been a waste of time. Fifteen companies had said that they would like to meet me on arrival, and one had virtually promised me a top managerial post. In addition, I was on the short list for Director of Soccer Coaching for New South Wales, coupled with managing the Australian Soccer team.

That day I told a friend, George Hardwick, what had happened and he suggested that I should write to Ted Croker, the secretary of the Football Association, as he may have some influence. I did this and Ted kindly mentioned the matter to Mr Davis, who was the Agent General for New South Wales. He was based at New South Wales House in London, and in no time he invited me to visit him. Within days, I was sitting in his office. He said that he could not make a decision, but that he would certainly recommend me.

A few days later, I received a letter from the Immigration people saying that if we were accepted medically in England, and then we passed a chest X-ray in Australia, we could be permanent residents. The latter revelation was surprising, as it must be very traumatic to arrive in Australia, and then be sent back due to failing a chest X-ray!

However, we could not have been happier or more relieved, and we immediately booked an appointment with the doctor who was appointed by the Australian authorities. We had to go to Stockton and both Leni and I were apprehensive, as we did not know what standard of fitness was required. My back was getting better by the day, but still, would it be good enough?

I walked in the room and the doctor was waiting. He said, 'Hello, Stan, how are you these days? Going to Australia, eh?'

I said, 'Yes, John, and I hope that you will be able to pass me!' John Merson and I went to Stockton Grammar School together! Anyway, John passed me, and then we were free to sell our house and arrange our journey.

We had a few furniture removal people to give us quotes, chose one, and told them that we would let them know the date they would be needed.

Fluffy and Bambi our two darling cats were too much part of our lives to leave behind, so another job was arranging their passage. This culminated in putting them in a local cattery, from which the carriers would collect them to fly them to Sydney, where they would go into quarantine.

We then arranged to spend some time with Derrick and Vera in the Wirral, and Johnny and Margarete at Shoeburyness, from whence we would go to Heathrow. Our intention was to fly to Singapore, spend a couple of days there, and then go by cruise liner to Sydney.

Selling the house was a source of much worry. A house, which was a duplicate of ours, four or five houses along from us, had been on the market for about a year. By this time it was empty as the owner, a bank manager, had been transferred to Penrith. I was confident that because of its beautiful internal and external decor, carpets, and built-in furniture, someone would walk in and say, 'I am going to have this.'

I put together an attractive advertisement, and we had three responses, only three, but all good ones.

The first to look around finally bought it, but after a couple of sleepless nights for Leni and me. A young man, his fiancee, and his mum and dad, all liked it immediately. 'Dad' kept on about the fact that there would be no mortgage, that he owned a credit drapery business and had plenty of cash, and that the following day he would bring a large cash deposit, and I could get on and organise the legal side.

He was to be at our place at 9 am but it got to 12 noon before we heard from them. 'Dad', it was, saying that the house was overpriced by £1,000, and that if we would accept £1,000 less, they would buy it!

On the strength of his promise the day before, we had booked our trip to Australia and notified the carriers when to come to collect the household contents. Because of all of this, I would have grudgingly accepted, but Leni took the phone off me and told 'Dad' that she would not accept, and that he should keep his word. He said that he would think it over, and contact us again on the morrow.

We did not even go to bed. We just sat up and talked and cried and worried, until it was daylight again. Our other two possible purchasers had not maintained their interest, and here was Leni being tough with our one prospective buyer!

There was a knock at the door at 9.00 am. It was 'Dad'. They had been up most of the night too, and had decided... to pay the asking price! Leni has never let me live it down!

There were no more problems. The carrier came and went, as did the cats. We spent our last day in Thornaby, which held so many memories for us, at Vera and Santino Palleschi's. They were very kind and there were lots of tears as we left in a hire car, en route for Little Sutton, and Derrick and Vera's.

During our four years in Thornaby we were fortunate to meet Bill Matthews, who was an Anglican priest, and team leader of the four Church of England churches in the town. He was domiciled at St Peter ad Vincula, an ancient church on the village green, but responsible for the other three as well, all of which had a resident vicar.

Our friendship has lasted through all the years; this is of course a source of blessing to us, but it is about a tragedy in which Bill became involved that I wish to write.

Bus 'trips' have always been popular on Teesside. Of course for many years this was the only way that most people could get around and see the countryside. One day in about 1973 or 74, such an outing took place, and over forty locals set off to see some of the magnificent North Yorkshire Dales countryside. Tragically, somehow or other the coach left the road and crashed down the hillside adjoining it.

The result was that there were more killed, I believe it was forty, than ever before anywhere in the world, and whenever there has been a major bus crash since, it has been mentioned. All of these victims were from Thornaby. I think that all except the driver were women. As soon as the horrific news came over the radio, Bill set off for the crash scene and was there in quick time to comfort the survivors and the dying.

With so many killed from a small town, it meant that there were many relatives in need of a priest's help; husbands, children, brothers, sisters, and parents. Then there were the funerals and, although the deceased and/or their near ones may not have been regular communicants at one of Bill's churches, they all needed a funeral.

Can you imagine Bill's responsibility? When it was all over, I asked him how it had affected him, and it was his reply that makes this story so well worth the telling. He said it was a great example of how tragedy can bring people together, and he added that it had welded the community in a way that no other experience could achieve. He added that his faith was strengthened, by the way those involved stood up to their tragedies and found comfort in the church of Jesus Christ.

CHAPTER TWENTY SEVEN
WE EMIGRATE TO OZ

Shortly after our arrival at Little Sutton we were shocked to receive a telegram from Margarete saying, 'Change of plans, come to Perth.' We had to scramble to re-direct the cats and the furniture to Perth, and we were lucky to be able to do so, as in neither case had the shipment yet proceeded.

We were glad to be with our old friends, but the prospect of saying goodbye loomed over us. We slept in a bedroom next to dear Carol's, whom we loved like our own. She sobbed her heart out all night and we felt like criminals to cause her so much heartache.

We had known her since she was a baby. She had spent holidays with us, and she was one of our very favourite people. And as I write this fifteen years later, she still holds the same place in our affections.

And of course loyal, 'always there' Vera and Derrick, would have to be 'goodbyed' too, and we have never shone in this regard. We set off for Shoeburyness with tears streaming down our cheeks.

John and Margaret French were as welcoming as always, and we had a lovely time with them, but every second the thought of leaving hovered over us.

I took the car back to the local car rental office and John drove us to London Airport. As we walked into that lounge, which admits only the travellers, I looked back to see my old pal waving to us.

The flight to Singapore was uneventful, except for a stop in Saudi Arabia. We were picked up at Singapore Airport and taken to the Ming Court Hotel, which was really excellent. We were excited at spending a few days in a city that held memories of Somerset Maughan, and the old British Empire, of which we used to be so proud.

We enjoyed our stay, but we were disappointed at the lack of things to see. Shopping was excellent and we bought a few items of clothing.

In the backs of our minds there was always the nagging worry about succeeding, and when the time came to go aboard the ship, we had mixed feelings. All of the planning was done by me in a spirit of optimism. This was going to be the new life in the new country. When there were still months before our departure, I was confident. Now it seemed that the nearer we got, the more scared I became.

It was not made better by dear Leni constantly ending any positive statement of mine with, 'Yes, but what if...?'

And now we were about to take the last step. However, didn't the brochure tell of the six days of luxury aboard the SS Karbarovsk, of lying by the pool and enjoying the good life?

We boarded the ship on or about 19th July 1975, and we revelled in the thought of six days deluxe cruising, with gin and tonics around the swimming pool, and a quick dip when the weather was too hot. The word 'cruise' always seemed to exemplify leisure, comfort, joie de vivre, and all of the good things in life.

Quickly we discovered that the glossy leaflets that we had read back in England were, to say the least, misleading. 'Where is the pool?' was one of the first questions we asked, after we had stowed our luggage into the inadequate 'cabins'. The answer was that there was no pool. This was just the beginning of a calamitous voyage.

July is summer in England, but it is winter in the Southern Hemisphere. And in any case, there is no real winter down there, is there? For the first day and a half we were in the lee of the islands (in the Java Sea), but for the next four and a half days we were in the open ocean. And the waves! They were unbelievable. We were thrown from pillar to post.

Our first meal had been a pleasant afternoon tea, as the ship was leaving the Singaporean Docks. We shared the table with three nursing sisters, all bound for the Royal Perth Hospital, and by coincidence, all from Teesside. We slept reasonably well the first night because the ship was still in calm waters, and we went to breakfast the following morning shortly before the appointed time of 8.00 am.

The crew were all Russian and, whilst the lesser genre were courteous and helpful, the stewards and stewardesses were more like prison warders as they strode around, with large bunches of keys on big steel rings fastened to their belts.

At 8.00 am, to our amazement, they locked the dining-room doors, and refused to open them for latecomers, even those whose tardiness was a mere two or three minutes. By each door was a large blonde woman, reminiscent of Nazi concentration camp female guards.

We were told that news bulletins would be published on board at different points on the ship, and they were; all Tass Agency reports.

There was a cinema on board and we did see a few good films, but their content was worthy of comment. There were some pure propaganda, showing the wonders of Communism, and others were subtly condemning the USA by virtue of the amount of crime, drugs, and racism they contained.

We formed the opinion that the Karbarovsk was a spy ship, and that its main purpose was to preach Communism. A visit to its so-called library was proof of that.

As we ploughed into the open seas the weather worsened, and the ship was tossed about like a cork. We were all violently seasick and thoroughly miserable. I found that the worst thing about a bad sea journey was that you could not get off! After two days everything was at its worst, and the thought of 'four more days to go' was horrifying.

Conditions did improve about a day out from Fremantle, at about the time that we were all called to the large cabin, which was used for entertainment, where our names were called out and we went up to an Australian official who was checking visas, etc.

We had become friendly with an Aussie named Bill, from Brisbane. The first time I heard his surname was when it was called out re his visa. 'Haddock, Bill Haddock.' I thought, 'He is the image of 'Finnan' Haddock, with whom I played football for the school team.'

'Bill,' I said, 'this is amazing, you are the image of a pal of mine I went to school with. He was a fighter pilot and he was killed in the war.' 'He wasn't,' said Bill. 'Yes, this person was,' I said. 'He was from Wheatley Hill.' Bill staggered me by saying, 'Yes, that's my Uncle Fin. He was shot down, presumed killed, but the French hid him until the war was over. He is now a doctor in Grimsby and I have just been on holiday with him!'

So, more than thirty years after I thought Edwin (Finnan) Haddock was killed, I discovered on the high seas, 11,000 miles from home, that our good looking school team's inside left, and a very talented footballer, was in fact alive and well. When we eventually moved into a house, and had our furniture delivered, I got out a photograph of the school team, and asked Leni if she could tell which was Fin, because Bill was so much like him. She unerringly pointed her finger at the right one.

Shortly after we had docked at Fremantle, a message came over the loudspeaker asking Leni and me to come to the Purser's office. This worried me, as I had been concerned that we had been accepted for New South Wales, and we were disembarking in Western Australia. We responded to the call with our hearts in our mouths.

Happily, instead of it being a negative situation, it was a very welcome and positive one. We had almost forgotten that we had filled in a coupon in the 'Sunday Express' that had been advertising houses in Perth, as well as claiming to have an employment bureau.

The firm was RDC and their representative, Des Fahey, was deputed to meet us. His intention or hope was to take us to a furnished flat belonging to RDC, for us to live there until we bought one of their new houses. We told Des that we did not want to feel indebted to a builder, and that we would rather stay at a hotel until we found ourselves furnished accommodation. Kindly he took us into Perth and we enjoyed our first views of the spectacular Swan River, and the city, as we were driven along the Kwinana Freeway to the Forest Motel.

It was 25th July, the middle of winter, and a beautiful sunny morning. After thanking Des, we went to our room to freshen up and Leni washed a few bits of clothing in the bathroom, and then hung them on a line on the balcony, whilst we went for our first walk around Perth. After a couple of hours we returned to find the clothes bone dry, and this was winter! What was it going to be like in the summer, we wondered?

I wrote to Margarete in Sydney, giving her the Forest Motel's telephone number and a time to ring me. It was wonderful to hear her voice. She was speaking from a telephone box, and I was disappointed that Tim had not bothered to accompany her, despite it being dark. I was to get many more examples of his lack of care. I could never have let Leni go off in the dark alone. Nevertheless, it was good to hear her voice. She rang regularly, and eventually she was able to tell me when they would be arriving on the romantically named transcontinental railway, the 'Indian Pacific'.

In the meanwhile, we found a quite large furnished flat for a reasonable rental, and thought that it would be big enough for the four of us, as we had all lived together in England. It was close to the city and it seemed ideal.

So the first problem had been solved. There were two more; a job, and then we would want to buy our own house. Things were coming together, and Leni was so happy when she met our daughter at the station, for she had often doubted seeing her again.

However, it was not long before there was friction. Tim did not like the flat. It was ideal for the time being, with a very low rent, and situated half a mile from the city, where many of the jobs were. It was good enough for us, including Margarete, but not for Tim. But as always, anything for peace, so we all moved to Como, near the river. I still cannot think why.

Tim had a job to go to at Fremantle and Margarete got a beautician's job in a city store. So they had two incomes immediately.

I had to start from scratch. I knew no one in Perth on arrival, but we had to survive and then 'go ahead'. Our capital was AUS $9,000, not much with an uncertain future, a car and a house to buy, and no job, but ever an optimist I was like Mr Micawber (that resilient optimist from Dickens's novel David Copperfield). I knew that something would turn up, provided I started looking.

I let 'The West Australian' newspaper Sports Editor know that I was in Perth, and he wrote a nice piece in the Saturday edition, giving my address and mentioning that I was looking for a job. This never resulted in work, but it did succeed in making me a few contacts. Before the print was dry, there was a knock on the door and Vic Ireland, a friend from England, was standing there, much to my surprise, as I did not know that he lived in Perth. He was a mature student at WA University (University of Western Australia), and he was very kind and helpful. Incredibly, he immediately loaned me a motor car, which was marvellous for us. However, the first time I drove it, I got my one and only ever to this day, parking ticket! I parked where it said a one hour limit. I put the stipulated coin in the meter for an hour's parking, and came back in forty minutes, but I did not know that I had parked on a 'Clearway' which started at 4.15 pm, and it was 4.30 pm by this time.

The Soccer Federation of WA also got in touch, and on 31st July, Leni's birthday, one of their executives, Dennis Silver, architect, took us out to lunch at the Concert Hall. This was most appreciated. Dennis also tried to find me a job, and did in fact get me one with a well-known firm of Estate Agents, but the area that was available was not suitable.

John Williams, a member of the Upper House of the State Parliament, was also most helpful and tried hard to get me a job with the State Government, but there were no vacancies, due to there being a bit of a recession at the time. John was also on the Soccer Federation executive. Our relationship was of a tenuous nature, as he was a Wolverhampton Wanderers supporter in the days when I played for local rivals West Bromwich Albion, but I learnt to forgive him for that!

I answered every suitable advertisement in the newspaper and got several interviews, but no jobs. I did not intend to look for work in the life insurance industry, but I was forced to, and I walked in a few life offices in the main financial street, St George's Terrace. My reception was always frigid, because my references were such that the interviewer could see that I had held a much higher position than he currently did, and therefore I posed a threat, so I gave that up. I did try for a job with Australian Fixed Trusts, which operated a little like IOS's Mutual Funds, but I embarrassed the manager, unwittingly, by asking questions that he could not answer. This showed the paucity of his knowledge and, of course, I just had to get a 'Thank you for coming for an interview, but...'

One direct concrete example of being refused a job because the interviewer thought I was too good, surfaced in a most unusual way. I had an interview for a sales manager's post, and I really thought I would get it, and I mentioned it to Vic Ireland. To my surprise, he told me that I was not getting it as, believe it or not, on the previous Friday night he had been talking in a bar with some acquaintances, when the conversation turned to soccer. One of the group said that he had just interviewed a footballer, Stan Rickaby, so Vic asked him how I had fared, to be told that I was not getting the job, as he feared that if I did, he could see me deposing him!

CHAPTER TWENTY EIGHT

AT LAST WE GET A JOB

I was never desperate, as I knew that one day we had to be lucky. We thought we were when we read that a very nice motel by the river wanted a husband and wife team to manage it. Leni is a trained hotel housekeeper, but we were refused because we did not know the geography of Western Australia! I said that we would soon learn and we offered to work for two weeks for no wages, but even that ploy failed, and yet the jobs were advertised again.

We saw an ad for a kitchen consultant, and reading further, it said that Modular Kitchens were seeking a person to design and sell kitchens to people who wanted to modernise the place in which the lady of the house spent so much of her working time. The earnings were the main attraction for me; but what did I know about kitchens? I had worked for hundreds of hours doing the dishes; but was this a qualification? But how about Leni? She was in her element looking at show houses, Ideal Homes exhibitions, and the like. Had not she seemed more knowledgeable than the 'expert' who had discussed the kitchen layout, when we had our house built in West Hagley?

I rang Modular Kitchens who were advertising on TV at that time, so they looked a go-ahead firm, and asked if they would consider a husband and wife team? I would do the measuring, quoting, and the selling, Leni the actual design. Let us talk about it they said. So we did and they took us on!

We spent some time in their splendid showroom, finding out about their products, their systems, and something about plumbing, tiling, electric wiring, etc, and then we went out with their other consultant. All of these things motivated us and the day came when we were given our first appointment.

It was with a single man, who had then recently finished his time in the army, had bought a small house, and wanted a new kitchen. Of course, we were very nervous, but we had not to show it. What would he have thought, if he had known that had he asked the question, 'How many kitchens have you sold to-date?' I would have replied, 'Well, when you put your signature here – one!'

He did buy, and we earned $108! Not bad for two or three hours work. That first month produced a cheque for $2,400! But we never reached that amount again. It was a lot of money for 1975, and we bought a nice car for $1200 cash and we were away.

I used to ring the office at 9.00 am every morning, Monday to Saturday, and they would generally give me two addresses, and the times would be either morning, afternoon, or evening. They could be in any suburb in the very large Metropolitan area.

By constant reference to street maps, I soon became an expert on the best routes to various places, to the extent that Perth-born neighbours would ask my advice when wishing to go somewhere.

We would always chat to the prospective customer, about such as the news of the day, prior to getting down to business. In this way, we broke the ice, and in so doing, we learnt the opinions of a cross section of the Perth public. We often surprised people when they asked how long we had been in Western Australia, and we would say four or six months, or however long it was at the time. Our general knowledge was such that they thought that we had been here for years.

For newcomers the job was ideal. We worked together; we enjoyed a good income; we got to see the whole area; we learnt quickly about what was happening and what had happened in the past; we were able to get down to the beach in the good weather, if not in the morning, then often in the afternoon (because we had an appointment most evenings); and all in all we thought ourselves lucky.

With a good income we had no difficulty in getting a mortgage, and soon we were lucky to find a lovely house in North Beach (we paid off the $32,000 in about seven years), and moved in. Our furniture had been in store, and our two cats in a cat home after being released from quarantine. It was a marvellous feeling to see our beloved 'home' re-established here in WA.

This happened in December 1975, so we were able to celebrate our first Christmas in our own home. Meanwhile, Margarete and Tim had also done the same in a new house three or four miles up the road. They were a mile from the Indian Ocean beaches; we were 400 yards from Mettams Pool, the safest and the best beach of all of the Metropolitan beaches. We have beautiful inland views and have now lived in the house for more than 27 years.

By October 1976 we had installed 144 kitchens, quite a remarkable achievement. Amongst our customers were a judge, a psychiatrist, an architect, a member of one of the WA pioneeer families, several doctors, and lots of others from many different occupations and countries. We did one for only the second 'Leni' I had ever met, my Leni being the first.

On the 1975 Melbourne Cup Day, we knocked at the door of a house just as the great race was about to begin. We had never heard of it, and we could not understand the atmosphere we met when we went inside. 'Ssh, Ssh' they said, and we had to sit and wait.

A successful sale was documented with a signature by the customer on the design, a copy for them, plus a contract. The contract was tricky, with written-in additions, and people always studied it, looking for loopholes, as there had been many home improvement 'scams' going on.

We arranged for the judge to come to the showroom on the Saturday morning for he and his wife to choose colours, pay the deposit, and sign the contract (because, whereas most customers signed and paid at the time of the consultation, I was afraid that the judge may have found something wrong with the contract).

He came in on time on the Saturday, his wife chose the colours, and he gave me the deposit, asking where he had to sign. I had stayed up late on the Friday night, sweating over the contract, but he did not even look at it. He was the only customer who never did. Why? It has been suggested to me that he would just know that no one would cheat him, and therefore assume that the contract was all right!

When we 'sold' the psychiatrist I was afraid that I was using the wrong words; that he would read something into them that was not there; or that he would interpret my body language wrongly. Maybe he did, but he still bought our kitchen.

The kitchen we did for the pioneer family was one of the best. Leni quickly decided that the kitchen was in the wrong room; that the kitchen and a particular bedroom should be changed around. I was horrified. Sale lost, I thought, who was going to pay for what included bricking-in doors and windows, and cutting new ones? The cost would be horrific. 'What a great idea,' they said, and agreed immediately. They gave Leni a special bottle of 1970 wine, which we still have, unopened.

We made many friends and we only had one awkward customer. She was a coloured Asian schoolteacher, who adopted a very belligerent attitude, and we had to tell her in the end that we were no longer interested.

Of course, we designed perhaps 500 kitchens, 350 of which were not bought by the prospective customers, and we often thought that they wanted to pick our brains, get us to do the design, and then get their local cabinet maker to make it. We became experts and could weigh up a kitchen, sometimes in seconds, and then solve the problem – for someone else to benefit from.

A perfect example was an Italian-Australian petrol station owner. His kitchen was really very difficult and we spent hours trying different ideas. Eventually, Leni came up with the solution: make the kitchen smaller – and they thought it great.

We left it a while and then rang them, to be told that indeed they had got an Italian cabinet-maker to do the job.

A year later, I drove into a petrol station in Scarborough Beach Road for a fill up. I went in to pay to find our friend behind the till. He was delighted to see me as he had intended to contact me. The cabinet-maker had made a mess of the kitchen and could we put it right? Well no, actually.

The easiest sale we ever made, or to be accurate I made, as this was one of the rare occasions when Leni was not with me, was to a Greek lady. I mentioned that we had a new Italian kitchen – incidentally, all of our kitchens were Italian – called 'Esse 4'. It was all white and I told her that it was new that week, and that so far we had not sold one. She responded, 'Does that mean that if I bought one it would be the only one in Perth?' 'Yes,' I said. 'Then I'll have it,' she said. The design was easy, the contract no problem, the deposit immediate. In and out of the house on the West Coast Highway in a couple of hours, and $240 better off.

Naturally, we got better and better at our jobs, and as many older houses, which were the kind we encountered most, were quite similar in design, it made our work easier. For a few months we did very well, but in mid to late 1976 all of the talk was of recession, and to most people this meant the fear of unemployment, resulting in them still asking for a quotation, but concluding by telling us to wait a few months until things picked up.

Working on commission this was no good. We kept working, making fewer and fewer sales, and then the company said in the October that there would be no more leads until February! The directors would deal with all enquiries, they said, so we had to consider what to do. I applied for various jobs, and during that time I came across a Danish maker of kitchens, who said that he had received a few enquiries from the south of the State, but that he would never get around to visiting them.

He gave us a price list and the names and addresses of the enquirers – we rang them to say that we were on our way. We were away four or five days, sleeping in the car, travelling long distances, and earning a large amount of money. Our first call was at Collie at 8.00 am, where we were thanked for coming, and they bought as soon as we produced the design and the price. We sold one at Harvey and one near Boyupbrook, en route to which we saw an eagle swoop out of the sky, grab a large snake, and fly off, with the reptile swinging round in the air as it tried unsuccessfully to escape.

We sold another at Narrogin, but the best was to a timber merchant at Manjimup. When we arrived, we were disappointed to see that they had a booklet from a very expensive German firm. However, we pressed on as the kitchen still had to be designed, and the one we came up with, they loved. 'If you can make it with doors and fittings similar to the German, give us a price' they said, and admitted that the competing quote was over $10,000. The merchant said that he would provide the jarrah (the local hardwood for the doors), all planed and profiled, and we gave him a price of $5,000, which included $450 for us. It was the best kitchen we ever put in – and the most profitable.

It was amazing to learn, during our short reign in the kitchen world, how housewives who had spent years in kitchens knew nothing about good design, and even more so that their husbands, whose kitchen function was limited to taking a tinny or three out of the refrigerator, generally wanted to make the decisions, even to the colour scheme. We often suggested that the wife, who spent a lot of time in that room, should choose the colours, but the little wife often gave way to her macho Aussie husband. Sad, but true.

So what were the basic kitchen rules? Of course, sometimes the size or the position of the doors or windows precluded the ideal design, and there were not many like the Swan Valley pioneering family, who would agree to changing doors or windows. The first obstacle with which we were faced was often 'I want a nice big kitchen!' Now a nice big kitchen could mean lots of extra walking, which was not necessary and negated the whole idea of kitchen planning, so we tried to talk them out of it. We showed them how they could have a refrigerator and a pantry next to one another at one end of the kitchen, with a worktop next to them, so that when the groceries were brought in, they could be put on the worktop and then easily put in the two food 'cupboards'. Worktop space was 'a must' next to the cooker, whatever the type, and cupboards on the wall and under the worktop were sited for ease of putting away the washed dishes. A sink with a drainer on either side was important, and we had a variety of solutions for the utilisation of the space in the corners. If we could site the sink in front of a window, we did, so that the user could look outside, rather than on to a blank wall, when they were washing-up.

There were different shapes and sizes of kitchens – narrow galley kitchens; three-sided, which were in the majority and lent themselves to good utilitarian design;

and four-sided, which would include a breakfast bar with stools or chairs on the outside of the kitchen, generally in the family room.

Leni was a wizard at all of this, and as ever, her sense of colour and colour co-ordination was outstanding. My forte was in measuring and designing accurately. A fitter once told me that all of our kitchens just 'slid' in. My arithmetical skills ensured that I never once misquoted. Our foray into kitchens was an interesting and rewarding experience, and it was a pity that it came to an end. It was that gremlin.

Our country trip had been very rewarding financially, but the money would not last forever, so I was back to scouring the job vacancies in 'The West Australian'. I had the usual run of no replies or two-line answers saying, 'Thankyou for your... etc, etc, but... etc, etc,' and then I saw a position for which I knew I was eminently suitable. The Anglican Church, my church, needed a manager for their most prestigious homes for the aged, 'Moline House' at Karrinyup, only a mile from our home. I knew that I fulfilled all of their requirements and I applied immediately. I soon had an interview with the executive director, Barry Hawley, and I commenced there in early December 1977.

CHAPTER TWENTY NINE
THE ANGLICAN HOMES SAGA

At last I had the perfect job. I was involved with providing security, welfare, and comfort, for 234 people over the age of 55 years, in three different kinds of accommodation. There was an eight-floor high-rise building of self-care units for singles and couples, with recreation rooms on each floor; a shop; a doctor's surgery; an office, which included a bank agency and a deposit fund agency; a dining-room; a kitchen; and it was all surrounded by gardens. On either side of the main building there were 29 hostel units, making 58 in all, where the rooms were cleaned for the residents, they were helped with showering, given their medicines, etc, and they were provided with meals in the main dining-room. They also had recreation rooms where they could play cards, etc, and make a cup of tea or coffee, and biscuits were provided.

Then around the perimeter of the multi-million dollar development were 58 self-contained cottages with their own gardens.

Every resident paid a rent, and the office collected the payments. We had one secretary; two lady supervisors; a chef; four or five kitchen staff; two or three cleaners; and two part-time handymen/gardeners. When I took over, I was unhappy about some of the staff. The laws of libel prevent me saying too much, but sufficient to say that the previous manager – who had been appointed when the high-rise and the hostel-units had been built two years before (the cottages being older) – had actually eloped with one of the kitchen staff. He was married, and his wife worked in another of the Anglican Homes. He had selected the staff and one of them I had to terminate, due to exposing herself in one of the single men's units.

The place was badly organised, there were no signs to tell visitors where to park or where the various facilities were, but even worse was the lack of cohesion. Every floor of the high-rise was a separate entity, with people criticising one another simply because of the floor they were on. They also did not mix with one another or with the hostel residents. The latter were generally older and less mobile, and often could not carry their trays from the counter in the dining-room to their tables. I decided that all this had to alter, so I organised games in the hostel, such as bingo, and invited high-rise people to join in. This became very popular and people got to know one another. Then I put up a notice asking for residents from the high-rise to append their names to a roster, whereby they would help in the dining-room by carrying the hostel residents' trays to their tables. This was most successful.

On the social side, I organised coach trips during the week, and I got in touch with the Regal Theatre and the Perth Entertainment Centre, and got them to give us a quantity of free seats for the first night of some of their shows. Again people mixed and got to know one another.

A real highlight was when I organised a week's holiday down in the Porongorups, a range of hills in the south of the State. Forty people had a wonderful time, and Leni and I looked after them. Mrs Hastings, in her late seventies, told me that it was the first holiday of her life.

One night the chalet hotel owners asked if we would like a game of bingo, and I ran it, calling the numbers, etc. So you can imagine my surprise when the executive director showed me a letter from a resident, accusing me of not assisting the old people, for instance, when getting on or off the bus, and refusing to join in the bingo sessions.

The most difficult thing to do is to contradict lying statements, as there always remains the stigma that 'there must have been something in it'.

This letter was the most remarkable document with which I have ever been associated. The writer was not on the trip, and therefore, had no firsthand information, and yet he was prepared to libel me. Strangely, I had always looked upon him as a friend.

There must have been some kind of misunderstanding of something that was said by a person or persons on the trip, because it was all totally untrue. As 'caller' at the bingo sessions, I did all of the organising, called all the numbers, and checked all of the cards. Who could do more? And as for helping people on and off the coach, Leni and I did this every time the coach stopped or started. See how difficult it is to refute lies?

I asked a solicitor to write to the libeller and within a week he paid $1500, and I took it and kept it. Despite the fact that the letter was a lie, I am sure that it was the foundation of the attack on me a few months later, resulting in my losing my job.

As time went on, I looked into all of the items of expenditure to see if I could effect changes to reduce costs. Then I approached other firms, asking for quotes, and I made some quite dramatic changes. I saved a large amount of money on food without any reduction in quality. Similarly, with disinfectants and cleaning products, I reduced the costs a great deal by negotiating with a small local company, who were prepared to buy more machinery to accommodate our demands.

I could not have been happier in any job. Leni and I used to go back in the evenings to visit people, and often on a Sunday morning we would go and take part in their church service. If we needed a relief supervisor, due to illness, Leni would fill in as she did when the secretary was away, and she was by far the best supervisor and most loved by the old folk.

Our first year showed that I had run Moline House $30,000 under the agreed budget, and shortly afterwards Hawley sent for me. He said that I had proved my ability and he felt that I was under-extended. He had problems at the swish 'Sundowner' Anglican Homes for the Aged, and he asked me to manage it too. The Sundowner had been a luxury hotel, with a swimming pool surrounded by cabanas, a magnificent dining-room of red velvet decor, and there was a beautiful ballroom with a stage for dances, receptions, etc. It had eight floors with thirty self-contained units to accommodate fifty-one people.

I accepted the extra post with alacrity, especially when there was to be a car as part of the job. I had problems with the supervisor who was not the type of person I would have chosen, but she seemed to be well in with the hierarchy, which included the Archbishop, so I had to accept her.

Again, I changed things very quickly, regarding suppliers, and also re the relationships between the residents. Most, if not all, of them were wealthy, coming from the Cottesloe and Nedlands area, and there was more than one new BMW in the residents' car park.

As usual the place was neglected. In the ballroom there were some magnificent curtains all around the room, but they were in a dreadful state, in need of sewing and falling off the rails.

I talked to the residents one day and told them that I wanted them to take care of the place, and that it would be good for them to be involved. I asked for volunteers to take part in sewing sessions to repair the curtains. This was an instant success and people got to know one another as they improved their own comfort. We had been given a large number of books from local libraries, and they had just been left lying around, so I asked for people to act as librarians, to list and index the books and to man the library at certain hours. Another success story.

Shortly afterwards Hawley sent for me again. The Archbishop had told him some time previously that he wanted a 'Sundowner Club', with all the people in all Anglican Homes as members, and then membership to be offered externally, to all over the age of 55. Hawley confessed that, although the club had started, it needed managing, and he and the Archbishop asked if I would take on this further responsibility. So now I had three jobs.

To say that the Sundowner Club was a success story, is a gross understatement. When I took over there were few members and very little was happening. I took hold of it and it became probably the biggest old peoples' club in Western Australia (WA). On the first Friday night of every month, we had a dinner and cabaret. We were fortunate to have a superb chef who put on some magnificent meals at minimum prices. Dining tables were spread around the ballroom floor in cabaret style, and we had a number of smartly dressed waitresses. Everyone dressed up and we all had a great time.

I knew people in WA show business, such as Guiseppe Bertinazzo, Director (and Founder) of the WA Opera Company; and the president of the Gilbert and Sullivan Society, named Jack Clancy. They always supplied us with the State's best talent and Guiseppe, whose mentor was none other than Beniamino Gigli, himself sang on several occasions. Two friends, Ken Murray on piano, and Peter Burger, a South African baritone, provided lots of sing-along episodes and I always acted as compère.

We started painting and pottery classes, and indoor bowls became very popular. It really was a joy to see the pleasure that the members experienced.

The Club grew so big that, according to some law or other, it had to become incorporated. The three local councils and the State, along with me, were on a Steering Committee leading to incorporation.

The final act in this process was a public meeting, which we held in the Sundowner.

As the Club's leader, I chaired the meeting, and on the platform were representatives of the above bodies plus Hawley, the executive director. He had spent little time at the Club and therefore knew few of the members, so I did the obvious in my opening remarks, by introducing him along with the local government and State government representatives. Leni and I thought that he resented that, although he had no need to, as I had praised him as the original prime mover of the Club.

At Christmas, I put on a super party for the members and the Homes' hierarchy, and I acted as Father Christmas. It was a great night and a few nights later, I did the same for all of the staff of all of the Homes, Nursing Homes, and the

Hospital. At the end of the latter, Hawley invited Leni and me to have a drink with the Archbishop and others in the Penthouse suite. It was past midnight and we had had an exhausting day, seeing to the party, the first ever held for all of the staff – and my idea – and so we declined with thanks. Leni thought that Hawley was not pleased.

Some time prior to Christmas, I was sent for on two different occasions by Hawley. The first was to accomplish another wish of the Archbishop, which was to utilise the floor below ground level, by creating a Disabled Workshop. I advertised for an experienced manager, got one, and together we got some projects going. These included repairing a large quantity of deck-chairs, which we repainted, re-canvassed, and sold at a good profit. Then we got the people involved in taking buttons and zip-fasteners off old dresses and selling them, etc.

So how many jobs was that I was doing at the same time? Moline House, Sundowner, Sundowner Club, and the Disabled Workshop. A total of four, but I was not yet finished. He sent for me again, saying that as I had been so successful with all of these jobs, he would like me to be, in addition, liaison officer of all of Anglican Homes – Homes for the Aged, Nursing Homes, and St George's Hospital!

So that was five jobs, and he said that I should have a look at the new cars available in a price range which I have forgotten, and to let him know so that he could order one for me. The car I had been using was an old Ford Cortina.

Not many people can write in detail of such a personal success story. When I joined Anglican Homes, managing Moline House was looked upon as a big full-time job, and yet here I was doing that successfully, plus four other jobs, and for very few extra dollars.

The chief welfare officer called one day, and during our conversation I mentioned that Barry (Hawley) wanted to see me the next day, and asked if she knew what it was about. She said that it could only be to do with salary increases, so that pleased me.

I knocked at the chief executive's door at the time appointed, he shouted for me to enter, we shook hands, and he chatted about his newly decorated flamboyant office. Then he said something that I did not catch. I begged his pardon and he said, 'I want you to resign.' Of course, I knew he was joking; I was here for a well deserved rise in salary. I laughed, but he said, 'No, I am serious, I want you to resign!'

I was thunderstruck and I asked him why. He said that there was one male surplus in the establishment and that, unfortunately, I was the one to go. When asked why me, he said that we did not communicate with one another. I would have thought that doing five jobs spoke for itself. Then he said, 'You told Colin about the new catering system.' I was even more amazed at this, and I answered, 'Of course I did. You told me to, as you announced it at the Sundowner Club meeting, and you agreed with me that as there were people from Moline House at the meeting, who would go back and tell Colin, it would be far better coming from me.' (Colin was the Moline chef). Hawley was in complete disarray and waffled on about a better job being available as catering manager of all of the institutions, and that I should think it over and ring him. I rang to tell him I did not want it, but before I had the chance to tell him, he told me that he had changed his mind.

He wanted me to leave immediately, but I told him that I could not as, for instance, that very evening Leni and I were taking 40 old people to the Entertainment Centre where I had got them free seats for 'The Gondoliers', on the opening night!

I stayed until the end of the week and this must have embarrassed Hawley somewhat, as I opened the mail as usual, to find that he had cancelled orders with the food wholesaler, and the disinfectant detergent manufacturer, and went back to the old suppliers, despite having to pay thousands of dollars a year more. Why did he do that? We can only conjecture.

His fait accompli was when he actually appointed as manager of Moline House, the man who had been running the Disabled Workshop. He had no administrative skills, and we had taken him on for his practical skills in the workshop.

If that is what it is like working for the Church, I thought, I would be better with heathens, especially when I discovered that the Archbishop had gone off to England for eight weeks, on the day I was sacked, and that he was the only person to whom I could appeal. I could go on, but just writing about it makes me feel ill.

Enough to say that the two local priests, Bill Adams my rector, and Allan Patterson the rector of Scarborough, whose parish included Moline House, both became upset and had thoughts of leaving the church. My final comments on the matter are that if that is what you get for working successfully for the church, then you can expect little for working elsewhere.

The gremlin had won again.

CHAPTER THIRTY
ET CETERA

Since our arrival in Western Australia (WA), John Williams had been very kind to us, introducing us to various people. One day he asked us to lunch in the members' dining-room at Parliament House, and he took us on a tour of the building. Others were also looking around, and one to whom we were introduced was the Soviet ambassador, on a visit from the Australian capital, Canberra. A few minutes later, John spotted Sir David Brand, ex-WA Premier and long-standing servant of the State. He was in the chamber. We had quite a chat for a few minutes, and were very impressed by him. To our surprise and concern, a couple of hours later, the television news reported that he had suffered a heart attack.

John also invited us to a number of football matches, including the 1975 Grand Final, and a game between the State and Russia. We met various people to do with the game, and this led to me being asked if I would like to stand for election, to the executive of the WA Soccer Federation, in December 1977.

I accepted and I was duly elected. Meetings were held on Monday nights, and often went on until after midnight. I tried to take part and make a contribution, but everything was so different to how it was in England. It is my opinion that they were all glad to have me elected, to be able to say that Stan Rickaby, ex-West Bromwich Albion, etc, was a friend of theirs, a member of the executive, etc, but that they did not really want to know my opinions. It was a frustrating time and although elected for two years, I resigned after a year, but with no hard feelings.

Just about the time I was thinking of resigning, purely by coincidence, Floreat Athena, a Greek ethnic soccer club, started making approaches to me to coach their club. I had several phone calls from their secretary, but I always refused. My private unspoken reason, was that the playing standard was such that I did not feel that they could do the things that I would want them to do. I know it is a good job that not all ex-players are like me.

However, after having a couple of lunches with the club's secretary, I decided to give it a go, but on a different basis to that which had been proposed in the initial discussions.

They had wanted me to coach their three teams, the first team, the reserve team, and the under 18's. It would have meant starting at 5.00 pm every Tuesday and Thursday with the youths, then 6.30 pm the reserves, and finally 8.00 pm the senior team. This was not on, neither was the Saturday stint – 11.00 am kick-off for the young ones, 1.00 pm the second team, and 3.00 pm the seniors. All Saturday would have been taken up, plus all Tuesday and Thursday evenings.

When they relented and said that I could coach the first team only, I decided to give it a try. Whether this was a ploy from the start I do not know, and whether the flattery regarding my coaching methods was honest, or just to egg me on, I don't know either, but within a few weeks they asked me to coach the second team, 'just for a while', followed by the same for the under 18's.

This was ridiculous, as was another fault of the ethnic teams. They would bring players over from the UK, sometimes good players, or quite often players who were virtually finished, and sometimes a member of the club would personally pay all expenses. When this happened, the member would expect his player to be picked. This led to great pressure being applied to the coach when choosing the team, and this happened to me. Although the teams were doing quite well, all these problems were coming to a head together, and included was my frustration, which I had feared at the outset, that the players would not have the skill that was needed. Some were very good, but others exasperated me.

I was asked to attend a committee meeting after Thursday night training, where amongst other things, I was told that I would have to attend all other meetings to discuss whom I had picked to play on Saturday. That meeting finished quite soon for me, because I resigned. From an initial work load of seven hours per week, to one of seventeen or more was totally unacceptable. I had been right at the beginning. Coaching in WA was not for me.

During those early days in WA, I was invited to take part in two television programmes, and Leni and I were invited to the presentation of the Sportsman/woman of the Year awards, which was held in Perth, for the first and only time, because of the State's 150th anniversary celebrations.

My first appearance on TV was on Channel 2, which is the ABC channel, and was intended to expose me to the soccer clubs and to prospective employers. Although people told me that it was a good interview, nothing to my advantage materialised that I know of, but it was very interesting. Prior to my appearance, they showed some of the horse-racing of that afternoon, and I was amazed at the way it was done. I still do not know if it is always done in this way, but incredibly, the race commentator watched a silent television set, and he commented on the film in the studio. Naturally, I always thought that he did the commentary at the racetrack!

My second and last appearance was on Channel 9, a commercial channel, which had the rights for the FA Cup Final from Wembley, in 1976. I was to join well-known British coloured comedian and ex-professional footballer, Charlie Williams, to give pre-match comments and then to discuss the first half during half-time, concluding with post-match comments. I hoped that this might have led to an annual appearance, as the Channel wrote a letter of congratulation and said that I would be always invited on future occasions. But there were none, as the FA Cup programme has come to Perth via Sydney ever since. Charlie was appearing at a Night Club in Perth and made us all laugh when he said that, although he had only been in Perth six weeks, he had a better suntan than I had, although I had been here a year!

The Sportsman of the Year awards were interesting, and Leni and I met lots of Australian sportsmen and women who had won the prestigious awards in previous years. We also met a number of politicians and, all in all, it was a most enjoyable evening.

One Sunday morning in late 1979, a group of friends were enjoying a cup of coffee with us after church, when the conversation turned to a television programme the previous evening, which showed the awful situation in Kampuchea and highlighted the commencement of an Australian fund to help the people there.

It was known amongst our friends that I had organised and compèred a number of cabaret type concerts for the old folks in Anglican Homes for the Aged, and Phyllis Murray said suddenly, 'Why don't we put on a concert for Kampuchean relief?' Everyone said, 'Yes, why don't we?'

I was asked to organise it, but everyone present immediately made suggestions as to how they could help. We had the ideal venue within four hundred yards from our house. The 'Charles Riley Hall' belonged to Stirling Council, and one of our number, Peter Rose, was a councillor, so he said that he would soon fix that up.

It was known that the hall would seat about five hundred, but that there was nowhere near that number of seats in the hall. Someone knew where we could borrow a few hundred, and John Wilmer said that that was his job, that he had a large truck, and just to leave the chairs to him.

Peter was an advertising executive and said that he could easily get programmes printed, if I would do the writing-up of the artistes, and what they were going to do. He added that Brownes' Dairies was a customer of his, and that he was sure that they would give us a good quantity of cold drinks, such as iced chocolate-milk, and orange juice, if he were to explain our purpose.

There would be a lot of manual work, placing and cleaning the chairs, cleaning the stage and the piano, and on the night, selling programmes, acting as ushers, looking after the needs of those taking part, etc, and Ken Murray and our ladies Doreen, Leni, Marie, and Phyllis, agreed to look after those tasks.

Peter also got the tickets printed free, and on receiving them, we soon got started selling them. We sold 750 at $2.00 each, and at that time we could not even say who the performers were. This was my task and I enlisted the aid of my friend, Guiseppe Bertinazzo, then director of the WA Opera Company and a soccer fanatic, and I also brought off a real coup. I had been to a concert at the magnificent Perth Concert Hall just prior to this time, where the star performer was Katie Zukoff, a Russian concert pianist, and after ringing a few people, I found out where she was staying. She had a lady managing her engagements and she agreed immediately to let Katie take part.

I was delighted, but then someone said, 'But what is she going to play on? Surely, not that old upright piano in the hall?' Well, we could not find a grand piano, but someone knew a piano tuner! And that's who we got to try to tune up the unprepossessing instrument, which was also all scratched and filthy. Leni spent a lot of time improving its appearance, and that was that.

It was a joint North Beach Catholic and Anglican appeal and we sold our tickets through the churches. We tried to incorporate the local Baptist Church, but they would not sell tickets or come to the concert, because it was to be held on a Sunday. I believe that they had an appeal of their own.

Whilst selling tickets outside Our Lady of Grace Catholic Church one Sunday morning, a young man named Pat Cahill asked me if we needed someone to organise the audio and the lighting. 'Well,' I said, 'that is nice of you, but we have lights on the stage and a microphone.' How naive can one be? He said that he did these functions for the big pop stars and their concerts at the 8,000-seat Entertainment Centre in Perth, and he would like to do it for us.

Going on a bit, it is suffice to say for the moment that he worked with an assistant all day prior to the show, and it took him most of the Monday to disassemble the equipment!

The only untoward occurrence throughout the whole sequence of events was that Leni and I noticed that there were quite a few South-East Asian people in the Catholic congregation, but they all declined when we asked them to buy a $2.00 ticket.

Meanwhile, I was having great success in getting the cast together. I did not have one refusal. Having it on a Sunday night was obviously an advantage as none of the performers were engaged.

The great day came, and so did John Wilmer with his hundreds of seats, all covered in thick dust. It was a hot day, but the perspiration generated by the unloading and placement of the seats, was nothing compared to that generated by the cleaning of them by our ladies.

We counted the seats. There were a few over five hundred. We had sold 750 tickets, but had not some said, 'We'll buy a ticket, but we won't be able to come'?

The evening came. Would all of our performers turn up? So many things could go wrong. We had the programmes but there were lots of printing errors, some humorous, some unintelligible, but they were free, and they had been done in a hurry. The drinks for the interval, so necessary on a warm night, had not arrived, but Peter assured us that they would, and he was right, they did.

In fact, everything and everybody turned up, except the 750, thank goodness. We had been terrified as the crowds rolled in, and the seats filled up alarmingly fast because they all seemed to arrive at once. The starting time was 8.00 pm, to enable those who went to evening church services to get to the show on time.

I had intended to sell the programmes, but when the rush arrived, I told everyone to give them away, but to ask for a donation instead, to avoid the necessity of giving change. This worked incredibly well, as we received much more than we would have, had we sold them.

Because of this, I decided not to sell the drinks either, and we passed around a few buckets to collect donations. I had told the audience in my opening remarks that the drinks were free, but if they would like to donate, they could. Again, this was a great success and we again made more than we would have had we sold the drinks.

Well it really was our lucky night; everything went perfectly and guess what? About 500 people attended, the hall was packed, the atmosphere was great, and we really brought some culture to North Beach.

I thanked the people for coming, made a few announcements, and then handed the microphone over to Alan Robertson, a well known Perth radio personality, and he did a wonderful job for us. Sadly Alan died a few years ago, at a relatively young age.

Suddenly, the lights went out. It was pitch black as the two Croft sisters went to the microphone. Then I found out what our audio/lighting man meant. The girls who were from the Catholic Church, and were professional entertainers, were to sing the Lord's Prayer to the accompaniment of one of them on guitar. A flash of lights, and a crucifix, created by clever lighting, was thrown across the sisters. It was quite remarkable and much appreciated by the audience.

A few weeks before the concert, Leni and I had been to Scarborough High School with Eion and Beverley Martin, to see their son, Shawn, in an excellent performance of the musical 'Oliver'. On our behalf, they had asked the school principal if they could perform some excerpts from the widely acclaimed show at our evening. He had agreed straightaway and they were much enjoyed by all.

I kept my fingers crossed for the appearance of our Russian pianist, in case she was unhappy about the upright piano. She came on to the stage to great applause and she played the 2nd and 3rd movements of Beethoven's Appassionata. It was truly beautiful, and in the second half of the programme, she played a Rachmaninoff 'Prelude', and a 'Study' by Chopin.

WA opera singers, tenor Edward Holding, bass Neil MacLeod, and soprano Ruth Atkinson, entertained us, with accomplished accompanists Deirdre Foyster and George Karko.

A marvellous evening ended with a speech of thanks from Government Minister Ian Viner, after a fitting finale, when the Croft Sisters led us all in singing, 'Amazing Grace'.

Much had to be done afterwards. All the seats had to be folded up, those belonging in the hall put away, and the borrowed ones put ready for John Wilmer to pick up in the morning.

We left at 2.30 am, and the last to leave of those who helped us was Father Mullins, the not so young Catholic priest.

We gave the Right Honourable Ian Viner $2,200 to take to Canberra to present to the Fund.

The following Saturday night, in the Entertainment Centre, a concert of big national and international names, advertised over and over again on television, raised $10,000. Se we were quite proud of ourselves. We said we must do it again, but we never did, and sadly over the years the prime movers have drifted apart. Life is strange. Our little group were always so friendly, so happy to see one another in the church, on the beach, or in one another's homes, but today the camaraderie has all gone.

When I left Anglican Homes, I was given a reference that, in normal circumstances, would have ensured me getting a good job immediately. It told of my management of Moline House and the Sundowner Centre, although no mention was made of the Sundowner Club, the Disabled Workshop, or being Liaison Officer for the rest of the Group, despite the organisational chart showing this. It said that I was '...capable in various areas and, in particular, financial management, as he is very capable at studying budgets and taking appropriate cost saving measures where possible. He is able to communicate well with people, and generally gains the acceptance and support of staff.' He went on that the only reason for my termination was, '...the changing in staffing structures, and were not as a result of any inefficiencies on the part of himself.'

But I never had the chance to show the reference to any other employer. I applied for several 'homes' jobs, but only ever got one interview, and I was left with the thought that as soon as anyone contacted Hawley, he put them off.

Ah, well! I was quite used to the game of looking for work, and I soon got another job. I worked for a firm of accountants, particularly to do with tax minimisation. I found it very interesting and I was soon earning more than at Anglican Homes. My mental arithmetic facility was soon honed up, and I was always quicker than anyone to work out complicated tax saving systems. I could often beat colleagues to the answer, even though they used calculators. The boss was always amazed and he boasted of me to clients.

I was able to get him a lot of new clients and, all in all, it was a happy environment. I used to report to the office two or three times a week, and the rest of the time I was calling on clients or prospecting for new ones.

But whereas it was bright on the work front, it was gloomy at home, for Margarete had told us that in October 1980, Tim had decided to take her and our grandchildren back to the UK. We knew that the informal way of life in Oz did not suit him, and he felt that they would all be much happier in England.

As the time approached for Margarete, Tim, and our grandchildren to return to England, Leni became more and more depressed at the prospect. It would not have been appropriate for us to go too, because they did not know where they were going to settle, and in any case, we did not consider that our financial position was strong enough to go back.

It worried me constantly, and I could see the sadness in Leni's face as her thoughts centred on the prospect of losing her 'little family', as she so fondly referred to them. I wracked my brains to try to find some sort of solution. We did not want to move, to sell the house that we loved, but I realised that once they had gone it would be a fount of memories of her grandchildren. After all, were not the two downstairs bedrooms known as 'the children's bedroom', and 'the kids' playroom', both fitted out accordingly?

CHAPTER THIRTY ONE
WE TRY TO GET AWAY FROM IT ALL

One thing that occurred to me during this black period, was that supposing we could get 'husband-and-wife jobs', where we could live in, and rent out our house for a period until things became clearer. This would occupy our time and minds in different surroundings, without the daily reminders of the children and our daughter.

More in hope than expectation, I started to read the 'Situations Vacant' and 'Professional Appointments' columns of 'The West Australian' newspaper. Almost immediately, a headline seemed to stick out and beckon to me. 'Christian couple required to work in Arnhemland.' Could this be it, I thought, as I read what the qualifications and the requirements of the job were?

Retail or wholesale experience was needed to manage a store in a remote Aboriginal community in Arnhemland. I had had plenty of the second requirement in the food industry in England and, as I had spoken to hundreds of retailers who were our customers during that time, I was aware of their systems and also their problems.

Stock control, a knowledge of bookkeeping, ability to train staff, plus a willingness to respect and work with aboriginal people, were some of the necessary attributes. Also, it was important that applicants should be active members of the Christian church.

Surely, God was helping us? This seemed tailor made for us. A two-year contract was offered, with a rent-free home, six weeks holiday a year, and all travelling expenses paid for.

I wrote to Darwin immediately, and I soon received a reply enclosing a form on which I had to give a full résumé of my past, both re employment and church membership. References were required from two people including the church minister. The organisation was the Arnhemland Progress Association, 'ALPA' for short, and it belonged to the Uniting Church.

It did not take us long to answer and then we just waited to see if God wanted us to do this work.

Eventually, we had a phone call, inviting us to attend an interview in Perth with the Reverend Robert Stringer, who was the Uniting Church's leading minister. The appointment was for a Saturday morning, 7th August 1980.

People in Western Australia will remember that day well, because it was the day the above-mentioned minister was arrested by the police at Noonkenbah, for lying down in the path of a bulldozer, and demonstrating about proposed mining in the area. It was front-page news at the time, and the Reverend Stringer obviously put this before interviewing Leni and me.

There was a very much-publicised confrontation, between essentially Charles Court's Liberal Government and the Aboriginal community, with regard to allowing mining in the area around Noonkenbah.

As always, the Uniting Church played a leading and very vocal part, and various church members and ministers went up North to confront the mining company. They lay down in front of the bulldozers and a strong police presence eventually had to arrest several people, including, as I mentioned earlier, the Rev Stringer.

Support for Aboriginal causes was paramount with people of the Uniting Church, certainly in Western Australia (WA) and the Northern Territory, although Leni and I sometimes thought that they let their emotions get the better of their common sense.

Nevertheless, we did have an interview at the appointed place and appointed time, but with two other people, a minister and an Aborigine.

We were questioned at length about our past, whether or not we had the ability to manager a store, and many loaded questions were asked, quick-fire at times, to determine if we really had any animosity towards Aborigines.

In all we were there about two hours, but we left without any idea of whether or not we had been successful. The time of Margarete and family's departure loomed nearer with no news at all. It seemed strange that what appeared to be an urgent situation, seemed to have died, and we could only assume the worst. We started to doubt that we would be called to Arnhemland.

I was still working for the accountants in the city, but I found that my heart was no longer in it, and I had frequent telephone conversations with Leni, and I only had to hear the tone of her voice to know how she was feeling.

Then Tim and Margarete's furniture was collected, and for two or three days before their flight, they stayed with us. As we looked at our two grandchildren whom we adored, we dreaded the parting. We decided not to go to the airport, as it would have been too traumatic for Leni and me. On the night before, Margarete, who had been keeping a stiff upper lip in line with her husband, broke down in the children's bedroom. But it was too late. The die was cast, and on the morrow, the dreaded knock on the door heralded the taxi driver for whom it was just another fare. To our surprise and some comfort, Tim cried as Leni hugged him; the children did not seem to appreciate what was happening, and with a husky 'I love you' from Margarete, they got in the cab.

We just went downstairs and collapsed in each other's arms. What was life about when your own flesh and blood left you of their own volition, to be separated by 12,000 miles? Emigration has caused more heartache than any other condition of man. Initially, it is only those left behind who experience it, as the migrants are all excited about the new life in a new land, but eventually most of them miss the family back home.

In our case it was a little different, as our family was returning to the old land, but the result was the same. Most immigrants in a new land continue to call the land of their birth, 'home', and eventually when it is too late, they realise how important a part their families and friends played in their lives. Proof of this comes from us living in WA, and talking to many in this situation. Mum and dad die back 'home' and erstwhile hidden feelings of guilt surface.

The wrench of parting had again happened to us, but God did have a plan, as around about the end of October, we had a letter asking us to go to Darwin for a further interview. This was marvellous news and it certainly brightened our day. We flew overnight from Perth to Darwin, stopping at Broome and Derby, and at about 7.30 am we alighted in the tropics. We had a wonderful week, better than any holiday, and during which we flew to Elcho Island and Goulburn Island, both in the Arafura Sea.

Of course, the most important event was the interview and it really was quite difficult. Leni and I sat together on the perimeter of a circle of ten chairs, containing five Aborigines and five white Australians. They varied from a white chartered accountant to an Aboriginal tribal elder. They all wanted to be sure that Stan and Leni were the right people to manage a community store, and we were asked a wide variety of questions. There was little comment following our answers, thus we were not sure whether or not we were in tune with them. Eventually the meeting broke up, and we were still not much wiser.

It was not clear either, where there was a vacancy, and this was no more evident when we were taken to Elcho Island, which had not been mentioned in any of the discussions. John Ford introduced us to the Aboriginal Council and we held a meeting with them. The site of this meeting was surprising, to say the least. We all sat on the ground in a circle under a coconut palm tree. As the meeting progressed, it seemed to us that we were being considered for their store, and as we broke up, the council president walked with me in a most friendly fashion. They also took photographs as we sat there, and all in all it was very convivial.

During our time there, we were shown around the whole community, and naturally we had a good look at the 'store'. To our surprise, it was in fact a supermarket, trolleys and all, and the aborigines could buy everything from Levi jeans to Kellogg's Cornflakes.

Eventually, we said our goodbyes and flew back to Darwin. The pilot was quite a character, a jack-of-all-trades, working in the stores when necessary, but primarily pilot of the Uniting Church aeroplane. It was a six-seater Cessna, and whether or not it was intended to be humorous or a source of comfort I do not know, but on the back of his seat for all to see were the words, 'God is my pilot, I am only the co-pilot.'

Our next trip was to South Goulburn Island, which is about 300 kilometres east-north-east of Darwin. Elcho Island, by the way, was a further 180 kilometres east, 60 kilometres from the mainland.

This visit seemed mainly for the purpose of seeing another ALPA store, and we stayed overnight to give us plenty of time. We were given a small house in which to sleep and we faced our first night on a tropical island with great trepidation. Our fears were well founded. The wife of the store manager showed us in, showed us where the various rooms were, wished us a pleasant sleep, and invited us to breakfast at her home next morning. Much was to happen between those two events.

We decided to make a cup of tea, have a shower, and get a good night's sleep as we were very tired. Gallantly, I said that I would make the tea, whilst my wife had a shower, but I had no sooner switched on the electric jug when she shouted, 'Stan, just come and have a look here!' Thinking it must be an animal of some kind I dashed to the bathroom. I have never seen so many insects in my life. The room, in particular the bath, was crawling with them, millions of them, so I hurried in the pitch-black tropical night to the store manager's house, and he got us two tins of insecticide, which eradicated the problem after a considerable amount of time. First battle won. The second debacle was in the room where we were to sleep. That the bedroom was not up to the standard of the Geneva Intercontinental or the Cyprus Hilton was a fact, of course, but this place was really dirty. So we decided to more or less sleep with our clothes on, but the worst was still to come. I went into the kitchen again, the electric jug was boiling, but where were the cups and saucers? I opened a cupboard and two big eyes stared out at me. Everyone back in Perth had warned us, 'No, I wouldn't go there if I were you, crocodiles, snakes, and goodness knows what else,' so they were right, on our first night on a tropical island. It had to be a big snake – the eyes were so far apart. What was I to do? Was discretion better than valour? Did we really need a cup of tea that much?

'I cannot find any cups,' I called out. 'Well don't worry love, I am very tired, so don't bother,' Leni answered. For a few moments I felt relieved, but how could I sleep with the thought of what was beneath the kitchen sink? I went back with great misgivings, and paused in front of the cupboard, my heart beating louder than when I stepped off the Infantry Landing Craft into the water off the Normandy beaches.

What was I to do? I know, have another quick peep I thought, or I shall be here all night, and if I do not go back to the bedroom soon, Leni will be coming looking for me. So I slowly opened the kitchen cupboard door, and perhaps there was more light this time, maybe because I was standing in a different spot, but those baleful eyes still stared at me. It was the biggest frog I had ever seen! So I left it alone, being brave by definition.

On the morrow, we met a few of the island's 'dignitaries', including the Aboriginal Uniting Church minister. Jessie Dunbar, whose husband Lex was the island's carpenter, made us particularly welcome. She asked us to her home for morning tea, and what a beautiful surprise awaited us. Although Jessie is Australian, from way back I believe, she had the nearest thing to a typical English country cottage that I have ever seen. Roses around the door, roses either side of the garden path, chintz curtains on the windows, and as we entered, the delicious aroma which could only come from freshly baked bread. Butterfly cakes in pretty paper cups were on the table, as was a large crystal glass jug containing a delightful homemade lime drink, made from the limes picked from the trees in the back garden. The furniture of dark wood complemented the pretty woollen rugs, strewn about the polished wooden floor.

Jessie was a truly beautiful person, a committed Christian who had helped in the church at Goulburn for many years. A few months later we were to be especially grateful for Jessie's hospitality and generosity.

Whilst on Goulburn, we were taken to a particularly beautiful spot on a lovely beach, and we saw a magnificent sunset behind some rocks out at sea, that were in the shape of a beer bottle on its side. We were told that Malcolm Frazer – the then Prime Minister – and his wife, along with his deputy, Ian Viner, and Naari had met the people of Goulburn on this very beach a couple of years before. We were able to discuss this after our eventual return to Perth, as Ian and Naari go to our Anglican Church at North Beach.

We were pleased to have had the opportunity of visiting these two islands and particularly to have seen the stores. With due respect to all concerned, we felt that we could do a better job than was evident at Elcho and Goulburn. When we got back to Darwin, we were taken sight seeing and that really was something.

Darwin, the capital city of the Northern Territory, home to 40,000 from the 55,000 people who live in the Northern Territory, should be visited by all people who think that maybe it is not possible for different races to live in harmony. At lunchtime it is a revelation to walk through the Smith Street Mall, and to see hundreds of girls from the various offices and shops, obviously of different racial origins, sitting chatting and eating their lunches, beneath sun umbrellas at circular tables.

At night the scents of the tropical plants, bushes and flowers, mix to produce a heavenly aroma which seems to pervade the whole of Darwin. During the period of the Bougainvillaea Festival, around about April/May, the gardens in the public parks and house gardens, are magnificent. Competitions are organised to choose the best, and everyone works very hard to make sure that they give themselves the best chance of winning. We walked around one suburb at about 9.00 pm and many householders were still at work putting the final touches to their already beautiful displays.

More about Australia's most northerly city later. Eventually, we had to leave, but as we boarded the Perth plane, we still did not know if we would be accepted by both the white and black members of the Uniting Church in Darwin, and the Arnhemland Progress Association.

I went back to work, but most of the time I was thinking of Arnhemland. We had been given lots of literature on living in remote Aboriginal communities, and in the hope that that was where we were bound for, we spent our evenings in study and discussion. We often paused to consider whether or not we were doing the right thing. After all, two years is a long time if you have made a mistake, and do not like living a lifestyle which is not only foreign to you, but to all but a few white Australians.

Then, of course, we were not even Australians. A male Pom and a female half-Pom/half-German, with little prior knowledge of the Australian Aborigine, were perhaps less likely to enjoy Outback Australian Aboriginal communities than just about anyone. Would today's 'black fellah' still remember the horrendous treatment apparently handed out by our predecessors in the early days?

The books we read seemed to intimate quite definitely that there were real problems for the uninitiated entering the almost private world of the Aborigine. 'Culture shock' was the expression that almost every writer used to accentuate the phenomenon. Apparently, it came in a number of guises, from children whose noses seemingly dripped permanently with mucus, to body smells, food reprehensible to the white culture, and spiritual or religious ceremonies, which were unknown to European-Australia.

Time went on and we started to think that our application must have been unsuccessful, even though the signs had all appeared to be positive. Then we had a phone call one evening from John Ford, ALPA's manager. There was a problem at Lake Evella; could we go, almost straight away?

Well, that was positive and meant that we were wanted. Great news, but we intended to rent out our house. If we left it empty for two years, vandals could ruin it. So we had to refuse, but John told us that we were wanted anyway, to get on and find a tenant, and to let him know the date when we would be able to fly to Darwin.

We soon found ideal tenants, a real estate agent with his wife and daughter, and we booked our flight. On the morning prior to the night when we flew off to the North, we went to church and the priest blessed us. There was a bigger weekday congregation than normal and most of them were there to say 'au revoir'.

CHAPTER THIRTY TWO
CROKER ISLAND

We were amazed and delighted when we got to Perth Airport, for there were about twenty friends there to see us off, even though the plane left after midnight.

We settled down for a flight that would take until about 8.30 am, which demonstrates the enormous distances involved in internal flying in Australia.

We were met at Darwin by John Ford, who took us first to his house where we were to stay for a few days. Later in the day we went to the Arnhemland Progress Association's (ALPA) head office in Smith Street, to start to learn the systems used in the various stores spread over the 'Top End' (the nick-name for the far North of Australia), as our services were required virtually immediately.

However, it was not at the community of Lake Evella, but at Croker Island. John Ford told us two main things about the community store and the island, which is in the Arafura Sea about 250 kilometres north-east of Darwin. And how right he was in both instances. He said that there were staff problems in existence, and that it was the most beautiful tropical island of all the Northern Australian islands.

After a quick introduction to each of the wholesalers in Darwin, from whom we would eventually be buying a large variety of goods, we were on the tarmac of Darwin airport, to be flown to our new home by the Uniting Church plane. On our previous trip to the North, we had got used to small-plane flying, but we were given further confidence when we sat in our seats immediately behind the pilot and saw that it was the same one who proclaimed that God was our pilot.

Of course, Leni and I were quite nervous, not about the flight, but about the moment of truth which would soon be arriving, the moment when we took over the reins of a quite complex business, aided by local Aboriginal staff.

We flew over barren Western Arnhemland, and then over the magnificent clear blue Arafura Sea. As we started to approach the Croker airstrip, we looked down and we could see literally thousands of fish coming up to the surface, as their silver scales reflected the sun's rays, creating an incredible mass of flashing light.

As we were actually crossing the coastline, we could see crocodiles basking in the sun, pointed out to us by the pilot. John was certainly right about the beauty of the island. To see the golden beaches, the cliffs, the jungle, the bush, and the plains took our breath away. At this, we started to think how lucky we were to be going to work in this island paradise.

On landing we were picked up by the vacating manager in a red utility, which proved to be our vehicle for use for work and pleasure. He took John, Leni, and me to Minjilang, the name of the Croker township. There we met the vacating manageress and the staff.

We were shown around the store, which was well stocked, and which sold just about everything needed in a house, except furniture. Clothing, food, refrigerated goods, fruit and vegetables, electrical goods, toys for the children, cool drinks, and so on.

In the afternoon the store closed so that we could take stock, a most laborious task in the tropical humidity, as there was no air-conditioning, only ceiling fans. At that, we were responsible for the Croker Island ALPA Community Store.

Our first evening was one to remember. The council clerk was leaving the following day, after several years' service, and the people put on a corroboree as a farewell celebration, and we were fortunate to be invited. Sitting in the dark, the only illumination being a few small fires, and the seemingly billions of stars and the moon in the black velvet sky, with a gentle warm breeze blowing, we were thrilled to be able to listen to the ancient rhythms of the didgeridoos and the sticks.

For the uninitiated, the didgeridoo is a hollowed out trunk or branch of a tree, and the player produces many sounds from it, including those of birds and animals. The sticks are used to beat out the rhythms, and the combination of the two produces an integration of sound that has been heard across Australia for thousands of years.

The music was the accompaniment to the strange, stamping tribal dancing, which told the stories of the 'dreamtime', when the Earth was created. All of this was so interesting and exciting, but there was one incongruity, which just about ruined the spectacle.

I noticed these black dancers, their bodies painted with bright colours, all had something in their hands. One hand was gripping a square box and I kept my eye on this, waiting for the end of the dance to see what it was. These representatives of an ancient people, which is reputed to have been here for 40,000 years after migrating from Indonesia, held packets of cigarettes, ready to light up at the end of their exertions!

When it was all over, we went to the house which was to be ours on the morrow, our predecessors being still in situ, and had a barbecue, given to welcome us and to say goodbye to the three who were leaving the island. The retiring council clerk offered us some advice, which we adhered to all of our time up North. He said that a lot of European-Australians endeavoured to be like the indigenous people, that is they sat in the red soil to discuss affairs with the Aborigines, and they ate Aboriginal food, some of which was really repugnant to them, and did their best to ape their hosts.

His advice to us was to act like Europeans, to keep to and to be as proud of our traditions as they were of theirs. We decided to do as he said and, in retrospect, we are quite sure that we did the right thing and we are certain that not one Aborigine ever felt slighted.

We took over the store or supermarket, which it really was, on Tuesday, 11th December 1980. Our staff consisted of Ruby and Norma on the two tills, Maureen, who did the cleaning around the store, generally accompanied by her gorgeous little baby girl, and an elderly 'porter' who was in the books as a storeman.

There were four premises involved in the store operation; the 'shop'; the bulk storage, for fruit and vegetables; a freezer-room for ice cream, frozen meat, fish, chickens, and other frozen foods; and a large grocery bulk store.

My 'storeman' became a porter because he could not read or drive, and the hardest job was at 7.00 am, when it was necessary to go to the bulk store, cold-room, and freezer, to load up essentially what had been sold the previous day, in order to restock the shelves.

Therefore, I had to list what was needed and find it, and pass it down to my rather unsuitable storeman, who would put it on a trolley. After a few trips back and forth to the 'ute' (Utility Vehicle), we would drive back to the 'shop', which was about 400 metres away. Then off-load on to the trolley, which my helper pushed into the shop. Finally, I priced everything with a 'gun', and depending on the number of customers, we all helped to stock the shelves. By this time I felt quite physically tired, and the day had just begun.

Because of the rules of Aboriginal society, serving everyone could be quite complicated. For example, a brother and sister beyond puberty could not look at each other, and a son-in-law could not look at his mother-in-law. These were two of the laws from ancient days, to prevent incest.

Fine, but what about when Ruby and Norma's numerous male relatives came into the shop? One of our two assistants could be straightening up the shelves or cleaning the fridges, etc, when the other's relatives came in. We had to watch out for this and be quick to step into the breach.

The people of Croker had a very poor work history, particularly the men, with their attitude to working in the store. It was regarded as 'women's work', so it was with a sense of relief that I recruited my first volunteer. My 'porter' was proving unsatisfactory and he was being paid for doing very little, so I welcomed the newcomer with open arms. He was a gentle delightful character, with a beaming smile and I took to him straight away. He was a good driver, strong, and very cheerful. 'Can you read?' I asked Archie, and he answered 'Yes,' immediately. This was terrific, so just to make sure I pointed to a large bag with the word 'Sugar' in large letters on the top. 'Please read that,' I asked. After looking at the five letters for quite a while, he turned the bag around making the word upside down. Poor Archie, he was so willing. Anyway, I took him on, and he always did his very best and he was totally reliable. How we take things for granted. We enjoy reading books immensely, whilst poor Archie does not even know whether the letters S, U, G, A, and R, are the right way round or not.

He and I were talking outside the store one day, and he was pointing to some long grass on the other side of the road. He said that when the Methodist Mission ran the island,the grass was always beautifully cut, and the lawns rolled and flat. He regretted that everything had been allowed to run wild.
These comments serve to introduce a little history of Croker Island. No one knows how long the original Croker Islanders had been there, nor how the wild pigs, and wild horses and ponies, had got there. In fact the first recorded history seems to start in 1916, when the Reverend James Watson was sent by the Methodist Australasian Conference to Darwin, to convert the Aborigines to Christianity. His was a hard life in those far off days, and his first mission was established on South Goulburn. Of interest to me was that one of the first Aboriginal children to be taught in the school he established, was Lazarus Lami Lami, of whom more will be written later.

Goulburn and Croker are part of Western Arnhemland, itself part of the wild expanse known as Arnhemland, which was 31,200 square miles of largely unexplored territory at that time. It was a wild land of immense variety with wide plains, rugged escarpments, gorges and waterfalls, thick jungles, and mangrove swamps. Green tidal rivers snake their way to the coast and islands such as North and South Goulburn and Croker, lie dreaming under a tropical haze in the milky-blue warm waters of the largely unknown Arafura Sea. The wildlife includes buffalo, snakes, crocodiles, turtles, and an incredible variety of birds and insects.

The missionaries were, of course, faced with enormous problems, not least of all was language, as there were a number of different ones over the 'Top End'. There were other problems, to do with their different social organisation, and a number of tribes practised polygamy.

During the twenties and thirties, Elcho and Millingimbi islands saw the birth and growth of Methodist missions, as did Yirrkala, a community on the east Arnhemland coast. The first step towards creating a mission community on Croker was taken when the director of the Department of Native Affairs in Darwin, Mr E W P Chinnery, proposed that part-Aboriginal children in various areas of Australia should be protected from perversion and moral corruption, by being deposited in the 'Top End'. He recommended that the churches should be responsible for these children, with the help of some Government finance.

It took a long time, but at last Canberra agreed to support the plan. For their special 'children's settlements', the Roman Catholics decided on Bathurst Island, the Anglicans selected Groote Eylandt, and the Methodists chose Croker Island. Two Methodist missionaries explored Croker and found good soil, coconuts, and wild horses and pigs. Minjilong, the large bay, was recommended as the site, and they told of fish, turtles, trepang beds, and crocodiles, of which they caught two of the latter! Some missionaries!

On 25th November 1941, the first forty-four children were transferred from South Goulburn to Croker. There were over fifty more to follow and the group's ages were from one to eighteen. Taken from their Aboriginal mothers, for they were the fruit of liaisons with white men, the staff had many a sleepless night due to the children crying for their real mothers.

There was to be no peace for them on Croker because, due to Pearl Harbour and the advent of Japan in the war, it was considered unsafe to remain on the islands, which were very vulnerable to air or sea attacks. Incidentally, the church at Millingimbi was eventually bombed.

Arrangements were soon made for various white families, Fijians, and others, to leave and go back to the mainland. Apparently, they had a horrendous journey, with some finishing up in Sydney and some in Melbourne, but they were safe; the Croker children were not. The only safety feature for them was a large cross, made of whitened stones, to let fliers know that it was a mission station. Radio was bad when we were there on the island, but in 1942 it would have been much worse, and the marooned Croker islanders knew little of what was happening in the world outside.

The 'advance party' looked for accommodation for the ninety-six children, but their first hope was to be dashed. Dalmar, the Methodist children's homes in Sydney, were to take sixty, but then this Christian committee had a change of heart, due to information about working with half-castes. After prayerful consideration, they had changed their minds. Perhaps they were only half God's children.

Meanwhile, back in Croker, life proceeded. Easter was celebrated and we are told that on the Saturday were baked a hundred big buns, three hundred biscuits, five fruit cakes, and seventy-four loaves of bread. But Easter Tuesday was to be the big day, the day when an Anglican missionary, who gave three weeks of his life, and at great personal risk took the children and deposited them on the beach at Barclay Point, on the mainland opposite South Goulburn. What had happened was that three organisations in the Eastern States had opened the door to these unfortunate children. It took them forty-four days to arrive in the East and they had to cross the great continent travelling by lugger, dinghy, canoe, truck, military convoy, train, and on foot.

Surprisingly, as the war was by no means over, in July 1944 an advance party of eight of the older boys returned to Minjilang, and their purpose was to help to erect the buildings necessary for when the remainder came back. Amongst them was Robert Shepherd, who was the manager of Bamyili (of which there is more, but later) when we went there. This is typical of life in the Northern Territory, that you meet people you know in all kinds of odd places, or as in this case, you read of someone and then in time meet him, despite the enormous size of the Northern Territory.

It was not until April 1946 that the rest of the children returned to their homes. In each cottage, of which six were awaiting them, an older girl acted as a 'cottage mother'. Another welcome surprise was the farm that had been created, and there were bananas, pawpaws, peanuts, sweet potatoes, watermelons, pineapples, custard apples, mangoes, and citrus fruits. There was also a goatyard, a pigsty, a well-kept vegetable garden, hens, roosters, and chickens awaiting them.

All of the above is of great interest to Leni and me because thirty-four years later, all that remained were the pigs running wild, lime trees left to their own devices, and custard apples, such a tree being in our back garden.

As well as the part-Aboriginal children, living on Croker were the remains of the Iwaidja tribe, but the Methodists endeavoured to keep them apart. Leni and I were to meet these members of an ancient people, because by the time we went there, the half-bloods and full-bloods were integrated. This had started in 1966 and progressed from there.

So that was the history of our new home as far as we could discover, but more important was for us to get to grips with the many problems that confronted us on modern Croker Island.

Communication was obviously a necessity and we were informed that the manageress usually used the radio transmitter, which was housed in a council building. Now this was going to be a problem, for Leni could not be called a technological type, as her top achievement in that area at home would have been switching off the radio (and even then she would often just pull out the plug). So I courageously volunteered to take her place, and I became the radio operator!

One day I went across to use the radio at our appointed time of 12.00 noon, intending to speak to our office in Darwin. We were allocated an hour every weekday to conduct any business we may have had. The biggest problem of being so isolated was communication with the rest of the world. The only telephone was a radio-telephone and, although we could ring anywhere in Australia, everyone in the tropics could listen in.

The problem was compounded by the amount of static we experienced, particularly in the wet season when electric storms played havoc with the airwaves. In addition, the Royal Flying Doctor Service (RFDS) had precedence over everyone else, quite naturally, but it could be very time wasting.

On this particular day, reception was quite good and I was just waiting for the time to reach noon, when the RFDS came on the line. What occurred next was one of the most unusual things that ever happened to me. On an airstrip somewhere in Arnhemland, a lady was about to have a baby. The aircraft was ready to take the expectant Mum to a maternity hospital in Darwin, but it was apparent to the accompanying nurse that they would never make it.

I felt quite embarrassed and intrusive as I listened to what happened next. The nurse told Darwin that she had no experience of attending a birth. Darwin said that she should not worry because they would remain on the air, and tell her what to do. By question and answer, the nurse was told how to go on. She reported on the changes that were occurring in the patient, and she was advised how to attend to them.

When the birth was imminent and happening, I was perspiring profusely. For one, I was in a tiny room at midday, not far from the Equator, and two, I was listening to a miracle, albeit in a very embarrassed state. I was delighted when the nurse told the doctor that the baby was born, and shortly afterwards they went off the air and I was able to make my call to head office.

A further surprise awaited me. What I did not know was that the drama had been enacted on the Croker Island airstrip, and that the nurse was Sister Daisy Yamirr, Aboriginal nursing sister, someone we of course knew very well, and the new mother was her sister, Mary.

Another experience I had with the RFDS was also unusual. It was only a few days after we had arrived on the island, and a young lady in the RFDS uniform came into the store. As soon as she spoke I knew where she was from. I asked her if she was from Middlesbrough and she averred. So here were two Teessiders meeting in a place which does not even merit a spot on most maps, and could hardly be more remote.

Arriving in early December meant being thrown in at the deep end, because Aboriginal communities prepare for the festive season similarly to the people of white Australia, meaning a very busy time for the store. We took a large amount of money at the tills, increased by special foods for the holiday and dads and mums paying whatever remained of the cost of sophisticated toys, which are equally important to the black child and the white.

Christmas Day was the most unusual we had ever experienced. Previously, going to the first Holy Communion of Christmas, starting at about 11.30 pm and finishing about an hour into Christmas Day, was the way we liked to begin the celebration of the birth of our Lord Jesus Christ. But there was no such service on Croker Island and we looked forward instead to a service on Christmas morning. However, fate played a trick to cancel out even that. A male Aborigine died a few days before Christmas, and his funeral was to be on the afternoon of Christmas Eve.

Friends and relations were to fly in from all points, as funerals are very important occasions. It was slightly amusing that these ancient people now flew everywhere. Obviously, a few years ago, the funeral would have to be very much delayed, as the mourners would have to come by dugout canoes and other similar craft.

Unfortunately, despite the modern means of travel, some important family members still could not arrive by the 24th, so the ceremony was put off until after Christmas, there being no local flights on Christmas Day.

It was here that the old habits or beliefs conflicted with their relatively recently acquired Christianity, and it was obvious that the former was more important than the latter. The rule was that there could be no Christian services whilst there was a dead Aborigine awaiting burial. So the Uniting Church building was closed over Christmas.

This was a blow to Leni and me. Not only were we 12,000 miles from our family, not only was there only one other white adult in the community, the rest having gone off to the Southern State for their holidays, but we could not go to church on Christmas Day. We decided to have our own service in our bedroom using the Australian Prayer Book, and a tape of our favourite carols recorded before we left Perth.

Jesus said that when two or three are gathered together in his name, he would be in their midst. And we knew that he was, on that tropical Christmas Day.

We also recorded a tape to send to our grandchildren, and in it we described our feelings on that holy day, when even though we could not go to church, being together as a family was the essence, even if it was only in the spirit.

On Christmas night we took part in a very pleasant ceremony, which had been established some years previously. Several months before, parents had selected toys for their children from the store, and as is also the habit in the mainland Australian cities, they had paid a deposit and paid the balance over the intervening weeks.

And on this night we had to bring all the toys, bicycles, etc, to the Community Hall for distribution. As a child's name was called out, they would trot up to the front to receive their gift to the applause of all present. It gave Leni and me the opportunity to dress up a little, as prior to this we had been very much in casual garb.

Our Community adviser, Kevin Washfold, remained on Croker with Melany and her brother, his two children, whilst his wife, Mary Anne, went down to Melbourne, because of her mother's serious illness. We went over to see them in the morning, and during our visit, a lot of the children's Aboriginal friends dropped in to wish us a happy Christmas. We took a photograph of them crowding around the door, their black faces split in two by their brilliant white smiles.

I was never very keen on anything to do with hunting and fishing. I certainly ate meat and enjoyed it, but whilst I also ate fish, it was a matter of having to, and not by choice. I suppose that I was a bit of a coward in that respect. It was all right for somebody else to kill or catch the animals or fish which I ate, but I also always had the feeling that it was cruel. And I am still of that opinion to this day.

Nevertheless, I was persuaded by Kevin to go fishing, and unwittingly I was involved in a little hunting too. After several invitations, against my better judgment, I went off in his boat, whilst Leni and the children stayed on the beach. I knew nothing of the piscatorial art and I had to be taught everything. As we left the shore, I could see the silver backs of fish darting about under the boat.

We went out about a kilometre into the Arafura Sea, my mentor baited the hooks on a hand-line for me, and I cast it over the side. It was not long before I felt a big tug on the line, and instead of presumably hauling it in, I shouted, 'Kevin, Kevin, I've got a bite!' passing the whole lot to him.

He landed a large fish and proceeded to try to kill it, by continually sticking a knife in it. Blood spurted everywhere, including all over me. I felt terrible, and wished that I had not relented and agreed to go fishing. Also the smell of blood permeated the atmosphere of the boat, and when it combined with the ever existing oil fumes it was positively sickening.

I was pleased when Kevin started up the motor, thinking that we were returning to the island, but unfortunately, this was not so. We were going 'spinning.' It meant nothing to me, but I soon discovered what it was about. Without using bait we just raced through the water, pulling behind us two fishing lines with bright metal 'spinners' attached. I had no sooner thrown in my line than I felt a fierce tug and I had obviously caught a large fish.

Within seconds Kevin had caught one too, and we were back to the stabbing and the blood. I was very happy when we reached the shore and I was able to wash in the sea and rid myself of the blood, which was all over my stockings, shirt, and shorts.

Whilst we were out on the sea, we saw several very large stingrays leaving the water and making a huge splash, as they re-entered. More frightening was a huge white shark, which circled the boat several times before thankfully swimming off. I managed to get a photograph of it.

We hooked the trailer carrying the boat, back on to the four-wheel drive and drove along the beach. Shortly we came across a few of our friends cooking fish on a wood fire.

Ruby was there with her mother, Illajilli, and Isabella, her sister. They had cut the fish up before washing it again in fresh water from a stream, which ran into the sea at that point.

One of the strange facts about the Aborigines on Croker was that very few went fishing. The Arafura was full of fish, but only a handful caught fish.

Considering the amazing quantity of fish in the Arafura Sea, it really was very bad. Leni and I were once sitting by the side of a rocky pool, dangling our feet in the warm water, and quite large fish were swimming around. Similarly, there were lots of oysters adhering to the rocks around the island, and yet the local people bought tins of smoked oysters from the store.

There were many turtles on Croker and their eggs were much loved by the people, but they did not seem to be too keen on looking for them. One Sunday afternoon we went for a trip to the 'fourth bay'. We parked the 'ute' as near to the beach as we could, avoiding some sacred sites, which were marked by pieces of rag fastened to bits of wood stuck in the ground.

It was perhaps April before it was possible to swim in the sea, once the dreadful killer sea wasps were absent. We were crossing the beach when we noticed a number of tracks, which were known to us as those of turtles, and they led to a spot, which we recognised as one where eggs had been buried.

On the Monday, in the store, we happened to mention that we had discovered these hiding places. A few young people showed immediate interest and asked where we had seen them, but we refused to tell them because we thought that if they wanted eggs they should get around the island and find them. The young people were mostly very lazy and could not be bothered to go off 'hunting' for eggs. The word 'hunting' was used in unusual ways. It seemed that if the Aborigine went searching for food, be it wild pig, eggs, or even honey, he called it 'hunting'.

Before our arrival on the island we had read of the 'sea wasp' and how dangerous it was. Similarly, we had read of crocodiles and other 'nasties', but after a few weeks, during which none of these things had been encountered, we got to thinking it had all been exaggerated. For example, we had not seen one sea wasp, despite us walking along the edge of the sea after work every day, until one day Leni suddenly spotted what was obviously a sea wasp. It was very much like the jellyfish that we used to see periodically in the North Sea at Redcar. However, the latter gave only a mild sting, but the Northern Australian version's sting could be fatal. Another difference was that the English variety had only small tentacles, the sea wasp could have tentacles as long as six or seven yards, trailing behind them and every bit deadly poisonous.

Then having seen one, we could see literally hundreds of them as our eyes got used to peering below the surface of the water.

The only crocodiles we ever saw on Croker were from the plane, whenever we took off or landed. Crocodile stories in the North of Australia are similar to fishing stories elsewhere, that is, often exaggerated and sometimes invented. For example, several people told us about a recent crocodile encounter, but it was difficult to decide what was true or not true, particularly when some said it happened at the barge landing beach and others said it was at Minjilang Bay. The two bays are on different sides of the island.

The barge landing, now that brings back memories. Memories of moonlit, balmy tropical nights, and hours of backbreaking work. Once a month the barge arrived from Darwin and it delivered all of the goods for the store. This included fruit, vegetables, frozen foods, ice cream, and all of the many and varied goods we sold.

The first two or three barges arrived during a weekday, when it was easy to mobilise a dozen Aboriginal lads, to assist us by forming a chain and passing on the goods. We would send a couple of trucks to a stretch of concrete known as the 'barge landing', and then I had to be on-the-ball when they got back, to make sure that everything was stored in the proper place. The worst job was always stacking the frozen food in the freezer room, because I had to count it and read the labels in dim light, whilst working in sub-zero temperatures.

Then we had the barge arrive on a Saturday night, three times in succession. This was catastrophic. We would have just a few hours notice that the barge was offshore and waiting for the tide. Finding a few Croker Aborigines to help load the trucks at the barge landing and to unload them at the store, bulk store, and cold rooms, was a problem at the best of times, but on a Saturday night it was impossible.

Our unloading 'gang' consisted of the lady (white Australian) who ran the bank agency, her son and daughter, Leni, me, and one young Aboriginal boy. On a black tropical night lightened only by moon and stars, we had to unload goods from trucks and recognise what they were; clothing, groceries, electrical goods, etc, as they all were stored in different places. Then the frozen foods and ice cream, a big job to check and stack in daylight, were very difficult to sort out at night. By the time they were passed on to me in the freezer room, they were damp through partial thawing and, consequently, the labels were almost unreadable.

The cold room where we kept the confectionery, fruit, and vegetables, was almost as big a problem. Finally, there was always a large quantity of tins of soft drinks, and they were kept in yet another place. This other storeroom was supposed to be difficult to break into, and some young boys were prone to attempt this, often with success.

By the time the last item was safely stored and checked, it would be 3.00 or 4.00 am. We would all be shattered, but the community were not interested in our plight. It was this cavalier attitude towards the store that started Leni and I wondering if we could stand if for much longer.

As already mentioned we had a nursing sister, and the services of the Royal Flying Doctor plane. In addition, a doctor visited the island for half a day every three weeks, and a dentist came over occasionally. However, for us the pièce de résistance was the quite modern ambulance. It could only happen in an Aboriginal community. Quite unofficially, although everyone was cognizant of it, the ambulance doubled as a vehicle to assist in fishing pursuits.

The first time we ever saw it, two people who shall remain nameless, were emptying it – not of stretchers or first aid equipment, but of nets and various items of fishing tackle.

It smelled, not of disinfectant, but of fish and salt water, and to say it was filthy or unhygienic is an understatement of gigantic proportions. Leni's comment was that she would never go in that ambulance, however ill she was, because she would finish up with blood poisoning and I could not but agree!

We had a 'cinema' on the island. I have forgotten how often it opened, but it did get some good films. The building was quite big and well ventilated, for, in addition to a couple of ceiling fans, there were several huge holes bashed into the walls. They also served as entrances for Aborigines, whilst the white contingent used the door and paid their entrance fees.

One night we had to button our lips, for prior to the main film there was a documentary produced by an Aboriginal organisation, no doubt funded by the Government and, therefore, the taxpayer. It was brought to Croker by two or three men from another community, Millingimbi, and purported to show the lack of decent living accommodation in that place. It showed a row of camp-fires with Aborigines sitting around them, but as we had recently visited there, we knew that if the camera had moved slightly to the right, we would have seen a row of single-storey houses. It was an example of racism, Aboriginal style.

Saturday afternoons were always very pleasant for us. Sometimes we would go to a place that was as near to Paradise as could be found in the Southern Hemisphere. We loved to drive the 'ute' along a jungle track as far as was possible, then we would walk the last few hundred yards until we reached what Australians call a 'billabong'. It is a fresh water pool and this one was quite spectacular. It was surrounded by the jungle and large trees reached down to the water, whilst myriad-coloured birds, many of them of the parrot and the budgerigar species, swooped into and under the water and out again, thoroughly enjoying themselves.

We used to take our cassette player, some of our favourite music, a couple of folding chairs, liquid refreshment, and with perfect weather, the temperature generally about 30° to 33°C (86° to 92°F), we could not have been happier.

We varied our billabong trips with visits to the corral, where the Aboriginal stockmen broke in the wild horses. It was very exciting and Leni used to love to sit on the top of the high railings with the Aboriginal girls. The riders always dressed attractively 'cowboy' style, with smart checked shirts, jeans, leather riding boots, and large sombrero hats. Similarly, the girls wore brightly coloured dresses, which looked beautiful against their black skins. Aborigines make great riders and they exercised well-tuned skills in overcoming the horses' desire to throw their unwelcome encumberments.

These same riders seemed to spend quite a bit of time parading their horses around the rough red community roads, presumably to catch the eye of the girls.

The new council clerk had what appeared to be a good idea. There were large numbers of animals roaming the island, including cattle, which were supposed to be kept within a large area of what is best described as 'plains', being grassed and therefore providing food. The job of the stockmen was to keep their eyes on the cattle and to maintain the fences to keep the animals within and under control. But they never really got on top of their jobs and many cows roamed throughout Minjilang. I cannot remember the number, but it was many hundreds, and as the island was struggling financially, the clerk thought it would be good to sell off a few hundred.

He ordered a barge from Darwin, and the stockmen's job was to get the cattle to the corral at the barge landing. It was the talk of the village, especially of the girls who proudly claimed that their heroes, best known for breaking in horses and showing off, were to start 'mustering' on the Monday, and to carry on all of the week prior to the barge's projected arrival on the Saturday. Achieving daily targets was very important, as the barge was to cost several thousand dollars.

Well Monday was very exciting and most of the conversation outside of the front of the store, where the people liked to gather for a chat, was of the mustering. We awaited the results with bated breath, as this was to be the financial saviour for Croker Island. How many did they drive to the barge landing that first day? Well, none actually.

Tuesday was infinitely better as two animals were securely tethered, ready for the eagerly awaited barge. Wednesday was less than successful as a nil figure was recorded, or I should really record minus two as, unfortunately, Tuesday's pair had escaped.

We weren't doing very well at all. Ideas were wanted urgently. Helicopters! We who had lived in the developed world had seen 'copters driving cattle in large numbers in other places, so why not in our neck of the woods? Leni and I were first to know of their arrival early one morning. Suddenly there was a tremendous roar and looking out of our window all we could see was a huge cloud of red dust, as the blades whirred and faded to a halt. A second followed, and then we could get on with the job again.

The two experienced pilots were briefed by Keith Williams and off they went to do what our stockmen had failed to do. But our cattle were not so silly as their mainland relations. No, as soon as they saw and heard these frightening invaders from the sky, they headed off, but for the jungle, not, unfortunately, the barge landing.

Panic set in. Instead of a beef bonanza, we were to have a cattle catastrophe. We had to pay for the stockmen and the 'copters, but what about the barge? Fortunately, Keith, a great rider and good friend of ours, knew someone at the barge firm. After a good deal of persuasion on the radio-phone, the firm agreed to cancel the contract and we escaped even further losses.

That was not the only disaster during our stay on that beautiful island, an island that, incidentally, could be very profitable and self-supporting. Cyclone Max was another special situation. Whereas the cattle fiasco could also be seen as hilarious, particularly writing about it years later, Max was a very frightening event. Since Cyclone Tracy had decimated Darwin at Christmas 1974, the hint of another approaching was the cause of much worry and tension.

The first we heard of Max was when it was reported to be 40 kilometres north-west of Millingimbi, heading for Croker Island, with winds in the centre at 160 kilometres per hour. Soon we were given a red alert and the threat was to be a reality.

A crowd of people, who assembled in and around the store, asked what they should do. There were two 'cyclone-proof' buildings on Croker; the community building, which included the church; and the electricity generating station. The latter had been 'knocked out' before by Keith Williams forgetting to order the oil! But this time, we were concerned that the electricity lines from the generator to the buildings could be blown down, so we issued all householders with electric-torches and candles, which had been stockpiled for such an emergency.

What should we do? Leni had the answer. We should go to the church that evening and pray. This we did, and Mick Yamirr delivered the greatest expression of faith I have ever heard, and equivalent in inspiration to those people saying their Rosary in the cellar in Germany. He said, 'We are not worried. Why should we worry? We know that if we die tonight we will go to a happier place and a better life than this.' Everyone went home. We went to bed. There were tremendous winds and incredible rainstorms, but we slept through most of it!

Fortunately, Cyclone Max veered away from us, caught the southerly tip of the island, knocked down one house, killed two dogs, and set course for Darwin. If it had hit, it would have been worse than Tracy, but our prayers were answered, as it veered away from the Northern Territory capital and blew itself out in the Indian Ocean.

Another night of torrential rain brought much worse results. Our little wooden house was on a slight slope, with a road above our front garden. The back garden ran down to the store, or to remind you, the supermarket, and then behind the store was the new bulk store, which had been built since our arrival. Thus all three buildings were on a slope which ran from the road to the other side of the bulk store. And on the night of the great deluge, the water ran off the road, down the front garden, through the house, under the front door, out under the back door, down the back garden, through the store, and through the bulk store – soaking everything, carrying large quantities of red mud, and flooding all of the area.

I had to get up at 1.00 am and with a spade dig deep ditches around the house to run off the surface water. This I did by the light of a torch. I worked all night and I had to go into the two stores and try to restrict damage to goods. Unfortunately, such things as breakfast cereals and, indeed, toilet rolls, were in cardboard boxes on the floor and at least all of the bottom layers were soaked. Leni and I took the boxes apart and spread out the damaged articles on boxes and shelves above the level the receding water had reached.

We were shattered, and after a night of no sleep, we had to clean all three buildings. Red mud two inches deep covered every square inch of the three places. What a job, and frankly, Croker Aborigines were not noted for hard work, so it was left mostly to Leni and me, and especially Leni.

And it was Leni who gave me and herself an awful shock. She was approaching the bulk store around which were deep ditches, especially dug for the eventuality of flooding, when she slipped in the deep red mud and fell into the ditch. It was about three feet deep and full of water. I had to drag her out, and this was most difficult as it was so slippery that I was afraid that I was going to follow her.

Heavy rains were frequent in the 'wet season', and they often washed-out sections of the few roads which existed. The council had a squad of labourers headed by a white Australian, who were responsible for road repairs and they were quite impressive.

The rains also put the airstrip out of action on a regular basis, and this had an adverse effect on life in general. Apart from regular supplies, including mail, bread, fruit, and vegetables being disrupted, people could not get to and from

Darwin. Then there was a social effect, insofar as it was a popular habit to go up to the strip to see if you knew anyone on the plane. This was not just a matter of meeting Croker passengers or visitors, but there was always the possibility that on board was a friend or relative travelling on to another island, very often neighbouring South Goulburn.

Just a word about the bread. In 1980 we were selling bread for $1.80, and yet ten years later here in Perth it still costs just a little over a dollar. The cost of freight was about a dollar and it really was ridiculous, as living on Croker was a master baker, but his bakery had been destroyed in the years after the missionaries left. Of course, we should have had our own fresh fruit and vegetables grown by the people, but the Aborigines there were incredibly lazy. An example of the laissez-faire attitude of the locals was to do with one senior member of the community, who had what was euphemistically called an 'out station'. Water had been laid on for him, a house and a 'ute' were provided, and he was to supply the store with his 'produce'. We never received a thing.

The funding, which was the word used, instead of cash, was supplied by one of the Government's bottomless pockets. Funding is the 'in word' that disguises the fact that other peoples' taxes are being wasted, and if the taxpayers could have seen the almost new 'ute' which had run out of petrol near the 'out station', and had been dumped and left to rust away, some of them would certainly join the ranks of the tax dodgers.

And things do not change in the business of Aboriginal affairs. As I write this, seven or eight miles away from here is another typical example of the terrible wastage which goes on virtually unchecked. Writing this will be considered racist, but the facts are that in the Nyoongah community, water reticulation was installed over a large area, and under the tutelage of a white Australian, it was planted with a variety of vegetables, including cabbages, lettuces, turnips, parsnips, etc. I remember admiring the market garden as the rows of vegetables peeped through and then grew to the stage where there was a first crop for market. The avowed intention was to go to the Perth markets early in the mornings, and Ken Colbung, the admirable ex-regular soldier and Aboriginal leader, was enthusiastic as he talked about a self-supporting community.

However, the powers that be dispensed with the white supervisor and expected the Aborigines to carry on the good work, but a few weeks later when I went up, the water had not been turned on for some considerable time, and Ken's horses were let loose on what was supposed to be the community's great success story.

When I asked Ken's wife, Betty, what had happened, she said, 'Oh they all said that they were better off on the dole.'

Now back to Croker and a few animal stories. One I have in photographic form of Leni, unable to get to sleep due to some snorting in the front garden, chasing a wild pig with a stick. When we arrived on Croker, there was a feral cat living around the house, and Leni, ever loving God's creatures, set out to tame it by tender loving care, and we have a lovely photograph of it drinking its first bowl of milk on the patio. By the time we left it was domesticated, which is more than I can say about the possum in the ceiling. We often heard it in the ceiling at night, but we never ever sighted it. 'Tommo', an aborigine who was in the Army Reserve, had a beautiful dog called Shandy, and as it had taken over Leni, who used to walk it on the beach, he asked her to look after it when he went off to his annual army camp. This she enjoyed immensely, and our best 'animal' photo is of the cat and dog eating from the same bowl!

Leni often had to chase cattle out of the back garden, due to them escaping through the fences the stockmen failed to secure, and as we were warned in a leaflet given to us prior to travelling north, we had to keep a watch out for a variety of members of the animal world. Some comments to make us look forward(?) to our arrival included, 'Crocodiles and sharks are a deterrent'. 'Sea wasps (deadly) prevent swimming from April to October'. 'Frogs look at you when you are having a twinkle'. 'Cockroaches, ants – a problem in the house'. 'Dogs – outnumber people'. 'Green ants – in trees, give a nasty bite'. 'Snakes'. 'Spiders – redback's bite can be fatal'.

The reference to frogs puzzled us, as no doubt it is puzzling the reader, but it was not long before Leni discovered and experienced what it was all about. We were told to put the light on in the toilet, but this evening she failed to do so, and her shriek was the result of not seeing what was sitting on the toilet seat!

As a regular lifetime church member, I had heard many reasons why people didn't attend church, but in a letter back to the church in North Beach, I told them of another one – It can be dangerous, in fact fatal. On Palm Sunday, our service was to be held under 'the big palm', which was a huge palm in the middle of the village. Obviously, a very good idea, but to get there we had to walk along a narrow path through some bush. Leni walked ahead of me, but she failed to see what I saw in the middle of the path. I yelled, 'Stop, Leni!' and she did. We had just passed Tommo's 'humpy' (a kind of hut) and he shouted, 'What's the matter?' I replied, 'It's a snake.' At that Shandy's owner grabbed a spear, jumped on top of a small upturned boat, and threw the wooden handmade weapon at the snake, which disappeared into the undergrowth. Tommo leapt off the boat, dashed into the bush and emerged triumphantly with a four or five foot long King Brown snake, wriggling on the end of the spear. It is one of the most poisonous snakes in the world!

One evening Leni was sitting up reading the newspaper in bed. Suddenly, I heard a scratching, rustling sound emanating from the paper, which I grabbed and placed on the floor. Opening it, I found a six inch long centipede. These monster insects are very dangerous and particularly to people like Leni, who suffer from allergies of all kinds. I stamped on it and killed it, but it was a frightening episode. She had already survived an encounter with a centipede in the bush at North Beach. She had only been wearing thongs on her feet when we had gone walking with Eion and Bev Martin. Leni had shrieked suddenly as the centipede fastened itself to her right heel. She suffered from the poison, which caused swellings, for several weeks.

I have a photograph of a frill necked lizard, a most unusual Northern Territory reptile, and I snapped it as it was crossing the road to one of the bays. I stopped the 'ute' to take the photo, and it appears to be snarling or spitting at us. That was the late afternoon when we nearly got into dire trouble. We went for a walk along the beach, and left the 'ute' at the end of the road that ran through jungle. When we got back to the vehicle the tropical night had fallen, which we had watched happen, the sun disappearing visibly below the Arafura Sea horizon at a speed that has to be seen to be believed!

So it was dark. And the 'ute' would not start! And I did not have a torch. And if I had, I did not know sufficient about car engines to be able to diagnose a fault. Desperately, I pressed the starter, but the engine would not start. Eventually, there was little life left in the battery. It was pitch dark, and we could hear the eerie sounds of the jungle. We were about twelve miles from civilisation. I could not possibly walk back, as the jungle road was impenetrably black, and even if I had wanted to try, I could neither have taken Leni with me nor left her behind. What a predicament. No one would come looking for us, because no one knew where we were, so it looked like a night in the 'ute', in the jungle, and near the beach, which could have been home to some crocodiles.

And we had no liquid with us, a very bad mistake, quite inexcusable. But then, a touch of the starter and the engine roared to life! It was one of the most welcome sounds I have ever heard, and we drove back to Minjilang quicker than we had ever done before.

When we went on such trips, we had been warned not to venture on to sacred sites. Apparently, these could be anywhere, and so before leaving we always told one of the community leaders so that he could tell us what to look for.

We had been told from the outset that we had to respect Aboriginal culture, which included such as sacred sites, and of course, we did, but there were occasions when we felt that the taxpayer was being taken for a ride. Let the reader make up his own mind about the following story.

Leni and I were invited to go to Elcho Island for the opening of a Supermarket training school, one Tuesday. As we had business to do in Darwin, John Ford invited us to stay at his house on the Friday evening through to Tuesday. This was the first time we had left Croker Island and a weekend in beautiful Darwin was most attractive to us.

We got the lady from the Bank agency to look after the store for the Friday afternoon, Monday and Tuesday, and we went to the airstrip to be picked up at 1.00 pm. We ought to have been forewarned that things were not going to go according to plan, when the plane was three hours late, due to having to turn back to Darwin with engine trouble. None of this seems to be connected with taking the taxpayer for a ride, but hold tight, as there are two stories in one here.

Eventually, we got to Darwin and it was really nice to renew our acquaintance with this cosmopolitan and most Northerly Australian capital city. My first visit on the Saturday morning was to a hairdresser. It was a gentlemen's, but all of the 'barbers' were young women, and I somehow felt embarrassed when one sat me in a chair, but I was even more so when she asked me if I had seen my hair at the back, as she put a mirror behind me. When I saw the reflection in the mirror in front of me, I could not believe my eyes. One would have thought she had used a knife and fork! Yes – Leni had been having a go!

After a pleasant Sunday when we went to the Uniting Church in Smith Street and met many of our new Northern Territory friends, we spent Monday visiting various wholesalers and the ALPA offices. Early Tuesday, we flew off to Elcho Island in time for the opening of the school, which was to train Aborigines from all over the territory in skills applicable to running, and working in, an ALPA or any other community store. There were speeches from Government officials and from some Aborigines, one of whom handed out printed copies. Amazingly, it was purely political, regarding Land Rights, and in it we were told to get a copy of a booklet entitled 'My Mother the Land'. They were available at Galiwin'ku, the name of the main village on Elcho. I obtained a copy and here is a reprint of one of the articles, which is typical of Aboriginal mythology.

It is written by Dhamarrandji, a Clan leader who lives on Elcho Island.

'The two Djar'kawu sisters made this madayin [sacred object] I have here. They made it themselves. They had the authority to make it just like it is: white feathers of the nurrunurru [spoonbill], bees wax, red feathers of the lindirritj [parrot], more bees wax, and gunga [pandanas] for the dilly bag itself, which we call Mindjalpi.

Yolru men didn't have any authority before this time, before the day Djar'kawu came with the sacred Mindjalpi. But on that day they brought it, they cut some baltarr [forked sticks] and hung the dilly bag on them. Then they went off to look for some shellfish and crabs. The men were watching all this, and as soon as the two sisters had left, they decided to take over the dilly bag with its power. The original dilly bag didn't have a lid; it was completely closed in. So the men cut the top off and began to sing. As soon as the Djar'kawu sisters heard the marrwat [special songs], the younger sister said, "They took our bag from the forked stick."

"Never mind," said the older sister, "let them have the power, because we call them wawa" [brother].'

So that's how the men got the authority over the land. And from that time the men hunted the women away from the sacred dilly bag.

So today, the dilly bag which belongs to the men in each mala (clan) is the proof that that mala has the authority over that land – because the dilly bag came from Djar'kawu.

This dilly bag, here as I write, is proof of ownership of Marapay, my homeland centre at Buckingham Bay.

As I wrote earlier, the reader can make up his or her own mind as to the validity of land claims, in this case regarding Marapay, the writer's homeland centre at Buckingham Bay.

I said that there were two stories and the second one started to unfold immediately after our plane took off, at 2.00 pm on Tuesday, heading for Croker Island, estimated time of arrival, Tuesday 4.00 pm – actual time of arrival, 8.30 am on Friday. There has to be a story when a journey takes about sixty-seven hours instead of three.

We left Elcho and very soon afterwards the pilot lost radio contact with Darwin, so he looked for somewhere to land, and eventually through a gap in the clouds, for it was very cloudy, he saw an island with an airstrip. We landed safely and the pilot went into the village to use a land radio, discovering in the process that the island was Millingimbi. There was nothing his base could do for him so late in the day, and as it was not possible to repair the radio, they said that they would send a pilot who was willing to take over the aircraft, and fly it without a radio.

He arrived on the Wednesday morning. Meanwhile, we had spent a comfortable and interesting night with the local ALPA manager and his wife. It was useful to be able to compare things, and our premises fared very badly in the comparison. They had modern accommodation with air-conditioning and several excellent Aboriginal staff, including an assistant manager, quite different to our situation. The aircraft bringing the new pilot landed and took off straightaway with the other pilot, who, it transpired, had our aircraft's keys in his pocket! When the new man realised this he said that he would go into the village and get a mechanic. This he did and we listened to a conversation they had outside the plane, whilst we and an Aboriginal lady whom we knew, sat in the tropical heat created by the sun blazing on the metal skin of the aircraft. The pilot asked the motor mechanic to 'hot wire' the engine to get it started, but the latter said that it was a very dangerous thing to do and against the law! This was too much for the lady, who disembarked like a shot out of a gun.

We didn't follow her, despite the mechanic's protestations, but we got a tremendous shock when we heard the engines burst into life! The Aboriginal lady decided to stay with friends and, at last, we took off for Croker, still without radio of course.

The journey seemed to be without further complications, and we were just thinking of what time we would get home when the pilot announced that he would have to land as soon as was possible as he was unhappy about one of the engines! He thought that we must be nearing South Goulburn Island, so as he could not radio their airstrip, he would go down to a lower level to see if he could find it. This was great. I could not stop thinking of the description given to the 'Timor Sea', years before in the days of England to Australian air races, and the like. Now the Arafura joins the Timor, and therefore if the latter deserved the tag 'shark infested', so did the former.

We were in luck, if that is what you call it, as the sought for South Goulburn Island came into view. We landed, and who should be on the airstrip but our dear friend made on our previous visit. Jessie picked us up and took us to her delightful cottage. By this time we felt most unwholesome, having perspired freely and the ever present red Northern Territory dust having made us look like Red Indians, so we could not get under a shower quickly enough. And what then? Our clothes were damp with perspiration and filthy, so we were unable to put them back on, and our suitcase had gone on to Croker on the regular flight from Elcho to Croker on the Monday!

I spent the evening and the night wrapped in one of Jessie's bed sheets and Leni was able to borrow one of our hostess' dresses, whilst our clothes were being washed. Jessie was as hospitable as ever and she drove us back to the airstrip on the Thursday morning, and guess what? Despite assurances that there was nothing much wrong with the engine, they had not the wherewithal to fix it, so back we went to Jessie's again! By this time we were very concerned for the bank lady looking after the store, even though we were enjoying the rest. At 7.30 am on Friday, a special plane arrived from Darwin. It flew us to Croker where we arrived at 8.30 am! And the bank lady was truly delighted to see us!

There were a few white Australians on Croker. There was an adult educator, a community adviser, an engineer in charge of the roads, a temporary council clerk, plus their wives and a few children and a male and female teacher. And Leni and I.

The teachers were responsible for teaching about 37 children, and the first thing they did every morning was to give each child some special biscuit and a drink, to ensure an adequate consumption of protein, vitamins, and minerals.

The school was perfectly adequate and looked fine to us, so it was a surprise to see a comprehensive painting job being undertaken. There had to be a reason, and we soon found it. On 12th March, my birthday by the way, the Northern Territory's Chief Administrator, equivalent to a State's Governor, was to visit Croker and naturally he would visit the school. I was told that the cost of the refurbishing was $40,000, an extravagant waste of the taxpayer's money, by the way.

The Aborigine always knows what to say and do to please the Government official, especially where funding is involved, or when it is felt that a show is necessary. So it was decided that all of the school-age children should go to school on the great day, all 37 of them. They were not so silly as to only have the normal 7 or 8 attending. But it was all to no avail as 12th March was the day of Cyclone Max!

One excellent decision taken by the Aboriginal Council was to disallow liquor of all kinds. I do not recall ever hearing of anyone contravening this edict.

Another praiseworthy quality was their church attendance. Despite the Missions, as such, being banished in the early seventies by the Australian Government for being paternalistic, attendances at the church services were very good. There were a number of 'elders' who led prayers and preached sermons, including Mick Yamirr, whom I have already mentioned, and Daisy Yamirr, his daughter. It was always surprising to see the difference in appearance of Mick and his girls over the weekends. They lived opposite us, and on a Saturday Mick would be wearing a 'naga' (a piece of material) draped around him, a silver stubble on his chin, barefooted, and with a staff in his hand, and looking like his forefathers must have looked for thousands of years before him, except that the 'naga' would have been of animal skin. The girls were always topless on Saturdays.

The following day in church Mick would wear a nice business suit, be clean shaven, and wear shoes, the antithesis of the day before, and the girls would be dressed in their Sunday best.

The Croker congregation sang beautifully and Keith and Liz Williams would often organise an evening of hymn singing in the church. Keith played the guitar and we sang mainly modern 'chorus' type hymns, very rhythmic, but also a few traditional, one of which is now a great favourite of mine. The refrain or chorus goes, 'Trust and obey, for there is no other way, to be happy in Jesus, is to trust and obey.' Now, whenever we sing it in church, I think of our dear Aboriginal friends, thousands of miles away on a tropical island, but seemingly with us in spirit. They had their own hymn in Iwaidji and every service started with it. It was haunting. I took a service by invitation one Sunday and I recorded it, and I love to listen to that Croker hymn. Incidentally, I was treasurer of the church during my stay. Leni loved the church there, and she liked to read the lesson.

Shortly after our arrival we were introduced to an old lady called Hazel, who was one of the traditional land owners, and we used to go some evenings to her surprisingly poor accommodation to sing hymns. She was dying of emphysema, and our hymn singing was a great joy to her. Incidentally, she had been a heavy smoker, as unfortunately, a lot of Aborigines are. Just another bad habit inculcated by the 'Balanda', as the whites are called.

Another of the traditional owners was Illajilli, a lady who could have won 'Miss World', had she entered it. She will always be remembered if only due to the man she married. Earlier I wrote of a member of the first Bible school on South Goulburn, in the early days of missionary James Watson, Lazarus Lami Lami by name. It was he whom Illajilli married, and it was he who became the first Aboriginal Methodist minister.

They probably had more children, but we knew daughter Ruby best of all, and shortly before we left, son Ronald was being trained as council clerk after working on the mainland for a mining company. There was also a gorgeous girl, Isabella, who certainly was Illajilli's daughter, but despite Aboriginal beliefs that Lazarus was the father, he could not have been as he had been dead several years.

Ruby, of course, was the Ruby who worked in the store, and she was quite a character. She came in one day telling us of a cheque for a few thousand dollars she had received as a member of the traditional land owning family. There were two similar situations whilst we were on Croker, one being payment for the killing of numbers of buffalo on their land, and the other to do with royalty payments. I cannot recall what Ruby's cash was for, but I do remember well what she bought with some of it. She bought a pool table and charged everyone fifty cents to play on it! A tough girl was Ruby. She seemed to be involved in most things going on.

One day Leni sold a dress to an old man who bought it for his little granddaughter, and unknown to Leni, Ruby had wanted it for her daughter. After lunch one day, our assistant failed to report for work. When we enquired why, we were told that there was a fight in the village, and that the indefatigable Ruby was the instigator. She had seen this child wearing the dress she wanted and she had attacked the poor old man.

It was not uncommon for her, and sometimes Norma, not to return after lunch, and it just meant that Leni and I had to do their work, our own having to be left until the evening. We had complained often to John Ford. We were discovering why our predecessors only stayed six weeks, after working several years in some other community.

After only five weeks, John wrote to us after a visit, telling us that he and his executive committee had received many good reports about Leni and me, realised our difficulties re the laziness of the staff, and would support us if we decided to sack them.

This strengthened our hands, but we endeavoured to encourage them, and to some extent, we were successful for a while. However, we eventually decided to get rid of Ruby, as she was holding us to ransom. Sack Ruby! Sack the daughter of Lazarus and Illajilli! It could not be done, we were told, and in a way they were right for, although we did it, it was not popular with some of the most vocal of the community.

A month or two later, a Fijian Uniting Church minister was appointed to Croker, and he was opposed to ALPA, saying that they took all of the profits from the island. This was patently untrue, as the system was to pay profits back to the community, but with Ruby a thorn in our flesh, and he calling meetings to inflame the people and turn them against ALPA, our position became untenable. Although we did not believe that it could happen, there were rumours that we would be attacked. The Fijian was hardly a man of God, as far as we were concerned.

We had worked hard and well. We were much admired by many in the community, but the minister and the supporters of Ruby would not let the matters rest. It was ALPA out, and Ruby in, and it was not worth us continuing, so we radioed John Ford and he agreed that we should leave. The church plane arrived and we flew to Darwin, to stay for a while in a Uniting Church apartment.

Looking back, it was a great let down. Things beyond our control created antagonism, which could not be easily dissipated. What we did discover was that, whereas Aborigines want to be treated like the remainder of the Australian community, in practice it just cannot happen. Indeed if this did happen, the people of Croker would be much worse off. Things may have changed since we left, but I doubt it. For instance, the islanders could go to Darwin any time they wished, but the people of Darwin could not step foot on Croker unless invited and acceptable to the council. Apartheid?

Of the 108 people over the age of 15, 53 Aborigines were employed, and a Government report states that only 2 or 3 drew unemployment benefit. Looking back, this is a surprise to me, but the 53 listed as employed were certainly supported by some Government subsidies. The report concludes that the bulk of jobs depend directly on subsidies.

I am told that the Whitlam Labour Government decided that the Missions were too paternalistic, and that the Aborigines should be allowed to develop, presumably to be equal to the white Australian. Certainly some have. One has been a State Governor General, many are in the professions, some of the greatest Australian sportsmen have been, and are, indigenous; Members of Parliament, State and Federal, including Cabinet Ministers, have taken advantage of the opportunities which are available.

But as in the white community, there are those who do not want to work, and want everything given. I think that the situation at the moment, is that you cannot criticise anyone other than Anglo Saxons, or you are considered racist.

I think that the pendulum has swung too far the other way. There are many things the Aborigines could do for themselves, and a prime example is on Croker Island. It is part of Australia, and yet people on the mainland are forbidden to go there. It is a most beautiful tropical island and should be made into a holiday paradise. Chalets could be built for accommodation; the inhabitants could grow the fruit and vegetables; the baker could bake the bread, etc; the cattle could provide the milk, cheese, and meat; the people could provide the music and dancing and corroborees; and everyone would prosper. Fishing trips could be organised, trips to other islands could be arranged, and all of the 'Top End' communities would benefit. What a prospect! But no doubt some armchair philosopher would find fault with the proposition. They always do.

Shortly after we left Croker Island a deputation from the World Council of Churches arrived in Australia, to look into how the Aborigines were treated. One of the places they visited was Croker, and their report included comments on how they saw the Aboriginal situation on that lovely island. If their report on the other communities they visited was as inaccurate as that of Croker, then the visit was a waste of money and time. They succeeded in raising world-wide concern about the 'plight' of the Aboriginal people, but really it was ludicrous. They published a statement made, they said, by the chairman of the council and it was in perfect English, describing the awful problems the people were facing. All I can say is that two things must have happened in the fortnight since we had left. One, 'Jumbo', the chairman, must have had some tuition in the English language that managed to transform him from someone who had little command of the tongue, into a person who could have been a teacher of English. And two, conditions must have deteriorated incredibly rapidly. It really was untrue.

The leader of the deputation was an East German communist and he would have been better employed helping his own people struggling under the yoke of the 'hammer and sickle'.

We had appreciated and enjoyed our few days in the Northern Territory capital as always, but we were becoming concerned about our future once again.

Despite our eventual disappointment at Croker Island, we felt even more than previously that we had a mission to work with the Aboriginal people. Had not all of the church and Aboriginal study literature warned us that the big problem was 'culture shock'? And yet we still did not know what it was, sure proof that for us it did not exist. Yes, we felt that we had both sympathy for and empathy with, the Australian Aborigine.

We looked at one or two projects in Darwin involving Aborigines, but whereas we loved the city, perhaps even more than Perth, it was the remote community which attracted us. We called daily at John Ford's office in Smith Street, and one day he appeared to have no good news for us, because after asking our usual question re employment prospects in another store, he started his response with, 'Well, no not really. Bamyili need a store manager and manageress, but I would not advise you to go there.'

This did not sound very good, but we were determined to get back in action as soon as possible. 'Where is it?' we asked. Looking at the map, it was about a 450 kilometre drive from Darwin, 'down the track' as Territorians described the road south, to Katherine, then after about 45 kilometres, travel east-south-east about a further 50 kilometres to Bamyili.

'Can you fix an interview?' we asked. John replied that this was no problem as he was on a committee of management to do with it. We could not get there quickly enough.

To do so we hired a car and drove down to Katherine. The trip was very interesting as it was our initial sortie into the Northern Territory. We had heard of going 'down the track' quite often and here we were experiencing it. As we drove along, we were intrigued to witness a herd of buffalo, something we had never seen before. They had been brought to the territory many years before by Afghans, and had proliferated to the extent that they were considered a menace. Many had brucellosis, making them unfit for human consumption, and they did an enormous amount of damage to the topsoil in many parts of the Northern Territory. They were very strong and solid, and if a car ran into them, although the buffalo might be killed, the car would generally be a total wreck.

We had seen many kangaroos in Western Australia, but never wallabies, and we were able to rectify this omission just after we left Pine Gap. There were two beautiful specimens standing together quite near to the road. We also saw an Australian wild dog, the dingo, roaming through the bush. It was very alert, ears standing up straight, and its almost golden coat glistened in the sunlight.

We had stopped for a while at the Tavern at Pine Gap where we had a drink, a sandwich, and a wash. It was interesting to talk to some genuine denizens of the Outback, who had ridden in from a nearby cattle station. We were surprised that Australia had genuine cowboys with stetson hats, and kerchiefs around their necks.

Our next stop was Katherine, which is marked on the maps in large print, but whose population, 4,500, was not as large as that of many villages in England. We had to report to the Yulngu Association, and we quickly found their offices. First we met Ray Fordinail, a very charming Aborigine, who was a leader of the local people, and who in later years, was to be chief spokesman in many important meetings with Prime Minister, Bob Hawke, regarding the transfer of ownership of Katherine Gorge to the Aboriginal people, and similarly, with Land Rights and the ownership of the great Kakadu National Park.

Next we met 'Meggsy', their accountant, and as we seemed to satisfy them both, it was arranged for us to visit the Bamyili community, a further 94 kilometres away. We drove south about 45 kilometres, and then turned left and the rest of the journey was on a rough unsurfaced road. Every time a car passed us going in the opposite direction, we had to plough our way through clouds of red dust.

All there was between the main road and Bamyili was the tiny community of Maranboy, which consisted of a police station and nothing else, although it too figures on most maps of Australia. We were to get to know the police who were stationed there, very well, in future days.

CHAPTER THIRTY THREE
BAMYILI

On arrival in Bamyili we were very pleased with what we saw. The grass had been cut and everything looked very neat and very tidy. We compared it to Croker Island and felt that it looked much cleaner and better organised.

A meeting had been arranged for us with the Aboriginal Council, and we met them in the council building. We liked the people immediately and felt that they liked us. It really could not have been friendlier, and we were happy with the salaries, etc. I remember Elizabeth, a rather large Aboriginal lady, suggested that we should be employed, and this led to the rest giving their approval too.

The current manager had only been there for four weeks, and it had been too much for him. He had got off on the wrong foot and his wife never joined him. This was not the happiest of auguries, but we were determined to succeed, and to benefit from our Croker experience.

We were told that beer was the biggest problem in the community, so we were forewarned. A further bit of information was that in an attempt to stop the losses, which many similar stores had experienced, Bamyili and four or five others had formed a kind of co-operative, employing a general manager and an assistant who would act as internal auditors. This was certainly necessary, as the stories of managers stealing were horrific.

The penultimate manager at Bamyili had been taken off the plane at Sydney Airport bound for London, with a case full of cash. As often happened, apparently, the Aborigines would not allow the police to charge him. Another manager had lost the store a lot of money, but somehow or other the accountant had 'lost the books'!

The position of the store as it was explained to us, was that it owed suppliers about $80,000; the community owed the store $21,000; the place was unbelievably filthy; the refrigeration was archaic; and there was a truck, misused by everybody, with a 'feature' that as you sat in the driving seat, you could see the road going by – through the holes in the floor.

The worst thing was that most of the main suppliers refused to supply, due to being owed too much. It was obvious that we had a tough job ahead of us, but

I felt that I would rather do something of this nature, than take on a position with little opportunity for achievement and improvement.

We drove back to Darwin, had a few days holiday at the Darwin Motor Inn, and after thanking John Ford for his recommendation, we rented another car and drove again to Bamyili.

It was arranged that we should work with the incumbent manager for a few days, to learn his routine and then, after a stock-take by the 'internal auditors', take over. This we did, and the day came when our predecessor drove off, and we were in at the deep end. My list of responsibilities is worth recording. I was the store manager, the licensed milk vendor, the licensee, the manager of the service station (petrol, diesel, oil etc), the postman, the newsagent, and although the community had a bank agency, just about all of the people cashed their cheques through me. This latter duty was very onerous the way it was organised. People had got into the habit over the years of just walking into the office at any time at all, to change their cheques. This meant cash lying around all the time, and constant interruptions.

I soon changed the system. To begin with, I had a sliding window and a shelf put in the wall of the office that faced the store, and I set certain hours when cheques could be cashed. This saved a lot of time. For some unknown reason, newspapers had been sold from the office, resulting in more interruptions, so I put them out by the tills to be sold in the same way as everything else.

A further innovation was stopping credit. For years a 'book' had been kept and most of the people just did not worry if they had spent their income, as they could always get what they wanted on credit. The majority of the customers were on social security and received a fortnightly cheque. They were better off than their white counterparts in the cities, because few paid rent, or paid for electricity, water, or rates. They had no travel expenses, unless at their own choice they travelled away from the community.

I could see no sense in credit, so I told the council. They did not like it, but I was adamant. Even the school's headmistress came to see me to tell me that I could not do this, as it would mean hardship for some people. I told her that I would not try to tell her how to run her classroom.... Aborigines are known for sharing. It is part of their culture, so I told them to borrow food, etc, from relatives until the next cheque arrived.

After a couple of pay-days, very few even asked about credit, but I did not succeed in getting back the $21,000 owing. I got a few thousand, but it was eventually far too time consuming and as we were starting to make a profit, I did not bother about it. It was the community's loss and in a way their fault, for permitting credit in the first place.

The store, like most of the buildings in Bamyili, was only about five years old, but it had not been looked after. There was not one display unit in the place. When Leni went to use the toilet for the first time, she came back to tell me of the horrific state it was in. I examined the men's toilet and, as expected, it was the same. No attempt had been made to keep them clean, and we immediately put the area, which included the bulk store, out of bounds. Two Aboriginal girls were given the job of cleaning them and under Leni's expert supervision, they were soon pristine clean. We decided to bar customers from that part of the building, except when the trying on of clothing necessitated privacy.

The petrol pumps were an obvious place to lose money. Vehicles could appear, the drivers drive off without paying, and all the hard work in the store could go for nothing. I made Cain, a fine Thursday Islander, responsible for the key for the pumps, and all petrol purchases. This completely solved the problem, as frequent dipping of the tanks proved. Furthermore, petrol could only be bought at specific times. Our first Saturday afternoon and Sunday morning in Bamyili taught us a lesson, as people knocked at our door for us to go to the store half a mile away to get the petrol 'to visit relations in the hospital'! We soon put a stop to that.

I had air-conditioning in the office, but it was not effective. On examination it had possibly never been cleaned before, as it was clogged with the all pervading red dust of the Outback. It took a few minutes to clean and I had a cool office.

In a room, barred and bolted, at the back of the store, we found hundreds of dollars of discarded clothing, which had got dirty, hanging on the racks. Leni took them home, washed them, and in the course of time sold them all. We also found a box containing twenty or thirty pairs of good quality leather children's sandals... for Aboriginal children? They even played soccer bare-footed!

We had a phone in the office and I was straightaway on to the suppliers to whom we owed so much money. Most of them knew me from Croker, and they all readily agreed to recommence supplying us on my guarantee that we paid cash for every order, and paid off the debt over an agreed period.

At Croker we had to do most of the work, but at Bamyili we decided that things had to be different. We had been led to believe that staff had to be treated with kid gloves, and we saw where that got us, so we decided at the outset that if the staff were not all there at opening time we would not open. This happened quite often in the early days, but eventually all got the message and we invariably had the full complement. If one was missing, we would sit on the rail, which surrounded the store, the customers would shout, 'Stan – when you open the store?' and I would reply, 'When the staff all here.' Someone would ask, 'Who not here?' I would tell them and a few of the customers would go and fetch him or her.

As time went on, we succeeded in making dramatic improvements to the store. The refrigerator, so vital in the tropics, was in a poor state and we spent quite a bit of money repairing it and restoring it to as good as new. Everything in the store was priced, and the prices were according to percentage profits applicable to the different goods on sale – electrical, clothing, hardware, food, etc.

I soon realised that we had too many staff. One known as Hickey was actually paid for 'keeping dogs out of the store', a job the remainder of the staff could easily do. Aborigines love dogs, but they do not look after them. They are generally filthy, mangy, and ill fed. Leni used to get quite distressed by this and was determined to effect a change. When funds permitted, she bought large sacks of dog biscuits and after the store closed, she sprinkled them all over the concrete block, which fronted the store. She did this to make sure that even the little dogs could get something to eat. She also had all of the staff trained to keep buckets filled with water. Every evening the community's dog population turned up for a feed! She even got some of their owners to buy shampoo and various powders, etc, to kill the parasites which covered most of the dogs. Leni reckoned that they looked upon her as a mad Englishwoman, but really she did a marvellous job for both the human beings and the canine population.

We were making great progress. How different to when one of our tasks had been to examine all of the food stocks to see if they were all fit to eat. I asked Leni to take stock of the biscuits, and as she moved the packets, dozens of cockroaches ran out. She was horrified, and later in the day, she sorted out the desks on which stood the tills and the same thing happened. We destroyed all the food that could have been contaminated, and told the council that we would not continue until the store and the storerooms behind were entirely fumigated. This was done and the distressing problem was eliminated.

Due to prudent trading, we were able to keep our agreements with suppliers as to repaying our debts, and things got better and better. We were soon showing a good profit and I had the time to search for better suppliers. One Sunday after church in Katherine, we dropped into the Katherine Bakery from whom we bought all of our bread and cakes, and over a cup of tea we chatted about each others' businesses. It transpired that the Bakery owners also had a transport business, and that a huge truck and attached enclosed trailer went fortnightly to Mount Isa, picked up a load of copper and delivered it to Brisbane in Queensland. It then returned with a load of flour and other bakery items. Now I had recently found that a Queensland wholesaler was immensely cheaper than our suppliers in Darwin and Katherine, but that due to the distance involved, about 2,200 kilometres, the cost of freight gobbled up the margins.

Could they bring us a load at the same time, I asked? They said that the trailer came back with room to spare and that if I could afford $500 a trip, they would bring me all I needed. I reckoned up how much per dollar of purchases this meant and it was infinitely cheaper all told, so I agreed immediately. For example, we could buy tins of soft drink for 19 cents and have them delivered to the store, sell them for 30 cents, and make 57% profit – whilst 50 and 60 cents a tin were the prices in the Katherine shops.

The system worked perfectly. When the truck arrived, I got a dozen young men, and they passed the boxes man to man, like a chain, and for a can of beer each, it was all unloaded and stocked in the storeroom. It was shortly afterwards that people discovered that we were much cheaper than the Katherine supermarkets. Eventually, we topped $16,000 in takings in a week, and I found out that this was twice that of Cox's, the main shop in Katherine.

An early change in routine I made, was to do with the dreadful 'floorboardless' Toyota truck, which did a 188 kilometre round trip to town every weekday, and the petrol and the driver were paid for by the store. The driver went to the wholesaler and brought back a minute amount of groceries, he went to the bank on behalf of the council and he went to the Post Office for the mail. Now various other people used to go to Katherine daily, so I got them to go to the bank and the Post Office, and I cut out the ridiculous grocery pick up. Of course, there was no job for the driver, but I was there to make a profit not to throw money away.

Leni and I had also used the awful Toyota to go to Katherine at weekends for a change of environment, and a bit of peace, but when we were doing so well, the council told us to buy a car for our personal use. Aborigines always bought huge cars and they were both surprised and disappointed when we turned up in a $4,500 Daihatsu Handivan! Our idea was to buy something cheap, in which we could pick up any odds and ends we still had to get in Katherine, and which had no room to carry a load of Aborigines! This may sound awful, but whenever we drove the Toyota, all of the community expected to be picked up and dropped off. We worked hard enough without that.

There was talk of a satellite being launched that would bring TV to the remote areas of Northern Australia, and we told the council that the store profits would be able to pay for it. They were delighted, as they were when we suggested that we could afford to put on a Christmas Party, with plenty of food, and presents for all of the children.

Aboriginal children, even in the Outback, like the same toys as the city kids. Mums and dads were booking sample toys, which we had on display, and putting by for later payment, as early as August. Tonka toys for the boys, dolls for the girls, and BMX bikes for both boys and girls, were very popular choices. We had our back storeroom full by the time the festive season arrived.

Whenever we went into Katherine, which took us about an hour and a quarter, we looked forward to tea and cakes at the Countrywomen's Association (CWA), at their delightful cafe in the main street. One Saturday, we drove in and discovered that they closed at 1.00 pm and it was ten past, so we went across the road to the Chicken and Pizza Bar, and thereby hangs a tale. I asked the lady for two cups of tea. She put a tea bag in each cup, poured boiling water on them, immediately topped them up with milk, withdrew the tea bags and passed the cups to me. It looked and tasted like warm milk. As politely as I could, I told her that we preferred that the tea bags be left in the boiling water until the tea was quite strong, so she emptied the cups and did as I asked. She was a Scottish lady, or so her accent suggested.

A few weeks later we arrived in town late again, parked in front of the Pizza Bar as there was a space there, and wondered where to go for a cup of tea. Glancing through the cafe window, Leni said that she thought the cafe must have changed hands as there was a different lady behind the counter. So we went in and spoke to her.... She replied in a broad Black Country English accent, so I asked her where she was from. 'Wolver'ampton,' she said. I told her that I guessed so, and that we had lived in the adjoining town, West Bromwich, or very close to it. Then I regaled her with the story of our last incursion in her cafe. She roared with laughter and said that that was her sister Edith, and that there were three sisters and their husbands in partnership.

I was most embarrassed, but I could hardly believe it until Elizabeth explained that their father used to be in the RAF. He had been stationed in Scotland for a few years when Edith, the oldest of the girls, was born, thus the Scottish accent. The sequel still goes on today, as we became good friends with Elizabeth and her husband John, and they eventually moved to Perth where they settled down. As a matter of fact, shortly I am to propose a toast at their daughter Helen's wedding.

At Christmas we were invited to stay at Elizabeth and John's and we actually had dinner at Edith's, where we had a good laugh about the tea bags.

On Christmas Eve, Leni and I went to the Midnight Service at the Anglican church, and we arrived shortly before twelve o'clock. Strangely, people never seem to like sitting in the front pews, and this was so this night. Leni and I have never been like that, and we were quite happy to walk straight to the front. This led to a strange coincidence. Every Christmas Eve for years before, I had always read the magnificent verses from Chapter 9 of the book of the prophet Isaiah, from verse 2, beginning with, 'The people who walked in darkness have seen a great light' through to 'unto us a child is born, unto us a son is given', to 'his name will be called Wonderful Counsellor, Mighty God, Everlasting Father, Prince of Peace',and down to 'The zeal of the Lord of Hosts will do this.' And every year since, I have read it here at St Michaels, North Beach.

Just before this tropical Christmas Eucharist, Father Stacey announced that the first reader was unable to attend, so was there a volunteer from the congregation who would like to read in his stead? Now I had no intention of volunteering, because surely a regular church member would want to do this? There was a tense silence as the rector looked along the rows. No one volunteered and finally his eyes rested on the front row and on me. He then asked me specifically, 'Would you like to read?' It really was amazing. I was more than happy to oblige, particularly as it was Isaiah, Chapter 9!

Katherine was a great little town and I have regretted that we have never been able to re-visit it. Distances are enormous here, Perth being 4,000 kilometres, or 2,500 miles, from that superb little Northern Territory township. I would recommend it to anyone. We used to love Katherine Gorge and Helen and I used to swim in the warm waters. There were crocodiles there too, generally basking on the rocks in the sun. Leni used to implore us not to go in, but I had read that freshwater crocs are harmless. Since then I have also read that this is not always true!

The salt-water variety are, of course, highly dangerous, and have been seen 300 kilometres from the sea. However, those under two metres long are not dangerous, so I tell people to carry a tape measure! Seriously, apparently salt-water crocs are vegetarians until two years of age, when they are also about two metres long. So don't forget the tape measure!

People in smaller countries find it difficult to comprehend the distances between some towns in Australia, and if faced with the prospect of driving 188 kilometres (116 miles) to see a movie, I guess that most would stay at home and watch television. But we didn't have TV and on occasions we did drive to the Drive-In cinema in Katherine, just for the evening, and we really did enjoy 'the trip out', to use Leni's expression.

One night after seeing two good crime films, my favourite sort, we set off back to Bamyili. We were just leaving the town's environs when I spotted something quite large in the middle of the road, and I had to swerve smartly to miss it. It was a huge snake, and talking to an Aborigine the following day, he said it would have been a python, as they often lay on the tarmacadam, which apparently remained warm all night. A few minutes later we saw a strange looking marsupial, probably a wallaby, but it ran in a strange way, with one paw held out in front of the other. My friend said that they called it a 'left handed wallaby' as it was its left paw that it always held in front.

Something of interest often occurred on our trips to and from town. One day we really had a fright. As we drove along past open bushland whose main feature was the giant anthills, which are a strange phenomenon of the Northern Territory, we were surprised to see clouds of dust to the left of us and seemingly approaching us. Suddenly we had the eeriest of experiences, as our car was assailed by a roaring wind, which bounced the car along for several seconds, before moving into the bush on the other side of the road. The car was struck by clouds of dust containing lots of small stones or gravel, picked up by the roadside. They rattled the underside of the car and really gave us a fright. We were very lucky that we came out of it unharmed, as it was a 'Willy Willy' (a tropical cyclone/hurricane).

On the same road was a sign saying, 'Caution, buffalo crossing'. Now we knew that these enormous animals ran wild all over the countryside, but we did not think that they could read! The story was that for their own reasons they chose to cross only at that particular spot. Another day we saw and photographed a large number of wild horses. Often we saw the Australian wild dog, the Dingo, and one of the most beautiful sights was of two baby wallabies in exactly the same pose in a gap on the side of the road.

There was always something of interest to see. A common sight was the road trains, which traverse the continent, and which take a lot of passing on the narrow 'track' through the Northern Territory. I thought that the diesel trucks plus trailers of postwar Germany were big, but they paled into insignificance when compared to the gigantic road trains plying from Eastern and Southern cities to Darwin.

Whenever we travelled, we did as recommended by the police and took plenty of drinks with us, as if you broke down in temperatures of, for instance, 45°C (113°F), you could soon dehydrate. One Saturday morning en route to town, we came across a broken down car with an Aborigine standing by it. It was about 10.30 am and he told us that his friend, whose car it was, had gone back to Bamyili, about 45 kilometres away, at 10.00 o'clock on the night before, and he was still waiting for him to return with someone to tow his car in. He had had nothing to drink and was in quite a state. We let him have a couple of bottles of soft drink.

Buffaloes were easy prey for the huge road trains, and we frequently saw their carcasses on the side of the road. It was remarkable how quickly these bulky animals were reduced to skeletons, by the incessant heat from the sun and the ravaging of the various termites.

Holt Thompson was the school principal, his wife was Chal, and one night we called at their house for a chat. After sitting me in a chair, Holt said that an hour before he had found a King Brown snake, the second most venomous snake in Australia, and one of the most venomous in the world, under that very chair. Their front door had a gap of a couple of inches underneath, and it must have slithered in through the gap. Holt was not particularly perturbed, being both experienced through twenty-odd years in the Northern Territory and also through an interest in snakes, including having had a twenty foot Python as a pet!

Another animal story is to do with a calf named Matthew. An Aboriginal lady kept it as a pet and she used to walk it everywhere with her, just like a dog. And talking of dogs... there was that story about 'Mud'. Walking home for lunch one day, Leni thought that she saw a movement in a large bush, which was shaped like a cave, near our house. Thinking it might be a snake, I was sent to investigate. The sight that met my eyes was so appealing. Four lovely little puppies were taking milk from their mother. A fifth lay dead at the back of the 'cave'. As soon as Leni saw them she fell in love with them, and for several weeks she fed Mud and her family, until she could find homes for them all. Mud was well-known in the community, but no one would say whose dog she really was. We looked after her until we left, and one of the conditions of the new people who took over from us, was that Mud was part of the deal! Meanwhile, she behaved impeccably, following us backwards and forwards to work, but never attempting to follow us into the store. She would lie outside waiting for us for hours.

Bereft of electronic aids for pleasure, we had to find our own ways of entertaining ourselves, and the obvious alternative was through reading. Sometimes we read separately, but often we read to each other, and particularly detective stories. However, at other times we read from a university textbook entitled, 'The Essential Prose'. There were pieces from all of the world's great writers, and at the end of each were questions for discussion. We thoroughly enjoyed ourselves those evenings in the back of beyond, and we had to laugh after our return to Perth, when we were invited to join an undoubtedly well-meaning organisation 'Marriage Encounter', where couples spent weekends with others at weekend retreats, 'to give them the chance to talk together'!

We had been reading to one another in bed one night, and we were just settling down to go to sleep when, to our amazement, there was a hammering on the door. I called out, 'Who is it?' and the reply was 'It's me, Cain.' I opened the door to see our best store assistant bleeding profusely from three holes in his arm. He seemed afraid for his life and indeed he was. He asked if he could stay as his attackers were hiding under our house, which incidentally, was on stilts. Leni took him in and bathed his wounds, bandaged them up, and told him to go to the medical centre on the morrow. After some time, he left and later in the day, as it was then early morning, he did as he was bidden, one of the results being that Leni was told off for interfering with something that was nothing to do with her. Sometimes you cannot win! Eventually, we heard the whole story as to why Cain was attacked. There was nothing unique about it, something to do with consorting with another man's wife.

Cain was a tremendous worker, who ran everywhere. Even in the store he ran down the aisles. He had worked there ever since it opened in 1975, and he paid me quite a compliment one day. I had been showing him how to do something or other when he said, 'Stan, you know you are the first manager who has ever taught me how to do anything. The others just left me to find out for myself.'

As time went on we learnt more about Bamyili''s history and it was a sad story of wasted money. Governments, both Labour and Liberal, of recent years seemed to be so keen to placate or please Aborigines for political purposes, that immense sums of money had been wasted.

I had seen the burnt out shell of a building for some time without enquiring as to what had happened to it. It had been an egg producing business, with battery hens laying sufficient eggs for the community to supply the shops in Katherine as well as other communities. No one knew how the fire started, but it certainly was not put out, it had been just left to burn out until only ashes remained.

A particularly colourful character was David Blanasi, who went on tour with Rolf Harris and taught him the didgeridoo. He made them as well and he made a special one for us, as Leni used to dress him up when he went off to appear in one of Australia's cities. Unfortunately, David, who was multi-talented, used to drink too much beer and, of course, he could afford to buy a lot of it. He painted the walls of the school with wonderful Aboriginal designs and I am glad that I took photographs of them.

The Bamyili dancers were also in demand, performed regularly for tourists in Katherine and, occasionally, in the big theatres of the Eastern States.

The news that there was to be a visit from Aborigines from other communities was always greeted with pleasure, and it was no exception when we heard that several people from Millingimbi were coming to Bamyili. I have recounted our experiences on that island before, and even for us there was a feeling of excitement as the time of the visit approached, partly because we rarely saw new faces, and partly because there was a chance that we might know one or two of the Millingimbi people.

Living in the communities around the Northern Territory, although often many hundreds of miles apart, it was surprising how many people you got to know. You met them on airstrips, on planes, at meetings, at the wholesalers, in the churches, and I think that due to the vast distances involved, when we did get together, the occasion was much more convivial than bumping into friends, say, in the supermarkets of the Southern and Eastern cities, for example.

I have mentioned before that the Outback Aborigine's concept of time was not highly developed, and the Millingimbi visit was a good example. For two or three weeks before their actual arrival, we kept on hearing that they were 'probably coming tomorrow'. Remembering the saying that 'tomorrow never comes', and particularly in Aboriginal culture, we were quite happy in the knowledge that one day they would arrive.

Eventually the Reverend Nero Timothy told us the purpose of the visit, and to say that we were pleased is to play down the elation we really felt. The word 'visit' did not do justice to what was about to happen.

We had heard of a great Christian revival, which was spreading right across Arnhemland, and it had been intimated that it had begun in Millingimbi. Yes, at last the crusade was to come to Bamyili, and the people spreading the Gospel were called 'The Millingimbi Gospel Singers'. Now we were really excited, and even Aboriginal time has to pass eventually. Then the great day came.

There were eight of them, five young men and three young ladies, probably all between the ages of eighteen and twenty-three. Just looking at them was enough to see how joyful they were and we could not wait to hear them in action.

Similar to 'pop groups', the young men were experts at wiring up electric guitars to loud speakers and putting up floodlights, etc. This they did by the side of the church, and although no time was ever announced, one evening we saw lots of people drifting towards the church. We could not get over quickly enough and after tuning their three guitars, they began to sing and play. As we had already appreciated, Aboriginal voices have a distinctly different sound and their singing was beautiful. Some hymns they sang in their own Millingimbi language, and some in English, with a different accent to the locals.

I have heard Africans and black Americans singing in films and on television, and they have always enjoyed swaying and stamping to the rhythms. The people of Bamyili were the same and thoroughly enjoyed such as 'Father Abraham'. If you know it you will remember that it goes, 'Father Abraham had many sons, many sons had Father Abraham, he is one of us and so are you, so let's all praise the Lord. Stand up, sit down,' etc, etc. They sang out very loud and they really loved doing the actions.

Other hymns they sang were; 'Turn your eyes upon Jesus' (Look full in his wonderful face, And the things of earth Will grow strangely dim In the light of his glory and grace.); 'All good gifts around us'; 'At the name of Jesus, every knee shall bow'; 'Jesus, friend of little children'; 'The Lord is my shepherd'; 'Christ for me'; 'Things are different now'; 'Every person in every nation'; ' Fix your eyes upon Him'; 'I met Jesus at the Crossroads'; etc.

Outdoor services were no different to indoor, as there were lots of dogs in attendance. People sat just anywhere; squatting on the ground, sitting on fallen tree trunks, younger ones up the trees, and some like us sitting in fold-up chairs.

Initially, they were going to stay a few days, and quite often as we made our way home, we thought that they were moving-on on the morrow, but there they would be again as soon as the sun went down. Incredibly, they were with us for a fortnight. Now we knew why their arrival was so delayed. Obviously, once ensconced in a community, they did not want to leave.

I think that we went every night. We certainly wanted to and we enjoyed every minute, and it was fortunate that we did, because living just across the road we would have heard every word anyway.

At the end of every gathering, the Reverend Nero spoke to the people and thanked the visitors. As always, he would find the right words, and he explained what following Jesus Christ meant. 'It was one thing to thoroughly enjoy an evening of music and sing lively hymns, but it was another to live the Christian life, to love God, and love one's neighbour be he black or white,' he would say.

At the end of every message, he would invite anyone who wished to know more to go into the church. And to discover what he was telling the new converts, we also went in one evening.

Knowing Nero by this time, it was no surprise to find that he told them that being a Christian was no easy option, and that love and service to others were paramount. Having fully explained what would be expected of them, he blessed them in the name of the Trinity, and bade them goodnight.

The results of the crusade were excellent, and church numbers of both people and dogs grew dramatically. The newcomers included one Donald, and his story is worthy of recounting in full.

Donald was a real character. He was tremendously handsome, about fifty-five years old I would guess, his hair was more silvery than any I had ever seen, and he always seemed to have silver stubble around his face, although it never succeeded in becoming a beard. He was a gentle person, as many Aborigines are, and he had a distinguished air about him, when he was sober that is. Very friendly, he was a regular customer in our store, and thereby hangs a story or two.

As previously recounted, we did not allow credit in the store. It was cash or else they could not buy anything. However, for a while after bringing in that rule, several members of the community would still try it on. They would turn up with their trolley at the till and then after going to the trouble of putting the goods in carrier bags and putting them all through the till, we would be asked to 'put it in the book'. Eventually, everyone got the message, but definitely the last to accept it was Donald.

He would get his 'sit down money' as their social welfare cheques were called, and instead of making it last a fortnight until the next one, he would spend it all on beer, in the bars of Katherine, or via the six cans he could buy over our counter. On his affluent days, he would try to do both.

So, long before the next dole cheque arrived, he would be out of food. One day he worked out a method of overcoming our rules, being without cash, but hungry. I happened to go to the back of the store, an area that could not be seen from my office or the tills, and there was our Donald with corned beef literally all over the lower half of his face, and the remnants still in the tin, which he held rather sheepishly in his hand.

After remonstrating with him, I told him that next time I would report him to the council. He paid for his stolen food from his next cheque, but that was not the last of Donald's illicit dealings. No, the next could almost be called hilarious, were it not wholly illegal.

One day, I was standing at the front of the store, listening to Donald complaining that the deluxe blue silk shirt he was holding, all crumpled may I add, was in fact too small for him. My main concern was that Donald had tried on the shirt, and not being the most hygienic person I had ever known, it worried me that we could hardly sell it again. Whilst thinking, for instance, that Leni might be able to wash and iron it successfully enough to resell it, the truth of the situation never occurred to me. Of course, it should have. Would our Don have spent $15 on a silk shirt when instead he could have bought fifteen cans of his favourite brew?

Always insisting that my wife was responsible for clothing, I called out, 'Leni, please come and have a look at this shirt Donald has brought back.'

Even though it was our most rascally customer, I was not ready for Leni's response. 'What do you mean, it's too small? I have been looking all over for that shirt. I knew I hadn't sold it. You pinched it didn't you?'

Donald immediately recanted and awaited his fate, but who could help loving the old rogue? I took him in the office and told him once again that this was not on. He promised never to do such a thing again, and to my knowledge he didn't.

This further misdemeanour gave me the opportunity to get to know our miscreant better. He told me that he was brought up by a white Australian family. This explained his surprisingly good knowledge of English, and after a few more reminiscences, it was necessary for me to go back into the store.

Sometime later, on one of the crusade evenings, as we walked across the arena, deciding where to put our seats, whom did we see but Donald? We could not have been more surprised, and we went straight to him. He was stretched out on a log, and as we approached, I could see a grin start to creep across his face. 'I am so pleased to see you here Donald,' I said, and his reply will live with me forever. It surely deserved to rank with Sir Francis Drake's reply, when his game of bowls on Plymouth Hoe was interrupted because the Spanish Armada had been sighted, saying 'I can finish the game and beat the Spaniards too.'

'I thought that I would give Jesus a chance,' were the words that Donald uttered. How does one reply to that?

After I regained my composure, I asked him what he actually knew about Jesus, and he told me that when he was with the family previously mentioned, they took him to church regularly. To prove his point he joined in with the hymn that was being sung, and another surprise was the quality of his voice. It was altogether a surprising but also a very pleasing experience.

At last the loudspeakers were taken down and the Millingimbi Gospel Group moved on to win more souls for Christ elsewhere. They were very much to be admired, and often nowadays, I play a cassette I recorded on one of those wonderful evenings.

The Reverend Nero Timothy had had his batteries recharged, and he pursued his vocation with even more vigour than before. We had a rather special relationship, because in addition to our mutual interest in the church, we had arrived at Bamyili at the same time.

Nero had a delightful wife, Norma, and three children. They came from their home community of Boroloola, and he often used to refer in his Sunday morning sermons to the days when he used to be a stockman there. In his simplistic way he would introduce humour, and invariably it would be about an experience he had had in Boroloola. I am sure that his congregation remembered the point of his messages because it was linked to a funny event in his life.

One such example was when the New Testament reading was from Paul's second letter to the Corinthians, chapter 9, verse 26. This refers to Paul's exhortation to the Christians in the church in Corinth, which he had established. To run straight to the finishing line, Nero repeated the verses we had already heard, and concentrated on the theme of submitting to discipline and he told us of an occurrence on a New Year's Day in his earlier years.

As always, when he was about to say something humorous he would start to laugh, and then he took quite a time to control himself. As he laughed we could see the large gap in the middle of his front teeth, and this alone made me have great difficulty in stifling my own mirth.

The story went that every January 1st the community had a foot race, and Nero told us that he often used to win it. I could quite believe this, as he was slim and had incredibly long legs, and was a very smooth mover. However, there was another athlete who always gave Nero a good run, and it was thought that this particular year might be this other athlete's year to actually win.

There was a problem though, as the threat to Nero's supremacy was in prison! Surprisingly, he was allowed to run, and he came to the town under escort from two warders. They were off and across the bush they went. I believe it was a 400 metre race and, although Nero won, his challenger was not far behind. Nero went through the tape and stopped. His opponent also ran over the finishing line, but kept on running.

As our preacher got to this point, he roared with laughter, and the whole congregation with him. When we all recovered, he extrapolated the points that we should be disciplined in our faith and keep striving for salvation, just as the runner strives for the finish line.

Our first visit to the church was surprising to say the least. Having worshipped in the Aboriginal church on Croker – where apart from the way people dressed, the environment and the service were little different to the churches in white communities – we were amazed to find that the people brought their dogs with them. Anyone who has seen dogs belonging to tribal Aborigines will know that they are not looked after as they should be, and it was a most unsavoury sight to see them in the church.

We sang hymns in two languages, English and Kriol, accompanied by guitars. A favourite was a Croker favourite too, with the beautiful chorus sung after each verse, 'Trust and obey, there is no other way, to be happy in Jesus, is to trust and obey.'

The Kriol hymns were sung to the same tunes as their English counterparts, and to give you an example, the Kriol words of the well-known hymn 'Turn your eyes upon Jesus, (look straight in his beautiful face)' were 'Danim yubula ai langa Jesus, (Luk streit langa in shainiwan feis)'

We also had an assistant minister, Dale Naden, who worked at a trade during the week, and assisted with the service on Sundays.

Sometimes we would go into Katherine to go to church, for a change. Although at the time a town of a population of only about 4,500, there were eight active churches; the Assembly of God; Anglican; the Aboriginal Inland Mission; Uniting Church; Roman Catholic; Baptist; the Lutheran Church; and the Salvation Army.

We divided our favours between the Anglican, Catholic, and Uniting Churches, and because of this we knew most of the people in that isolated township.

One of the highlights of our lives happened because of this. We were at Mass at St Joseph's, the Catholic church, when it was announced that of all people, Mother Theresa was to visit Katherine on the following Wednesday, and she was to preach at a special Mass.

The prospect of seeing this lady, who we looked upon as a living Saint, was very exciting. We knew that the Sisters who served the church were members of the Order she had created. They were all very well known in the Katherine area for their work amongst the poor and needy, including Aborigines.

Every Sunday they would form a choir in the church, and from early morning they would go around the town in a small bus and encourage Aborigines to come to Mass, picking them up as they went. They also cleaned the church and looked after the garden. During the week they did a lot of visiting both black and white families, and one of their Order's rules was that they could only accept a drink of water.

They were seen regularly around the town and were easily recognisable in their white robes, with a blue stripe around the head-dress. Mother Theresa had created the Order known as Sisters of the Poor, whilst living in Calcutta, India. Initially, in a convent there, where she spent most of her time in prayer, she eventually became aware of the poverty and the disease prevalent in that city.

She left the shelter of the convent, and went into the streets to help these poor unfortunates. Horrified that people were literally dying in the streets, she set out to help them, and if they could not be saved, she endeavoured to bring comfort and dignity to them at their death.

Eventually, as her Sisters spread further afield, she also became involved in finding people willing to adopt Indian babies, and it was to do with this work that she came to Katherine at this particular time.

Her visit was twofold, to check on the babies already in Katherine, and to meet other people who had expressed a wish to adopt a child.

Mother Theresa spoke to a packed church on this warm evening, and she inspired us all, I am sure, by her humility. She had truly consecrated her life to help others, to help some at the end of their lives, and to assist others who were just beginning theirs. My thoughts centred on how much this little frail lady had achieved and was still achieving in her life, and relatively, how poorly I had done. I am sure that I was not the only member of that Katherine congregation who felt that way.

Being a Catholic church, the people had to be predominantly of that persuasion, and indeed I might have been the only Anglican, but be that as it may, I had two pleasant surprises to come. When the Mass had ended, we all stood whilst the priests, their attendants, and Mother Theresa left the altar and walked up the centre aisle of the church. Whilst not being a Catholic, I certainly was one of the tallest there and because of this I always sat at the end of the row, whether in a theatre, a football match, or in a church, to be able to stretch out my legs.

The future winner of the Nobel Prize for Peace walked up our side of the aisle and stopped by me. To my amazement and my pleasure, she put out her hand and shook mine, and we spoke together for a minute or two. I was so taken aback that I cannot remember a word that was said. But I do recall friends saying, 'And you an Anglican!'

Eventually, we all wandered out into the church gardens where there were seats and tables ready for a buffet meal. Leni and I sat with two or three friends we knew from our periodic visits to St Joseph's. Just by chance, it was the table nearest to the garden entrance. We were all chatting away, remarking about the beautiful evening, and of Mother Theresa's talk. We were told that she had gone off to meet some of the ladies who had adopted the babies she had brought on her previous visit, and consequently the proceedings would be delayed until she arrived back.

We knew when she neared the gate because a few members of the local Press suddenly appeared, and moments later our most honoured guest entered the garden. She walked straight to the nearest table, and spoke to the nearest person, which was me! We talked about the gardens and the Katherine area, just generalities, but it certainly was an evening to remember.

So tiny in stature, so immense in achievements and influence, and so humble in her simple garb; that was Mother Theresa.

Katherine's Anglican and Catholic priests had perhaps the biggest parishes in the world. They stretched from Pine Creek in the north to way past Mataranka in the south, and from near the Western Australia border in the west to the Gulf of Carpentaria in the east, something like 4,000 square miles, which is about the area of the whole of Ireland.

Of course, the population was not great and they lived in a few small townships and cattle stations.

We used to have regular visits from Father Cooper and Father Stacey out at Bamyili, and Holt and Chal Thompson used to put their home at the Fathers' disposal, and that of those who wished to attend. Holt and Chal were both Catholic, but were, like us, quite ecumenical, and we all found the Eucharist to be of equal importance, be it dispensed by a Catholic or an Anglican priest. Holt and Chal Thompson are worthy of much more than a passing comment.

Chal was from Kuching in Sarawak and she was a marvellous gardener. Caring for natural resources was something very important to her, as she told us that back in Sarawak, there were no welfare payments, no handouts, and that cultivating a vegetable garden could be the only sure means of survival.

Every house in the community of Bamyili had its own plot of land, all of which was highly suitable for growing vegetables, fruit, and flowers, and yet there were only two which had been tended, Chal's and her next door neighbour, the police aide, who obviously tried to copy her. He was greatly to be admired, as he was the one Aborigine who knew the taste of fresh vegetables straight from the garden.

Behind the Thompson house was a most beautiful billabong, the Australian name for an inland fresh water pool. Amongst the denizens of the billabong were fresh-water prawns and, although I am not able to enlarge on the qualities of this particular delicacy as I have never wished to taste shellfish of any kind, I am told that for crustacean buffs they are something really special. Holt and Chal and their two sons, Martin and Leslie, were particularly adept at catching them. Down by the pool they kept a most magnificent female goat, which provided them with milk, and around the gardens they bred turkeys, whilst free-range chickens provided them with plenty of fresh eggs. They had mango trees, pawpaw trees, and banana trees – all of which produced fruit in profusion – and potatoes, tomatoes, lettuce, capsicums, and other vegetables, which ensured that their table was the best supplied in the community. Chal was able to pay for seeds and fertilisers out of the proceeds of produce she sold to us in the store. For instance, she sold us the most beautiful mangoes and pawpaws, and we gave her half of what we got for them.

As soon as people got to know that Chal had sold the store some pawpaws, a queue soon formed to buy them, and yet the sad thing was that they could all have grown their own on their piece of fertile Bamyili soil. At some time, the council had planted pawpaw trees on verges around the community, but the children would not allow the fruit to mature. Similar to English children who would steal sour green apples, take a bite and throw them away, so also would the Aboriginal children do the same with pawpaws.

In Australia one hears a lot about Aboriginal Land Rights, and no doubt they are entitled to land, after all they have been there for 40,000 years. However, this emotional issue seems to encapsulate the use of land. Much is made of expressions such as 'My mother the land,' but it is possible that there is not an indigenous race in the world that has done so little with the land. Few have ever planted a seed. Certainly, in Bamyili only two had done so.

One day I was talking to Johnny O'Farrell, whose name suggests that he is a man of Erin, but who was, in fact, the full-blood Aboriginal Chairman of the Bamyili Town Council. We were talking about vandalism, which is not only the prerogative of city children, and he recalled the days he spent as a child on Bathurst Island, which is in the Arafura Sea near Croker Island. 'We would have to go to school every weekday,' he said, 'and as soon as we got home we would go and help in the gardens. We did not have to do it, but we wanted to do it. Today kids would rather destroy things,' he concluded. Yet he still did not have a garden programme for his community.

As I have written before, when you are in a remote area, it is always exciting when visitors arrive from elsewhere, so we were very happy to learn one day that a group of teenage schoolgirls were visiting us from Bathurst Island. This island has a great reputation for its culture and its art. We never got there, but we saw a lot of their paintings and basketwork in the shops in Darwin.

The girls were dancers and singers and we really had a treat in store. They danced barefoot of course, and they were dressed in tops and skirts made from material that they had coloured and designed themselves. Their dancing was a revelation and they were accompanied by didgeridoo players, and other young men playing the sticks.

Unless you have seen lots of Aboriginal girls, you cannot appreciate just how truly beautiful some of them are, and the Bathurst group was an outstanding example.

The following night was also a night to remember, but for a somewhat different reason, as I am about to explain.

Parker pens have been known as excellent writing instruments for many years now, and the most expensive one I ever had was solid gold, with a beautiful design covering it. However, I lost it in a most stupid way. Leni bought it for me when I was doing very well with IOS, and one day I put it on the ledge of the front window of my BMW 1800, to see it roll down and to my horror disappear through a vent. I could not get at it, so I decided to leave it until I had the car serviced, but I forgot all about it, until several weeks after I had traded the car in for a BMW 2000 Tilux!

My next 'Parker' was given to me by Elizabeth Short of the cafe in Katherine. It was not as glamorous or as expensive as the previous one, but would you believe that it had life saving propensities?

It was black and made of steel and I used it all of the time in the store office in Bamyili, and I kept it in my shirt top pocket when not in use. And a good job too.

Every Friday night I stayed late in the office, as we always took 4,000 to 6,000 dollars and this would be in all denominations of money, as well as in cheques. Preparing the bank pay-in-book and balancing the tills was a long job, and one needing much concentration, so I always told Leni to go home and to leave me to it.

The toilets were at the back of the store beyond the fans, and as temperatures frequently reached the high forties – Celsius – it got pretty hot and airless back there. As written previously, Leni insisted on cleanliness and hygiene, and to prevent the toilets being used by all and sundry, we removed the door handles, and the staff used deftly hidden spoons to get in. They inserted the handle in the square hole and that turned the lock.

One Friday night I needed to go to the toilet. I grabbed the spoon, opened the door and walked in, but absent-mindedly I had replaced the spoon in its hiding place.

When I realised that I was locked in, I searched my pockets for anything that might help, but all I had was the black pen. A round peg in a square hole, now that wouldn't work, or would it? I pushed it in and turned it vigorously, but nothing happened. Panic set in and I stood on the toilet seat to see if I could reach and see through the louvred window, but it was too high. I tried shouting, but I had little hope of being heard, because the store was away from the houses and the chance of anyone walking past at night was extremely slim. Leni would start worrying if it got to midnight and I was not home, but not before.

It was only about 7.00 pm and the air was getting hotter and thinner, or so it seemed, as I put my shoulder to the door like they do in the films. The net result was a painful shoulder.

The black pen was my only chance of salvation, so I plunged it back into the square hole and desperately pushed and shoved. The door opened, how or why I do not know. I still have the black Parker pen with scratches where it had engaged the square hole in the lock, and which will forever remind me of an hour of panic in a toilet in the tropics, or should I say of terrible trauma in a tropical toilet?

One of the problems of a community store was that it was in fact owned by the community, and this encouraged some individuals to think that, therefore, it was all right to help themselves. We had to be constantly on the look out.

However, what we could not control were break-ins at night. We had about five such crimes and always on a Friday night. The culprits were invariably caught, as they always stole beer, and in a relatively small community, it did not take Aboriginal members of the store committee long to find who was blind drunk on the Saturday morning.

As the various culprits found methods of entry, the council strengthened the particular area, until we felt that the store was impregnable. However, we were soon proved to be wrong.

One Saturday morning we entered the store to find obvious signs of things having been disturbed. Looking around we soon found the point of entry. A window had been replaced by very strong iron bars, but to our amazement, they had been sliced through at the top and bottom and removed. We soon found out how, as the community plumber, Cyril McCartney, discovered that his workshop had also been broken into and his giant pair of bolt cutters had been stolen!

Frank Ranch, who was on the store committee, and who was always willing to help, said that he would find who had done it. He was a very experienced Aboriginal tracker, and he soon got to work outside the store, which was surrounded by sand. There were hundreds of footprints, but Frank quickly spotted some leading away from the back of the store. He told me the names of his suspects and I went into the office to ring the police who arrived about 10.00 am. Prior to this, someone shouted to me that Frank wanted me. I was taken to behind the store and led along a barely noticeable path created by the breaking of very tall grasses.

Every few paces I was shown an empty beer tin, and eventually by merely following both the trodden down grass trail and the beer can trail, we found the culprits. There were two of them and Frank had correctly identified them! They were fast asleep in a drunken stupor, and it took hours before they came round to find themselves in the Katherine lockup. They also stole two umbrellas and they would have been just as useless as stealing two pairs of shoes. Have you ever seen an Aborigine with an umbrella?

When such a robbery occurred, there were two different schools of thought about it. One was a quiet admiration of the feat and the other was of annoyance that community members should steal from the store, which was owned by the community.

Leni and I used to be most annoyed, because apart from the obvious, that people should not break in, we had the job of quantifying what had gone and tidying things up again. Worse was the paper work, before the police could leave and, of course, irrespective of any private arrangements we might have made in Katherine, we could not leave until the matter was completed.

The perpetrators would usually get a few weeks in prison in Darwin, but it can only be said that they seemed to enjoy it, as on their return they would regale their mates with stories of who they had seen and they would tell of the good food they had enjoyed. With stories of lawbreaking and police connotations in mind, I must tell you about the time when the whole community looked up to me for the strength, fortitude, and courage I showed in a difficult situation – or words to that effect.

It was four o'clock, and our two Aboriginal storemen, whom we had trained successfully to sell the beer and to balance the books every day, had just opened the 'canteen'. They knew well that under the laws of the Northern Territory, it was illegal to sell beer to anyone who was already drunk, and that as the licensee I could lose my licence, which was effectively the community's licence.

I was in the office working and I could hear the normal hum of conversation that accompanied the opening, but suddenly the level of noise increased dramatically. Leni came running in, declaring that I was needed to sort out a big row that was going on between our two staff members, and several drunken men who demanded to be served.

I went outside to be met by demands from twenty or thirty, obviously drunk, patrons that they should be served with the mandatory six cans of beer. I told them that as they had been to the hotel in Katherine and had had too much to drink, they could not be served and that was that. There were two or three ringleaders, and they approached me cursing and swearing. I told them that there was no way they were going to get any beer. One of them was wearing a huge cowboy hat and he told me that if I did not change my mind, he would have me 'off the community' the following morning. I told him that if he did not go away, I would get the police and have him arrested. He scoffed at that so I said that he was looking for trouble. 'What do you mean, trouble?' he demanded. 'Just stand there for much longer and you will find out,' I threatened.

It was plain that he was implacable, so I went back to the office and rang the police at Maranboy, which was about 25 kilometres away on the road to the Katherine/Tennant Creek highway.

Within half an hour the police truck arrived, and I told them who the ringleader was and in a flash he was locked in the back. The police presence resulted in the rest of the crowd going home.

So I was quite pleased that I had been able to show strength, and that the police support was immediately available.

That evening as the incident was talked about throughout the community, my reputation as a tough and resolute manager reached incredible heights.

You see what I did not know was that the cowboy-hatted drunk was Gordon Bullumburra. 'So what?' you might ask. Well, unknown to me he was the traditional landowner (TLO), and as such was very similar to the old English Lord of the Manor. And anyone who stood up to and, indeed, had the TLO arrested, was very much admired and revered.

Would I have done the same if I had known that the rabble-rouser was the TLO? Frankly, I have no idea, but probably not!

The matter did have a surprising ending, for at about 11.00 am the following morning, Gordon Bullumburra came into my office and apologised profusely. So all was well.

When we first started, Leni used to sell the beer, on the basis of a maximum of six cans for a male and four for a female. This was the council's edict, but of course a wife often gave her four to her husband. It was considered that Aboriginal staff would be pressured to break the rule if they were behind the counter, but we proved them wrong. We had two lads on duty, we issued them with a quantity of beer and some cash as a float, and on checking afterwards, everything always balanced and only on the one occasion which I have recorded earlier, did we have to sort out a difficulty for them.

Drink caused many problems at Bamyili, but there were times when it was the cause of humour too. An example occurred one Sunday. We had been to the Anglican church in Katherine and we decided to call at the thermal pool at Mataranka before returning home. Mataranka is one of the tourist attractions of the Northern Territory, and is situated in what is known as the 'Never Never Land' from the book, 'We of the Never Never' by Aeneas (Jeannie) Gunn.

To get to the pool we had to walk along a path through jungle type terrain, eventually opening out to the beautiful tropical pool surrounded by some magnificent trees. Leni and I were well known in Bamyili and Katherine, particularly by Aborigines, and we liked Mataranka because we were able to have a little peace and time to ourselves, as we had never seen Aborigines there. Until that Sunday morning that is. Roars of, 'Hello Stan, hello Leni!' greeted us.

There were seven or eight young blokes, and only one female, Elizabeth. They were delighted to see us, but we were not so sure that it was so vice versa, as it was immediately obvious that, Elizabeth excluded, they were all drunk. Her husband was a noted boozer, and he was the most vocal of them all, shouting to me that he would bet me six cans (of beer) that he could walk across the bed of the pool.

The water was perhaps five or six metres deep, and it seemed impossible to do, but this inebriate would not risk six whole cans of precious beer. Consequently, despite his attempts at persuasion, I continued to refuse, until he said that he would do it anyway.

He picked up a large heavy stone, put it on his shoulder, climbed down to the bed of the pool, walked across to the other side, and then climbed out! He then said, 'I'll do it again,' and walked back over! It was almost worth six cans.

We admired Elizabeth, and we were intrigued by her activities as a housewife. She lived with her oft-drunken husband in a small house opposite the store. As was the Aborigines' habit in the dry season, they all slept outside, often on the grass, but Elizabeth's house had a block of concrete outside, on which she used to make the matrimonial bed. Often we would see her picking up the blankets etc, as we arrived in the morning, and it was the care with which she folded the bedclothes, etc, that we admired. It all seemed so primitive, and yet to her credit she took such care.

Eventually everything was running like clockwork. We had good girls on the tills, good storemen to do all of the physical work, and Leni was a gem on the clothing side, especially with the young women. She would get them anything they wanted from pretty underwear to lovely tops, skirts, frocks, and jeans, and she got great pleasure from seeing lots of people in the community nicely attired. Our record week sales, was $16,750, more than twice the average of when we took over.

We had sorted out the shop times so that we were open fewer hours, but we were more efficient. Previously, for example, the store had been open 8.30 am to 1.00 pm on Saturdays, but with a populace who could easily shop on Fridays for their main groceries and who could fill up with petrol first thing on Saturday, it was pointless us sitting around waiting all Saturday morning. We changed to 8.30 am to 9.30 am and soon everyone got used to it. This then gave us a nice long weekend, which we could spend with Liz and John Short in Katherine. The main objection to the change of hours came from an expected quarter. At 4.00 pm every Friday, when the council workers finished for the week, the card-schools started. The women were the heaviest gamblers and it was possible to win, or lose, one to two thousand dollars. We really could not see why they could not do their shopping first or come in early on Saturday morning. The council supported them as they always did, but we used our normal blackmail of threatening to get the next plane to Perth and again we won the day.

Every month a meeting was held between the council and the main participants in organising the life of the community. This included me as the store manager and, for example, Nero Timothy as the Aboriginal church minister. We had to give a report as to our activities, and these reports were included in the monthly magazine 'Barunga', put out by the council. This was very useful for us to get our message across, and to keep the people informed as to the progress of the store and as to new products we may be selling.

Nero told of the number of people baptised, and how they were baptised by immersion in the billabong. Of course, the water and the air temperature was always warm, unlike perhaps immersion in the North Sea at Redcar in the winter!

A sad, indeed horrific, incident happened one Sunday when a baptismal service was to take place in the afternoon. A very lovely girl, whom we knew well, but whose name I have forgotten, was to be baptised that day. After morning church, she was travelling to nearby Beswick with her fiancé driving, when somehow or other she was thrown out of the passenger front door and killed instantly. We are not to reason why.

Few people in this modern world will have enjoyed the lifestyle we experienced at Bamyili, and enjoyed is the operative word. We had no television as the satellite was not available at that time, the radio crackled so much that it was pointless putting it on, there was no cafe or social centre to visit, and the tropical night was illuminated not by street lights but only by the moon and stars.

As already related, we were always very pleased when visitors arrived from other communities, for religious, social, or any other reason. We were thrilled to serve in the store several members of the cast of the Aboriginal film, 'We of the Never Never'. Bamyili was close to the area known as the 'Never Never' and several of our people were actually in the film, including our driver.

There is a football story worth recounting with relation to visitors. Peter Miller, a superb Aborigine, a teacher at the school with the ambition of becoming the first native school principal, and coach to the Australian Rules football team, told me that we were to play a team from Roper River 'tomorrow', in a pre-season practice match. Incidentally, he told me because I had been invited to be president of the Bamyili Football Club! My one claim to fame is that I am definitely the only English soccer international to have been president of an Aboriginal Aussie Rules Club!

On the morrow at about 3.30 pm, I noticed the team out on the 'oval', as all sporting venues appear to be called in Australia, practising their skills. We carried on working in the store, but every few minutes I peeped out to see if the opposition had arrived. Not surprisingly they hadn't, and eventually, we closed, and on the way home I had a word with Peter, who said that they must be coming another day. Now this was said without rancour, not even tinged with disappointment. Only forty-thousand years without clocks or calendars could have bred a lack of the need for the concept of time!

A few evenings later, Peter knocked at our house door, just as we had settled down for a well-earned rest. The Roper River mob had arrived, without cigarettes, food, or drink. To Peter and to all Aborigines, this meant that Stan and Leni must open the store. I can imagine what a Woolworths' manager would say if his rest time was so interrupted. The request became much more onerous when the electricity failed and the lights went out. As often happened, there was a problem at the power house. Probably no oil!

Try to imagine what it was like. A tropical night with an in the store temperature of about 35°C (95°F). Twenty odd Aborigines milling around the aisles by the light of hand torches, filling trolleys with all kinds of merchandise and turning up at an electrically worked till, except there was no electricity, and they were all in a hurry.

I did as I had done before when power-less, except always previously it had been in daylight. I transferred the contents of one trolley, one by one, into an empty trolley, all the time using a torch to read the prices, and adding it all up in my head.

Incidentally, on a similar occasion on a Friday afternoon, with dozens of Aboriginal mums doing their week's grocery shopping, I also served Peter Miller. Peter, quite wisely, took his purchases home, listed the prices on paper, and checked them and the addition, to find it correct. He was so impressed that he came back to the store to tell me and to congratulate me, and he also spread the news amongst the people.

The 'footie' game was played the day after the Roper team's arrival, with no recriminations or questions as to their tardiness.

Not long after this incident, something very similar, but much more hilarious occurred. We were playing our neighbours, Beswick, who lived 20 kilometres up the road from us, and the scenario was as for the Roper River team, except the distance to travel was much less – but the result was the same. Our team had lots of skills practice, and did plenty of running. Peter concluded the practice by saying that maybe they would come 'tomorrow'. Incidentally, I got to feeling that the word encompassed not just the following day, but all of the 'tomorrows'.

The coach came to see me the next day with what certainly appeared to him to be a reasonable explanation. 'Ah!' he said, 'I found out what happened. You see they were coming by bus and just before they got to the turn off for Bamyili, they took a vote on whether to turn left and go and play footie, or to go straight on to Katherine and go to the pub. Most of them said to go to the pub, so they did!' I asked him if they were in their footie clothes and he said that they were. Well as long as we found the reason. It seemed pretty obvious that if the position were reversed, Bamyili could have easily done the same. And why not?

'Our' first league match was against Katherine at Katherine, and we went to support the team in my honoured position of President. Peter asked me to speak to the team. I was happy to do so, and I tried to convince them just how brilliant they were. Outback Aborigines are mostly shy people, and are apt to underestimate themselves. There was certainly no reason for this in sport. Fleet of foot, with tremendous reflexes, they excel at every ball game, and I tried to get this over to them.

Peter then did an outstanding job of organising the team. Everyone knew what their particular tasks were, and his final remarks or accolades, were for four obvious mates who stood together at the end of the row. 'And you four blokes,' quoth Peter, 'it's good that you kept off the grog this time.' In a later explanation, the coach told me that at the last match of the previous season they had turned up drunk, and that the club had been warned that if this happened again they would be banished from the league.

A further few words about the Aboriginal in sport. One year in Perth, the first six best players in the WA Football League were all Aborigines! Strangely, although the first Australian cricket team to tour England were Aborigines, this in 1867, very few have graced the baggy green cap since. Evonne Goolagong showed what they really can do, but they still seem slow in coming forward.

At Bamyili the police aid's daughter, Kathy Ryan, was a good example. Barefooted, as are most Australian children when young and playing games, even football and soccer, Kathy was a wonderful natural athlete. She ran like the wind and without any coaching excelled at sprinting and jumping. She won four events at the local school sports, then she did the same at the Katherine Area sports, and she followed up with similar wins at the Northern Territory Championships. Full of enthusiasm, I remarked to the school principal that Kathy could become an Olympic champion, but Holt Thompson said sadly that she wouldn't because she would start having children at fourteen. I was reminded of this when I heard some beautiful teenage girls talking about social security payments, and they reckoned that the way to go was to have four children as this was the optimum payout, and more than that saw a decline in the average per child.

Yes, 'sit down money' is the way most community people live. A few worked in the town's institutions, such as the Council Office, the medical centre, the bank agency, and the store, but most enjoyed a good standard of living on social security. Alice Brown was a good example. Owner of a very British name, as were most of the people, Alice was the least beautiful of the local women. She had one tooth at the top and one at the bottom, and unfortunately, it has to be said that she may never have had a bath or a shower. One had to keep a few feet from her, but Leni and I learned to love her as a humble, kind human being. Alice cried her eyes out the day we left, but that is going on a bit. She received $145 a fortnight and her problem was how to spend it. She did not pay rent. She did not pay for electricity. Her food needs came nowhere near her income.

One day she bought a stereo radio, which cost all of her cheque and a fortnight later, she bought a bike for her grandson.

The local lads and lasses were very particular about which clothes they bought. Leni once made a great purchase of beautiful denim jeans. They really were stylish, but the young ones looked only for the label. No they were not Levi or Amco, so irrespective of the $14 price, and the quality, they stuck on the shelves.

We were more successful in introducing them to some different foods, one of which was sold hot, ready to eat. We bought a special heater for a variety of Heinz meat dishes in rip top cans, and they went like wildfire, particularly for breakfast. We also converted many to health promoting fruit and tomato juices, and we were complimented by visiting Health Department people.

We had an airstrip and often Government people came from Katherine and Darwin. They generally wore 'cowboy' hats, as I called them, smoked pipes, and sat in the council office, invariably with their feet on the desk. They talked about 'funding', never about money. They flew in, pontificated, the Aborigines told them what they wanted to hear – they were very good at that – and then they flew back, experts on Aboriginal affairs. What a joke.

You have to live in the community, not even on the overlooking hill where a few white teachers were, to know about what went on. If I was Minister for Aboriginal Affairs I would consult such as Holt, who has spent almost all of his adult life in two communities, not people who fly in and out once a month.

Leni and I used to visit the churches in Katherine as often as we could. After the service at the Anglican church one morning, we were having a cup of tea in the church garden when a person came up to us and said, 'I believe you live in Bamyili, don't you?' We said that we did, and I asked him why. He said that he had been working out there for the last two weeks, making a new ablution block, which was costing $72,000. I said, 'But what for? There are already two blocks there and they are not used much, and certainly not for the right purposes.' He agreed, but added that it was nothing to do with him. He was told what to do and he did it.

Another example of laissez faire was to do with Johnny O'Farrell. His car was old and he decided that he needed a new one. He told me that he would ask for a grant of $2,000 from one of the Aboriginal funding agencies, and then borrow the remainder from the Katherine branch of the ANZ bank.

Only a very few days later I saw this beautiful new vehicle with Johnny at the wheel. He stopped to show me it. Admiring it, I commented that he had got his $2,000 grant alright, but he replied that he had been given the full purchase price!

Much was made of a forthcoming Aboriginal election. It was for the National Aboriginal Conference and a lot of energy was expended by Governments encouraging everyone to vote, but on the day, a Saturday, it seemed that just about everyone had left the town and hardly anyone voted. The person who was elected for the area was someone we knew from Beswick. He was a noted drunk, and that had been his condition every time we had seen him. He came into the store one day to tell me that he had won. He told me of his own office in Katherine and, in particular, of the bottles of sherry and wines that were in situ. This really was placating Aborigines in a most cynical way.

As I have written before, you cannot expect a people, who for many thousands of years lived lives untrammelled by the conventions of time, to suddenly embrace the European work ethic and its time constraints. However, I did tell Holt that there was indeed an exception to these rules, and that it was Reggie, who had been immaculate with his time keeping, and extremely efficient making display units for the store. The cautious Holt had known Reggie from the day he started school until that moment, and it was a disappointment to me to have my judgement questioned, as Holt told me that even Reggie could let me down. And he did in the perfect Aboriginal way. One Monday morning there was just no Reggie. When I asked the rest of the staff, they said that he had gone to Roper River on the Friday night, but that they did not know for how long. There was no message from him. He just went walkabout.

The sequel was equally typical. About three months later we went to open the store one morning, and there was Reggie smiling as always, all ready to start work. As was his habit he bid us a 'good d'y,' and it was obvious that it had not occurred to him that he might have been replaced. There was no apology, no explanation, and no job. However, when business eventually warranted one more employee, Reggie was the first we thought of.

The store started to make two to three thousand dollars a week net profit, and our only creditors were current trading debts. In the 'Barunga', their monthly magazine, I wrote, 'We have all been working hard in the shop to improve it for the benefit of all the community. We have made it look much nicer, and it is now easier for you to see and find things by using pegboard and hooks. Then we have bought many more products so that you have a much bigger variety to choose from. We have lots of things for Christmas, lots of toys, clothes etc, so that you can buy all of your presents in the store. All has gone well and our monthly sales have gone up from an average of $44,600 to $57,900 per month, an increase of 30%. This is all thanks to you, our customers, and to the hard work of the staff. For all this Leni and I say thank you, it is a pleasure to serve you. Finally all the staff wish you, our valued customers, a very Happy Christmas, and may God bless you all as we remember the birth of Jesus the Prince of Peace.'

And then it happened. I was walking back to work after lunch and I suddenly felt breathless, and I had to stop. I stood there for a few minutes and I did not know what was happening, but I knew it wasn't good. I realised that it was to do with the heart, and with the nearest hospital 94 kilometres away, and the nearest fully equipped one at Darwin, 420 kilometres away, I knew that it was back to Perth for us. I could not tell Leni as she would have died of worry. She had been suffering from asthma quite a bit, so I decided on a plan. We would go to Katherine to see a doctor; I would ask if a change of climate would help her; if the doctor agreed, I would ask if we should return to Perth.

The scenario turned out to be correct, and the doctor recommended a return home. We regretted very much the thought of leaving as we were really enjoying our lives in the Outback and the enormous success we achieved. A proof of the latter was that, apart from the original stocktaking, and then the final stocktaking, Charles Hegi the General Manager of the 'Co-Operative', had not visited us once. He explained that we were going so well, and the other community stores so badly, that there was no point in his interfering.

The mention above of walking to work reminded me of a previous day when returning after lunch. I was half way across the Oval, when about ten Aboriginal boys aged about six to twelve came racing across to me. They surrounded me and one said, 'You are a Christian, aren't you?' I said, 'Yes, I am,' and he replied, 'We are.' They then started to sing their favourite 'Father Abraham had many sons' as they danced around me for the last fifty yards to the store. When I opened up, they continued their singing, as they danced around the aisles. I felt so happy.

And, of course, there were many happy memories, many friends made and it seemed to be our lot in life to have to leave friends behind. We told the council of our decision and they implored us to stay, with all kinds of promises, but I knew that it was no good. Our biggest concern was to find someone to replace us who would be honest, and who would carry on with the methods and systems that we had created.

Our immediate predecessor, Ray Hewitt, who had stayed only four weeks, was an experienced store manager, and we had been in touch with him all of the time we were at Bamyili, in his new role as a salesman for ALPA, our previous employers. I told him that we were leaving and rather to our surprise, he said that he would like the job back. Of course, he knew that he was taking over a profitable business, not a loss maker, as he knew it. His wife had agreed to work with him, so I recommended him to the council. There was much opposition as they considered that he had let them down before, but I was able to persuade them to take him on again. It would have been awful if another rogue had taken over and stolen the vast profits available.

You see it would have been so easy to cheat the Aborigines in many ways. Some were both numerate and literate but plenty were not, and they could have been cheated when their cheques were cashed. Whenever I changed a cheque for such a person, I would give them the requisite number of notes and they would crush them in their hand. They would then fill their trolley with groceries and a dishonest person could give them the wrong change. Finally, he could fail to pay for his own groceries and literally take money out of the till.

Getting Ray prevented all of this happening and, eventually, he and Heather arrived to take over.

On our last evening we spent most of the time with Holt and Chal, talking things over. I mentioned the disgraceful mess of the 'Community Hall' and the 'Club', both of which had been vandalised and were completely wrecked. In the club, we had found large chest freezers full to the top with bread, which had, at one time, been frozen, but the freezers had been turned off leaving the bread to go mouldy.

In the hall, the once magnificent kitchen resplendent with its stainless steel shelving, bench tops, etc, and magnificent ovens and cooking equipment of all kinds, was now a catastrophe. All of the above had been ripped out – the effort must have been superhuman – and thrown into the hall. All of the hall's lights and ceiling fans were smashed. As the ceiling was very high, it was quite an achievement to smash them. The 'security' doors all had holes in them, and this must have taken a lot of doing. Certainly, it could not have been done without others seeing it being done.

I told Holt that I had heard that it was going to cost $5,000 to replace the doors, and that this after only five years. Holt was surprised that I did not know that these refurbishments had been done every year since the place was built! Equally horrific stories were to do with the cost of refurbishing houses, up to $14,000 being spent on one house. Before I left I took a photograph of a row of houses which were derelict, without doors or windows which had been taken out in the dry season, and burnt on the camp fires.

Whilst appreciating that after perhaps 40,000 years of wandering through the massive continent, not having to work, and building humpies to shelter themselves whenever necessary, it is not to be expected that in the course of a few generations Aborigines can be as domesticated as we are. Still, the situation has got out of hand and immense sums of Government money, or rather taxpayers moneys, are totally wasted.

Holt told me that when I returned to Perth, I should not bother to approach Members of Parliament, State or Federal, because they would not want to know. It was not for them to rock the boat as votes were involved, and I had cause to remember his words.

We decided to have a holiday before returning to Perth, and we accepted the offer of Enid, Leni's ex sister-in-law, who lived in Adelaide. She had often invited us to come and see the capital city of South Australia, and this was the perfect opportunity.

We elected to go by coach to see something of the country, and we booked on Pioneer coaches. On the day we left, we found out just how much we were liked, or hopefully, loved. So many of the women cried as we said goodbye, and we wondered if we had made the right decision. Ray and Heather Hewitt had arrived the day before and it did not take us long to make the changeover. Ray – having been the manager before me, and in the interim having visited us on behalf of the ALPA wholesale company, selling us various products – soon settled in.

Heather is one of the most remarkable people I have ever met. In 1957 Heather Hinch, as she was then known, arrived on Goulburn Island as a trained nurse, and with an interest in Aboriginal languages acquired when at the Summer Institute of Languages (SIL) in Darwin. The islanders spoke Maung and, at that time, there were few words known to the missionaries. 'Yes, no, good, and bad' were about the limit of their vocabularies and they had no idea how to go about increasing their knowledge.

Heather went about collecting words, but due to having to nurse and teach, because the teacher had left the island, she had little time for language study. However, she had unravelled the intricate verb system and discovered that Maung had sixteen verb classes!

In 1966 she attended a further SIL course, this time in Brisbane, and whilst there she met another nurse and persuaded her to accompany her to Goulburn, where she took over from Heather, and allowed her to concentrate on Maung full-time. However, this did not last long, as she was frustrated once again by being sent to Croker Island to nurse as their nurse had left. She was there for ten months and felt that she was never going to do what she really wanted to do.

Whilst on Croker, she delved into the Iwaidja tongue, but whereas she realised that they were from the same group, she also realised that there were many differences.

On her return to Goulburn, at last she was able to progress.

Now dear reader, I want you to imagine that you have been cast upon a desert island where the natives speak a language unknown except to them. It is purely a spoken language. Just imagine the peculiar sounds issuing from their mouths.

How would you like to learn first to speak that language, then write it down, then determine the grammar and, finally, translate the Gospel of St Mark into that language?

Heather Hinch, now Hewitt, did just that, and I believe that she was awarded the OBE for her tremendous work.

I have a tape which I play at Christmas, that tells the story of Jesus' nativity from St Mark's Gospel, spoken by an Aboriginal Uniting Church Minister in the Maung tongue. Listening to it, I always marvel at Heather's achievements, as all I can understand are the names and place names such as 'Jesus', 'Mary', 'Jerusalem', 'Nazareth', and 'Bethlehem'.

Now let us return to Bamyili and our preparations to go back to city life. As usual, the indefatigable Holt Thompson had volunteered to transport us to the coach stop, which was at Mataranka, where the hot springs are located. The last act of our association with the Aboriginal community was when the shop committee presented us both with wristwatches, and a handwritten note from the ever reliable Cain Jawai, thanking us for all that we had done for the community.

Holt drove us slowly out of Bamyili, with people waving to us all of the way, and dropped us off at the coach stop. He promised to visit us at North Beach, but he has not, to-date, but his wife Chal keeps in touch with us, by exchange of Christmas and birthday cards. Another chapter of our life was over.

CHAPTER THIRTY FOUR

WE RETURN TO PERTH

It is difficult for people in such countries as the UK to comprehend distances as we know them in Australia. We left Mataranka at about 6.00 pm in daylight, and our first stop was Tennant Creek, which was 667 kilometres 'down the track'. The track, by the way, is a perfectly good bitumen road, although I have heard awful stories about the days when it was just red earth. This distance is almost the same as Brighton on the South Coast of England to the Scottish border. Then we carried on to Alice Springs, or 'The Alice' as it is affectionately known to Aussies, a further 1,522 kilometres. Interestingly, we sometimes went off the road to deliver mail to outlying townships, and this included one with, I believe, Lutheran missionaries who all wore the type of beards I associate with the Pilgrim Fathers, as we have seen them in films.

The date was mid March, still the 'Wet' (the wet season), and we encountered unbelievable rainstorms. Somewhere between the Alice and the Lutheran community, we came upon a steep hill. Red mud had seeped into the road from the verges and the result was a quagmire. Our first knowledge of it was when we heard the wheels racing and losing traction, so that terrifyingly we realised that we were going backwards! We finished up stopping at the very bottom of the hill. If another vehicle had been approaching, an awful accident could have occurred. The driver had to make about five attempts before he made it to the top of the hill. How he did it, I do not know, but what would have happened to us if he had not succeeded did not bear thinking about, for we were hundreds of kilometres from anywhere.

As we travelled further south, we left the 'Wet' behind, and we experienced just the opposite, dry roads that were very dusty, and the need for air-conditioning. Unfortunately, the latter did not work, so someone 'helped' by opening the roof ventilation, and in came the red dust covering everything and everybody. We made a stop at a roadhouse at 2.00 am and managed to have showers.

After 48 hours on the road and having covered 2,722 kilometres, tired but happy, we arrived in Adelaide to be met be Enid. She lived at Reynella, which is vineyard country, and we had a thoroughly enjoyable fortnight when we saw lots of things and places of interest. Adelaide city centre is especially appealing. The streets are symmetrical and both the cathedral and the famous cricket ground, where Ashes matches have been contested for many years, are right in the middle.

We visited the Art Gallery, seeing traditional paintings, contemporary art, and then the most amazing examples of 'art' I have ever seen. Believe it or not, taking up one huge floor was a 'display' of old refrigerators, arranged in groups with different colours of paints daubed across them. I ask you???

Leni and I were delighted to be taken by Enid to Hahndorf and the Barossa Valley. A Germanic area where grapes are grown and German-type wines made, we were surprised to see many shops with German-type printing on them. We went to look at the main Lutheran church in Hahndorf, but it was locked. As we were leaving, an old man rode up on a bike. He said that he was the verger and that he could unlock the door for us. Naturally, we were pleased and I asked him what part of Germany he came from, for he had a heavy German accent. He told us that he had never been to Germany, and that he was born and had lived all of his eighty years in the town.

That was a real surprise and I was amused when he added, '…but my brother has been to Germany'. Although all of the inhabitants spoke English, a lot of homes must have kept up their German. Our verger asked me my name and when I replied, 'Stan Rickaby,' he said, 'Oh, the owner of the German Arms hotel at one time was Ralph Rickaby.' He was probably a relation as two Rickaby brothers came from England in the 1890's to South Australia and established a small fishing village, called 'Port Rickaby', on the Spencer Gulf.

We enjoyed visiting the Adelaide Hills, likening it to England due to the villages, which had an English feeling about them, and sometimes had what looked like village greens. But when we were there, Leni commented that she would not like to live in those hills because she considered them a great fire hazard. The following Ash Wednesday, it all went up in flames and many were killed.

With fond farewells and thanks to Enid, we settled into the plush seats of another Pioneer coach for the 2,781 kilometre trip to Perth, including the seemingly endless Nullabor Plain. We stopped at the Great Australian Bight and were thrilled at the views. We had at one stage a very pleasant and chatty driver who, amongst other things, told us that he had just won a fortune in a lottery and that this was his last trip. We all expressed our congratulations and best wishes. When the driver got off at Eucla and a new one got on, it was the middle of the night and I could not sleep, so I went and sat behind the driver's seat and had a chat with him. When I mentioned what his predecessor had told us, he exploded! 'Rubbish,' he said. 'That was his last trip, but only because he has got a job driving a bus in Perth.' You cannot believe anyone!

It took us 38 hours to reach Perth, arriving at 7.00 am in Adelaide Terrace, where we were pleased to see our friends Phyllis and Ken Murray waiting for us. They took us home and it was wonderful to enter our house and to see that it was just as lovely as our memories suggested. There had been no damage done by our tenants, and we were able to settle in without a problem.

Phyllis and Ken were superb and insisted that as it was Saturday, Leni should have the weekend off from cooking, and that Phyllis would provide all of our meals until Monday. This was a great welcome home.

After the euphoria of the homecoming, we came down to earth on the Monday when all of the workers were going to do their various chores, and I was without a job. So once again, I started looking around for a position. Soon I saw a company advertising for someone with experience in the investment area. It was a commission only situation, but a nice office and some existing clients were provided, as was Press advertising.

Gold, silver, and diamonds, were the leading products. It was interesting learning about them, but I never felt that I could honestly suggest that diamonds were a good investment. There were so many conflicting stories about their value, as it seemed that there was a book value if the client wanted to resell, but to find a buyer willing to pay that price was another thing.

Silver seemed a better proposition, as it was down in price after the historic highs of (I think) 1980, and it was suggested, in fact it was ordained, that these were good reasons for it to go back up. I remember two reasons. One was that the 'slumbering giant', China, was starting to buy silver, and the other that a new photographic process involved the use of silver and large quantities would be needed, thus pushing up the price.

I had some success with superannuation, and I produced tables demonstrating its efficiency and superiority over fixed interest investments, such as building societies. I showed the dynamic effect of the compounding of tax-free regular investments over those that were taxed, but when something is that good, most people think it cannot be true. We also sold 'time share' investments, but whereas they may have been good holiday situations, there were many 'incalculables' in the argument. Another risky investment was in the commodities, or futures, markets, where clients could win or lose fortunes in one night, for it was a night time occupation being in touch with overseas markets.

I also looked into and dabbled with real estate, without much enthusiasm or much success, all the while looking for something better.

Regarding the dynamic futures market, a very sad event occurred shortly after I left. I heard on the news one day of a murder in the city. When I saw the name of the victim, and read that he had been found dead in the morning, having been killed during the night, I guessed what had happened. I told Leni that the murderer would have lost a large amount of money, and that the person who had been managing his account would have been held responsible, and so in his anger the client would have attacked him. It transpired that I was right. The client was tried, convicted of murder, and sentenced accordingly.

During this period a family catastrophe occurred. Tim and Margarete, seemingly living an idyllic lifestyle in a lovely cottage in Tealby, Lincolnshire, with our two dear grandchildren, parted. Our daughter rang us in the middle of the night to tell us that Tim had moved out, she could not afford the mortgage, etc, and that she had no car, no income, and was having breast problems. All of the circumstances from then until now are too painful for me to record, sufficient to say that she, Toby, and Elizabeth arrived back in Perth, devastated, on 22nd November 1982. We had paid their fares.

After the sad events of recent years, it needed a bit of luck to cheer us all up, and it came from a most unexpected quarter. Margarete and Toby walked through their front door to hear a voice on the radio, which they had left on, asking all mums who had a four-year-old Australian son with blue eyes, to ring up Channel Nine for an interview for a commercial television advertisement.

Margarete rang, arranged an interview, and attended with some apprehension. Toby was asked a few questions and the TV people were so impressed with him that they gave him the part immediately, and told their secretary to cancel all other appointments. They came home on cloud nine – no pun intended.

It was for the airline, Air India, and to make it, Margarete and Toby flew to Singapore, Delhi, and Bombay, segments being filmed in each city. Margarete played the part of Mum, and it turned out to be a really excellent advertisement. They had a great time making it, flying first class and living in the best hotels. The producer said that Toby was a natural, that although barely four, he had been given up to six instructions at a time and performed them perfectly.

They were not paid for the ad, but Toby did receive $200 for his picture being used on the biggest advertisement hoarding in Perth – that outside the railway station. It was enormous, and for many months whenever I drove down Wellington Street, there was Toby kissing the Indian air hostess, just as he did in the last frame of the film.

In Perth, corner shops are called 'Delis', being, presumably, short for delicatessen. When they were being interviewed, they were told that Toby would ride an elephant in Delhi, but when he got home he told us that he was, 'going to the Deli on an elephant'!

For a long time he was recognised by everyone who saw him as 'the Air India boy', and it became a source of embarrassment to the young lad, especially when lots of mums told him that their little daughters kissed him on the television screen whenever they saw him.

Toby has a natural acting talent, and 'The Australian' newspaper wrote an article on him, actually referring to him as 'Australia's newest star', although his mum has never looked for more work for him, I still think that he will be an actor one day. He is very clever academically, and plays lots of sports, including table tennis. I thought that I could play quite well, but being beaten about 21–10 every game, eventually seemed to tell me that it was time to hang up my bat. Toby is the extrovert, whilst his sister, Elizabeth, is more introverted. She is a beautiful girl and they get on together really well. They have always spent a lot of time with us and this has been a great blessing. We have had some lovely times and I am sure that this will continue. They are now in London, but our hope is to rejoin them in England.

Elizabeth had an exciting experience when she was in England in 1981. The TV series 'Nanny', with Wendy Craig starring, made an episode in Tealby, and Elizabeth took part. It was when the children were evacuated during the war. She was in quite a few scenes and the video-copy is a very nice memento of her childhood.

However, I must return to my oft-repeated search for a better job, due to not being happy with what I was doing. I faced the prospect in a positive manner, always with a feeling of excitement, not knowing what wonderful opportunity dwelt just around the corner.

CHAPTER THIRTY FIVE
THE BAIL HOSTEL

Having enjoyed working together in the outback so much, Leni and I decided to look for a 'husband-and-wife job', part-time or full-time, live in or work from home.

We looked at a few motel management situations, but they were all rather run-down businesses, where liquor sales were the major part of their takings. If instead, it was an up-market place, there was always the problem of not having managed a motel before. It seemed that whenever I queried why we were turned down, it was for that reason.

We had always tried to overcome this at the interview, by stressing Leni's qualifications as having been deputy head housekeeper at a four-star hotel in England and the fact that I had managed old peoples' homes. The latter was much more difficult than managing a motel, but we did not seem to get this over to the interviewers.

On two or three occasions we went to the motel later, just to see what kind of people got the jobs. Invariably, the place was dirty, saying little for the manageress, and the manager would have little idea of public relations, or staff management – essential in what is now known as the hospitality industry.

As an expert on cleaning, which done properly really is an art, Leni has always complained that all and sundry seem to think that anyone can clean. It is just not true. Cleaning has many skills, and Leni would never accept anyone for a cleaning job, unless they had those skills, or they were willing to learn them.

A good example was back in West Hagley, in Worcestershire, when we decided that due to her involvement in IOS, Leni should be relieved of some of her housework. She engaged a charming lady who purported to be a cleaner. She arrived on time on her motor scooter, and we really liked her attitude. When told that she would have to do things Leni's way, she agreed immediately, commenting that the house was so beautifully cleaned and polished that she would love to know how to do it herself.

For the first few days Phyllis earned her pay very easily, because Leni did just about all of the work. She showed her the daily and weekly routines, which made certain, to use her words, 'things never really get dirty, making your work much lighter.'

This insistence on a system and on cleanliness had remarkable repercussions later, here in Australia, as will be related eventually.

But for now, back to the search for a husband-and-wife job. One day we saw an advertisement from the Probation and Parole Department, who were to open the first Bail Hostel in Australia, at Fremantle, and they required two married couples; one to live permanently at the hostel, and the other to relieve them on their two days off.

It was hardly what we were looking for, but the reader by now will realise that we were like chameleons, and that change was not entirely unusual for us.

We applied for the job, and were able to obtain an interview, so we went down to North Fremantle to have a look at this Bail Hostel. There were workmen everywhere, converting an old primary school into a hostel. It only took us twenty minutes to get there, so it was not far from home, if we were to get the job.

However, our luck was no better than before. It is strange how you can spot a rejection letter as you take it out of the post box, as I have previously written. We were not really surprised, as we gained the impression that an ex-policeman or an ex-prison officer would be preferred.

Not to be deterred, we kept looking and a new type of situation was being advertised. Very attractive retirement villages were being built, and they all employed a husband and wife to manage the place, with free accommodation and a small salary.

There was one not far from North Beach, so we applied and we really did think we had a good chance, but there was to be a further disappointment. It was decided that the wife should be a trained nurse. This surprised me as Moline House had been six times as big, and had much older people on average, yet did not find it necessary to have a trained nurse on the premises.

Always positive, I knew that we would find something sooner or later, and when it came it was a pleasant surprise. The letter had the name of the sender in the top left hand corner. It was the Probation and Parole Department!

After ripping open the envelope with great haste, as always where letters re possible employment were concerned, I read the last paragraph first. Would I ring to make an appointment for a further interview? Of course I would, and I did, to learn that the ex-police inspector and his wife, who had been appointed relief managers, had not liked the job and had resigned. They would carry on until we were ready.

Of course we were ready, right now. We had some 'in-house' training, which was to do with the philosophy of the Bail Hostel, the rules appertaining to its running, and the nature of the actual work. Then we attended the Central Law Courts in Perth to be shown the bail system, and to meet the various officers with whom we would be dealing. Finally, prior to being trained in the hostel itself, we visited Fremantle Prison and the Canning Vale Remand Centre, as it was explained to us that I would have to go to these institutions, and other Police Station lock-ups, to pick up people who had been released on bail, to reside in the Bail Hostel.

We then spent a few days in the hostel, where we were allocated a one-bedroom flat. I worked with the manager and Leni with his wife. As had been our lot on other occasions, we could not see why the incumbents had been preferred to us.

However, I think that as time went by, we felt that although the couple who worked five days a week obviously earned much more than us, two days (or forty-eight hours in residence) a week was enough. We also worked when the managers were on holiday, so our annual income was quite adequate.

After some months, we all realised that we were being exploited. For some time our pay slip would just show an amount, tax deducted and net pay, but there must have been a change in staff or in procedures, because one day we noticed a further statistic had been added. We were being paid for seven and a half hours a day!

A normal day would go like this. I would be up at 6.45 am as the residents had to be up at 7.00 am. I would go around all of the rooms and call them, and then have to go back down again as often some would go back to sleep. They all had to shower and to be at breakfast at 8.00 am.

They had daily duties, which covered the cleaning of the common-room and the meal tables, and washing up afterwards. In addition, they had to vacuum their own rooms, make their beds, etc. The raising of the Australian flag, and its taking down at sunset, were also daily tasks. Once they had done their duties satisfactorily, they could go, as long as they signed the book and indicated if they would be in for lunch and tea.

They had to be back in the hostel by 10.00 pm every night, and there were various other rules, which were explained to them on entry, with a warning that if they did not observe them, they could be returned to prison.

Leni had to do all of the cooking and planning of meals, and she had to ensure that the cleaning was completed. She also had to wash and iron sheets, towels, pyjamas, etc, and be responsible for their repair etc.

The full complement was twenty-four and, although the hostel was rarely full, it was often around the twenty mark. This involved a considerable amount of work for her, and after entering the kitchen at about 7.15 am, she would be on the go until the dishes were put away after the evening meal at about 7.30 pm.

This was a normal day, but on occasions I would be at a prison in the evening to pick someone up, and she would be in total charge of some twenty people. Of course, she could not rest, as it was necessary to walk around the building frequently to make sure that nothing untoward was happening.

Many a day I would be out at the various courts around the metropolitan area, and Leni would have to carry out her own duties, but also she would have to deal with the many matters that I should have dealt with. Some days the telephone would not stop ringing. She could be in the kitchen, or out in the garden hanging out the washing, and the phone would ring in the office. Off she would dash, unlock the office door, and rush to the phone just as it stopped!

And for all of this she was paid for seven and a half hours. We were both on duty twenty-four, even if seven of them were in bed. I had a phone call at at 2.30 am one morning, from the police who were on night duty, and quite frequently the police would make enquiries in the evenings. They were getting paid for it, we were not.

My day invariably involved trips to the courts or the prisons. When on duty, I was responsible to the court to produce the defendant when required for hearings. The system was such that, despite the accused being palpably guilty and not denying it, the lawyers often would advise them to plead not guilty, thus ensuring several court appearances before finally being found guilty and sentenced. Some were in the hostel for many months, during which time they could not get on with their lives. However, some used it as a kind of club, and were quite at home there.

When a person was admitted to the hostel, he or she had to read the rules, and then sign an acknowledgement that they would adhere to them. There was nothing punitive in them, as clients were innocent until proven guilty, but in their particular cases – for instance if they were of no fixed abode, or they were from the Eastern States – they would have been held in a Remand Centre, which was a wing of a prison, had it not been for the hostel's existence.

The most difficult rules to administer with some residents, were being in by 10.00 pm, not getting drunk, and doing their chores properly. To compound these problems for us, was the fact that the 'powers that be' were too lenient at times. If from the beginning these rules had been enforced, we would have had very little trouble.

In the event, what happened was that I would explain the rules, pointing out that every establishment, job, or organisation, had rules for the benefit of all. However when the new resident went into the TV-room and mentioned the various rules that had been explained, they were told that you didn't have to take too much notice of them – by the other residents!

We locked the doors at 10.00 pm, and anyone who was late had to ring the bell. I would go to the door and admonish them, saying that I would forget this instance, but not to be late again. Quite often this would be sufficient, as the prospect of going back to Fremantle Prison or the Canning Vale Remand Centre, was far less attractive then the comparative comfort of the Bail Hostel. Of course, some were not co-operative and when it was apparent that they would not subscribe to the regulations of the institution, they were arrested and taken away.

We used to keep a daily log of happenings, of ins and outs, of breaking the rules, and a file was kept on each inmate. I used to say that the logbook could be used as the basis for a television serial. Instead of 'Z Cars', or 'Cop Shop' it would have provided scripts for years for, 'The Bail Hostel', every Tuesday and Thursday evening!

One evening I was alerted by someone that a new inmate was drunk and making threats to a fellow 'guest'. The latter was in bed, but apparently they had had a drunken argument, and when I went to investigate, the newcomer was stamping around all of the rooms demanding a knife, as he was going to kill his inebriated new 'mate'. I remonstrated with him, but he was obviously 'beyond the pale', so I rang Fremantle Police Station to have him picked up, warning them that they would need two or three big lads as our parolee was in a highly dangerous state. They sent three and he was taken after a struggle, and he yelled lots of four-letter words and obscenities at me as they led him off.

We rarely had parolees, but we did in this instance, so I was particularly sad at having to take such action. He could well have breached his parole and finished up in prison again, for the balance of his original sentence.

This incident occurred when I was 'in attendance', but I could well have been out picking up a new client from a prison. This demonstrates how dangerous it was for my wife at times, and also how ridiculous it was to be paid for seven and a half hours, or fifteen for the two days, when in effect we were 'on guard' for forty-eight hours.

And what kind of people did we deal with? Well, the drunken parolee threatening murder had just finished a sixteen-year sentence for the attempted murder of a policeman. So the scale was from him to a young homeless first-offender, via some with horrendous numbers of 'break and enters', who we once called burglars. There were also women accused of selling drugs; one fifty-year-old man accused of incest; a 'devout' Catholic who stole the collection from a northern WA church; an accountant who had a predilection for mixing up his money with that of his clients; and many many others, covering most crimes against property or the person.

The Catholic had always been a churchgoer, and loved to serve the priest, so it came as a bit of a shock, and I must add as some amusement, to know that he had nicked the collection.

He, like many others who passed through the double front doors of Stirling House, had such a penchant for telling untruths that I am sure he actually believed his prevarications. During the several months he spent with us, he unfolded the 'story' of his life.

Born in a small town in New South Wales, the name of which I have forgotten, he left school at fourteen, and started work in the shearing-sheds of that State. According to him, he preferred to work with the cooks and eventually he was sufficiently accomplished to become a cook himself.

He married and they had a son and daughter. Unfortunately, his wife died and this upset him so much that he took to the drink, and wandered from shearing-shed to shearing-shed.

His good news whilst in residence with us was that his daughter, by now a nursing sister, had told him that she was coming to WA to work and to set up a home to include him. His son was doing well as a diesel fitter and it was even anticipated that he would come too.

One day his supervising Probation and Parole Officer came to see me as he was preparing a pre-sentence report, and he wanted my comments on 'Paddy's' behaviour whilst in the hostel. He had been in touch with the police in New South Wales and the information he received was rather surprising. Our recalcitrant had never been married, was not known at the 'address of his daughter' or that of his 'son', both of whom were figments of his imagination!

Being a cook, he decided that he would look for a job and to our amazement, he quickly got one as a chef in a Fremantle restaurant. We thought it strange when on the day of the evening when he was to start, he asked Leni if she could tell him how to make 'Chicken Kiev'. Would there be a chef in the world who could not produce this popular dish? Other than Paddy, I mean.

She showed him and at 5.00 pm he went off to start his duties. At about 8.00 pm the owner of the restaurant rang. Where was Paddy?

To be funny, he had 'chickened' out (Kiev?), and not turned up. He did later at the hostel. Drunk. 'Our' accountant, 'Peter', brought with him his wardrobe. Fortunately, this did not mean a wooden fabrication, but unfortunately it did mean by far the largest collection of haute couture clothing I had ever seen.

Our humble premises were certainly not of the style to which he was accustomed, for which hostel habitué had 24 magnificently tailored suits of the finest cloth, 62 shirts, many of which were silk, and a profusion of ties and socks?

His wife had left him as he had more than once brought shame to the family, due to his illicit dealings, and in a small WA town news travels fast. But I liked him and felt sorry for him. He got two years and it was ironic that the next time I saw him, he was in green prison-denims, working on the lawns fronting Fremantle prison.

It was about this time when we decided to become Australian citizens. We had talked about it many times and had intended to do something about it. We had already been to a citizenship ceremony when our friends, the Shorts, were 'nationalised'. That was at Gosnells, and every council organised their own. Therefore, we applied to the Stirling City Council and shortly afterwards we were called to the council chambers at 4.00 pm one day, to find in the region of thirty people with like-minds.

The proceedings on both occasions were similar in two ways. The first was that the programmes included the National Anthem, the oath of allegiance, and the presentation of a New Testament suitably inscribed. The second similarity was the manner in which they were both conducted. People went to the front in groups of about ten, and swore the oath of allegiance to the Queen, that is Queen Elizabeth of Australia, and to their adopted country. At least some did. Something like half appeared not to speak or understand English, and they certainly did not swear – I felt intentionally – that allegiance to the Queen. In these cases it was a farce.

Its effect on us was to give us dual citizenship, British and Australian, and probably triple for Leni, having been born in Germany.

I was reminded about this subject when I mentioned Fremantle prison, as it is known as Her Majesty's Prison. Now back to the Bail Hostel!

There was always something happening and never a dull moment. We had had this 32-year-old mother-of-three with us for a while and we had got to like her. Her children, all littlies, used to visit her, and Leni was always kind to them. But then, as so often happens, she disappointed us, by disappearing. She did not obey the rules, so her bail was withdrawn and a warrant for her arrest was issued.

That was that, we thought, but it was not to be the end of her story. We had a bit of a shock one day. We had a phone call from the police, saying that a Post Office had been held up and it was believed that a particular young man from the hostel was involved. They described the suspect, and I knew straightaway that it was not who they thought it was, as the description was awry. However, this seemed to put us on our guard, thinking I suppose that maybe some of the others might have been involved.

However, work had to continue and Leni went into a recently vacated bedroom to vacuum and dust. Suddenly one of the chaps turned up, came into the room, saw Leni vacuuming, and made his first mistake. He volunteered to do the cleaning, in fact, insisted on doing it. Now this is ridiculous, thought Leni. He was bone-idle and would never make such an error as to volunteer for work, what was he up to? So she declined and he reluctantly withdrew. Suspicious, Leni then searched the room and found a locked cash box in a bedside cupboard. We rang the police, and they soon questioned our disappointed volunteer helper and his mate, and arrested them.

More was to come, as they had a boss, someone who had organised it, who committed the robbery and passed the proceeds to our clients. And that someone was Mrs Big, who unknown to us had taken a room in a house at the end of the street opposite the hostel, which she could see from her window. Maybe she signalled to her accomplices, but whatever the method, she must have found a way to contact them.

She also 'mistress-minded' an armed robbery at a chicken takeaway and one other, the details of which I have forgotten. For her share she was sentenced to seven years imprisonment at Bandyup Womens Prison. She fainted on sentencing and the last I heard of her, she was apparently 'Queen Bee' at the prison. It was such a shame, and especially for her children. She will be out by now and I hope that she has been able to rebuild her life.

One of the most serious occurrences at the Bail Hostel during our tenure was also not without its humour, or maybe more appropriately, its incredulity. The smell of cannabis being smoked, and the discovery by Leni of two 'bombs' or smoking apparatus, heralded a raid by the Drug Squad. In fact, they made two whilst we were there. The discovery of heroin hidden in a hollowed-out section of the window frame of one of the rooms was bad news, but the fact that they found cannabis growing in the hostel gardens was almost hilarious.

Finding bottles of beer in the garden was almost trivial compared to the above, but it was just another way to break the rules. Curiously, one of the clients, about whom the Parole Department wrote in the local press as one of the hostel's success stories, was involved in another one of our incidents worthy of recording in the logbook.

She was an attractive auburn haired girl of obvious Scottish family background, although her parents lived in Queensland, and she had a useless drug-addicted 'boyfriend', who used to write to her from a prison in South Australia. Why basically nice girls get themselves involved with such people I will never know. She had never been arrested or appeared in court before, and when I went to pick her up, she was crying and trembling as I accompanied her from the Perth Central Law Courts. Yet after a few weeks in the hostel, she did as most of the others did: she went with them on their court appearances, and the fear of such happenings disappeared.

Eventually, she became no different to the others and one night stayed out. The following morning I saw that her car was in the car park. The driver's door was wide open and there were large dents in the bodywork. She had obviously had quite a bad accident. I went to her room to find her either drunk or drugged out of her mind. She could offer no information about where she had been or where it had happened. And she was a big success story. Or so the hierarchy said.

I had to laugh one night. A client had not returned and I decided to have one last look outside to see if he was trying to get in, prior to my going to bed. Suddenly a figure loomed up in the dark, but it was not someone coming in, it was someone going out. He had got through the window. When I asked him where he thought he was going he said that he had a date with a girl at a Night Club! And he insisted that he could not let her down! Incredibly, I had to argue firmly with him to get him to go back to his room.

We had a number of people on drug related charges, and as is well known, the drug habit is no respecter of persons. One very likeable young man stayed with us for some time, and when he left – his case having been settled, I cannot remember how – we thought that he had learned his lesson. Both of his parents were academics; his father a lecturer at the University in Canberra and his mother in Perth. Sadly, 'Paul' reappeared one day. He had taken a van and driven it down south where he managed to turn it over, but again it was to do with drugs. And the worst thing that happened was when a truly beautiful young lady teamed up with one of the young men and failed to report in one night. The following morning she was found dead in her car, overdosed, and he was unconscious. She came from a very good English family. What a waste.

We also had a resident beaten up by the police. His brother was a policeman in the country, and he was the kind of lad who had done something silly and probably would never repeat it. I think that he stole some food from a delicatessen when he was unemployed. Anyway, we found him to be the perfect resident, polite, co-operative, and never a problem. He also found a job, which was cold canvassing on houses. Very hard work, but he stuck to it. Imagine how shocked we were when he came in one afternoon, his face bruised and swollen, and with various marks on his body. He said that the police had questioned him about some break-ins, and because he had refused to admit to crimes he had not committed, they had beaten him up.

I sent him to a doctor so that we had expert evidence available concerning the nature of the injuries, and 'Terry' saw his legal adviser to lodge a complaint. Eventually, I was questioned by a senior officer of the enquiry team, but I realised that 'Terry' had no chance, because the officer suggested that he had been beaten up on the way home after his questioning! What rubbish, but that was the end of the matter.

When on duty it was my responsibility to make sure that the residents appeared in court for their hearings or trials. Although most of them used to go under their own steam, when necessary I had to take them in the car, and quite often others would ask for a lift. One lad from the Eastern States asked me for a lift one day, as he wanted to go to Subiaco. I dropped him off, and that evening the East Perth lock-up rang to say that he would not be back as he was under arrest, accused of three break-ins at Subiaco! I had been used to take him to the scene of his crimes!

One of his pals said that he did it to get some money together to travel back East, as though it was perfectly normal.

We learned a lot living with a vast variety of recalcitrants. One, 'Bill' was charged with incest with his fourteen-year-old daughter, in the back of a car driven by his son. A sordid affair, and a dreadful thing for the girl to have to live with, but the point I wish to make is that Bill was seemingly no different to anyone else, your neighbour, for instance. One may have a picture in one's mind of a rapist, but Bill could not have been more ordinary. Another fact in the case was that his wife took him back.

CHAPTER THIRTY SIX
COMMUNITY SERVICE ORDERS

Whilst working at the Bail Hostel, the managers who relieved us after we had relieved the full-time managers, Gordon and Georgina Dowling, told us of Gordon's other part-time job. He was an area liaison officer looking after people who had been sentenced by the courts to terms of community service. It sounded very interesting, and Gordon said that there was an advertisement for a relief officer at that very time, so I applied, thinking that two part-time jobs made one whole job, and both were with the same department of the Public Service – terrific!

Bureaucracies are well-known for 'red tape', and so this is probably why I was interviewed at length by my bail hostel bosses, before I got the job. It was even hinted that maybe I was too hard on hostel residents. Well, if trying to get them to obey the rules laid down by the same bosses was too hard, then I suppose I was too hard!

The job was to move around the various branch offices relieving officers who were off sick or on leave. The Community Service Order (CSO) system was that the courts could sentence people who would otherwise go to prison, to anything from 40 to 240 hours of community service. The work was to be done at approved projects, which had to be within certain guidelines. For instance, the work had to be of benefit to the community and worthwhile for the 'client', and furthermore, the work should not be that normally done by a paid employee. The trade unions were in the vetting process and they were very hot on the latter stipulation.

The client theoretically had a year in which to do the work, but the Area Liaison's task was to get a contract signed to complete the hours as soon as possible. Where clients were placed, what work they did, and how quickly they completed the hours, depended on such criteria as employment status, mobility, physical ability, and personal skills (e.g. painting, clerical, typing, etc).

It was determined how many hours a week could be worked, and a contract was signed explaining the client's obligations and instructions, and detailing when, for how long, and where the work should be done. Most clients reported to the nearest office on the Tuesday following the court's sentence, when the above was all sorted out.

Finally, I was accepted, allowed to do two jobs for the same department and they dovetailed perfectly. During my days at the hostel, I was available to the various probation officers on both counts. Most Tuesdays I was at a branch office interviewing CSO clients, and the other days I worked from home.

During this time I came across a modern day Fagin. He had a shop of his own, but this was not sufficient for him. He persuaded three teenagers to 'work' for him. He would select the targets, decide how to break into them, take one or more of his apprentices with him in his car, and sit outside waiting for them to reappear with the goods, cash, etc. He then paid them their share and sold the goods. They were all caught and I was involved with one of the youths who had really let his mother down. She was running a cafe, working very hard for the benefit of her family, and her son spoilt everything by his actions.

It does not take long to become immune to what are, initially, shocks caused by the identities of some clients. Having been to most courts, and knowing the names of judges and magistrates, I was intrigued when I saw the name of one offender. His was an uncommon name. Could he be related to the magistrate of that name? Yes he could, he was his adopted son.

At the Bail Hostel, I learnt quite a bit about the waste of money by government bodies. I had received quite a schooling in the Northern Territory. It was no different in Western Australia. A big store shed, or garage, was built behind the hostel. I asked what it was for, to be told it was for storage. Knowing that there were large empty cupboards inside the hostel, I could not make out what was to be kept in there. No one else could either, but it cost a lot of money – 'money which had to be spent before the end of the financial year', as I discovered. When the man came to put it up, he told me that he could not understand why it was being made so strong. Apparently, the gauges of the steel girders and sheets were far too substantial, and just not necessary. But that is government. In private enterprise, it would not have been built at all, but supposing the need for extra storage arose, a much lighter and cheaper structure would have been erected.

I would have been quite happy to run both jobs in tandem, but Leni and I were getting progressively more frustrated by the doings – or the lack of doings – of the 'full-time' hostel manager and manageress.

I found myself putting in all of the systems necessary to run the place efficiently, and most of the paperwork was being left for me. Deliveries of foods and other supplies were conveniently arranged to coincide with our two days of duty. There was obviously no supervision of the clients to make sure that the rosters, which were left for me to organise, were adhered to, and thus the place was always dirty when we arrived on Wednesday mornings. When the two went on holidays, we took over and found out the whole picture of a week's procedures. We confirmed that which we already knew; that we were being used.

Eventually, we dropped hints to our superiors, but it did no good. I knew that Leni was fed up of her counterpart's almost total lack of activity, and we told our boss so. He tried to persuade us not to rock the boat, saying that Leni's standards were too high, when he should have been saying that the other person's were too low. Then the latter told the boss something, I have forgotten what, that was untrue, so we saw him and told him that we were resigning. He tried to dissuade us, and when he saw that we were determined, he asked us how long it would be before we actually left. 'In the morning,' we said. He asked us to think it over and to ring him at home that evening. I rang him and to his obvious disappointment, I confirmed that we were leaving in the morning.

This was all rather brave as the same person was also my boss on the CSO front, and I thought that I might be eased out of that, but it was a matter of principle.

At that time, I was still the relief Area Liaison Officer. I rather enjoyed that, working in different areas from the various offices. In this way I got to know far more about the community service orders situation in the Perth metropolitan area, than anyone else. I also knew all of the officers and offices. The systems were different in every office, and I thought that one day someone might ask me about this. I could have improved the efficiency of the whole thing, and saved the department a lot of money. But that is not how State Government departments operate.

I must say that I found everyone very friendly and helpful, wherever I was. One day, I was talking to the officer who was responsible for the North-West area, which included my own suburb of North Beach, and he told me that he was retiring, so I applied for his job, and got it. Other officers had also wanted it, but I was lucky and I was appointed.

Being a relief officer was very interesting, but having your own area is better, because you are responsible for its progress. You have to be always on the lookout for new projects and try to make sure that you then place the right people into those projects.

We have had many success stories. Many projects could not have survived if it had not been for us supplying free labour. We also have our own workshop, and we have performed minor miracles in there. For example, we have always sent CSO clients to work at the St Vincent de Paul depot (SVDP) in Osborne Park, which is a North Perth suburb. SVDP is a Catholic welfare organisation. People give them used clothes, furniture, household goods, books, etc, and they sell them, or give them away to the needy, having first cleaned or repaired them if necessary. One day the manager said that they had to send to the council tip more than 60% of the furniture that they picked up, due to their inability to repair it. Now they deliver it to our workshop. We repair it and re-stain it, if it can be repaired, and if not we take it apart and keep the wood for repairs to other furniture. The value of our service to the community in this venture is tremendous.

We have built a children's playground, made toys for poor people and the children of prisoners, and been involved in tree planting in new areas. The list is endless and the job satisfaction boundless. This week a lady rang me. She had just completed 150 hours of community service at an establishment which teaches disabled children to ride horses. Thanking me for putting her there, she said that when she was sentenced, her life was at its lowest ebb. It was hardly worth living, but now she was 'living on a higher plateau' and working with disabled children had turned her life around. She has now carried on as a volunteer and she is working towards qualifying as a riding instructor.

A little Irish nun, in her seventies, could be considered unlikely to have much effect on today's 'tough guy' young criminals, but the facts are different. Sister Rita, a Sister of Mercy and a retired teacher, has been what we call a Project Volunteer for several years. We have sent people to her convent to do the large gardens, to paint the rooms, and females to help in the kitchen and do cleaning. Very often we have sent problem clients – those who are the least motivated, even bloody-minded, some needing and getting psychiatric help – and always the required hours have been completed. She has performed miracles.

The public often complain that we are too lenient with some offenders on community service, saying that if they do not turn up as per the contract we should send them back to court where they would be re-sentenced, sometimes to prison. But CSOs are to keep people out of prison for their own sake and to save the great cost of incarceration, and then it is hoped that both they and the community will benefit by the work that is done. It is easy to send them back to court, but that is failure. It is far better if we can find the real reason for non-attendance. An example would be Michael X, who had obvious psychological problems, caused through rejection by his family. First, I arranged for him to work in the office of an Aboriginal community. He agreed to this, but on arrival he got into an argument with someone, and it transpired that he had certain opinions about Aborigines to do with the fact that some of them do not want to work. I then sent him to St Vincent de Paul. Michael was really very intelligent, despite his complexes, and I think that the foreman might have sensed this and treated him harshly in consequence.

Anyway Michael came to the office distressed and fearing the worst. I rang Sister Rita and explained all of this to her. As I expected, she told me to send him along. I did and he performed wonders and worked as many as ten hours a day. He was valued as a human being and loved by Sister Rita, and he responded as all of the others had.

Monica Armstrong has been a project volunteer for about twelve years. She has been bedridden for most of that time with many ailments, which include arthritis over most of her body. Medical science has performed some minor miracles, but being a widow, whose grown up family live a long way away, she has relied on the 'Silver Chain' for home nursing and daily house cleaning, and us for gardening, painting and general home maintenance. We have done an enormous amount of work, but the most important result of the exercise has been her effect on the people we have sent to her. Seeing her so crippled seems to have had an electrifying effect on our 'clients'. Similar to Sister Rita, malcontents have come up trumps and worked hard, been punctual, and have rarely let her down.

I have a long history of examples of successful clients and successful projects. I am now an honorary probation and parole officer and a sessional supervisor with nearly eight years service, and it is the job which has given me the most satisfaction. Shortly we are to be involved with 'Home Detention', which will be yet another opportunity for me to find satisfaction in my work.

CHAPTER THIRTY SEVEN

CHURCH AND OTHER AFFAIRS

Once more I must turn back the clock again, to encompass happenings other than my work. In June and July of 1984 there was much excitement in North Beach and its environs, as the Anglican and Catholic Churches set up groups of lay people to examine a report of something known as 'ARCIC', or 'Anglican, Roman Catholic, International Commission'.

ARCIC was a commission which was composed of Anglican and Catholic bishops and it met in Rome between the years of 1971 and 1981. Its purpose was to discover what were the problems preventing the unity of the two great Churches, and to see if progress could be made towards unity, which must happen if we are to carry out Christ's great commission that we 'love one another as I have loved you.' Much progress had been made and it seemed that the two main stumbling blocks were to do with differences over what happens on the altar when Holy Communion is being received, and with the fact that the Catholics do not recognise the validity of Anglican orders.

The first problem is to do with what the Church of Rome calls, 'transubstantiation', meaning that Jesus Christ is physically present on the altar when the bread and the wine are being taken, whereas the Anglicans believe that He is there in spirit only.

As Leni was baptised a Catholic, we had solved our differences by simply going to both Churches, and taking the view that Jesus had said, 'Where two or three are gathered together in my name, there I shall be in their midst.' That was good enough for us, and whether He meant in spirit, or in person, did not matter to us.

The second problem is a matter of the Catholics believing that St Peter was the Bishop of Rome, that he and the apostles were the first priests, and that the validity of the ordination of present priests is derived through the direct lineage of the bishops to St Peter. Because the Church of England broke away from the Roman Catholic Church, the Catholics feel that the Anglican priests do not have this continuity from St Peter, and are thus unacceptable.

Following on from this, of course, was the problem of the Anglican Communion accepting the Bishop of Rome, the Pope, as head of the proposed united Church.

Knowing that I know the Mass as well as I know the Anglican Eucharist, Lewis Firman, our rector, asked me to contact the local Catholic church to see if discussions could be arranged. This I did, to find that their priest had done nothing about ARCIC, and if I had not had contacts with their laity, there would have been no discussions.

However, their Max de Mamiel was as enthusiastic as I was, once he understood what it was about. There was excellent discussion material available. It was split up into several subjects, which included the three problems mentioned above, and the Maryan doctrine was examined, whereby the Catholics ask Mary, the mother of Jesus, to intercede with Jesus (the Anglicans believe only in praying directly to Him). There were notes on how the sessions should be run. Each week at the end of the evening, study notes were issued, regarding the following week's subject.

About seventy people took part, roughly half-and-half Catholics and Anglicans, and Max and I organised six groups to meet in various houses. Half would be of one denomination and half the other. To start it all off, I suggested that we all should meet at the Catholic church, 'Our Lady of Grace', for their 6.30 pm Saturday evening Mass, and then to meet again the following morning at 9.00 am for the St Michael's Holy Communion (Eucharist). I knew that this would be a big first step, as I knew that very few of the seventy were aware of each other's services.

This was a big success and created a bond between Christians. A group met at our house the following Tuesday night, and I knew what was going to happen. We said a prayer to begin with, and then I asked them what they thought about the two Eucharists. They all told of their utter amazement at the similarity, that the really important parts were identical. Of course, the Creed, or the Credo (which is Latin for 'I believe'), is the most important statement in both services, and in a very long prayer, the only difference was a matter of semantics – the Catholics say, 'he became incarnate from the Virgin Mary and was made man,' whilst the Anglicans say, 'he was incarnate of the Virgin Mary, and became man.' Really, is it worth arguing about?

At the end of the meetings, we joined up with all of the groups from other suburbs, at a wonderful service at a large Catholic church in Perth. The enthusiasm was tremendous, the atmosphere electrifying, and lots of people from both persuasions went up to the microphone to declare that nothing of any importance stood between us and unity, so let us unite!

And this is how it should be, but I believe the two biggest problems are human. I firmly believe that, for example, the two Archbishops of Perth would not want to give up their positions and great houses; and that theologians seem to lack the simple faith, which Jesus gave us, and they are always looking for reasons 'why not'. The Church is supposed to consist of the people, but they are never consulted.

The Anglican Church have what is known as a synod every year. There are three factions involved; the bishops, the priests, and the laity. The Archbishop starts it all off by saying what he wants to happen, and few clerics would argue with him. Then they say that the people are represented. But are they? All churches send two representatives, and they vote purely as they want to vote. They know nothing of the peoples' views. The only way to find out whether, for example, we want women priests, is to have a referendum in all churches. Instead, we sent two people, a man and a woman, and I have no idea how they voted on women priests. They could have even cancelled each other out for all I know.

The selection of reps for synod is ridiculous too, as only homemakers and people with jobs where they get paid if they are absent, are available. Of course, all of the clerics get paid, but if I were a representative I would lose two days' pay!

On a more positive note, I was invited by two schools to speak to their pupils. The first was at the Lymburner Primary School, where I was asked to make a speech on Anzac Day (a commemoration of the WWI Anzac landing at Gallipoli), and the second was at Guildford Grammar School. I spoke to half of the school one day and to the other half the next day. My subject was 'Being a sportsman and a Christian', and I was following in the footsteps of many illustrious Australian sportsmen, including the then Australian Test Cricket captain, Kim Hughes.

Since leaving Bamyili, we had always felt sorry that it had been necessary to do so, as we had really loved working with Aborigines. There had been disappointments and some deprivations, but there had also been much satisfaction and a lot of appreciation for what we had done. Occasionally, we looked in the 'Situations Vacant' columns in the newspapers and one day in 1985, we saw something of real interest. A leading firm of Australian accountants were advertising on behalf of Aboriginal clients, for a manager, with work also available for a wife.

We applied and we were asked to go to Alice Springs for interviews. When we got there, it was explained to us that there was a group of Aboriginal communities spread over a large area, with Alice Springs as their base. The job was to operate from 'the Alice' and to run the wholesale side of the business, and to provide relief for managers and their wives when they were sick, or during the changeover of staff. We met the accountant first and he appeared to be very happy with us. He arranged for a meeting with some representatives of some of the communities, and some of the managers, a couple of days later.

When we met, things could not have gone better. One manager said that he had been to Bamyili when we were there and he told the meeting of the great job we had done there, and yet another told of his visit to Croker, with the same plaudits. We seemed to answer all of the questions to their satisfaction, and we discussed terms and conditions. For the next few days we acted the tourist role, visiting all of the places of interest or beauty, of which there were many. When we called again on the accountants they said that all was agreed, but that in typical Aboriginal affairs style, no one had said how and when we would start. One of them took us to the airport and said that he would be in touch as soon as possible. Every now and again he would tell me on the phone that he was still trying to get a decision from them, but that being sometimes 1,000 kilometres from one another always slowed things! Several months after our visit they told us that no one else had been appointed, so to still hang on....

We had been in Australia ten years and nine months, and had developed a longing to revisit England, so we decided to go for six months and to rent our house out.

Margarete drove us to Perth International Airport, accompanied by Elizabeth and Toby. It was 1 April 1986, the beginning of autumn in Western Australia. After the usual preliminaries of checking tickets and passports, we weighed in our luggage. We were all quiet as we realised that shortly we would be saying our goodbyes, not to meet again for more than six months.

We appreciated that our daughter was in a parlous position, but we thought that our trip to England might open some different avenues for all of our futures. Margarete had not really wanted to come back to Australia, so if we found an opportunity whereby we could all go back to England, this could be a solution for us all.

Leni gave them a cheque to go on holiday to Mandurah, a seaside suburb to the south of Perth, and also some cash to go into Perth, have a meal, go to the cinema, or whatever they wanted to do. Months later we discovered that they were all so sad to see us go that they just went straight home.

CHAPTER THIRTY EIGHT
HOLIDAY IN ENGLAND

It was a heartbreaking parting, and we wondered if we were doing the right thing. We flew to Singapore on British Airways, and it was very pleasant listening to the accents of the British stewards and stewardesses. As I sat thinking of being away more than six months, I felt that it was such a long time, that it would never pass. As I write, we have been back for over five years.

We stayed over two nights in 'Singers' as the Perth 'yuppies' call Singapore, and we were able to do a little shopping and buy a few presents.

We thought that things were quite a lot dearer than they were on our visit in 1975, taking inflation into consideration. For people from Europe, a stay in Singapore is no doubt very attractive if only for the warm atmosphere, but living in Western Australia, where it is even hotter, the attraction used to be the cheapness of most things in the shops.

Our view is that there is little to see and to stay a week or two must be quite boring. The tourist spots are mostly quite bizarre, and they are generally dirty. However, it is the people who make your stay enjoyable. On both of our visits, we found them to be so helpful and pleasant. The hotels were excellent, as was the food, and particularly the breakfasts. A chef told me that he fries 2,000 eggs every morning. Certainly there was no need to have much lunch after a gargantuan breakfast.

The next leg of the flight was via Air Lanka, the Sri Lankan (ex-Ceylon) airline, which flew us to Colombo. Leni was a bit worried about this because of the activities of the Tamil terrorists, but we were happy to accept that this was happening in the north of the island. The plane was a Boeing as usual, but it might have been the original. The carpets, seats, and other fittings, were worn out and did little to inspire confidence, but the Sri Lankan staff could not have been more helpful.

Having read of the problems of the terrorists, we were not pleased at having to wait for three hours on Colombo airport, but we were very pleased with the aircraft, which was to take us to London. It was almost new and very comfortable. The food and the service were superb, and we thoroughly enjoyed the trip to Gatwick Airport, that included a short stop at Dubai.

As we crossed the English coast, I had marvellous happy feelings of anticipation. I was about to set foot in my native land after nearly eleven years absence. Although by then an Australian citizen with an Aussie passport, I was totally English at heart. Our anticipation was intense, and we were very excited when we were told to 'fasten your seat belts' before landing.

We were quite quickly through the Customs, due to the system of passing through uninterrupted if you had nothing to declare.

As we walked along the moving pavement, coming towards us on the next pavement was the well-known and easily recognisable figure of Major Ferguson, 'Fergie's' father, and Prince Charles' polo manager.

A very pleasant gesture by our friends, Mike and Sandy Leathley, awaited us at the end of the pavement. As we looked around for Mike, we saw a chauffer complete in a smart blue-grey uniform and peaked cap, holding a notice with 'Mr and Mrs Rickaby' on it.

We walked up to him and he grabbed our cases and took them off to a beautiful gleaming Rolls Royce. We felt that we belonged to this island race, but this incredible reception certainly confirmed it.

Moments later, Mike turned up. Always on the lookout for business, he had been chatting to someone who was in the Nursing Home industry. He gave us a tremendous welcome, and we really felt great. What could be better than to return to your native land and be picked up by a friend's Rolls Royce and chauffeur?

Mike's place, Holmesdale Park Nursing Home, is in the village of Nutfield in Surrey, and it probably only took about half an hour to get there. Standing in 25 acres of lovely Surrey parkland, it consisted of two sections – a straightforward Nursing Home for old people, and a residential part, which housed elderly retired ladies in suites of beautiful oak-panelled rooms, with a sitting-room, bedroom, and bathroom.

They ate in a delightful dining-room, which was truly elegant with its old fashioned decor and genuine antique oak furniture. The music room was furnished in classical style, and was very comfortable.

To be honest, I would never have thought that Mike would have enjoyed sitting down for an hour and playing hymns on the magnificent grand piano. In fact, I was not even aware that he could play. So it came as a great surprise one morning, when Leni and I were sitting reading, as we loved to do, for Mike to sit at the piano and start playing. Two old lady residents were there too, as our host went through an impressive repertoire of the old hymns, which we have known all of our lives. It was as enjoyable as it was surprising.

The view from the music room was particularly impressive, being of a small lake complete with a family of ducks and ducklings. Impeccable lawns and many old established trees of a number of types, including firs, oaks, and poplars, combined to make a landscape which always brought joy, whether it was cloaked in mist, glistening with hoar frost, bathed in sunshine, or lit by the several lamps around the front of the Home.

Before we left North Beach, we had received numerous invitations from friends to stay with them. Mike and Sandy said that we should stay with them for the six months and go off whenever we wished. Bill Matthews in London made the same offer, and other friends said to stay with them as long as we liked. The invitations were from Swanage in Dorset, Barnard Castle in Co Durham, Scarborough on the Yorkshire coast, St Ives in Cornwall, Thornaby in Yorkshire, Everton in Lincolnshire, Little Sutton and Heswall both in the Wirral, Balsall Common in Warwickshire, and Halesowen in Worcestershire.

Dear Carol in Heswall asked us to stay with her and Colin for six months, but her mother Vera wrote to say what a nerve Carol had, and we were to stay three months with each!

This made it very difficult, particularly as we wished to spend some time in Poole in Dorset, as well as Newton Abbot in Devon, and do some touring too. We had let our friends know when we would be with them, and for how long, but starting with Mike and Sandy's, it was obviously going to be impossible to stick to a schedule, for they wanted us to stay 'just another week' several times! How could you find the words to decline such generosity and kindness?

What happened was we got in an awful mess, having to ring up various friends to postpone our visits, sometimes for several weeks. There were their holidays to be taken into consideration too, and a good example was our trip to lovely Swanage, on the South Coast, to see our long-time friends, Busty and Jean Villis. We arranged to go in June but finally spent the first two weeks in August there!

Cyril, known as Busty, Villis was a stretcher-bearer with the 5th Dorsets and our friendship started in 1944. It was wonderful to see him and Jean again. They are now a retired couple, although kept busy doing all kinds of good works for relations, friends, and the community, whilst Busty still plays golf and Jean is well-known for her expertise in flowers and floral arrangement.

Whilst at Mike's we explored Surrey, Sussex, and Kent, including renewing acquaintance with Newhaven, from whence I sailed to Normandy in 1944. During our stay in Newhaven, I noticed that my old team, West Bromwich Albion, were playing at Brighton, so I rang the latter and they left me tickets for the game at the official entrance. This is something I miss in Australia.

We had often passed through Canterbury when we lived in England, and we had promised ourselves that one day we would explore the Cathedral, so we put this on our itinerary and we thoroughly enjoyed it.

It was awe inspiring to stand in the doorway through which four of King Henry II's knights entered the cathedral on 29 December 1170, to murder Archbishop Thomas à Becket. The story behind the assassination is that the king wanted to enforce the rule of law throughout the land, but standing outside that law was the clergy, who had their own courts and justice system. Henry actually appointed Becket because he was a friend and thereby expected him to be malleable, but alas, the king was devastated when the new Archbishop refused to comply. They quarrelled and Becket spent six years in France as an exile. Henry also spent a lot of time in his French territory, and whilst there he said, 'What cowards I have brought up in my Court. Won't anyone deliver me from this lowborn priest?'

The four knights took him literally and travelled to Canterbury where some monks had warned Thomas of the danger he was in. They persuaded him to go into the sanctuary, but he left and was a few steps from the cloister door when the knights arrived, and tried to drag him into the cloister as they argued with him, but when they failed, they slew him where he stood.

Henry was reviled throughout Europe, had to beg the Pope for forgiveness, and finally he had to go to Canterbury in public penance, walking barefoot the last part of the journey, and allowing himself to be beaten by the monks; whereas Thomas à Becket was canonised in 1173 as a Saint and Martyr. And Leni and I stood in awe and wonderment on the spot where the murder had taken place 815 years previously.

I am sure that it is the antiquity of Britain; its long history; its feeling of always having been, that acts as a magnet to me, and makes me want to return for always to be a part of that continuity. Another awe-inspiring incident occurred up in the North-East when we drove to the North Yorkshire National Park. After visiting several delightful villages, including the magical Hutton-le-Hole, we dropped into Kirkdale as we could see what was obviously an ancient church. What we found was truly remarkable.

A published history of this Saint Gregory's Minster tells that it was first built in 654, was badly damaged by Danish raids, and was rebuilt a few years before the Norman Conquest in the 1060s. Over the south door is a Saxon sundial, which is still in good condition. There is an inscription on it in ancient English that dates from about 1050 and it has been translated as follows: 'Orm, the son of Gamal, bought St Gregory's minster when it was all broken down and fallen, and he let it be made new from the ground, to Christ and to St Gregory, in the days of Edward the King and of Tosti the Earl.' Tosti was the Earl of Northumberland in about 1055.

Outside the church is a beck (stream) and we were amazed to read that in 1821, bones discovered in a cave by the beck were investigated by the Professor of Mineralogy at Oxford. They were identified as being of a great variety of species, including lion, bear, tiger, elephant, bison, deer, rhinoceros, and hyaena, of which there were the remains of three hundred! The mouth of the cave is only three feet high and so the professor concluded that the cave had been a hyaenas den, whose inhabitants dragged their prey whole or piecemeal into it. The discovery was a landmark in scientific history, and Kirkdale bones can be seen in many museums. You can still crawl through the narrow galleries, but all you will get for your efforts today is to come out plastered with clay!

We were having a wonderful time, revisiting places we loved, and also finding lots of places we had not previously been aware of. Quite often in Australia, we have heard people say that they had been to England and did not like it. Recently one said this after spending two days in London, en route for Norway! No one knows all of Britain. It would take a few lifetimes. During one of our trips to the Wirral, we had a remarkable experience.

One day we thought that we might have a trip along the North Wales coast, maybe go over to the Isle of Anglesey, and then return on an inland route. It was a sparkling day in early September, blue skies, bright sunshine, and all of the ingredients necessary for idyllic touring.

After about 45 minutes, Leni made the suggestion that with it being so clear, it might be a good idea to drive up the range of hills which had just appeared, ahead of us and to the left. Always wishing to please, I turned left as soon as I could and I started to climb. We were delighted to see a monastery, looking crisp and clear in the early morning sunlight. In all of our travels, we tried not to miss old churches and the like, so we pulled up outside of the main gate, parked the car, opened the gate and walked in.

There was a large vegetable garden in front of the building, and an ecclesiastic was hoeing some giant lettuces. We commented on the quality of the produce and asked if we could have a look around both the church and the grounds. As they were Franciscans, and thus self-supporting, he was more than pleased to show us through the building, where we bought a variety of souvenirs. Its name was Pantasaph and the monastery had been there since 1849.

The monk then suggested that we might like to explore the wooded hillside, pointing out that a path wound around and that it led to all of the Stations of the Cross. This sounded very exciting to us and so we set off. Better known to Catholics than to the other Christian denominations, there were fourteen 'stations', portraying incidents that occurred during Jesus Christ's journey to the site of His crucifixion and subsequently to His being laid in the tomb. We stopped and prayed at each Station, eventually reaching the awful scene of Christ crucified.

As we gazed up at the nails, and crown of thorns on the Saviour's head, we both commented that it was a shame that this most important of all of the stations should have been so neglected. It was badly in need of repainting and other repairs. However, there was nothing we could do about it, so we said a prayer and progressed to the last two stations, culminating in Jesus being laid in the tomb. Then we retraced our steps, and in a matter of a few minutes, we were re-approaching the crucifixion scene. As we got nearer, we were surprised to hear two voices in conversation. We had heard only bird sounds since we started our pilgrimage, and so it was quite a shock for us as we turned the corner to see two men standing below the cross, talking.

What happened then was quite amazing from several points of view. One of the two was a monk and the other was a workman in overalls, and he had with him a tool box and tins of paint. We introduced ourselves and I asked if they were going to repair the cross, etc, as we had only a few minutes before said how much it needed doing.

They both said that this was so, and at that I recognised the workman's accent. It was Teesside, or now Cleveland, where I come from. After saying how remarkable it was that after years of neglect, but only five minutes after our comments on the need for repair, here they were starting the work, I asked the workman about his antecedents. He was from Middlesbrough, and he was intrigued to know that at one time I had played football for them, as he was a very keen supporter of the team. As often happens between a player and a fan, this seemed to form a bond between us and our conversation was enlarged as we told them about our lives, of Australia, of living and working with Aborigines, and of our love of Jesus Christ, and how important He had always been in our lives.

Suddenly the workman, in a trembling voice, made a surprising confession. He said he was an alcoholic and he had come to Pantasaph to try to get rid of the addiction through prayer, Spartan living, hard work, and help from the

Franciscans. He had tried and tried, but that very morning, he said, he had packed his case and hidden it in the bushes, as he could not withstand the desire for drink any longer. That night, when it was dark, he had intended to walk out of his little room, pick up the case, and hitchhike the 150 miles back to Middlesbrough.

But, he said, having listened to us talking, he had realised that there was a good life ahead if he followed Jesus. The Franciscan said that God had sent us especially that day.

As we left them on the mountainside, we felt that we had been part of a miracle, and we prayed that the young man would find the source of true happiness in his life, Jesus Christ, and 'hold on to that which is good.' We hope that one day we might return to Pantasaph, to learn if they have news of my fellow Teessider.

My church in North Beach is to observe the Stations of the Cross this year, and for the first time we have plaques on the wall symbolising Christ's journey from the garden of Gethsemane to His crucifixion and the empty tomb. The rector has asked me to lead and organise it, as I have done in recent years with the Carol Service and Good Friday's Passion of our Lord. I told him about what happened at St Asaph and he said, 'Miracles do happen.'

This North Wales trip occurred when we were staying at Vera and Derrick Williams at Little Sutton, in that delightful peninsular, The Wiral, between Chester and Liverpool. Derrick was the lone sailor in our Combined Services football team, and we have maintained the closest of friendships over 46 years. And he hasn't changed. He walked my legs off every afternoon we were there. This was as predictable as his banana sandwiches at about 9.00 pm every night. Derrick still makes the best pork and meat pies I have ever tasted. Vera keeps very active and she has added a new 'sport' to her already lengthy list. She is actually in a darts team and plays in the league every week. On a more serious note, she also works voluntarily at a hospice, which for the benefit of readers who are not aware of their purpose, is a kind of nursing home caring for terminally ill patients.

We had a lovely time with them, and it seemed as though there had been no gap of eleven years between visits. One day they got all of the family together, Carol and Colin, eldest son Nicky, wife Margaret and family, and Roger, Nancy, and children. They have all done well and are prosperous. Nicky's story is interesting. He was a schoolteacher as was his wife, and for some years he was principal of a school in Germany that catered for the children of British Forces personnel. Ever since he was quite young, his main interest was bird nesting. He seemed to be part of a network, as especially in his teenage years, he used to shoot off to the North of Scotland or South Wales, or wherever an unusual or rare bird was nesting, on the receipt of 'bird's nest intelligence'.

Now this boyhood hobby has blossomed into a career. To the surprise of his family, he returned to England, bought a cottage in Lincolnshire, and proceeded to seek venues and institutions where he could give lectures on birds and their nests, eggs, etc. He has also developed into an ace photographer, many of his bird photographs appearing as colour plates in various bird books. His name, Nick Williams, appears below the pictures and we are very proud of five he has given us. They are brilliant and no description of mine would do them justice. They feature a robin, a puffin, golden eagles, an owl, and blue tits. The colours are fantastic, a word I rarely use, in fact, this may be the first time in this book, but in this case it is truly merited.

When we arrived at Carol's and Colin's house at Heswall, we had a very pleasant surprise awaiting us. Typical of sweet Carol, she had bought us a present, a particularly beautiful and well-chosen gift. It was the Readers' Digest 'Book of British Villages', perfect for our holiday, and inside the cover was a gift card saying 'To U Stan and A Leni, with love from Carol and Colin.'

Whilst in the Wirral we went to church two or three times, and we were gratified to see the number of children at the services. On one occasion there were about two hundred members of different organisations such as Scouts, Cubs, Guides, Girls' Brigade, Boys' Brigade, and the Sunday school. Unlike some churches, all of the church officers, i.e. wardens, clergy, church council, etc, lined the steps and talked to members of the congregation as they left. Leni and I were asked to the vicar's house for a cup of tea, as it was realised that we were visitors. It was the church that we had attended on the Sunday before we left for Australia. It was also very nice to renew acquaintance with that lovely Roman city, Chester. One of their churches, St Peter's, the Church at the Cross, was doing something practical to help third World countries, by selling coffee and tea from several countries, including some African, and we found them to be of good quality.

We also visited the cathedral, and found it so very interesting. Although we had seen it before, this time we were able to spend as long as we needed to really explore it. By the way, if you think of cathedrals and churches as things purely religious, you could not be more wrong. English history is to be found in every ancient church. Standing next to an effigy or walking through a door a thousand years old, gives you a feeling of awe. Someone long dead created it with tools and materials supposedly inferior to ours. His life is recalled through his work, but what have I created for posterity? Certainly nothing of note.

But back to Chester! People have indeed worshipped God there for over a millennium. St Werburgh, daughter of a king of Mercia, and a nun and abbess who lived in the seventh century, was buried in the church which bore her name and which stood in the same place as the cathedral now does, soon after 907. Many miracles were associated with her and they are featured in carvings in the quire. There is a beautiful stained glass window depicting her, in the west window. It is recorded that the church became an abbey in about 1092 and remained so for 450 years, until in 1540, Henry VIII dissolved it, but within a year it became a cathedral. If you are in Chester, visit the cathedral, and gaze on the tomb of a saint who walked this earth almost 1,400 years ago.

Now to the Midlands, and whilst staying at our friends, ex-IOSers, David and Kathy Parfrey, in Balsall Common in beautiful Warwickshire, we were able to visit many of our old haunts, including Coventry, Kenilworth, Warwick, Stratford, Leamington Spa, and Birmingham. Many very happy memories were recalled, and a special treat was when David took us for a trip in his aeroplane and we were able to view the castles of Kenilworth and Warwick, and the cathedral at Coventry, from the air.

Although we used to live half an hour from Stratford-upon-Avon, who could afford to be a few miles away from the home of the world's greatest playwright without paying a visit? We went around all of the places of interest, including the church where he was married, his wife's birthplace (Anne Hathaway's cottage), his birthplace, and of course, the theatre that commemorates him, by the beautiful river Avon. In one of the ancient houses a guide told us how the term 'the upper crust', which we know to mean the wealthy or high society, came into being. She told us that the bread was baked in the large oven we saw in the kitchen, and because of the lack of cleanliness and hygiene, the bottom half of the loaf was always covered in ash or dirt. So they cut off the top, the upper crust, for the gentry and the peasants ate the rest!

She also told us of how the servants kept warm in the winter. They used to smear themselves with goose-grease and sew themselves up! It does not bear thinking about.

After our first visit to David and Kathy's we went to see other dear friends in the Midlands. It was difficult trying to visit all of them. We were invited to have dinner at Peter and Jessica Fallows in West Hagley. They had lived at the back of us in our Hagley years and had moved since, but only to the next road. Their son, Julian, by then a partner in dad's solicitors practice (but a boy in the sixties, who used to watch TV with Leni), his fiancée, now his wife, Penny, and his sister, Catherine, gave us a wonderful welcome. Julian repaid Leni's caring in former days by seeing to her every need, and it was lovely to meet Penny. Catherine was as sweet as always, as was Jessica. It was most pleasant and memorable.

As was our habit of visiting churches, and particularly those in which we had worshipped previously, whilst staying at Kath and Arthur Noble's house in Halesowen, we took the opportunity of going back to the old church at Hagley Hall, the seat of the Lyttletons and the Cobhams. We knew the late Lord

Cobham in the sixties. He had been Governor General of New Zealand, also captain of Worcester County Cricket Club, and the Queen's Steward, being responsible, amongst other things, for organising her coronation.

As we entered, the vicar was at the door welcoming people, a very nice touch – quite unusual actually, and realised that he did not know us. We told him of our attendance in earlier days and took our seats.

The vicar made two announcements before the service, saying that one was sad and the other happy. Lady Cobham had died on the very day we chose to revisit our former church. Some of her family, all dressed in black, sat in the family pew, and thus ended an era. And the other announcement was to welcome Stan and Leni, who were revisiting after a 15 year absence!

I felt that the following subject should be treated outside of any chronological order. The Boro' or, as Teessiders pronounced it, 'The Borrer', is part of everyday life up in what is now called County Cleveland. 'Owd the Borrer gerr on?' would be perhaps the most asked question in that part of the world. Translated from the vernacular it means, 'How did Middlesbrough Football Club 'get on', or fare, in their game today?' We were brought up in an atmosphere of football being of vital importance to the working man, for that is how it used to be – the working man's game.

Today, we read of big corporations owning deluxe suites in the best positions on the grounds, of millions of pounds being spent on players, more millions paid by advertisers, and by the television networks – and the backbone of the professional game, the rank-and-file working class supporter, has been largely ignored.

The disaster at Sheffield Wednesday's ground will push the clubs to do more for them, as public attention has been focussed on the problem, but for years the working man stood in the terraces in the pouring rain, or whatever weather prevailed.

The 'Bob end' was the name for the terraces behind the goals before the war and for a few years afterwards. Supporters used to walk for miles to Ayresome Park, the home of the Boro', as a shilling was quite an investment for labourers whose pre-war wage was thirty shillings for forty hours work. The better off caught the Corporation bus specials and some went on their bikes, and left them at houses near the ground, who used to charge them a penny for looking after them.

The local newspaper, 'The Evening Gazette', gave excellent coverage every night, keeping the fans informed about injuries to players and about the next opposition. The 'Sports Gazette' on a Saturday gave full match coverage and all of the results local and national. People who could not go to the match, maybe for financial reasons, would hang about at the nearest bus stop, to await the first returning spectator to ask him the result.

The 'Boys' End' used to cost sixpence and an illustration of the value of that coin, is that I only managed to go to a match four times before the war when I was a boy. I always walked and it was four or five miles each way.

My first visit was magical. It was on a Wednesday afternoon and the school was given the day off. The game was England versus Wales, an international match, and for us lads it was the greatest day of our lives. I remember very little about the game, but I do recall that England's outside right was Stanley Matthews, who was to become a legend and the greatest player who ever played for England. Seventeen years or so later I was to play with him for England. If I had only known!

Other games I saw were Middlesbrough games versus Everton, Brentford, and Sunderland. The Everton game had a very controversial incident in it. Their centre forward was the greatest of them all. Dixie Dean actually scored sixty goals in season 1927–28, a feat that will never be beaten. But that day he enraged everyone of us in the Boys' End. Right in front of us he went up to head the ball, but he missed it and instead hit it with the palm of his hand into the net. The referee did not see it and gave a goal to Everton. We were really upset and booed Dean whenever he was near the ball.

The Brentford game also had an incident, which was rare in those days, although too common today. James, their centre half, was sent off for fouling, and he was the first I ever saw being sent to the dressing room. Since then, I have probably only seen two or three players similarly dealt with.

The Sunderland game was the game of the season always, as it was a derby game, that is, they were the nearest club to the Boro'! That it was the third Round of the FA Cup made it even more important, and the ground was packed.

Unfortunately, 'we' lost 2–0 and I remember that the star of Sunderland was Raich Carter, who in later years I was to play against, and later still he actually managed Middlesbrough.

My next visit to Ayresome Park was to be as a junior player, playing for South Bank Juniors in a North Riding Junior Cup Final. And then, of course, I was to play for the Boro, but this period of my life is written about elsewhere in this life story.

One of the things I looked forward to on our England trip was to revisit Middlesbrough's Ayresome Park, but I knew that they had problems. However,

I was stunned to discover that the club had been 'locked out'. This ancient club, part of the lifeblood of Teesside, and for so long a source of pride, was not allowed in their own ground. Apparently, their debts were such that the creditors had called for receivers to be put in. It was so sad, but we were allowed to have a look around after we explained the circumstances of our visit.

We sat in the stand and looked onto that hallowed turf, which was home to a long list of Boro' favourites for over a hundred years. So many had played for their countries; two – Wilf Mannion and George Hardwick – had even played for Great Britain; and the various teams over many years had been known for their good football, never rough, always fair – and yet the 1986 players could not even train on the ground. That day they were training on Redcar beach.

Whilst up in the North-East we caught up with two of my old colleagues from the Boro', George Hardwick, once captain of England, and Johnny Spuhler, who used to sprint so fast down the right wing that the fans said that he could catch pigeons. His running style was superb and a treat to watch. We saw George in his office in Darlington, but despite having written to one another for many years, we did not see him again, but we hope that there will be another day.

Our first stop in our native North-East was at Scarborough, that beautiful resort on the Yorkshire coast. We actually stayed with Bert and Margaret Palfreyman, whom we had met in North Beach! Their daughter lives here in Australia, and they make biennial visits and always attend our church. We thought that we knew something of North Yorkshire, but Bert proved us wrong as he took us to some magnificent places, including Thornton-le-Dale, surely one of Britain's most beautiful villages; Scalby Forest, with its unique forest 'museum'; and quaint and lovely Pickering.

When we left we made for Barnard Castle, the home of John and Nancy Spuhler, good friends since 1947 when I rejoined Middlesbrough FC. To get there I worked out a route through the Yorkshire countryside. It was a most beautiful day, warm, sunny, blue skies, and humming to the sounds of England that we had almost forgotten about. There is nothing in Australia, quite like a lovely English summer's day out in the countryside, with the sweet-smelling grass; the buzz of the bees and other insects, as they busy themselves in the golden buttercups, and other wildflowers in the meadow; the many bird songs emanating from the trees and hedgerows, and the sounds of farm animals mooing or 'mairing'.

We were idyllically happy twisting and turning around narrow roads leading to and over the hills, the sight of small villages with the old churches on the highest points. We visited Lastingham, an ancient village with an historic church, and a tenth century crypt containing the tomb and relics of 7th century Saint Cedd.

This interest in Lastingham was enhanced by the knowledge that our Canadian Rickabys listed it as one of the places where members of the family lived three hundred years ago.

We had told Nancy that we would arrive at about 5.00 pm, so when we entered the High Street at 4.00 pm we decided to park the car and have a walk around 'Barney' for an hour because there is nothing worse than visitors arriving early, before the hostess is ready.

But when we rang the bell at 5.00 pm precisely, Nancy appeared quite upset. She had thought that we were coming much earlier in the day and was very worried lest we had had an accident! However, we soon got over that, and once again, we had a great time. As always, Nancy was very involved locally, including being an office bearer in the Women's Institute, to which she took Leni. They, like us, are doting grandparents, and the first evening was taken up by discussing our respective grandchildren and the showing of photographs.

Johnny and Nancy both looked well, and told us how they played golf all the year round, and lawn bowls in the summer. We went on a number of trips, including one to nearby High Force, the highest waterfall in Britain, and Cotherstone, where my cousin June used to live. They wanted to see the estate and were amazed at what we showed them; two thatched gardeners' cottages with high and wide wrought iron gates between; the beautiful 'Dower' house 200 yards up the drive; and then as we walked around the bend we saw 'Lancelands'. This magnificent building was set in lovely grounds with a pool in front of the house and tennis courts behind. Adjoining the spacious gardens was the home farm, and the farmhouse where a manager lived with his family. June's husband, Tony, owned the shooting rights on the moors which started at the end of their property. However, Tony has passed on and June now lives in London.

June's mother, Auntie Margaret, now 95, lived in a Nursing Home in Barnard Castle, and we took her out for a drive in the car. She asked to go 'up the Dale' meaning Teesdale, which she said is the most beautiful of all of the Dales. She certainly was right and yet very few people in Britain would think of a visit to this enchanting part of England. If you have not been there, I recommend it.

During our Northern safari, one could have thought that as Aussies, we were following in the footsteps of Captain Cook. Although not deliberately so doing, we did visit Marton, where he was born; delightful ancient Great Ayton, a lovely village with a stream running through it, where the boy Cook went to school; Sleights, the very old fishing village where he worked in a shop; and Whitby, the historic seaport where the Endeavour was built and where he first went to sea.

Whitby is worthy of more than a cursory visit, as it is steeped in history. Due to the synod held at the Abbey in the seventh century, the dates of Easter were fixed for all time. The Abbess Hilda became a Saint and lived a remarkable life.

Another place well worth a visit is Buxton Spa in the Derbyshire Peak District. The journey is really special, as it matters not from which direction one has come, the views and countryside are spectacular. Outside a hotel I photographed Leni, as there was a plaque in the wall stating, 'Mary Queen of Scots slept here' – and Leni held a sign saying, 'and so did Leni', but unfortunately due to a reflection, it is not possible to read it!

Whilst in this part of England, one that I must confess we did not know much about, we were driving along a country lane, just admiring the scenery, the sun was shining, it was the first Saturday in July, a glorious day – when we saw a notice on a fence at a crossroads. It was so intriguing that, for people like us, as free as the birds and just letting things happen, we could not resist investigating. The sign said, 'Headon Well Dressing Two Miles', and an arrow pointed us in the right direction.

We conjured up in our minds what 'well dressing' could possibly be. We certainly were not the least aware of the delights that awaited us at the 'Headon Well Dressing Festival', which was its full title. It transpired that this event was best known in some of the villages of neighbouring county Derbyshire, but that Headon, in Nottinghamshire, had revived the ancient originally pagan custom in 1981.

To explain, Headon, the 'high hill' of the Anglo Saxons, has been inhabited since the earliest times. Men of the Stone Age, Romans, Vikings, and Normans, have all left their mark on this tiny village, and in the 13th century church of St Peter, are thought to lie the remains of one of the earliest Sheriffs of Nottingham, Simon de Headon, the King's Sheriff in 1259.

On the high ground where fresh water was often difficult to find, the well became a centre for religious magic and worship. In the Middle Ages the well names were changed to those of Saints and Headon's Ladywell was named after Mary the mother of Jesus.

We were taken to the well on a trailer pulled by a farm tractor, and although bumpy, we enjoyed the trip. The sight that awaited us was unique and remarkable. Above a brick arch, which protected the well, was a magnificent picture of the church made entirely from flower petals, with the words, 'Upon this Rock' and 'St Peter's Headon' woven into the picture. There were also 'banners' on either side of the main picture with '19' on the left and '86' on the right. The brick arch bears the date 1718, but behind lies one much older. The exact date is not known, but it was awesome to stand in front of the well, and imagine a Viking warrior or a Roman soldier stooping to drink of its cool refreshing waters.

We were taken back to the village hall and more pleasant surprises were in store. Refreshments included the ubiquitous cups of tea and lots of homemade cakes, scones, and sandwiches, were available and we certainly took advantage! So far, so very good, but more was to come. In front of the hall was a troupe of morris dancers performing English dances that go back hundreds of years. They were followed by mummers dressed in medieval costumes, and then a group of clog dancers entertained us with dances from a number of Northern Counties, including my own county Durham. During an interval we spoke to one of the girls and we said that we were on holiday from Australia, and this led to a very nice occurrence which typifies the Brits' affection for Aussies and all things Australian.

The last clog dance was to the tune of 'Waltzing Matilda'! We thanked them, and after our few hours of pure Englishness, except for the last dance, we went on our way. At that time of the year in England, the summer evenings are long and we were able to get up to Chester in daylight.

Readers will, I hope, excuse the lack of chronological order, as I recall interesting events during our holiday. Whilst at Kathy and David's in Warwickshire's 'leafy lanes', I enjoyed very much two special sporting occasions, one cricket and the other football. My old friend, Les Deakins, invited me to Edgbaston, to see a day's cricket. New Zealand were playing an England select XI, and I was invited to join the Warwickshire County Club's committee in their dining-room – I was very pleased at this and when I entered the room, what occurred was quite paradoxical. They all stood up and eagerly reached out to shake my hand. All of my generation, they were all remembering the Stan Rickaby they all recalled playing for West Bromwich Albion, and I was quite overcome. I was thinking how honoured I was to be meeting these distinguished Birmingham people of great note, but it was apparent that they were thinking similarly about me. One of them I knew quite well. He was Alan Smith, the secretary of Warwickshire at that time, and soon to be virtual boss of the prestigious and controlling Test and County Cricket Board.

I also renewed friendship with Ken Kelly, one of England's top sporting photographers for many years. During the afternoon session of play, I sat in the room where the players watch the game, and I had the pleasure to meet Gladstone Small, the twelfth man, but since then he has played many times for England.

Maybe at this juncture, I should record that since our trip, dear friend Les Deakins has died. We received his and his wife Nora's Christmas card, something that had been a habit for a very long time. A few weeks later we had a letter from Nora, telling us of dear friend Les's death. Cognizant that really it was very private, I would still like to quote from it as I hope that readers will derive the same assurance of the Hereafter as Leni and I did. She said in part that, '... I am so sad to have to tell you since preparing the overseas Christmas cards, Les's condition deteriorated and he passed to the Higher Life on Thursday, 19.10.89. .... There will be a great void in my life, but I know he is preparing a new home for us, and we will meet again one day.'

The second sporting occasion was when I rang the WBA chairman, Syd Lucas, who had been a rabid supporter and good friend in my playing days. It is pleasant to state that he got me the job in the offices of Facchinos Biscuits and Meddocreem ice cream, later leading to the Neilsons and Lyons positions. But it is sad to record that in all my life that was the only help I ever had, except for my appointment to Neilsons, which was due to Havard Knowles' invitation, itself a spin off from Syd's initial good turn.

WBA were playing a Moscow team in a pre-season game and I looked forward to it immensely. Incredibly, I actually got lost on the way to the ground! I, who knew Birmingham like the palm of my hand, got lost! But I just made it in time. Not knowing where to park, I slowed down near the players' entrance (what memories that brought back) and asked the official on duty where I could park. I was surprised that he said, 'Hello Stan, go in the official car park and tell them I said to let you in!' When I reached it, the man on the gate said, 'Hello Stan, fancy seeing you!' I felt at home again. I had not been to the ground for 17 years and I was still recognised.

It was an emotional moment when I took my seat and looked down on that green sward on which I had played so many times and where I had enjoyed so many triumphs, and finally bitter disappointment. And a little of the latter pursued me again. At the end of the game I was invited into the guests' refreshment room, where I could have joined the hangers-on, and imbibed a surfeit of intoxicating liquor, but that is not my habit. On such occasions I deliberately have a cup of tea, not that I do not like a whiskey or brandy and ginger ale. I waited quite a time for a director to leave the boardroom to say hello to one of the club's better servants, but in the end I just walked out into the night. Things had not changed.

We spent our last week back down in Surrey at Mike and Sandy Leathleys. It was very pleasant and relaxing and the weather held right into October. We walked a lot and paid another visit to London where we saw a show in a theatre off Piccadilly, with Eric Sykes playing the leading part. It was very funny and he is remarkable, his timing is perfect, and yet he is deaf!

A friend we made at Holmesdale Park Nursing Home, named Mrs Cox, was a most interesting person. She was in her eighties, and still lithe and attractive, which was probably the reward for her athletic life when she was a fencer and represented Great Britain in the 1924 Olympic Games in London. When we went to her apartment to say farewell, she insisted on giving us two of her books, which were part of the library built up by her deceased husband. They were parts one and two of 'The Life of Jane de St Remy de Valois' and were printed in Paris in 1791, which was two years after the beginning of the French Revolution.

Whilst at Mike's we took the opportunity of visiting my cousin Mary, June's sister, in London, and we enjoyed a happy reunion, which included a visit to the Cutty Sark (the famously fast tea clipper-ship) at Greenwich.

We had bought a car a week or two after our arrival, an Ital, and it had served us well during our 8,500 miles of driving up and down England. Obviously, we had to sell it before leaving, but this did not prove to be a problem. We got a good price and it worked out to have been cheap motoring – very much cheaper than hiring a car.

After saying our goodbyes to all the friends, both staff and residents, we had made at Holmesdale, Mike took us to Gatwick airport and with the holiday of a lifetime over, we flew off to Australia. Apart from a few hours delay at Singapore and some 'Europeans' trying to pinch our seats on the last lap to Perth, we relaxed and enjoyed the journey. Air Lanka was excellent, as was British Airways out of Singapore.

Due to the delay in setting off, we did not get to Perth until about 4.00 am, and we were both surprised and delighted to find dear Margarete, Toby, and Elizabeth, still waiting for us. It was wonderful to see them again and they took us home, and of course, we talked for hours, interspersed with hugs, kisses, and cuddles.

CHAPTER THIRTY NINE
BACK TO PERTH AND WORK

I went straight to work the next day and soon we had settled in again as though nothing had happened. Margarete and the children told us all about their trip with Ron to Kununurra, and huge man-made Lake Argyle, near which are the Argyle diamond mines, the scene of the discovery of some very fine stones. We saw a lot of each other for some time, I suppose trying to make up for the absence, and to tell each other what had happened in the long seven months of separation.

We were straight back into church activity. I was still editor of the magazine and I had missed only one issue, as they had not been able to organise what was the midwinter edition around about June. At Christmas, as always, I arranged the joint carol service with the Catholic church, and I put on a most successful Christmas party, the first we had ever had. It started with all the lights out in the church hall, and then there was a knock on the door. Someone opened it and I had arranged for a group of carol singers to don winter clothing, with blobs of cotton wool sticking to it to simulate snow, a young boy carried a lantern, and if it had not been about 20°C outside, it could have been back in England.

Shrove Tuesday, or Pancake Tuesday, had not been celebrated until I started it in about 1985, and it had become a feature in the church calendar. I had written initially in the magazine, that we should do as was done in many other countries, and have a party on the eve prior to Ash Wednesday, the beginning of Lent. I noted that this year, 1991, it did not happen, no doubt because I no longer hold an official position.

Pancake Tuesday 1987, was one that the congregation will never forget. Not for the party, but for the reason it was cancelled. Velma, our ex-rector Lewis Firman's wife, was always very active in the church, enthusiastically supporting everything, not least the pancake party. On that February morning dear Velma died. She was murdered by a young man. Apparently, I must have known him as he attended Sunday school when I used to teach and run it. The murderer was sentenced to life imprisonment. What a tragedy.

Poor Lewis. They were, as he said, "Darby and Joan" and inseparable.

For some long time nothing of any great import occurred in my personal or family life, except that Margarete got married again! Ron is a New Zealander, he had considerable success here selling real estate, and he hopes to be able to resume this profession in England.

In the church we encountered many problems, however. In common with many other main line churches, a number of the congregation started a push for change. I called them charismatic and many others and I were upset by them, as we did not want change. We were brought up with the Anglican liturgy and beliefs, and no one was going to change us. If some wanted change, then let them go to the several other churches, who were also charismatic, was our view.

Lewis Firman had left and taken up a position as chaplain at a church school, and for many months we had a priest in charge during what they term the interregnum. Eventually, we got a new priest and we hoped that he would sort things out. No doubt he thought he was doing the right thing, but by encouraging the charismatic group to hold their own services in a school hall, under the aegis of St Michael and all Angels, North Beach, was totally wrong, in my opinion and that of many more. It split the church and it will take a long time to recover.

I was sacked from the magazine editorship under the guise that I had too much to do, having been unwell once or twice, but really it was because of articles I wrote putting, "Another point of view." It would appear that we traditionalists were not allowed to hold a contrary opinion. The 'charismatics' were allowed to do anything, change anything, say anything, but when we offered a differing viewpoint, we were unkind, unloving, etc.

I still do all I can to help the church, and I always will, but St Michael's will never be the same.

However, while all these things were going on, my health must have been deteriorating and soon there was to be a crisis.

CHAPTER FORTY

OPEN HEART SURGERY

After taking pills for my heart condition for about eight years, without anything untoward happening, I was about to get out of the car to take Leni to lunch at a local restaurant, when I felt quite ill. I could not breathe properly, so I sat back in my seat for a couple of minutes, and then I tried again. I got out of the car and locked the door, but I only got as far as the bonnet when I realised that I had not the strength to make it. Leni wanted to call the ambulance, but never wanting to make a fuss, I declined and insisted on driving to the doctor. It was Saturday and fortunately our doctor's surgery opens every day of the week.

I crept along hugging the kerb and stopped two or three times at lay-bys, eventually reaching my objective. Doctor Pam Quartermass was on duty, and after examining me she rang for the ambulance, which came very quickly, and we were on our way to the Sir Charles Gairdner hospital.

They kept me in until Tuesday morning, doing lots of tests and putting me on a drip. They decided that my tablets had to be changed, as some kind of a build up had occurred. After lots of advice, my daughter Margarete took me home to pick up my car, and I drove straight to the office.

This was around September 1989, and for several months, as long as I did not exert myself, I felt all right. Until on 9th May 1990, we had our friends, Patrick and Yvonne Lynch, over for dinner. We washed the dishes and watched the television for a while and at about 12.30 am I felt more breathless than ever before. I knew that this was worse than previously and after one refusal to Leni's suggestion to ring for the ambulance, the intensity of my condition made me agree.

Again the service of St John's Ambulance was brilliant, and in no time I was lying on my back in the vehicle, with oxygen mask on and the attendant taking my pulse, blood pressure, and temperature. On arrival, I was taken again to the Intensive Care Unit, and kept there until the Sunday, when I was moved to the

Cardiology Ward. There it was decided that I should have open-heart surgery. I was sent home on the Tuesday, I went to see a surgeon at the Royal Perth Hospital in Perth City, who explained the operation, pointing out that there was a 2% risk of not surviving the surgery. I knew that, but having it articulated did not exactly help me. I was told to go home to await their call, and this happened quickly. I had to report to the Royal Perth Hospital on Saturday, 19th May by 6.00 pm, for an operation on Tuesday, 22nd May.

I felt sorry for Leni when she left me. She looked so sad, but fortunately our friend, Patrick, who had brought us to the hospital, was there to take her home. It transpired that Yvonne made a meal for Leni and they both did all that they could to comfort her.

The caring I received from the moment I got into the hospital bed was superb, as it had been in the Sir Charles Gairdner. I just cannot speak too highly of the staff of both hospitals.

On the Sunday I went to the hospital chapel, and with only one other patient, took Holy Communion. This helped me to 'get myself together', both physically and spiritually. Poor Leni kept visiting me, and in the afternoon Margarete and Ron brought Toby and Elizabeth to see me. It felt strange lying there not really knowing how things would go on the Tuesday, as after all, I had been told about that 2%.

I had plenty of consultations on the Monday with the anaesthetist, the surgeon, the nursing sister who was responsible for monitoring my progress, and the physiotherapist who explained the way to breathe deeply and to cough after the operation. I was told that I was probably going to be first in the theatre on the morrow, and at last it came to Monday night with just a few hours to go. I was given something to make me sleep, and with prayers to God for success with my 'op', I dropped off. The next I knew was being awakened surrounded by two or three people in white, busily putting me into a white robe, and injecting me. I cannot have been conscious much longer, and then the surgeons and anaesthetist literally had my heart in their hands. The miracle of modern medicine was initiated.

What were those unbearably bright white lights? Who were all these people in white garments scurrying about, and what were all the pipes and lines, which seemed to be issuing from my body?

'He is awake,' said someone who went on to explain that this incredible achievement of modern science had been performed successfully. Of course, I had known nothing about it, nor did I even have to worry about it, but for Leni and Margarete time must have almost stood still.

I kept lapsing into unconsciousness and waking again. Finally, I lay there sufficiently awake to realise that I was most uncomfortable, and that my back was extremely painful. It was the old back problem of the disc removal causing an inability to lie on my back. I wriggled around putting my hands under my body to try to change its position, even if only slightly.

So this was the Intensive Care Unit. There was no night, only day, as it seemed that all was blinding light. The ceiling was white and was a succession of small squares, and I must have examined every one as I tried to get back to sleep to escape from the pain in my back. Whenever the nurses realised my predicament they put something in my drip and I would lapse back to sleep again. Those days were the longest in my life. Earlier I wrote of my farming experience, when I was in the army and 'stooking' corn, and hating it, I hesitated asking anyone the time, because of the bitter disappointment which overcame me when I found that the clock had barely moved. This was just the same, but worse! There was no difference between night and day, as no doubt it was necessary for doctors and nurses to be able to see all patients at a glance.

A few hours after the operation I am told that Leni and Margarete came to see me. I did not remember their visit, which ended apparently by my asking them to go! I was told that everything had gone well, and this was great news. At about this time, I believe, I was encouraged to take deep breaths, and to hold them for a while before exhaling. The objective was to inflate the lungs fully, as one was not so, and to cough up phlegm. This was quite painful and the physiotherapist's visits were not wholly welcome at this stage.

The most horrifying thing was the bizarre dream I had over and over again. It seemed that whenever I had it, I woke up feeling scared. Strangely as I recount it, it seems to be funny, but I can assure you that it really was terrifying.

I was in a large hall, and both the walls and the floor consisted of pink tiles and pale blue tiles. This was so overwhelming that I never knew which part of the hall I was in. I was forever trying to escape, but after my frenzied efforts, I would be leaning breathlessly against the wall, looking up. I knew that there was a way out, and that towards the top of one of the walls was a small balcony, which led to our room. Now the point that we had a room of our own was another factor that bred more fear. You see, Ray Barlow, with whom I played at West Bromwich Albion, saw me trying to get out and he warned me that Joe Kennedy, another one of our players, would go mad when he found that Leni and I had the only double-room. Obviously, therefore, the team was staying here.

The most ridiculous occurrences were when a chorus of dancers and singers kept dancing across the hall. They sang a song, which I could remember for the first couple of days after the operation, both words and music. I intended to sing it to Margarete, to see if I had composed it, or if I had heard it somewhere else.

The troupe were accepted by me as perfectly normal during the dream, which was repeated many times, but that just shows how mixed up I was. All of the artistes were dressed the same, as one would expect. They had long cloak like dresses down to their ankles, and with square shoulders. They were also of a square pattern like the walls and the floor, and in the same colours.

Nothing too bizarre so far, one might say, but wait until I describe their heads. They all differed as heads are wont to do, but how about when I tell you that one's head was a kettle, and the others were a teapot, a cup, a saucer, a frying pan, a milk jug, a knife, a fork, a dessert-spoon, and a sugar bowl!

Every time I woke I felt that I had really experienced this, and I would lie in bed recalling the song and then slowly returning to normality. I had read about the possibility of bizarre dreams, in the truly excellent handbook, which I was given to read a week before the op, and it certainly happened to me.

Eventually I was moved to another ward. It was wonderful to get away from all of those lights. During all of this time I had only had a couple of small portions of soup, and the thought of food was repugnant. However, I did cheer myself up by thinking that this would mean a reduction in weight. This had been the bane of my life since I stopped playing football. You can imagine how shattered I was when one morning they got me out of bed to sit on some scales, and I had put on five kilograms! The explanation was that I had had large quantities of fluids pumped into me – I looked at my stomach and it was gross!

I received lots of cards from family, friends, and colleagues, who were also friends of course. The office card had lots of names and messages on it and was especially heartening. The day after receiving this one, I received another which touched my heart. Anne Marsden, one of our officers, had been away the day that the office card was sent, and on discovering that she had missed out, she sent me a personal card.

My favourite grandson, Toby ('I am the only one you've got,' he says), bought me a little bear in a glass capsule filled with water. When it is upturned, lots of little red hearts float around the bear and a notice on his chest says, 'Be mine.' There has never been any doubt about that.

I was only in the hospital for seven days after the operation, and when I left, Leni could not believe that I could walk to Margarete's car, awaiting me in the street outside. For two or three weeks the Silver Chain nurse called to dress my 'wounds', that is on my left leg from which a vein or part of it had been removed to be incorporated in the heart surgery, and on my chest where the ribs had been opened up to get at the heart. Just writing about it reminds me about the miracle that is open-heart surgery.

An important part of the recuperative process was the exercise programme to be done in the home. Leni and I did it together and it has been of great value to both of us.

I was back to work a fortnight after the operation, despite Leni's pleadings! But it isn't as if I dig ditches for a living. It has been mildly amusing to be asked daily how I am, and at the time of writing, now five months later, I am probably fitter than most of the enquirers.

Time went on and Margarete and Ron talked often about going to live in England. He had never been there, and as a Kiwi he had an immigration problem, but Margarete and I went to the British Consul's office in Perth, and we eventually satisfied all requirements. In effect, he had a year's work permit and depending on his employment success, he would be able to apply for permanent residency.

At about that time the England cricket team arrived in Perth. I watched a number of games on television but my hopes for regaining the Ashes were reduced to, yes, ashes. I had hoped to watch the final Test match on TV in England, but that too was not to be. Although I am both English and Australian, when the Ashes series is on, I am purely a 'Pom'. Being a Pom cricket fan is never a good thing to be in Australia. If we are winning, we dare not show our pleasure for fear of offending, and if we are losing....

Eventually, all of the problems facing what is always a worrying time were solved, and the dreaded day arrived when our family sold up and left us to go to England. This was our second such experience, and it got no better second time around. Patrick and Yvonne kindly took them all to the airport, leaving us to try to pacify one another through our tears. We had secured temporary accommodation for them with our old friend Bill Matthews in London. They stayed there a few months during which time Toby went to an East London school, Elizabeth studied at home, Margarete got a good job as a home economist, and Ron worked in a bakery. Then he got a good position in Norwich in real estate and they bought a house there.

But to digress once again.

One day in January 1988, a friend gave me an issue of a weekly newspaper which was published in Australia called, 'British Soccer Week.' After reading it and finding it to be really excellent, in fact, as good as anything in the UK, I wondered if they would like an article or two by me, so I dropped a line to Bill Cranny, the publisher, telling him of my experience as a footballer.

Immediately he rang, we met, and the article or two became more than one hundred, all of a thousand words each! I thoroughly enjoyed it. You may remember that the first job I was ever offered was as a junior reporter on the 'Evening Gazette', and I did a few articles for the 'Sunday People' and another magazine, but one hundred thousand words!

Eventually I found it difficult to find worthwhile subjects, as I had gone through the whole gamut of nostalgia, linking the happenings in the soccer world of my day to those of today. If we return to England it has been mooted that I will start to write again, this time interviewing old players and asking them a series of questions regarding their playing days, and leading to their opinions on how the game has changed and whether for the better or not.

CHAPTER FORTY ONE
SPANISH CATASTROPHE

Margarete had been back in England for a year and a half and we wondered what we should do for the best, missing our family as we did, so we decided to rent out our home again and go off on a nine months trip. We felt that we were lucky when we found a nice good-looking married couple in their late twenties, who needed to rent for a few months prior to buying. He was an Israeli Australian, she was from Mauritius, and he was transferring his cabinet making business from Melbourne to Perth. He said that he had door and window making machinery which was superior to anything here in the West. She was in the early stages of pregnancy and it was rather nice to think that the baby would be born whilst they were living in our home. All seemed well, so off we went. We had made a lovely new friend, Rosie Knight, in the year preceding our trip, and it was a wonderful surprise to find her waiting to see us off at the International Airport, which is twenty miles from where she lives with her husband, John. Lucy Corlett, a friend from our church, was also there, as was the ever-faithful Alan Smith, my friend from my accountancy days.

We changed planes at Kuala Lumpur and flew to Penang in Malaysia, where we spent a few pleasant and restful days at the 'Holiday Inn'. We found the taxi drivers very helpful and we were amused at the names they gave themselves, such as 'Danny Boy' and 'Van Gogh', so that their clients would easily remember them. As 'Danny Boy' was driving us through the countryside he pointed out the huge rubber plantations, explaining that rubber is their biggest export, and that it was all due to the Brits when Malaysia was part of the Empire. They planted all of the trees, and developed the whole business through to rubber production. We were pleased to hear praise for the British settlers, as in Australia they seem to be criticised for the things they did, that perhaps today may seem wrong (although probably normal 200 years ago), and very little praise is given for the enormous number of things they did right.

Then back to Kuala Lumpur where we caught the plane for London. It was an uneventful journey and I enjoyed it as always. Some people dislike flying, but the flying hotels of today I find very amenable. Total peace, no telephones, sleep when you want to, have a read, a drink or a meal, watch a film, all waited on – terrific. Also, I like to examine the goodies they bring around for passengers to buy, as one can often get unusual souvenirs and electrical goods like razors, at very good prices.

Getting from London airport to Norwich Railway Station was much more difficult than the 13,000 miles from Perth to London. On our last trip home, Mike Leathley's chauffeur was awaiting us with the Rolls Royce, but this time we had to make our own way. Incidentally, we have lost touch with Mike and Sandy, last heard of cruising the Mediterranean in the fantastic boat they bought with the proceeds of the sale of their nursing home, etc.

We were given a couple of wrong directions getting across London to Liverpool Street Station, and it was with relief that we settled down for the last lap of our journey to the great cathedral city and capital of Norfolk, Norwich.

Margarete was waiting for us with a huge bunch of flowers for her mum, and with tears streaming down her cheeks she escorted us to her home, less than five minutes walk from the station. Their house was only thirty yards from the charming River Wensum, and we were soon taken on an escorted tour, first of the house and then of the environs of the great ancient cathedral, leading to the centre of the city itself. If you haven't been to Norwich, you have been missing out. It is truly superb, with so much to see, such as four museums and lots of medieval buildings and places of interest.

Later in the day we met Toby as he came out of the Norwich school, which is attached to the cathedral. He looked very smart in his school uniform, and affectionate as always, he hugged his Nanna with tears in his eyes. His school actually dates back to 1096, and Lord Nelson is just one of its many famous former pupils. Being without a car, we walked home, chatting all the way, trying to make up for a year and a half of separation. It was only ten minutes walk and then we eagerly awaited Elizabeth, whose school came out a little later than Toby's. She looked gorgeous with her beautiful looks and blonde hair, and she was so happy to see us again. We all remembered how in Australia I often picked them up from school, how they ran down our stairs shouting 'What's for tea Nanna,' before they went into what still is today, 'the children's bedroom,' to take off their blazers, etc.

Of course, we talked until very late and they were all delighted with the many gifts Leni had brought them from Australia, Malaysia, and from Malaysia Airlines.

After a few days of walking everywhere, as the city is only a few minutes from Margarete's house, we bought a car. It was a very good buy, had three seat belts in the back, so that we could all get in, and for £2,200 and a high miles per gallon, we were delighted.

Margarete worked in a very select boutique in the city and after getting the children off to school, she walked to work. All three of them walked to school and work, something that very few people in the industrialised world are able to do these days.

It was a lovely English summer and with the long light evenings, we were able to go for car trips and walks and really enjoy beautiful Norwich and the surrounding countryside. It was so unlike Western Australia where it is dark by 7.00 pm, even in mid-summer. Our family were able to come with us at the weekends, although Toby went to school on Saturday mornings, and our daughter went to work. Leni and I used to love to go to church on Sunday mornings, quite often to the great cathedral, and sometimes they all used to come with us. However, one Sunday I was trying to get Toby out of bed to come to the cathedral when he said, 'Ah! Poppa I am tired.' When I told him that he should go to church every Sunday he had a good excuse up his sleeve. He said, 'But Poppa, I have been six times this week already!' You see, the school assembled in the cathedral at 8.45 am, Monday to Saturday, for a service. I have always said that our grandson should be a politician, as he always seems to be able to extricate himself from the most difficult of dilemmas. Needless to say, we let him go back to sleep.

Norfolk and Suffolk are two of the loveliest counties in Britain, with literally hundreds of ancient villages with their seven or eight hundred-year-old churches full of local history, and built by the wealthy merchants of those days.

There is a village named Worstead, which gave its name to the worsted cloth woven by the Flemish weavers who migrated to the village in the Middle Ages.

We covered three or four thousand miles between June and December, and between journeys to our friends, Peter and Jessica Fallows, in West Hagley, Worcestershire; Derrick and Vera Williams in Little Sutton near Chester; Carol and Colin Harkness in West Kirby; and Kath and Arthur Noble in Whitby, North Yorkshire. Yet when I looked through a book about East Anglia on our return home where it listed 34 places classified as 'Heritage Towns' we had only visited 8 of them! I also read that there are 164 museums and 69 ancient monuments, and then of course there are the Broads, 300–400 miles of waterways , a mecca for 'boaties' from all over Britain and indeed many countries in Europe. These remarkable waterways were created by people of the Middle Ages through digging peat for fuel! Driving through the beautiful countryside, we were often surprised to go around a bend in a country lane and see what appeared to be yachts in the middle of a field. If you have not been to East Anglia, make it your next holiday venue.

When we stayed in Hagley, I took the opportunity of seeing a game of soccer at the Hawthorns, West Bromwich Albion were playing Port Vale, the team we beat in the semi-final of the FA Cup when I was an Albion player. It was very nostalgic for me and at half time I was invited into the club restaurant where I met Johnnie Nichols, Jim Dugdale and a number of old supporters, all of whom recognised me, but there was also a very sad moment for me. Several people shook hands and after I shook the hand of one of them, John Nichols asked, 'You know who that is, don't you?' I replied that I didn't, and I was shocked when John said, 'It's Ron,' meaning Ronnie Allen, Albion's great centre forward for many years. I played more than 200 games with him after we both joined the club within a few days of each other, but at first I didn't know him. He was never very well-built, but he looked so frail. I was very worried about the way he looked.

Whilst at Whitby we took the opportunity of revisiting all those beautiful towns and villages in the Yorkshire Dales and the North Yorkshire National Park. The trees were in full leaf, and the gardens everywhere were at their English best – and these included that of our host. Again, if you have never visited North Yorkshire, you are missing out. Towns and villages like Middleham, Pickering, Goathland, Helmsley, and Hutton le Hole, are really lovely places, full of history and timeless beauty.

Then being only 40 miles from Teesside where I was born, and Middlesbrough for whom I played, we spent a day up there visiting a few friends and I went to Ayresome Park where my old club was playing Sheffield Wednesday. Again, I met a few old players including Harry Bell, Mick Fenton, and Harold Shepherdson. I spoke to the all-time greatest player on the phone, as he could not come to the game; Wilf Mannion, who lives in a Redcar council house. If he was playing today he would earn about £20,000 per week and be able to afford to buy a house, such as the one he is renting, every three or four weeks. Yes, we were all born too soon.

By this time it was into winter and Carol had said that we could have her Spanish villa whenever we wanted it, and for as long as we liked. We had always talked about the idea of living in Spain; to be two hours flying time from England, whilst enjoying the healthy climate of the Spanish Mediterranean coast, which is the best place to live for those with asthma, rheumatism, and arthritis, according to the United Nations Health Organisation. We mused about doing swaps with our friends in England. We would stay in their homes, use their car, etc, and vice versa. I had a contact in the Wirral who sold properties in Spain. He also was able to get cheap air tickets, as the airlines faxed him every day regarding flights not fully booked. So I rang them and he was able to get us a couple of tickets for £79, although he said that the week before he had had some at £29!

Leni was a bit mixed up, as I was always talking about going back 'home' to England, and now I was considering Spain, but I had come to realise that her asthma was really bad. She could get the benefit of the Spanish climate, and still get to see her family and friends in England. Margarete and the grandchildren could come to Spain whenever they desired, and as my plan was to buy a villa for us and an apartment to rent out, this extra income could pay for their air fares. So, although it was approaching Christmas, we felt that we must get on and try to make a decision about our future. So Spain here we come! Early on a rainy misty morning we were driven by Derrick to Manchester Airport to catch the 7.30 am Brittania flight to Alicante on the Spanish Costa Blanca. Having become used to the wide comfortable seats of the trans-world jumbo jets, it was quite a surprise to find that, for what was of course a relatively short journey, the seats were much narrower. This was obviously because we had only a little over two hours to endure, though being well over six feet in height and with a right knee which would not bend very much, it was a bit of an endurance test. Our company on the plane was very surprising too, as there were fifty or sixty wheelchair passengers aboard, going to the Mediterranean resort town of Benidorm. We discovered that during the winter, for this was 7 December, many Spanish hotels remain open at much reduced prices, presumably enabling them to keep most of their staff employed, without making much of a profit, if any. The airlines are apparently happy to join in, making a winter holiday package very affordable.

Little did I realise that a wheelchair was going to play a part in our 'escape to the sun' sojourn.

John Reid of Swan International organised cheap returns for us, and we were met at Alicante airport by his man in Torrevieja, who was to take us to Carol's villa and arrange to show us some houses which were for sale. All this seemed innocuous and normal, but please read on.

We got to the villa at about 1.30 pm and we were pleased with the accommodation and its location, only five minutes walk to the beautiful golden sandy beach. We had noticed a small self-service grocers shop as we were entering Caba Roig, the name of the suburb, and we walked the three or four hundred yards and bought a few immediately necessary items such as milk, tea, bread, butter, breakfast food, etc, and were pleased with the value for money.

Then we had a cup of tea and decided to go for an exploratory walk, and after a little difficulty in finding our way out of what was a very large, although attractive complex with several pools, tennis courts, etc, we made our way to the beach. It was warm and sunny and apparently a typical Costa Blanca winter's afternoon. On our way back, we had two conversations, one with a French couple and the other with a German who was carting logs from the drive to the back of the house. As in Australia, it can get cool enough to warrant heating of some sort in the winter.

The remarkable thing we discovered was that almost all of the villas and apartments were unoccupied, it being out of season, although we were told that there would be an influx of owners for Christmas and New Year. Most of the owners also spent their annual summer holidays at Caba Roig, and during the remainder of the year they endeavoured to rent their places out, thus deriving an income.

The French couple told us to call in any time over the holiday, and the Germans actually asked us for Christmas Day. We were very pleased to find such hospitality, confirming what we always thought, that Europeans are often more welcoming than are many Australians.

After our first night's sleep in Spain for nearly twenty years, we decided to have a look around nearby Torrevieja. The trip started brilliantly, as a car pulled up at the bus stop where we were standing and volunteered to give us a lift to the seaside town. Our first view of the place was not very flattering, as the weekly market had just finished and the town centre was a mass of empty boxes, paper, and such as fruit and vegetables, which littered the area where there had been many stalls. We proceeded to look around the shops and had a meal in a cafe.

The day was getting dark when we crossed the town's main square, and entered the main church. It was decorated for Christmas, and greatly thrilled us to see how the Spanish laud our Saviour. It was truly beautiful, and we found that whilst the English speaking world give and receive their Christmas presents on Christmas Day, and the Germanic countries and others do this on 6 December, on St Nicholas' Day, Spanish people exchange gifts on 'Twelfth Day' (i.e. 6 January, when the three kings brought the gifts of 'gold, frankincense, and myrrh' to the baby Jesus, in the Bethlehem stable).

After saying some prayers, including some for our 'little family in Norwich', we recrossed the square and whilst making our way to the bus station, I detected a delightful aroma coming out of a baker's shop. I couldn't resist popping in and I bought two apple pies which were still warm.

We caught the bus and I had a bite or two of a delicious pie, prior to getting off at Caba Roig. Uncertain how to get back to the apartment in the pitch dark, we dropped into a restaurant by the bus-stop and a lady told us the way, which started by crossing the road.

It was so very dark, no street lights, only a few chinks of light, presumably from house windows. There was nothing coming, so we hurried across, Leni leading.

...Then a blinding light coming from nowhere. 'Oh! Stan, Oh! Stan,' cried Leni. 'Don't worry, I am alright love,' I answered. 'You're not, you're not,' she argued. Then someone seemed to be picking me up, whilst another apparently went to ring for an ambulance. When I realised this, I told Leni that I was all right. I said, 'Don't get an ambulance, there is nothing wrong with me.' This seemed to bring no relief to Leni, indeed it seemed to worry her more. Then I realised that someone else was screaming, 'Get him off the road,' because apparently I was still in danger of being run over by another vehicle. I must have been only partly conscious, because I had no great pain. One man lifted me up in his arms and carried me the couple of yards to the verge, where he remained with me until the ambulance arrived. I believe the car driver was amongst those attending me, but on the ambulance's arrival, I think that he must have disappeared. Poor Leni must have been suffering more than me, as she could see physical signs of my many injuries, whilst I was actually protesting that there was nothing wrong with me. Then, I suppose I was trying to bring normality to the situation, when I remembered my one and a half apple pies. To show I had my wits about me, I said in an ever so matter of fact way, 'Oh! Leni have you got my pies?' When she replied in the negative, I chided her that they were lovely and that they must be on the road somewhere. I was ever so calm!

I was lifted into the ambulance when it arrived and I remember saying, 'Leni, this is awful. It is going to be so embarrassing when I get to the hospital, and they find there is nothing wrong with me!' What my poor terrified wife could see very plainly was that both of my shoes and my socks had actually been torn off my feet; my lovely green slacks were ripped badly and all bloody; my head was bleeding; and I was, all in all, in a poor state! Again, I asked about my pies, but there was no luck there either.

On arrival in hospital, it turned out that because of the bleeding they had to cut off my shirt, trousers, and underpants. Then they had to clean up my badly abrased left side and attend to cuts and bruises on most parts of my body. After all, I had been hit up into the air by a large, fast car!

Worse was to come. I was X-rayed for a considerable time and the results were; both ankles fractured, right elbow fractured, left collar-bone fractured. In fact, the first Spanish word I recognised was something like 'fractura, fractura, fractura, fractura.' So from my thinking that I was a fraud, and that I would be thrown out of the hospital, it now seemed certain that I would be incarcerated for some weeks. And what was coming up? Yes, Christmas and the New Year! The prospects were less than bright and I was so very sorry for my Leni. How would she cope? No car, no me to ease the daily problems and burdens, and all on her own in a foreign land, not knowing a soul. There was no point in letting

Margarete know, to ruin her Christmas, and we didn't see the point in spreading our misery over the Williams family in Little Sutton – so it looked as though we would be toughing it out alone.

But we were in for one or two surprises. One day an Englishman came into my ward, looking for me. He had been told that I was there and as a Spanish resident visiting a friend, he looked around to see if there were other ex-pats in the ward. His name was Sidney and he thought that it would be better to let Carol know, as her villa was now unoccupied, and other friends of hers coming for Christmas had been told of our occupancy, and they would have a shock to find no one there. In retrospect, this was a mistake and the upshot was that Carol actually flew to Spain to help us, leaving their restaurant at the busiest time of the year. It was very kind of her, but in a way it was more worrying for us as we felt we were a burden to her. Furthermore, she rang our Margarete, thinking that she was helping, resulting in our daughter being upset and of course unable to do anything for us. However, Carol was able to lighten Leni's load, by allowing her to sleep at the villa. Prior to this happening poor Leni had spent only one night in bed, when an English hospital visitor kindly took her with her, and brought her back the next day. Every other day and night Leni spent in a little chair by my bedside. I was so sorry for her.

And Margarete was left with a worrying guilt problem about whether she should fly over to Spain to be with us in our crisis. We let her know that her duty was to her children, and assured her that we would get through our problems in a few weeks.

Meanwhile, after hearing the word, 'fractura' so often, it was obvious that I was to be in a Spanish hospital for some time. The ambulance took me to the emergency ward at Arcos Hospital, where I was cleaned up and X-rays were taken. After a horrendous night for Leni, wondering what the future held for us, I was taken to a very modern hospital at Orihuela, where I shared a ward with a Frenchman. During the day, a doctor came around and examined the X-rays, and he was the person who uttered the Spanish word meaning fracture four times. By this time, I would think perhaps eight nurses and three doctors had done something for me, and surprisingly not one of them spoke English. I knew only a few words of Spanish and proper communication was impossible. Although English is now looked upon as an international language, all of these no doubt well-educated medical people had not learned any. It was very awkward and sometimes painful for me, as I was unable to tell the nurses my needs, and when they washed me or changed the bedding, they would often touch some of my many sore spots and abrasions. I had cramps quite a lot and I would dearly have liked to know the Spanish for the words, 'sore', and 'cramp'. Some months later I discovered that during General Franco's dictatorship, he forbade the teaching of foreign languages in schools and, consequently, a large section of the Spanish public had not had the opportunity of learning another language. Obviously most of the hospital staff were in this category.

Late on my first evening at Orihuela I was operated on. It was a long process as both ankles, my right elbow, and left collar bone, were all broken. The screws and wire inserted that night are still within my body and there seems to be no intention of them being removed.

That night was Leni's worst. She sat in a waiting-room whilst I was being operated on, but it was six hours of fear and worry for her, before she knew that all was well. The last two or three hours I had spent in the intensive care ward, but despite my efforts to get a message to Leni, due to the language barrier she had no news at all, until I was wheeled past her en route back to the ward. It was six hours of awful stress for her.

And what a state I was in. I had to lie permanently on my back, a position I found most painful due to the removal of the disc (mentioned in an earlier chapter) back in 1973. Both ankles were in plaster as were my feet and my legs up to near the knee, my elbow had a very heavy cast on it, and my left arm was in a very tight sling to allow the collar bone to heal without an operation. This meant me being totally immobilised, staring all the time at the ceiling and feeling utterly miserable, whilst pretending to Leni that I felt all right. I couldn't read, there was no TV or radio, and neither Leni nor I could get the nurses to understand any of our wants.

However, I must state that any treatment in the ward and in the operating theatre was excellent, and on my return to England and then Australia, specialists took X-rays of the four breaks, concurring that the Spanish doctors had done a fine job.

But I still had about another fortnight before I was allowed back to the villa. This included Christmas and New Year. On Christmas Day Leni and I sat trying to cheer up one another, mostly on the basis that it could have been worse – I could have been killed. English people visiting relatives or friends popped in to wish us well, and even brought us gifts. Carol gave me a radio with cassette player and Margarete had given me a cassette of carols from Norwich Cathedral. As all of the radio stations were Spanish, we played the carols over and over. What a Christmas!

As the days went slowly by we appreciated the help of several Brits who live permanently on the Costa Blanca. One of the most helpful was Sidney Thurlow and when we talked of our pasts, it turned out that he had had a number of furniture shops in the South of England. I told him that at one time I had worked for Firview Furniture, to which he replied, 'Oh! Ernie Rixon! He was a good friend of mine.' It is a small world, made even smaller the following day when a Scotsman visited me. He had been in the fire service in the South of England, so I asked him if he knew Mr Gillette, the father of Bill Gillette, Poole Town's centre forward, who worked on the Poole Fire Brigade. Of course he did, he said!

An interesting feature of life in a Spanish hospital is that the patients' family does a lot of the caring, the washing, the shaving, and the feeding. Lots and lots of the family descend on the hospital at visiting time, too many at times, for the smooth running of the wards, and we soon realised that much was expected of Leni. 'Familia? Familia?' asked a nurse, and I intimated that Leni was it. She had to shave me for the first time ever. We laughed about the nicks and cuts on my face afterwards.

On the day of my release, Carol brought Leni, who had slept at the villa, back in her car and it was only then that we were treated carelessly. Carol thought that if we used a wheelchair, she could get me into her car and out at the other end, but I was weeks away from even standing up, and our attempts to put me in her car failed. An orderly insisted that I should wait in a particular waiting-room. He pushed me into the room, which was incredibly hot, with the midday sun blazing through the window, in front of which I was left. Poor Leni, again unable to communicate due to the ever-pervading language problem, was desperately trying to find a way to get me to the villa, and it was at this stage that we criticised the Spanish hospital system for the first time. The orderly really did not care and it was not until a bilingual English lady came to Leni's aid, that my ordeal in the by now stiflingly hot room was over. She asked for an ambulance and on production of 10,000 pesetas, I was placed on a stretcher and at last I was on my way 'home.'

On arrival, one of Carol's friends, who was from beautiful Buxton in the Derbyshire Peak District, helped Leni, Carol, and the ambulance driver, to carry the stretcher into the villa, and to bring downstairs a bed which they set up by the louvred front door. I still had all the plaster casts on me and again I had to lie most uncomfortably on my back. However, to be out of the hospital signified progress, although it meant even more work for Leni, and going to bed every night must have been very welcome for her. Carol was still with us and she was able to renew friendships with fellow owners of the adjoining villas.

I had to go back to hospital to have the plaster casts removed, and it meant another there-and-back ambulance journey. Every such trip I made I was in the same position, that is, with my head by the rear door and my eyes looking upwards and outwards through the rear window. All I could see on my many ambulance journeys were the roofs. I have mentioned that family help in the hospital was a feature of Spanish health care, but I didn't think it would extend to 'do-it-yourself' plaster cast removal, and subsequently helping with the removal of stitches. The doctor just expected Leni to help with these tasks, which one would expect trained nursing staff to do.

With the casts off and the stitches removed this was real progress, but I couldn't walk, and indeed I could not stand up. However, I was much more comfortable in bed, and with the cast off my right elbow and the strapping off my left collar-bone, I was able to hold a book and read. It is strange how we take everything for granted, but something like this brings us to the realisation that it is important to take advantage of every minute of our lives. Just to be able to read was like winning a large lottery prize.

Carol's husband, Colin, joined her at their villa, having a few days holiday after the busiest time of the year in their restaurant. We were pleased for Carol, as her Christmas had been spoiled by my accident, but it had unpleasant consequences. For some reason Colin thought that I was able to get up and stand and/or walk, and that I was being a bit of a wimp. This caused some division between us, but as I could not even stand for two or three more weeks, Colin was proven to be quite wrong.

When I was lying on my back in the villa, unable to move, I looked for hours at the ceiling and eventually I knew every crack or mark. The worst aspect of this day after day ordeal was quite scary at times. With the front door open, I could see some white trellis in the small courtyard. Nothing scary about that it might seem, but there were also climbing-plants spread out over the trellis throwing shadows, and with the state of my health and mind at that time, those shadows were frightening. It seemed that every leaf, group of leaves, or flowers cast a shadow, which appeared to my tortured mind as grotesque. Eventually, they had a compelling fascination, making me study them over and over again. Whenever I woke from sleep, and this was often, as one does when one is trapped in a sickbed, my eyes sought those grotesque caricatures, for that was how they looked, searching for the head wearing a top hat, the lion's head, the rat, the pig, and a vast variety of silhouettes which seemed to be keeping watch on me.

So this was how our holiday went until a trip to the hospital resulted in my being declared fit enough to return to England. A girl called Jill, an English neighbour, rang Brittania Airways and they agreed that although our tickets had gone over time, we could use them to return to Manchester. Jill was a great help to us, as was Sidney. Without them, our disastrous holiday would have been even worse. We had to wait a few days for seats, and those were some of the longest days of our lives. But at last the great day dawned, and could everything go right? It ought to, after so many bad days. Yes, the ambulance arrived at precisely 9.00 am as ordered, and we set off for my last view of Spanish roofs (I was lying on a most uncomfortable stretcher; so much for Colin thinking I should have been on my feet a couple of weeks previously). It took forty minutes to get to the airport at Alicante. On arrival the driver jumped out of his seat and went off. Great, we thought, but the flight time was getting nearer and nearer. Eventually we nearly panicked as the flight time was past! No sign of the driver, I just could not contemplate another trip back to Caba Roig, and then all of this again. It was ten minutes after time, and by now Leni was crying. What had we done to deserve all of this?

At last the driver arrived, gave us the news in Spanish, so we were no better off, but he drove off and when he stopped, we realised that the ambulance was underneath a wing of a Britannia aircraft. Thanks be to God. Some kind of a hoist got me and my stretcher to the cabin door and then several strong men lifted me in to a seat. What relief. Every attendant was marvellous. Seventeen years away from the English, and didn't it feel wonderful to have them all around me, helping me? Giving me succour, as our forbears have given succour to multitudes of foreign people seeking peace and safety in 'England's green and pleasant land.'

We had got a message to Vera and Derrick to say that I would have to go into a hospital in Chester, and asking if they could arrange such, and for an ambulance to pick me up at Manchester Airport. Just by chance, there was a Manchester police sergeant on the flight and he insisted on taking charge of the situation, getting us straight through customs and into the ambulance via a stretcher-trolley. It was terrific to be on the road to the Wirral, but our ordeal was not quite over yet. Vera was waiting for us at her garden gate with the news that she had contacted the Countess of Chester Hospital, but they said that there was no way I could be admitted without a doctor being responsible. Vera had spoken to her doctor who had said he could do nothing! The suggestion was I should stay at Vera's! I couldn't walk. I needed nursing care. I needed 'physio' treatment and rehabilitation. So the ambulance driver, now fuming, drove to Vera's doctor, dragged him out of his surgery and demanded he should get me admitted. The doctor made a cursory examination of me to save face, and then rang the hospital, with the result that at about 6.00 pm on a freezing February evening, I lay down in a lovely warm bed. Malcolm Fraser, one time Australian Prime Minister, once said, 'Life wasn't meant to be easy.' I couldn't agree more.

After a couple of weeks of first standing, then shuffling along on crutches, then walking with a stick, I was allowed to go to Vera's where I continued my daily exercise programme. I remember my first walk out the back. I did fourteen paces. I got better and better until three weeks into February we bade farewell to Vera and Derrick, who had stood by me during what must have also been a trying time for them. It took two days to drive back to Norfolk, where we rented a cottage for a week, Margarete's house not being suitable for me with my injuries, and it was a little bit like heaven. Elizabeth and Toby stayed the weekend with us and Margarete visited us, as we did her. Then the day we all dreaded arrived. After tearful goodbyes we caught the train from Norwich to London and hence to Heathrow Airport. Malaysia Airlines were expecting me. A wheelchair was waiting for me, and right through to and including Perth airport, we had marvellous service from them, and they were able to find me four seats in a row in order to lie down, on both aircraft on which we flew. I had been told to keep my feet up as much as possible, something I still do.

It was 2.30 am when we got to Perth and dear Patrick Lynch was waiting for us, despite having told him by letter that we would get a taxi. Better than that, Yvonne, his wife, had beds ready for us, insisting that as it was about 4.00 am Saturday, we should stay the weekend.

Thus ended another one of life's vagaries, but then began the struggle to be able to walk properly.

With daily exercise, first indoors and then on the patio, I got strong enough to drive the car. Our first trip was short, to our favourite beach, Mettams, about 400 metres away. It was the end of March and contrary to the fondly held belief that Aussies are always down the beach, there was only one person in the ocean as I picked my way gently over the sand. I was thinking how clever I was stepping along on ankles full of hardware, until I realised the other person was Mr Ron Edwards, the ex-State Minister of Police. You see he lost both legs to above the knees when he stood on a land mine in Vietnam. 'There is always someone worse off than you,' was the thought that cheered me that early autumn day.

NOW, IN CONCLUSION...

So, hopefully, things will turn full circle and we shall once again be in our beloved England. Maybe we will be able to do what I would like to do more than anything else, and that is to retrace the steps I have described having taken in this book. To start outside 26 Hind Street, Stockton-on-Tees and then to visit every house we have lived in; to follow the steps taken by me as a soldier in England, Scotland, France, Belgium, Holland, and Germany; to see Leni's relations in Germany; to revisit the places on the continent where I played football or visited with Leni; one day to come back to Australia to see again our friends on Croker Island, Bamyili (now Barunga) and Darwin; and to bathe again in Mettams Pool, here in North Beach.

During the last few months prior to their leaving for England, I talked often to our grandchildren about life and the importance of planning and taking advantage of opportunities when they are presented. I tried to tell them how lucky they were to be able to receive guidance from 'us oldies'. I said that a common expression we used was, 'if only I had my life over again, I would ...' etc, etc, but that obviously we cannot do this. However, they can learn the fruits of our lifetimes, and thus be able to benefit in a way that we never could.

I told them how crucial the next several years at school were, that the quality of the rest of their lives depended on the amount of effort they put into their schoolwork now and in their ensuing school years. I will keep on repeating this message.

I know the mistakes I made, and I shall try to make sure that they do not make them.

And finally I would like to leave you with a piece of poetry I learnt when I was about fourteen, which has been a great help to me, especially when I have thought that the world was against me. It has brought me back to the reality that I am, and have always been, fortunate; that problems are there to be overcome, but that blindness is something else. How could one continue without one's sight? John Milton did. And this is what he wrote in 'Paradise Lost' (book III):

'Thus with the Year
Seasons return, but not to me returns
Day, or the sweet approach of Ev'n or Morn,
Or sight of vernal bloom or Summers Rose,
Or flocks, or herds, or human face divine;
But cloud in stead, and ever-during dark
Surrounds me, from the chearful wayes of men.
Cut off, and for the book of knowledg fair
Presented with a Universal blanc
Of Nature's works to mee expung'd and ras'd,
And wisdome at one entrance quite shut out.'

THE END